DEDICATION

To my colleagues Mike Stanbridge and Duncan Heyes, without whose constant support, encouragement and practical help this book would never have been completed!

EMPLOYMENT
ND HEALTH

PSYCHOSOCIAL STRESS IN THE WORKPLACE

By JENNIE GRIMSHAW

THE BRITISH LIBRARY

Employment and health: psychosocial stress in the workplace
ISBN 0-7123-0847-4

First published 1999 by
The British Library
96 Euston Road
London NW1 2DB

© 1999 The British Library Board

British Library Cataloguing-in-Publication Data

A catalogue record for this book is available from The British Library

Desktop publishing by Concerto, Leighton Buzzard, Bedfordshire.
Tel: 01525 378757

Printed by Atheneum Press Ltd, Gateshead, Tyne & Wear

Contents

INTRODUCTION AND OVERVIEW viii

GLOSSARY xi

1   THE CHANGING WORLD OF WORK AND
    WELFARE 1

    1.1   The traditional organisation 1
    1.2   The pressure for change 2
    1.3   The organisational response............................11
    1.4   Dismantling the welfare state..........................16
    1.5   Bibliography 18

2   WHAT IS STRESS?...32

    2.1   Definition of stress 32
    2.2   Stress models..33
    2.3   Bibliography 48

3   PSYCHOSOCIAL HAZARDS IN THE
    WORKPLACE...72

    3.1   Introduction...72
    3.2   Working hours...73
    3.3   Shiftwork...75
    3.4   Interpersonal relationships 78
    3.5   Violence and bullying 82
    3.6   Work–non-work conflict 85
    3.7   Role ambiguity and role conflict........................87
    3.8   Control in the workplace 90
    3.9   Monotonous work 93
    3.10 Job insecurity...94
    3.11 Bibliography 97

4   STRESS AND PERSONALITY: INDIVIDUAL
    DIFFERENCES IN THE STRESS PROCESS............160

    4.1   Individual differences in the stress process....................160
    4.2   Popular personality variables........................162
    4.3   Bibliography..176

5   STRESS COSTS AND CONSEQUENCES **200**

5.1   Introduction...200
5.2   Stress and health outcomes..............................200
5.3   Pathways to disease...202
5.4   Gastrointestinal disorders.................................204
5.5   Diabetes...205
5.6   Musculoskeletal disorders................................206
5.7   Cardiovascular disease......................................209
5.8   Stress and the immune system 212
5.9   Cancer...216
5.10   Mental health..219
5.11   Post-traumatic stress disorder..........................222
5.12   Behavioural responses to stress factors............223
5.13   Costs and prevalence of work-related stress......227
5.14   Legal consequences of work-related stress........229
5.15   Bibliography..232

6   STRESS MANAGEMENT: THEORY INTO PRACTICE **283**

6.1   Introduction...283
6.2   Classification of intervention strategies 284
6.3   Intervention evaluation.....................................285
6.4   Employee assistance programmes 287
6.5   Stress management training 291
6.6   Crisis intervention..299
6.7   Stressor reduction interventions......................302
6.8   Bibliography..312

7   NEW LABOUR, THE EU AND THE WORLD OF WORK **351**

7.1   The Third Way 351
7.2   UK economic prospects....................................352
7.3   New Labour and welfare...................................353
7.4   Private finance initiatives and privatisation of services..359
7.5   Minimum wage..361
7.6   The European dimension 363
7.7   Bibliography..371

8   CONCLUSIONS..**389**

INDEXES **391**
    General index 391
    Author index 410

Introduction and Overview

Objectives

The objective of this book is to present a summary, based on a survey of the research literature, of the present state of knowledge about work-related stress. I have aimed to give the interested lay reader sufficient background in the subject to be able to read, understand and evaluate the scientific literature. The study of stress is interdisciplinary, and I have drawn on psychological, managerial and medical sources to give a balanced overview. I have also attempted to set the subject of workplace stress into the context of organisational change, economic globalisation, the explosion of information technology and the reform of welfare. The effects of current UK government and European Union economic, employment and social policy on the world of work are also explored.

The review is aimed at practitioners in the fields of health and safety at work and human resource management, at trade unionists and at information professionals working in a business environment. It can be used either as a one-stop by those looking for an introduction to the field, or as a bridge to the research literature by those seeking to enquire more deeply.

Scope

The literature on work-related stress is vast and ever growing, and to make the task manageable I have confined myself to looking at psychosocial hazards only. Physical hazards such as the effects of extremes of temperature or exposure to dangerous chemicals are not covered.

Terminology

It has proved impossible to talk about this highly complex subject in entirely non-technical language. In order to help the lay reader, scientific terms are defined in footnotes at their first occurrence, and are also included in a glossary.

Overview

Chapter one looks at the changing world of work, where a job for life is a thing of the past, where career ladders are disappearing, and lifelong learning to enhance employability is essential. The introduction of new technology has led to the displacement of swathes of workers in both offices and factories. Downsizing and organisational restructuring due to financial stringency have spawned the evils of overwork, the long hours culture and massive job insecurity. Added to this, retrenchments in state welfare have left only a moth-eaten safety net to support the casualties of the new industrial revolution.

Chapter two introduces the concept of stress and explores the definitional difficulties surrounding it. Stress, or pressure, is an inescapable part of life. Most people enjoy, and benefit from, being challenged and stretched, and pressure only becomes harmful when demands exceed the individual's ability to cope. I introduce the three dominant models of the relationship between stress factors and strain outcomes. The job demands-control model developed by Karasek proposes that stress arises when workers are subject to high demands but have little control over how their work is organised. In the person-environment fit model, stress is caused by a mismatch between the demands of the work environment and the employee's ability to meet those demands, or between the employee's needs and the resources available to meet those needs. For example, an employee may need advice and help from a supervisor who is too busy to give it. Finally in Lazarus' transactional model, stress occurs when a situation is perceived as threatening or harmful and the threat or harm exceeds the person's ability to cope.

Chapter three looks at a range of stress factors in the work environment including long working hours, shift working, job insecurity, conflict between work and family life, difficult relationships with colleagues and clients, and lack of control in the workplace.

In chapter four I examine how personality traits influence an individual's response to stress factors. The chapter covers four popular personality traits: hardiness, locus of control, negative affectivity and Type A behaviour. The hardy person regards problems as challenges and not threats, feels in control of life, and is committed to, and believes in, the value of what he/she does. These personality traits may offer protection against the adverse effects of stress. A person with an external locus of control regards himself as at the mercy of chance or powerful others, while a person with an internal locus of control sees himself as the captain of his fate. Internal locus of control is associated with the ability to cope successfully with stress. People high in negative affectivity have a tendency to look on the black side, and are much more prone to anxiety. Finally, Type A behaviour pattern manifests itself in impatience, irritability, and competitiveness Type A people are always in a hurry and prone to setting themselves impossible tasks. This trait has been linked to development of coronary heart disease.

Chapter five examines the link between stress and serious illnesses such as coronary heart disease, cancer, gastrointestinal disorders and musculoskeletal problems. I look at the physiological changes that occur when an organism is under stress, focusing in particular on the expanding field of psychoneuroimmunology. This new interdisciplinary subject investigates stress induced changes in the immune system, and may hold the key to the link between stress and disease.

Stress management at the individual and organisational level is covered in chapter six. Evidence concerning its effectiveness is presented. I examine employee assistance programmes and counselling services designed to heal those seriously damaged by stress, multicomponent stress management programmes which seek to enhance coping skills, and organisational level interventions which aim to reduce stress factors in the environment through various forms of work redesign. Finally I introduce a practical framework for planning stress management interventions. Effective interventions begin with a diagnosis of the cause of the problem, have clearly defined objectives and include regular monitoring of results.

Finally in chapter seven, I look at the impact of UK government and European Union policy on workplace stress. Topics covered include the likely impacts of European Monetary Union, the Social Chapter, welfare reform, privatisation, and the minimum wage on well being at work.

Glossary

Additive effects

An additive effect occurs when two factors working independently of each other create impacts. When both are at work simultaneously, the effect is cumulative.

Adrenal cortex

The outer portion of the adrenal gland, fused with the gland's medulla and producing glucocorticoids and other hormones.

Adrenal medulla

Inner portion of the adrenal gland that secretes epinephrine and norepinephrine.

Adrenalin *See* **Epinephrine**

Antibody

A cell produced by the immune system that destroys foreign substances or microbes in the body.

Antigen

Any foreign substance or microbe in the body that can stimulate the immune system to destroy it.

Atherosclerosis

Arterial disorder characterised by plaques of cholesterol, lipids and cellular debris in the inner layers of the walls of large and medium-sized arteries. The vessel walls become thick and hard and blood flow is reduced.

Autonomic nervous system

Part of the nervous system that regulates involuntary vital functions, including the activity of the cardiac muscle, smooth muscles and glands.

B cell

A type of lymphocyte (white blood cell) that originates in the bone marrow. It is one of the two lymphocytes that play a major role in the body's immune response. (The other is the T cell.)

Biological rhythm

Any recurrent change in the physiology or behaviour of an organism that occurs regularly, e.g. circadian rhythm.

Buffer *See* Moderator variable

Burnout

Depletion of emotional resources leading to emotional exhaustion, reduced personal accomplishment and depersonalisation. Reduced personal accomplishment refers to feelings of inadequacy for the daily task, increasing discouragement, fatalism and pessimism about one's work, decline in motivation, effort and involvement in work and loss of creativity. Depersonalisation refers to negative, distant and insensitive attitudes to clients.

Catecholamines

Various substances, including epinephrine, norepinephrine and dopamine, that contain a benzene ring with two adjacent hydroxyl groups and a side chain of ethylamine and that function as hormones or neurotransmitters or both.

Circadian rhythm

Changes in physical or mental function (e.g. sleep, temperature or memory) occurring regularly at approximately 24-hour intervals.

Cognitive appraisal theory

The theory that emotions result from a person's evaluation of the situation he is in. Thus an individual will react differently if he perceives a situation as harmful to how he would react if he saw the situation as beneficial.

Cognitive therapy

A form of therapy that attempts to persuade someone suffering from a mental disorder to see the world in a more sensible and realistic way.

Cohort

A group of individuals selected for study because of a common characteristic, particularly in a longitudinal survey where the term refers to all individuals in the same age bracket.

Confounding variable

Confounding occurs when the relationship between two variables is distorted by the presence of a third underlying factor. For example, anxiety prone persons tend to exaggerate both the levels of stress in their workplace and the severity of the health complaints they suffer as a result. This tendency to exaggerate will artificially inflate the relationship between stress factors and strain outcomes.

Control (statistical method)

To statistically control for variables such as sex, age, socioeconomic status, etc., is to exclude their influence and effects from the analysis. The true strength of the relationship between two factors is thus brought to light.

Control condition

A group in an experiment that serves as a baseline against which one compares the effects of a treatment on the experimental group. For example, to test the effectiveness of a stress management intervention, it is necessary to compare workers receiving the training with a group who have not received training.

Coping behaviour

Any behaviour that enables a person to deal with or manage a stressful situation and reduce the distress arising from it.

Coronary arteries

Blood vessels which supply the heart.

Correlation

Statistical method which shows the strength of the relationship between variables under investigation.

Cortisol

Steroid hormone produced by the adrenal glands which functions to accelerate the breakdown of proteins to amino acids, to help to maintain normal blood pressure, and to regulate the breakdown of fats to release energy. Secretion increases during stress, especially that produced by anxiety or severe injury.

Cross-sectional study

Research study in which variables being investigated are measured at one particular point in time.

Decision latitude

In the context of Karasek's Demands-Control Model of work-related stress, the construct decision latitude is made up of skill discretion (the ability of the worker to use judgement and to assert control over use of skills) and decision authority (the worker's freedom to make decisions about task performance).

Demands–abilities fit

In the context of the Person–Environment Fit Model of job stress, refers to the match between work demands and the person's ability to fulfil those demands.

Depersonalisation *See* Burnout

Diastolic blood pressure

Minimum level of blood pressure measured between contractions of the heart.

Direct effect *See* Main effect

Diurnal rhythm *See* Circadian rhythm

Endocrine system

Hormonal system.

Epinephrine

Adrenal hormone that dilates the blood vessels in the skeletal muscles and stimulates the heart wall. Increases the rate and depth of breathing and the metabolic rate. Improves the force of muscular contraction and delays the onset of muscular fatigue. At the same time, the blood supply to the bladder and intestines is reduced, their muscle walls relax and their sphincters close. Epinephrine is released into the blood stream by the adrenal medulla in response to stress.

Glucocorticoids

Adrenal steroids that are concerned with carbohydrate metabolism. They maintain the blood sugar level.

Glucose

Absorbable sugar to which carbohydrates are reduced by digestion.

Glycogen

Form in which carbohydrate is stored in the liver. Is converted into glucose under stress.

Hardiness

Personality trait characterised by a sense of control (belief in one's ability to control events), commitment (an approach to life marked by curiosity and a sense of meaningfulness), and challenge (belief that change stimulates development).

Hawthorne effect

The phenomenon that if an attempt is made to reduce work-related stress through organisational level or individual level interventions, distress tends to decrease regardless of the technical content of the intervention. Well-being may be enhanced simply because workers are receiving attention or because they feel management is trying.

Heterogeneous sample

Sample where subjects have different characteristics, e.g. where teachers are compared to factory workers.

High-density lipoproteins *See* Triglycerides

Homogeneous sample

Sample where subjects have similar characteristics, e.g. all exhibit similar levels of mental ill-health.

Hypertension

Elevated blood pressure persistently exceeding 140/90 mm Hg.

Hypothalamus

Part of the brain that activates, controls and integrates the peripheral autonomic nervous system and the hormonal system.

Interactive effects

An interactive effect occurs when two factors, such as two different stress agents, combine to create an impact, such as a strain outcome. Strain would not be produced by one stress agent acting alone. For example, overwork may combine with lack of authority over task organisation to create strain, whereas a heavy workload combined with flexibility in planning work would present no problems.

Interleukins

Proteins with numerous immune system functions. Interleukin-1 activates resting T cells, endothelial and macrophage cells, mediates inflammation, and stimulates the synthesis of lymphokines, collagen and collagenases. Interleukin-2 has the ability to initiate the proliferation of activated T cells.

Ischaemic heart disease

Pathologic condition of the heart wall muscle caused by lack of oxygen reaching the tissues.

Leukocytes

White blood cells. Leukocytes engulf and digest bacteria, fungi and viruses, detoxify the toxic proteins that may result from allergic reactions and cellular injury, and function as immune system cells.

Lipid

Any of the free fatty acids in the blood, including cholesterol and triglycerides. They are stored in the body as an energy reserve, but are elevated in various diseases such as atherosclerosis.

Locus of control

A personality trait, being the extent to which people see themselves as being in control of their own lives (internals) or see themselves as being at the mercy of luck, chance and powerful others (externals).

Longitudinal study

Research study in which the variables being investigated are measured at two or more points in time, and results compared.

Low-density lipoproteins *See* Triglycerides

Lymphocytes

White blood cells produced in the lymphoid tissue whose function is the production of immune bodies to overcome and protect against infection.

Lymphokine

One of the chemical factors produced and released by T cells that attract macrophages to the site of infection and prepare them to attack.

Macrophage

Any phagocytic cell of the reticuloendothelial system. It is able to surround, engulf and digest microorganisms and cellular debris.

Main effect

Factor which has a direct effect on well-being, either enhancing it or reducing it, regardless of the presence of any stress agent. For example, people who have the support of friends and family are generally happier and healthier than those who are isolated, regardless of the presence of any objective stress factors.

Mediator variable

Factor responsible for the transmission of an effect, while not altering the strength or nature of the effect.

Meta-analysis

Statistical method of aggregating the results of a large number of research studies on a given topic.

Motility

Spontaneous, but unconscious or involuntary movement.

Moderator variable

Factor whose presence alters the strength of the relationship between a stress agent and a strain outcome. It will either reduce or increase the impact of the stress factor and ameliorate or exacerbate the strain outcome. For example if men and women react differently to a given stress factor, then sex is a moderator variable.

Myocardial infarction

Heart attack.

Myocardium

Muscle tissue of the heart.

Natural killer cells

Cells that attack and destroy certain virus-infected cells.

Negative affectivity

Personality trait, predisposing people to anxiety, anger, scorn, disgust, guilt, fearfulness and depression.

Neuroticism *See* Negative affectivity

Noradrenalin *See* Norepinephrine

Norepinephrine

Adrenergic hormone that constricts small blood vessels leading to an increase in blood pressure, increased blood flow through the coronary arteries, a slowing of the heart rate, an increase in the rate and depth of breathing and relaxation of the smooth muscle of the intestinal wall. It is released in response to stress, and mediates a host of physiologic responses that follow stimulation of the sympathetic nervous system. In response to stress the adrenal medulla is stimulated, causing the elevation of epinephrine and norepinephrine in the blood stream

Nuisance variable *See* Confounding variable

Participatory action research

Research method involving workers themselves diagnosing problems and developing and monitoring solutions under the guidance of a research team.

Peptic ulcer

Ulcer arising in the stomach or duodenum.

Phagocyte

A cell that is able to surround, engulf and digest microorganisms and cellular debris.

Pituitary gland

Endocrine (hormonal) gland suspended from the base of the brain. It consists of an anterior and a posterior lobe. The anterior lobe has a role in regulating growth and metabolism and influences the other endocrine glands.

Placebo condition

A group in an experiment that receives a bland substitute for the real treatment administered to the experimental group. For example, placebo groups may receive education about stress or training in personal development skills rather than actual stress management training. Improvement in both groups is an indication that expectancy effects are at work, i.e. that subjects are improving because they expect to, not because of the technical content of the training.

Prospective study

Research study undertaken on a group of people who are systematically observed over time in order to discover which conditions lead to the development of a particular trait or illness.

Psychosomatic illness

Disease occurring in an organ controlled by the autonomic nervous system, such as peptic ulcer, which may be caused or aggravated by emotional factors.

Randomisation

Arranging items or events in an unpredictable order, not governed by any rule. Allocation of subjects to groups is often randomised in experiments.

Retrospective study

Research on people who currently have a particular illness, character trait, etc., which aims, by examining their past, to identify causal factors at work.

Role ambiguity

Arises when the worker has inadequate information about what is expected of him/her, and manifests itself as confusion about objectives and uncertainty about the scope of the job.

Role conflict

Arises when the worker is subject to conflicting and incompatible demands such that complying with one would make it difficult or impossible to comply with the others.

Role overload

Can be qualitative or quantitative. Qualitative overload occurs when the work is intrinsically too difficult or complex for the employee to cope with. Quantitative overload occurs when the employee has more work than he/she can handle.

Serum

Clear fluid residue of blood, from which the corpuscles and fibrin have been removed.

Shiftwork

System of work organisation where some of the work is done at night.

Somatic

Pertaining to the body, and, therefore, physical.

Strain

Negative consequences for an individual of exposure to stress agents or sources of stress.

Stress inoculation training

A form of cognitive therapy designed to help people cope with stressful situations by exposing them to such events under safe conditions and teaching them techniques to deal with them.

Stressor

Source of stress or stress agent.

Supplies–values fit

In the context of the Person-Environment Fit Model of job stress, refers to the match between the worker's needs and the organisation's resources to meet those needs.

Sympathetic nervous system

Part of the autonomic nervous system that accelerates heart rate, constricts blood vessels and raises blood pressure.

Systolic blood pressure

Blood pressure measured during the period of heart contraction.

T cell

A small circulating lymphocyte produced in the bone marrow that matures in the thymus. T cells primarily mediate cellular immune responses such as graft rejection and delayed hypersensitivity. Helper T cells affect the production of antibodies by B cells; supressor T cells suppress B cell activity.

Trait anxiety *See* Negative affectivity

Triglycerides

Compound consisting of a fatty acid and glycerol. They make up most of the animal and vegetable fats and are the principle lipids in the blood, where they circulate, bound to a protein, as high- and low-density lipoproteins. The total amount of triglycerides and the amount, proportion and kinds of lipoproteins present are important in the diagnosis and treatment of many conditions including hypertension and heart disease.

Type A personality

The Type A person is very competitive, impatient, and hurried and tries to do different things at once, e.g. shaving while driving. May be prone to coronary heart disease.

Type B personality

The Type B person is relaxed, easy-going, not too competitive and not prone to feeling frustrated.

Type C personality

The Type C person is compliant and appeasing and tends to suppress strong emotions. May be prone to cancer.

Vulnerability factor *See* Moderator variable

1 The Changing World of Work and Welfare

1.1 The traditional organisation

'Organisation is about how people relate to one another when engaged in joint endeavours'
Meredith Belbin: *The coming shape of organisation.*

Large corporations and public sector bodies organised along traditional lines are hierarchical in nature. They are structured along functional lines, with separate divisions for finance, marketing, personnel, distribution and production. A separate management hierarchy corresponds to each function, with decision-making power concentrated at the top. The ideal span of control, ie how many subordinates report to a boss has been hotly debated, but the balance of opinion amongst management theorists favours five. It is common for organisation charts to show as many as 14 hierarchical levels between the production workers and the chief executive officer.

Such organisations are inevitably bureaucratic. Rules and procedures are set out to cover every eventuality, leaving employees and junior managers with little discretion. Adherence to laid down rules can cause otherwise sensible people to act in defiance of common sense. A particular example of this in the public sector is that departmental budgets have to be spent by the end of the financial year, irrespective of need. Money cannot be carried over, and if the budget is not spent, it may be cut the following year. The departmental objective then becomes spending the money at all costs!

Jobs are strictly defined using tight specifications. This only works if the interaction between all jobs is fully understood and if conditions remain stable. When things change, management has to either revise job descriptions, create new jobs to cover the work, or ask employees to undertake tasks outside their job descriptions, which can lead to resentment. This structure leads to fragmentation of work with responsibility falling between stools. Problems are usually 'the fault' of another department and are never addressed as a whole. For example, in the event of a faulty item being returned, a replacement will be sent with a note of apology. It is unlikely that the public relations department dealing with the complaint will try to prevent the fault recurring as that could cross job boundaries.

Promotion in traditional organisations tends to be through an internal market. There is an implicit understanding that hard work and loyalty will be rewarded by advancement up a hierarchical ladder, and that management and white collar workers at least can expect to retire after 40 years service with the same company. Life time job security is offered to an essential core of workers in exchange for loyalty and commitment, with the added incentive of possible promotion from entry level up to the executive suite. Finally, there is a sharp distinction between management and labour in responsibilities and practices. Managers and professionals do the thinking work, make the decisions, design workflows and tasks, and assign them to production workers to carry out. As a result, production workers become interchangeable, like machine parts. Demarcation is rife at the lower levels also, with workers hostile to the concept of undertaking work outside of their job description.

1.2 The pressures for change

A series of pressures came to a head during the 1980s which caused the traditional model of the organisation to become non-viable. Companies were forced to alter radically their relations with employees and the way they operated or face extinction. Privatisation returned public services in the UK to the private sector where they faced greater market discipline. Services remaining in the public domain were revolutionised by the introduction of quasi or internal markets and practices from the business sector to increase efficiency. Other changes were associated with developments in the world economy and advances in technology.

1.2.1 Changes in public policy

Postwar employment policies grew from the experience of the slump of the 1930s. This depression, which was associated with mass unemployment and widespread poverty at home and political instability abroad, is thought to have contributed to the triumph of Nazism and the outbreak of World War II. Postwar governments, both Labour and Conservative, were determined that this should never happen again and were committed to policies of full employment. Administrations of the 1950s adopted Keynesian strategies of demand management to sustain full employment and economic growth. However, by the 1960s trouble was brewing behind the facade of full employment and rising living standards. Antiquated plant, overmanning, poor industrial relations, low productivity and an underskilled workforce left the UK poorly placed to compete with the resurgent economies of Germany and Japan as they recovered after the War.

This situation was exacerbated by the use of politically motivated 'stop-go' policies of boom and bust whereby the government stimulated the economy before an election with subsequent retrenchment to damp down inflation. This created uncertainty in the business community which undermined investment and damaged the competitive position of UK industry. Eventually Keynesian demand management techniques began to come unstuck. Stimulation of economic growth led not to investment at home but to a rise in cheap imports from abroad, producing successive balance of payments and sterling crises. Government aid designed to expand new industries was used to shore up old ones while demand stimulation damaged the currency. Workers, frightened by inflation and the government's efforts to impose statutory wage controls, imposed ever higher wage demands which damaged competitiveness still further. Industrial conflict escalated and strikes abounded, culminating in the Winter of Discontent of 1978/9.

The Conservative governments of the 1980s and early 1990s abandoned the full employment policy and aimed to restore competitiveness through a programme of public and private cost cutting. The control of inflation by restriction of the money supply through interest rates became the overriding objective. Budgets were not to be used for demand stimulation and budget deficits were to be kept to a minimum at all times. Unemployment was to be solved by deregulation of the labour market and increasing flexibility to reduce labour costs and help increase competitiveness. The reduction of state intervention would foster enterprise, stimulate the free market and reverse economic decline.

Implementation of these ideas involved systematic weakening of the trade unions, abolishing the wages councils (which had the power to fix minimum wages), tightening the eligibility criteria for unemployment benefits, privatising public services, and stringently controlling grants-in-aid to both the private and public sectors. To promote employment flexibility on the supply side the strategy was to enhance incentives for the unemployed to seek work by reducing the level and duration of unemployment benefits, and targeting benefits to 'top up' the income of the low paid in work. On the demand side, employers were encouraged to hire labour by rebates on social security contributions and the removal of employment protection legislation for the low paid and for part-time and temporary workers.

International economic contraction caused by the second oil price shock of 1979 exacerbated the effects of this treatment and the UK economy collapsed in the early 1980s. Unemployment rocketed from 1.25 million in 1979 to over 3 million by 1985. Following a period of recovery in the boom of the mid-1980s, unemployment rose again sharply in the recession of the early 1990s. In May 1997, in the dying days of the last Conservative administration, it stood at 1.636 million according to the monthly claimant count figures issued by the Office for National Statistics. - higher than when the Tories took office. Possibly the true unemployment figure at that time was higher still as the count was based on numbers claiming the Jobseekers Allowance introduced in 1996. This excludes those with savings above £8,000, people whose partners are working more than 24 hours a week and those who left work of their own accord. Since the Labour Party came into power in May 1997 unemployment has been steadily falling, but in spite of this fall, the claimant count in November 1998 still stood at 1.33 million – higher than when Labour were last in office in 1979.

Whether the Conservative government reforms of 1979-97 in fact revitalised the UK economy and fitted it to compete on the world stage is hotly debated by researchers. While some are convinced that they have, others argue that they caused the people of this country untold misery through unemployment kept deliberately high to control inflation and the fostering of an insecure and unstable labour market where steady, permanent jobs have been replaced by low paid, insecure, temporary and part-time positions. A third view is that these changes in the structure of the labour market are merely continuations of trends which have been going on since the War, independent of government policies.

Britain attracted praise from the OECD (1997, ref. no.8) for its labour market reforms under the Conservative administrations. It singled out benefit cuts, reduced job protection and industrial relations legislation as key reforms of the 1980s which allowed the UK structural unemployment rate to fall from 10.2% in 1986 to 7% in 1996, whereas rates in France, Germany and Italy rose sharply. Similarly the World Economic Forum Global Competitiveness Report 1997 (1997, ref. no. 7) placed Britain seventh in the world rankings ahead of the rest of the European Union and every east Asian economy except Singapore and Hong Kong. Britain's success in increasing labour market flexibility, cutting tax rates and overhauling its welfare state received particular praise. By contrast, EU countries were seen as suffering chronic declining competitiveness as a result of rigid labour markets, burdensome social welfare systems and high government spending. However, the government responded coolly to what is often a controversial analysis, noting that the OECD ranks Britain 21st in the world economic league.

On the other hand neo-Keynesian economists like John Grieve Smith (1997, ref. no. 6) argue that Conservative governments deliberately and unnecessarily kept unemployment high in order to curb inflation. Government believed that unemployment could not be allowed to fall below 1.5-2 million without fuelling inflation. Abandonment of full employment along with accompanying measures to make the labour market more flexible led to a serious growth in inequality and insecurity. Flexibility became a euphemism for the casualisation of employment. Smith argues that unemployment and low pay stifle growth in the economy by cutting demand. The key question is how to run the economy at a higher level of demand which will stimulate growth and lower unemployment without increasing inflationary pressures.

Simon Deakin (1995, ref. no. 3) points out that labour market flexibility as a cure for unemployment does not get to the root of the problem and has costly side effects. The main disincentive for the unemployed is the precariousness and low pay of entry level jobs on offer to them. Entering employment often means giving up a secure and regular benefit in return for a low paid, part-time or temporary job. The situation is exacerbated by the means testing of benefits, particularly income support, so that families dependent on benefit will lose out if one partner takes a low paying entry job. Gregg and Wadsworth at the Centre for Economic Performance, (1997, ref. no. 10) analysed Labour Force Survey data for 1994/95 and found jobs taken by unemployed people had a median wage of £86.00 per week. These entry jobs were predominantly part-time (50%) and/or temporary (27%). Only 22% were permanent full-time posts. Losing one's job resulted in a substantial deterioration in job quality. People who lost good jobs were re-employed in lower grade occupations and roughly 20 in a 100 more jobs were full-time and permanent among jobs lost than jobs found. The vast majority of observed upward mobility toward the higher paying professional and managerial jobs and towards permanent positions came from those staying with the same employer and not from those entering work. An earlier study by Gregg and Wadsworth also showed that in 1992/93 only 20% of posts filled by unemployed people (ignoring job to job moves) were full-time and permanent, whereas 66% were part-time and/or temporary (50% part-time) (1995, ref. no. 4). The prevalence of job insecurity amongst the low paid was confirmed by Brendan Burchell of Cambridge University (1998, ref. no. 324). An analysis of the Social Change and Economic Life Initiative (SCELI) dataset showed that by the 1980s manual workers were 60% more likely to move into insecure jobs than professionals. The risk of moving from secure to insecure employment was heightened in the 1980s, partly due to the recession, but Burchell also contends that some of the insecurity was due to the legislation which made it easier for firms to dismiss workers.

The question of whether structural change or government policy has been responsible for the increase in job flexibility since the 1970s is taken up by John Philpott, Director of the Employment Policy Institute (EPI) (1997, ref. no. 5). Philpott concludes that Conservative employment policy on the whole moved with the grain of structural change rather than catalysed it. As an example of this he cites the fact that part-time working has been growing steadily for at least 50 years due to the inflow of women into the labour market. Many part-time jobs are taken by women to fit in with their other commitments, but this may arise in some cases not so much from choice as from a lack of good quality, affordable childcare. Philpott finally points out forcefully that Anglo-Saxon economics, whatever its virtue in promoting flexible work patterns, is not able to solve the problem of core unemployment amongst those with few or outdated skills at a time when there is a steady increase in the demand for higher level professional and managerial skills.

So, while labour market deregulation under the Conservatives may have improved the supply of low paid and insecure jobs, it did not solve the long term problem of reintegration of the unemployed. The said low paid and insecure jobs were more likely to be snapped up by people whose partners were already in work, thanks to a tough welfare regime based on means-tested benefits. There were other hidden costs as the public purse was used to subsidise low-paying employers through 'top-up' schemes for the working poor such as Family Credit (now Working Families Tax Credit). Labour market deregulation may well come to be seen as at best a mixed blessing and at worst a dead end and governments may have to look to other means at their disposal for managing labour demand.

1.2.2   Economic globalisation

The economic shocks of the late 1960s and early 1970s brought an end to thirty years of economic growth and stability and at the same time weakened the policies, institutions and structures which had underpinned the postwar settlement, such as the Welfare State and Keynesian demand-management to sustain full employment. The subsequent emergence of a neo-liberal agenda in the leading industrial countries, reinforced by the fall of communism, made the removal of these structures and institutions a condition of economic recovery. At the same time technological change in the form of electronic communications and transport links have been shrinking the world to a global village. Open markets and transnational corporations have become the new forces for economic growth and development in the world economy.

Strictly speaking, a truly global economy is one which is dominated by transnational firms and financial institutions, operating independently of national boundaries or domestic economic considerations. In such a world, goods, factors of production and financial assets would be interchangeable everywhere in the world. It would be no longer possible to identify a national economy and consider nation states as distinct economic entities with autonomous decision-making power in pursuit of national objectives. The world economy has clearly not yet reached this state. The current situation can be more aptly described as one of economic interdependence between countries where cross-border linkages among markets, production and financial activities have become so extensive that economic developments in any one country are significantly influenced by policies and developments outside its boundaries (Kozul-Wright and Rowthorn, 1998, ref. no. 22).

The impact of economic globalisation on working conditions can be analysed in three key areas: trade, international finance and multinational production.

1.2.2.1   Trade

Falling transport costs and protectionist barriers have created open world markets for goods and services. The OECD countries are now facing an upsurge in competition from new industries in Eastern Europe, Asia and Latin America. Transnational corporations are able to exploit the difference in costs that exist between First and Third world economies. Goods produced cheaply in the newly industrialising countries of the Third World are then exported to the First World. This has led to increased specialisation in production, so that, as industrialised countries have lost markets for low-skill intensive products, demand for their high-skill intensive products has risen. This has led to wholesale shifts of industry away from the OECD countries, causing large falls in manufacturing employment, increasing unemployment and/or falling real wages where a wage floor is not provided by unions or statutory minimum wages. Conversely, demand for skilled workers has risen and their wages have increased. Trade pressure implies the need to transfer resources, particularly labour, from declining to expanding industries, rather than a general loss of competitiveness. (Perraton *et al*, 1997, ref. no. 17).

1.2.2.2 *International finance*

From negligible levels in the 1950s, international finance has grown exponentially. The total size of the international capital market is now around US $6 trillion in outstanding loans. Turnover in the foreign exchange markets rose to over US $1 trillion every day in 1997, over 50 times levels of world trade. According to Diane Coyle (1997, ref. no. 28) these huge global financial markets developed to finance large-scale borrowing by certain governments, mainly in the industrial countries, although they are increasingly also financing private investment in 'emerging markets'. Capital can now be invested in almost any stock or bond market in the world at, literally, a moment's notice. Although some developing countries have opted out of the global markets by retaining restrictions on foreign exchange and foreigners' access to their domestic markets, most states have abandoned regulation of capital flows and are now competing for an international pool of savings. The greatest demand on this pool of international funds is borrowing by rich governments to finance spending for which their taxpayers are not prepared to pay. Repayment of this borrowed money is a problem for tomorrow's taxpayers, rather than todays.

The world's central banks and transnational financial institutions currently favour monetarist policies which prescribe low levels of government borrowing and control of inflation by restriction of the money supply through interest rates. International money will therefore be invested in countries which pursue prudent fiscal policies and do not spend too much more than their income. If their budget defecits grow too large, punishment in the form of swift and massive withdrawal of funds will be harsh. The currency will drop like a stone in value. Governments will attempt to defend their currency by raising interest rates, but this is rarely sufficient to end the crisis. The only solution for the beleaguered government is to cut public spending and announce an austerity programme. John Gray (1998, ref. no. 20) argues that the power of the markets dooms humane social market economies to extinction. Governments are now precluded from maintaining social cohesion through Keynesian interventionist policies that will guarantee full employment or through high levels of spending on public welfare. On the other hand Coyle (1997, ref. no. 28) argues that the markets are right and that governments which live beyond their means should be penalised. Mounting debts mean mounting interest payments which in turn increase the debt. Countries are trapped in a vicious circle, and sooner or later the day of reckoning will have come in the shape of massive tax rises and public spending cuts.

Susan Strange is also highly critical of the financial markets, arguing that traders will drive up the value of a market far beyond its actual worth, only to abandon it with equal rapidity. Speculation of this kind does enormous damage to the real economy of nations. Governments, still thinking nationally, have conspicuously failed to regulate and control the international financial markets (Strange, 1998, ref. no. 21).

1.2.2.3   *Multinational production*

Throughout the postwar period foreign direct investment has risen rapidly as multinational corporations (MNCs) have expanded across the globe. Multinationals' turnover has grown faster than world income, except during the mid-1970s, and they now account for up to a third of world output and two-thirds of world trade. The main impact of MNCs producing and selling abroad has been to create global competition. The degree of global competition varies across industries – obviously a taxi-driver in London is not in competition with one in Lahore. However, trade and multinational production have forced national firms across a range of industries to reduce costs and increase efficiency in order to compete globally.

Multinationals are often portrayed in the literature as being footloose, shifting production effortlessly within the firm in response to changing national conditions. However, this vision of MNCs shifting production costlessly around the globe is misleading, if only because they will not lightly abandon investment in plant, equipment, training, etc. More fundamentally, overseas production is undertaken because of significant advantages in production conditions abroad such as low wages, low taxes and little employment or environmental protection legislation. Small cost changes usually do not eliminate these advantages. However, few production advantages are unique to one country or location, so multinationals can and do pull out in response to changes in costs such as rising wages, increased taxation or restrictive legislation. Multinationals' ability to transfer technology abroad and the ability of foreign MNCs to tap into domestic innovation structures limits the effectiveness of national industrial and technological development strategies. Thus the ascendency of the MNC may have led to a shift in industrial policy away from national industrial development strategies and towards an emphasis on offering inducements for inward foreign direct investment. (Perraton *et al*, 1997, ref. no. 17). The role of national government shifts to negotiating the best possible deal for the country from its resident MNCs (Kozul-Wright and Rowthorn, 1998, ref. no. 22).

1.2.3   Information technology and automation

The impact of information technology and manufacturing automation has led to major changes in the world of work. In the automated factory human labour has been replaced by computer numerically controlled tools and robots. As early as 1982 a study from Japan quoted by Aronowitz (1994, ref. no. 23) 'suggests that amongst the most advanced robots currently in use displacement rates of 2-4 workers per shift are possible.' Michael Dunkerley (1996, ref. no. 24) quotes an example of a company he visited that was turning over £20 million per year and employed 200 people. The high turnover was due to the acquisition of robots each of which did the work of five men. The robots were run continuously over three shifts, twenty-four hours a day, and so were in effect doing the work of 15 people.

On the clerical side, information technology has facilitated the streamlining of administrative processes and the displacement of large numbers of workers. A hypothetical example from the insurance industry quoted by Cappelli (1997, ref. no. 39) makes the impact clearer. A customer who has suffered an accident or fire calls his insurance agent to file a claim. The agent passes the claim on to company HQ, where it is assigned to a claims clerk who checks that the policy is up to date. If it is, then the claim is passed to a company investigator who determines whether the claim is fraudulent and who is liable for the damage. The claim finally goes to a loss adjuster who determines the total damages and settles with the client.

The redesigned system relies heavily on information technology. The agent checks an online database to confirm that the policy is still in force and, using an expert system, estimates the likely validity of the claim. If the computer decides the claim is genuine, the agent simply pays the client. This information technology based system cuts out the role of the claims clerk completely and reduces that of the investigator and loss adjuster, whose services will not be required in most cases. The skills of the loss adjuster and investigator have been transferred to the machine, and a whole swathe of administrative functions has been cut out.

In the traditional organisation, middle management collected, collated and analysed information and presented it in ways that allowed decisions to be made. Now executive information systems allow the user to interrogate a database to extract the information needed and compare it to any other information of interest. At a stroke, these systems can be used to cut out whole layers of middle management. The transfer of skills to the machine also extends to the professions. The work of a doctor in diagnosis, for example, is in some senses routine and may be transferred to an expert system. In the field of software development itself, the routine aspects of programming are now being taken over by computer-aided software production (CASP) systems (Aronowitz; 1994, ref. no. 23).

Information technology not only displaces workers through the transfer of their skills to the machine, but also has the effect of deskilling remaining work. Once again an example will illustrate the point. The old style mainframe computers were large machines built out of hundreds of circuit boards. Skilled workers were required to assemble and test them. With the advent of the micro-chip, the circuits were automatically etched onto a piece of silicon. All the skilled workers required for manufacture of the old-style mainframes are gone and have been replaced by less skilled and lower paid assembly workers who slot mass produced parts into a plastic case and do a quick test to make sure it is working.

So technological change triggers a polarisation in the labour market. At one extreme there are opportunities for clever and highly educated people who can develop and implement new technologies and design and manage the industries based on them. At the other extreme low paid jobs in areas such as office cleaning, child and elderly care, retail service and catering provide the bulk of employment in the emerging service economy. Remaining office and factory jobs require lower levels of skills and specialist knowledge and skills are being transferred to machines. Middle income, medium skilled work which formerly enabled millions to live comfortably is disappearing, perhaps never to be seen again.

1.3   The organisational response

The interaction of government policy, economic globalisation and new technology have created a world of great turbulence. The organisational response to the new conditions has been characterised by restructuring and the development of flexibility in operations and employment practices. Cappelli (1997, ref. no. 39) suggests that four main principles have guided organisational redesign:

*   *Customer focused operating units.* The traditional functional divisions of marketing, development and manufacturing are being replaced by smaller units focusing on particular products and services. Each unit is responsible for all activities required for the delivery of a particular product or service, from development through production or operation to marketing, sales and promotion.

- *Devolved decision-making authority.* Business units are given responsibility for deciding strategy, but are also held accountable for results. They are typically focused around particular products and services for internal or external customers. Each unit incorporates as many functions as possible including planning, production and marketing. Relationships to customers are more clearly established and responsibility for decision-making is delegated so that managers have both more incentive and power to act. Accountability for results is more clearly pin-pointed, so they have stronger reasons to perform well.

- *Streamlined management control.* In restructured companies head offices are scaled back and management hierarchies thinned or delayered. Operating units are set financial targets and provided with incentives. They are then left to meet their targets without policy interference from head office. Management which fails to meet its targets can, of course, be summarily removed. This approach saves on personnel costs while expanding the span of control of remaining managers. The basic shape of the organisation becomes flat and broad instead of pyramidal.

- *Business process reengineering.* This approach, and its manufacturing equivalent lean production, involves the complete rethinking of which tasks need to be performed by organisations and how they are carried out. Reengineering streamlines processes through the introduction of new technology, reduction of paperwork, devolved decision-making and the removal of unnecessary checks and controls. Individual workers undertake a broader range of tasks, and are given greater power to make decisions. Simon Head (1996, ref. no. 38) gives a useful example of how reengineering works borrowed from its progenitors, Hammer and Champy. IBM Credit Corporation provides credit for IBM customers. Formerly, specialist workers were responsible for all sides of the business: clerical workers in one department logged in credit applications; specialists in the next department inserted special conditions for particular customers; another department fixed interest rates and the final section collated all the information and issued a quote letter. Reengineering introduced computer systems which enabled all these functions to be carried out by a single individual called a deal structurer. Reengineering at IBM increased the productivity of the credit business by 10,000% and displaced many clerical and middle management workers.

1.3.1   Downsizing

Business process reengineering and organisational delayering both offer companies improved competitiveness through downsizing to achieve massive savings in labour costs. Job cuts also follow the practice of subcontracting or outsourcing where firms concentrate on their core competencies and contract out support functions such as security, IT, cleaning, catering and building maintenance. Displaced workers in these areas may be hired by contractors, but often at reduced wages or inferior terms and conditions. Acquisitions and mergers can also lead to large scale job losses as combined organisations look to realise the economies of scale. In earlier times large scale redundancies were the result of recession (or the fear of one) and workers could expect to be recalled when capacity was increased in better times. Jobs cut through strategic downsizing, however, will be lost for ever.

The tide in the downsizing debate now seems to be turning. Employers have realised that unplanned, across the board job cuts made in a panic reaction to crisis can seriously damage the business. Cuts made on the basis of voluntary redundancy or early retirement programmes distort the balance of the workforce and lead to the loss of valuable skills and experience. Downsizing cuts labour costs and may in the short term improve profitability, but it does not of itself promote growth. Company growth and profitability in the long term depends on the possession of intellectual capital. Innovation, investment in research and development, management ability and a good marketing strategy translate into high performance, growth and job creation (Clayton and Carroll, 1994, ref. no. 33; Stewart, 1997, ref. no. 44). Employers, in their anxiety to cut costs, may compromise their ability to expand and adapt to new challenges.

Some companies and public sector organisations are also becoming increasingly concerned about outsourcing. The route is usually taken in response to a financial crisis, but without any clear analysis of what core competencies really are. In the case of IT, for example, it is becoming apparent that it is essential to retain a significant measure of in-house expertise so that the organisation can be an 'intelligent' purchaser of other people's services.

While it is generally agreed that downsizing is socially harmful and, if done badly, can damage the company, it is triggered by unstoppable technological and market forces which the company may feel powerless to resist. For companies in the grip of these forces, the alternative to downsizing may be extinction.

1.3.2   Work redesign

The central principle of work redesign in restructured organisations is increased employee power and responsibility, although empowerment may often be more rhetorical than real. The changes are, of course, not uniform across all employers who restructure, but perhaps the most typical innovation is the introduction of work teams. The core of the idea of teams is that employees take responsibility for a group of tasks, that there be a sense of responsibility for the team's product, that the workers be broadly skilled, and that there be an element of job rotation. Belbin (1996 ref. no. 36) identifies three types of teams:

• Operational teams, which are internal to a department or function

• Cross-functional teams, which involve co-ordination of departments or functions

• Strategic teams, which work concurrently on long term problems.

Introduction of team working of this kind is often linked to quality management and customer satisfaction initiatives or the flattening of organisational hierarchies as part of a general effort by the company to transform itself. Other changes in human resources management commonly linked to work redesign are the introduction of performance related pay and higher levels of training. The importance of training is obvious in that employees who are to be given more responsibilities need to be prepared. Performance related pay shifts risks from the employer to the workers, but on the other hand gives teams the power to reap the rewards of their efforts.

Work redesign and flattening hierarchies also have an impact upon career development paths. Now that there is no long corporate ladder up which employees can move, organisations are having to find new ways to motivate and reward staff. New approaches include committing the organisation to assist in the personal development of its workers to ensure their continued employability and assigning staff extra duties without formal vertical promotion.

1.3.3   Use of flexible labour

Business Strategies Limited (BSL) (1997, ref. no. 42) predict that nearly half the workforce could be covered by flexible arrangements such as temporary contracts, self-employment and part-time jobs in ten years time. The *Financial Times* also reported on 1st February 1996 that the number of short term contracts in manufacturing grew by 67.5% in five years as companies switched to just-in-time production methods. Flexible work arrangements offer big advantages to employers. Firms can push the effects of business downturns on to employees by terminating contracts or cutting part-time hours. Flexible employees are also more likely to have to meet the costs of their pension and sick pay.

Faced with fluctuations in demand, companies resort to all manner of exotic and creative labour practices. Harland and Wolff, the Belfast shipyard has switched from standard ship construction to bid for work in the offshore oil and gas sector but contracts and delivery schedules in the offshore business are more time sensitive than in traditional shipbuilding, leading to fluctuations in the demand for labour. In order to avoid having to pay redundancy and then re-hire workers, H&W has come to an agreement with a large employment services company, Randstad, under which employees temporarily surplus to requirements will be subcontracted out to employers in Europe and mainland Britain. A business services company cited by Casey Metcalf and Millward (1997, ref. no. 41) used up to 30 freelances in tandem with ten permanent staff to reduce fixed costs in a business where demand was lumpy.

Exotic and creative practices by occasional firms apart, however, Casey *et al*'s analysis of data from the Labour Force Survey (LFS) shows that the most common forms of flexible labour – part-time and temporary employment – have increased since 1984, but not dramatically. The proportion of workers in temporary jobs across all firms increased from 4.3 to 6.5%. The proportion working part-time increased from 20.4 to 25.4% in the same period. These figures confirm the findings of Robinson (1994, ref. no. 1) in his study of the structure of the British labour market that part-time employment has been growing steadily since World War II. Growth was in fact more rapid in the 1950s and 1960s than in the 1970s and 1980s. Part-time employment was 15% of total employment in 1971, 20.6% in 1981 and 24.6% in 1991. The bulk of part-time working is voluntary and done by women to fit in with other commitments. As for temporary employment, the LFS figures show that it did not rise during the 1980s and actually declined between 1991 and 1993. In 1984 5.7% of employment was temporary, in 1991 it was 5.8% and in 1993 5.1%.

The most dramatic increase in flexible labour between 1984 and 1994 appears to have been in overtime. As firms downsize and use fewer staff to cope with fluctuations in demand, paid and unpaid overtime has ballooned. Talk of massive growth in atypical working practices fuelled by the media has been exaggerated.

The real change is at the margins, with employers needing a few hours extra here and there and employees giving it.

1.4   Dismantling the welfare state

The welfare state was a central part of the postwar settlement, designed to provide free health care, decent housing and economic security for all. It was based on the assumption that the welfare of its people is the collective responsibility of the state, and that the power of the state should be used to modify market forces. It was intended to operate in an environment of full employment, stable families, job security and retirement of short duration but has come under pressure due to radical social changes including:

•   Increased entry of women into the labour market

•   Growth in single parent families from 570,000 in 1971 to 1.4 million in 1992

•   Increase in life expectancy from 67 to 73 for men and from 71 to 78 for women between 1950 and 1990

•   Permanent rise in unemployment following first oil shock in 1973.

These pressures caused spiralling costs which led the Conservative governments of 1979-1997 to engage in systematic attempts at welfare retrenchment. The Thatcher government which came into power in 1979 saw the welfare state as one of the prime causes of poor economic performance. Its funding required high taxation, it discouraged work and investment and encouraged dependency. The cushioning effects of social programmes led workers to sustain unrealistic wage demands that destroyed competitiveness. The ideology of the New Right decreed minimal state provision for need. Individuals were encouraged to provide for themselves and to help their needy fellow citizens directly through private charity and voluntary action. Anything more than minimum state provision led to welfare dependency and undermined the individual's commitment to self-improvement.

The implementation of welfare retrenchment policies based on this ideology at a time of economic turmoil, led to the weakening of the safety net just when many people were facing financial insecurity. Of particular concern were pension provision, the costs of long term care for the elderly, mortgage protection and unemployment insurance.

16

The Conservative government radically reduced the value of the basic state pension by changing the indexation in 1980 to uprating by prices instead of uprating in line with average earnings. By 1988 the new formula meant that a married couple received £65.90 instead of £79.90 per week, a reduction of 20%. The Social Security Act of 1986 lowered State Earnings Related Pension Scheme (SERPS) benefits and encouraged the take-up of private pensions by offering rebates in National Insurance contributions. Employees were also given the option of opting out of occupational pension plans and setting up personal pensions instead. The Blair government, in proposals announced in December 1998, confirmed that the link between the basic state pension and average earnings would not be restored. They plan to abolish SERPS and to use National Insurance rebates to encourage middle-income employees without access to occupational schemes to invest in 'stakeholder' pensions to be provided by the private sector. People earning less than £9,000 a year and those taking care of children and the elderly will be assured of extra comfort in their old age through National Insurance credits made on their behalf to a proposed new second state pension. The intention is to encourage all who can save for for their old age to do so, and to reduce the government's contribution to the pensions bill from 60% to 40% of the total cost. Unfortunately both personal and stakeholder pensions carry investment risk and uncertainty about the rate of annuity which can be purchased at the end. Unless policies change, pensioners in the next century will probably be on increasingly unequal incomes, depending on decisions made 25 years earlier about which type of private pension to choose.

Older people also face increasing worries about long term care should they become incapacitated. Since the 1990 NHS and Community Care Act, Health Authorities have been rapidly withdrawing from funding continuing care beds. Long term care is now financed by local government and is means- and asset- tested. Anyone with more than £16,000 in assets now has to fund care themselves, and people are being encouraged (or pressurised) into taking out insurance policies to cover the costs.

For younger people, the Jobseekers Allowance introduced in October 1996, was the latest in a long series of degradations of unemployment benefit. It is means-tested after six months, from which point it excludes those with savings above £8,000 and those whose partner is working more than 24 hours a week. Help with mortgage interest payments is now available only to people claiming income support or income-based Jobseeker's Allowance. Payments will only be paid after six months on benefit for loans taken out before October 1995 and after 39 weeks on benefit for loans taken out later. People are expected to take out mortgage protection policies to cover shortfalls. People in jobs therefore have to put aside a large and increasing percentage of income for insurance policies and precautionary savings. With the weakened welfare safety net and difficulties in finding another job after redundancy, there is an undercurrent of genuine insecurity in society.

1.5   Bibliography

1.5.1   Changes in economic policy

(1)
THE BRITISH labour market in historical perspective: changes in the structure of employment and unemployment
P Robinson
London: Centre for Economic Performance, London School of Economics, 1994. 86p.
(Discussion paper; no.202)

Uses data from the New Earnings, General Household and Labour Force Surveys and Censuses of Population to look at changes in the structure of employment and unemployment since the war.

DSC Shelfmark: 3597.120600

(2)
LABOUR market flexibility
M Beatson
Sheffield: Employment Department, 1995. 178p.
(Research series; no.48)

Assesses whether the British labour market has become more flexible. Explains that labour markets can adjust to changing conditions through quantities (employment or hours worked) or prices (wages) and covers both at the microeconomic and macroeconomic levels.

DSC Shelfmark: 7769.925000

(3)
LABOUR market flexibility: a cure for unemployment?
S Deakin
Benefits, issue 12, 1995, p.1–5.

Covers the impact of flexible labour policies in the UK and Europe. Concludes that while labour market deregulation may make part-time and temporary jobs more widely available, it does not offer a solution to the long term reintegration of the unemployed.

DSC Shelfmark:1891.465000

(4)
A SHORT history of labour turnover, job tenure and job security, 1975–93
P Gregg and J Wadsworth
Oxford review of economic policy, vol.11, 1995, p.73-90.

Argues that while job tenure has changed only marginally for the majority, entry positions available to the unemployed have become increasingly unstable and low paid.

DSC Shelfmark: 6321.016950

(5)
ANGLO-SAXON economics and jobs
J Philpott
London: Employment Policy Institute, 1997. 6p.
(Economic report; vol.11, no.1, 1997)

Suggests that structural change in the labour market operating alongside government policy has been an important determinant in spreading flexible working practices. Argues that Anglo-Saxon economic policies of deregulation and promotion of flexibility cannot provide a solution to cure unemployment, which requires a more interventionist approach.

DSC Shelfmark: 3654.390000

(6)
FULL employment: a pledge betrayed
J G Smith
Basingstoke: Macmillan, 1997. 262p.

Neo-Keynesian critique of tight fiscal and monetary policies pursued by Conservative governments from 1979 and now espoused by New Labour. The use of interest rates as the sole weapon for controlling inflation damped down demand and created mass unemployment. Suggests an alternative approach of stimulating the expansion of industrial capacity through demand management, and avoidance of a wage/price spiral through reform of the pay bargaining system.

DSC Shelfmark: 97/13441

(7)
GLOBAL competitiveness report 1997
World Economic Forum
London: World Link Publications, 1997. 250p.

Praises Britain's recovery from economic decline to become the envy of continental Europe following privatisation, deregulation and other structural reforms. Britain's rating reflects strong performance by 'Anglo-Saxon' countries, led by U.S.

DSC Shelfmark: Not found

(8)
IMPLEMENTING the OECD jobs strategy: lessons from member countries' experience
Paris: OECD, 1997. 34p.

Report cites Britain, the Netherlands, New Zealand and Ireland as role models for improving labour market performance through wide-ranging structural reform.

DSC Shelfmark: OP-OE/3682

(9)
MIRACLE or mirage: Britain's economy seen from abroad
K Marsden
London: Centre for Policy Studies, 1997. 51p.
(Policy study; no.150)

Concludes that Britain has one of the highest growth rates in the developed world, that it is the only one of the world's leading nations to have cut the effective tax burden since 1980, and that the fruits of prosperity have been shared by all when social benefits are included. Attributes success to Anglo-Saxon economics of deregulation and monetarism.

DSC Shelfmark: 6543.329570

(10)
A YEAR in the labour market
P Gregg and J Wadsworth
Employment audit, issue 4, 1997, p.13-24.

Statistical evidence shows that jobs taken by those out of work are of lower quality than the jobs they lost. This is, however, offset on aggregate by upgrading while staying with the same employer, and, to a lesser degree, by a series of job to job moves.

DSC Shelfmark: 3737.213700

1.5.2   Economic globalisation

(11)
THE LONG wave in the world economy: the present crisis in historical perspective
A Tylecote
London: Routledge, 1992. 338p.

Examines the theory of prolonged economic cycles in the world economy, in which upswings and downswings succeed each other at intervals of approximately 50 years.

DSC Shelfmark: 92/07502

(12)
THE EMPTY raincoat: making sense of the future
C Handy
London: Hutchinson, 1994. 280p.

Provides a vivid account of the pressures on organisations and individuals in the emerging international economy. Identifies problems thrown up as reduced demand for low-skill labour, accentuation of social divisions, job and career insecurity, overwork and reduction of leisure time.

DSC Shelfmark: 94/07500

(13)
THE EVOLVING global economy: making sense of the new world order
K Ohmae (editor)
Boston, Mass: Harvard Business School, 1995. 300p.

Attempts to help senior managers grapple with the practical challenges of steering their companies through the unfamiliar landscape of the newly evolving global economy.

DSC Shelfmark: 96/19777

(14)
When corporations rule the world
D C Korten
London: Earthscan, 1995. 384p.

A 'devastating critique of globalisation' which looks at the human and environmental consequences of globalisation in which the powers of nation states have been undermined by those of multinational companies with narrow financial aims that are pursued regardless of the consequences to society. Recommends a new approach to allow ordinary people and their political representatives to reclaim economic power and political influence from these elitist and undemocratic organisations.

DSC Shelfmark: 95/35800

(15)

IS the good corporation dead?: social responsibility in a global economy

J W Houck and O F Williams (editors)

Lanham, Md: Rowman & Littlefield, 1996. 318p.

In the light of economic globalisation, authors debate how to reinvent the good corporation in a form suitable for the twenty-first century.

DSC Shelfmark: 96/26532

(16)

STATES against markets: the limits of globalization

R Boyer and D Drache (editors)

London: Routledge, 1996. 448p.

Challenges the popular view that globalisation threatens the role of the nation state in determining national policy. The fundamental issues of competitiveness and market power in an increasingly borderless world are examined. Despite this threat to the nation state as an effective manager of the national economy, it remains the conduit for investment now and in the future. Only it can organise markets to ensure transparency, fairness, access and efficiency.

DSC Shelfmark: 96/20105

(17)

THE GLOBALISATION of economic activity

J Perraton *et al*

New political economy, vol.2, 1997, p.257-277.

Article analyses the evidence for globalisation in three key areas: trade, international finance and multinational production.

DSC Shelfmark: 6085.740000

(18)

GOVERNMENTS, globalization, and international business

J H Dunning (editor)

Oxford: Oxford University Press, 1997. 518p.

Describes and analyses the implications of the deepening structural interdependence of the world economy for the governance of economic activity of nation states.

DSC Shelfmark: 97/11727

(19)

SALMON day: the end of the beginning for global business

D Lamont

Oxford: Capstone, 1997. 300p.

Investigates how global firms prosper, why they fail and how they can avoid failure in the future. Shows how nation states can learn from the example of global firms and create successful agglomerations of power through free trade agreements.

DSC shelfmark: Not found

(20)
FALSE dawn: the delusions of global capitalism
J Gray
London: Granta, 1998. 262p.

Argues that attempts to create a global free market based on laissez-faire capitalism neglect the enduring human needs for security and social identity. As a side effect of global free markets, economic insecurity is increasing worldwide. Global mobility of capital and production triggers intense competition which forces the more humane capitalist economies to deregulate and trim back welfare provision.

DSC Shelfmark: 98/08700

(21)
MAD money
S Strange
Manchester: Manchester University Press, 1998. 224p.

Analyses the evolution of international financial markets over the past decade, including the impact of new technology and the development of new instruments such as derivatives and hedge funds, and assesses international efforts to regulate these innovations. Concludes that market operators are motivated by a blind pursuit of profit which leads to damage to the real economy as traders drive up a market far beyond its worth, only to abandon it with equal suddenness. Governments, which still tend to think nationally, have proved incapable of regulating financial markets, which now operate internationally.

DSC Shelfmark: Not found

(22)
TRANSNATIONAL corporations and the global economy
R Kozul-Wright and R Rowthorn
Basingstoke: Macmillan, 1998. 437p.

Papers deal with issues such as the nature and extent of globalisation, the changing role of transnational corporations in the world economy and the opportunities and obstacles facing national policy makers in the rapidly changing global economy.

DSC Shelfmark: 98/15580

1.5.3   Information Technology and Automation

(23)
THE JOBLESS future: sci-tech and the dogma of work
S Aronowitz and W DiFazio
Minneapolis: University of Minnesota Press, 1994 (1995 printing). 392p.

Explains, from a Marxist point of view, the impact of the computer on the world of work. Information technology is shown to lead to massive displacement and deskilling of human labour.

DSC Shelfmark: 94/26848

(24)
THE JOBLESS economy: computer technology and the world of work
M Dunkerley
Cambridge: Polity Press, 1996. 168p.

Readable summary of the impact of new technology on work, with interesting suggestions about how society could be remodelled in an age where intelligent machines produce all the necessities of life.

DSC Shelfmark: 96/32085

(25)
WORK out or work in? contributions to the debate on the future of work
P Meadows (editor)
York: Joseph Rowntree Foundation, 1996. 164p.

Examines impact of technological and social change on the labour market. Points to the rapid breakdown of the social contract between employer and worker as risks are shared and the impact of economic downturns are passed on to employees. Mass unemployment in the UK has led to loss of social cohesion and growing inequality as wealth is appropriated by those in work. Jobs being created require higher level social and technical skills, and there is concern about the availability of work for the unskilled.

DSC Shelfmark: 96/13825

(26)
THE END of work: decline of the global labor force and the dawn of the post-market era
J Rifkin
New York: Putnam, 1995. 350p.

Argues that the nature of work is undergoing a fundamental transformation as a result of global economic and technological developments in which human workers are being replaced by machines. These trends will affect white-collar, managerial and 'knowledge-based' jobs just as much as they have already affected the manufacturing sector. Societies will have to find ways of dealing with millions of people who are economically redundant except as consumers.

DSC Shelfmark: 95/07488

(27)
INNOVATION, organizational change and technology
I McLoughlin and M Harris (editors)
London: International Thomson, 1997. 228p.

Explores the organisational and managerial implications of technological innovation, including the use of business process reengineering, the concept of the vitual organisation, the social shaping of technology and the effects of technology on organisation.

DSC Shelfmark: 97/00593

(28)
THE WEIGHTLESS world: strategies for managing the digital economy
D Coyle
Oxford: Capstone, 1997. 250p.

Personal insights on the impact of new technology on the organisation of work, welfare, international finance and national government. Argues that the forces of digital technology and global business offer a route to a new era of human creativity and economic prosperity, and appeals to governments and individuals to embrace the new age where the goods which shape lives – global financial transactions, electronic commerce and computer code – literally have no weight.

DSC Shelfmark: 97/30345

(29)
POST-work: the wages of cybernation
S Aronowitz and J Cutler (editors)
New York: Routledge, 1998. 279p.

Essays directed at exploring the various economic and political changes underway, their consequences, and what organised labour and other social movements might do about them. Covers the impact of IT on the white-collar workplace, poverty, welfare policy and the guaranteed income, and the implications of global capitalism for education reform.

DSC Shelfmark: 98/28149

1.5.4   Organisational change

(30)
MANUFACTURING productivity
McKinsey Global Institute
Washington, DC: McKinsey & Co., 1993. Various pagings.

Using case studies of the motor, metalworking, steel and electronics industries, explains how Japanese use of just-in-time (JIT) manufacturing methods has achieved higher productivity levels than those found in the US and Germany. Points out that exposure to international competition and 'transplants' of best practices from leading companies abroad are significant drivers in raising labour productivity.

DSC Shelfmark: q96/01975

(31)
ORGANISATIONAL change and redesign: ideas and insights for improving performance
G P Huber and W H Glick (editors)
New York: Oxford University Press, 1993. 450p.

Explains the environmental turbulence which is forcing organisations to change to meet new challenges and explores the theory and implementation of the process of organisational change.

DSC Shelfmark: 93/23758 (missing)

(32)
REENGINEERING the corporation: a manifesto for business revolution
M. Hammer and J. Champy
London: Nicholas Brealey, 1993 (1995 printing). 240p.

Explains the authors' concept and methodology of business reengineering, which involves complete organisational redesign to meet the demands of today's markets through harnessing the power of the new information and communication technologies. Requires the identification and abandonment of outdated rules and assumptions which underlie business operations, and a complete rethink of how work is performed.

DSC Shelfmark: 95/23310

(33)
BUILDING business for Europe: evidence from Europe and North America on 'intangible' factors behind growth, competitiveness and jobs: final report to the European Commission by PIMS Associates Ltd and the Irish Management Institute

T Clayton and C Carroll
London, 1994. 59p.

Finds that innovation and intellectual property are the strongest drivers of competitiveness, but that investment focused on cutting labour costs usually destroys both profits and jobs. Research and innovation, management ability, providing customers with the choices they want and a good market strategy all translate into higher added value and more job creation.

DSC Shelfmark: Not found

(34)
THE RESPONSIVE organisation: re-engineering new patterns of work
C Coulson-Thomas (editor)
London: Policy Publications and Adaptation Limited, 1995. 3 vols.

A report produced as a result of the European Commission's COBRA Project. Volume subtitles as follows: Vol.1: Methodology: re-engineering organisations and processes for new patterns of work (159p); Vol.2: Best practice: key insights from European experience in business re-engineering and teleworking (169p); Vol.3: Resources: sources of support and briefings for effective business re-engineering and teleworking projects (138p). A useful antidote to reengineering 'hype' which suggests the increasingly negative image of BPR is fully justified. Most companies use it as a short-term fix to save costs, and few use it constructively to create new strategic capabilities, markets or products.

DSC Shelfmark: q95/33901 (Vol.1)
q95/33902 (Vol.2)
q95/33903 (Vol.3)

(35)
TIME pioneers: flexible working time and new lifestyles
K H Horning, A Gerhard and M Michailow
Cambridge: Polity Press, 1995. 198p.

Sociological study of the influence of flexible working practices on lifestyles.

DSC Shelfmark: 96/05877

(36)
THE COMING shape of organisation
M Belbin
Oxford: Butterworth-Heinemann, 1996. 128p.

Predicts the demise of the traditional hierarchical and bureaucratic organisational design. Based on social structures of ants and bees, envisages a hierarchy of teams working concurrently on short, medium and long term problems facing the organisation.

DSC Shelfmark: 96/20959

(37)
FLEXIBLE work
E Murphy
Hemel Hempstead: Director Books, 1996. 181p.

Explores how organisations are responding to technological change, globalisation and increased competition through business process reengineering, and the implementation of flexible working practices such as teleworking, job-sharing, flexitime, 'virtual office' solutions and multi-skilling. Draws on real-life case studies and examples from the UK and Europe.

DSC Shelfmark: 97/06412

(38)
THE NEW ruthless economy
S Head
Prometheus, vol.14, 1996, p.195–205.

Gives a concise account of general developments in the world of work, including lean production and its white collar equivalent business reengineering.

DSC Shelfmark: 6925.048000

(39)
CHANGE at work
P Cappelli *et al*
New York: Oxford University Press, 1997. 276p.

Excellent and comprehensive survey, from an American point of view, of organisational restructuring, work redesign, training and the effects of changes on employees.

DSC Shelfmark: 97/18594

(40)
THE CHANGING shape of work
R K Brown (editor)
Basingstoke: Macmillan, 1997. 226p.

Reviews the changing nature of the UK labour market, including the feminisation of work, the survival strategies developed by those without regular jobs, the effects of unemployment on families, management attempts to change organisational culture, and worker responses to total quality management. Emphasises transformation of work through the rise of atypical forms of employment and the migration of jobs from manufacturing to the service industries.

DSC Shelfmark: 98/04682

(41)
EMPLOYERS' use of flexible labour
B Casey, H Metcalf and N Millward
London: Policy Studies Institute, 1997. 180p.

Analyses data from the Labour Force Survey and Workplace Industrial Relations Survey to show that while use of temporary and part-time workers has increased, the most dramatic change between 1984 and 1994 has been an 87% increase in the number of employees working variable hours. Examines employers' reasons for using flexible labour and constraints they face in extending flexible working practices.

DSC Shelfmark: 7762.841000

(42)
FLEXIBLE employment and employment diversity
R Holt
London: Business Strategies, 1997. 75p.

Estimates that nearly half the workforce could be covered by flexible arrangements such as temporary contracts, self-employment and part-time jobs in ten years time. The growth in flexible work patterns will be driven by temporary work. Self-employment and part-time working will also grow, but more slowly than in the past decade. The growth in atypical employment will take place mostly in the service industries. Flexible arrangements benefit employers who can then transfer the effects of business downturns to workers.

DSC Shelfmark: Not found

(43)
INDUSTRIAL inefficiency and downsizing: a study of layoffs and plant closures
M B Krepps and A B Candell
New York: Garland, 1997. 145p.

Investigates the genesis and exodus of industrial inefficiency by analysing where corporate fat accumulates and how it is eliminated in response to competitive forces.

DSC Shelfmark: 97/28175

(44)
INTELLECTUAL capital: the new wealth of organisations
T A Stewart
London, Nicholas Brealey, 1997. 261p.

Suggests that knowledge is becoming the world's most powerful resource. Harnessing intellectual capital and exploiting it for profit needs new approaches and structures and the text lays down important ideas on the organisation of today's businesses. The arguments are presented persuasively in a mix of anecdote and statistics.

DSC Shelfmark: 97/09234

(45)
TOWARDS the virtual organization
R Hale and P Whitlam
London: McGraw-Hill, 1997. 239p.

Defines the vitual organisation as one which is continually evolving, redefining and reinventing itself for practical business purposes. The virtual organisation will institutionalise organisational change, enable individuals to optimise their potential to contribute, create new forms and shapes, develop dynamic communication strategies and create cultures which support continual organisational adaptation.

DSC Shelfmark: 98/02969

(46)
THE NEW organizational reality: downsizing, restructuring and revitalization
M K Gowing, J D Kraft and J C Quick (editors)
Washington, DC: American Psychological Association, 1998. 278p.

Presents a state-of-the-art view of changing organisational structure, its inherent problems and the ways in which solutions have been found. Includes theoretical articles, research findings and case studies.

DSC Shelfmark: 98/18938

1.5.5 Welfare reform

(47)
THE END of the line for social security: the Thatcherite restructuring of welfare
P Alcock
Critical social policy, vol. 10, no.3, Winter 1990/91, p.58-105.

Summarises the ideology of the New Right and its challenge to the social democratic notion of the interventionist welfare state. Shows how Thatcherism aimed to replace the welfare state with the opportunity state, and to encourage self-reliance and individual commitment to self-improvement. This philosophy underpinned the Thatcher government's minimalist approach to social security.

DSC Shelfmark: 3487.485500

(48)

DISMANTLING the welfare state: Reagan, Thatcher and the politics of retrenchment

P Pierson

Cambridge: Cambridge University Press, 1994. 213p.

Traces the historical development of welfare retrenchment policies in the UK and the US, and explains why some succeeded where others failed. Includes detailed case studies of housing, pensions and social security.

DSC Shelfmark: 95/12314

(49)

BRITISH social welfare: past, present and future

D Gladstone (editor)

London: UCL Press, 1995. 352p.

Comprehensive account of the development of the British welfare state after World War II, covering social security, health care.

DSC Shelfmark: 95/15708

(50)

INCOMES and the welfare state: essays on Britain and Europe

A B Atkinson

Cambridge: Cambridge University Press, 1995. 368p.

Analyses the impact of the welfare state on incomes and living standards of individuals and families. Investigates causes of the rise in income inequality in the 1980s, the role and economic impact of social security, and the pros and cons of targetting benefits in a reformed welfare state.

DSC Shelfmark: 96/10408

(51)

THE STATE of welfare: the economics of social spending. 2nd ed.

M Evandrou *et al*

Oxford: Oxford University Press, 1998. 363p.

Argues that the welfare state has coped reasonably well over the past 25 years with rising expectations, rising demands and a lid on the budget. Charts growth and changes in spending patterns since 1974 and measures what that spending has achieved and the growing demands on it.

DSC Shelfmark: 98/20612

2 What is Stress?

2.1 Definition of stress

The term 'stress' could be described as one of the most inaccurate words in the scientific literature. The root of the confusion is that the word has been used to describe both the sources and outcomes of the stress process. In popular parlance, people are said to be under stress when they are in a difficult situation or put under pressure. In this context the word 'stress' refers to a stimulus or input. We also say we are under stress when we are suffering from anxiety, depression or an inability to cope. Researchers have tended to be more precise in that each has used the word stress to mean only an input (stressor) or outcome (strain). Unfortunately they do not agree with each other in their usage, which makes comparison of results across studies difficult.

The fact that stress has many definitions does not mean it doesn't exist. In that respect it is a little like love. The word 'love' means different things to different people, but we all know what it feels like to experience the emotion. The feeling of being 'in love' or 'under stress' is not less real because it is difficult to define.

Pressure is an unavoidable part of life. In itself it is a neutral force. It can produce either good or bad outcomes, depending on individual adaptability and coping skills. Pressure can be the stimulus that enables us to learn new skills, experience excitement, and get things done. It can also be the force that causes depression and anxiety, breaks up relationships and can make people seriously physically ill. In this context pressure has become a stressor or source of stress leading to negative consequences or strains for the individual. The key to whether pressure is a positive or negative force lies in how the individual copes with or manages it.

Pressure is an essential stimulus for personal growth and achievement. Without it we atrophy. Attempts to eliminate pressure tend to produce new pressures. If an individual decides to drop out of the rat race and go and live on a croft in Caithness or on a beach in Spain, they will simply find themselves subject to a new set of pressures, such as the pressure of finding enough money to live on or the pressure of physical labour. Positively managed, pressure produces high performance. People perform best when stimulated, stretched and challenged, not when bored or constrained. However when the pressure is too great the individual begins to experience strain and performance is impaired. Tolerance of pressure varies from person to person. A level of pressure which produces good performance in one individual can produced strain in another. Williams (1994, ref. no. 60) helpfully envisages pressure as ranging over a five point scale. At the lowest point of the scale pressure is minimal and people will tend to become bored and lethargic. Williams calls the next point on the scale the comfort zone. There is some stimulation and challenge, but people are not really being pushed. As pressure increases, individuals move out of the comfort zone into the stretch zone. Here they are being stretched and challenged, are learning from their experiences, are growing and enjoying increased self-confidence and self-esteem. They feel stimulated, energised and confident, and function in a resourceful, successful state.

However, if the pressure continues to increase, people find they can no longer manage and become 'over-stretched. Coping mechanisms begin to break down and performance deteriorates as people exhibit signs of strain. The final point on Williams' scale he calls the panic zone. Here the pressure is so intense that people cannot take any more and are at risk of serious illness. In this area the strains become pathological and people may need professional help or have to make radical changes in their lives to return to normal functioning.

2.2   Stress models

In the current stress literature it is possible to identify three different, but overlapping, approaches to the definition and study of work-related stress. The first approach defines stress in terms of the physiological effects of a wide range of noxious or unpleasant stimuli. It treats stress as a dependent variable, as a particular physiological response to a threatening or damaging environment. This approach has been termed 'the physiological model'. The second approach focuses on the structural features of a person's interaction with their work environment. Two particular interactional approaches have been especially influential: the Person-Environment Fit theory of French, Caplan and van Harrison (1982, ref. no. 89) and the Job Demands-Decision Latitude theory of Karasek (1979, ref. no. 76). Finally, transactional approaches to stress focus on the cognitive processes and emotional reactions underpinning individuals' interactions with their environment. Transactional models such as those put forward by Lazarus (1966, ref. no. 94) define stress as a psychological state involving aspects of both cognition and emotion. The stress state is regarded as the internal representation of particular problematic transactions between individuals and their environment. Stress arises when individuals perceive that they cannot cope with the demands being made on them or threats to their well-being, when coping is of importance to them and when they are anxious and depressed about it.

We will now go on to examine these various models of work-related stress in detail. Three key approaches to, or models of, stress can be identified in the literature, two American and one Scandinavian.

2.2.1 The Stockholm School and psychobiology

The Stockholm school builds most directly on the pioneering work of Hans Selye. Selye defined stress as 'the non-specific response of the body to any demand made upon it'. His major contribution to the field was his outlining of the three stage general adaption syndrome (GAS). The Alarm Stage is an integrated call-to-arms which mobilises the biochemical resources of the organism. This is followed by a second Resistance Stage in which the organism begins to adapt to the stressors, reducing the extent of the earlier symptoms and preparing for longer term but still finite resistance. In the final stage Exhaustion sets in following prolonged resistance to the stressor, leading to a reversion to the earlier symptoms of alarm and the eventual death of the organism if the stressor persists. The School's approach emphasises the part played by arousal, stimulation and workload in stress. Its preferred methodology invariably includes a particular form of physiological measurement centred on the measurement of stress hormone secretions. Problems with the physiological model reside in the difficulty of distinguishing those physiological changes caused by stressors from those which are not. There are subtle but important differences in the overall pattern of response. For example Cox and Cox (1985, ref. no. 74) investigated the role of two neuroendocrine systems, the sympathetic-adrenal medullary system and the pituitary-adrenal cortical system in the psychophysiology of stress. They suggest that situations that give rise to anxiety may increase sympathetic-adrenal medullary activity, while situations associated with depression and helplessness may increase pituitary-adrenal cortical activity. Psychosocial factors associated with increased sympathetic-adrenal medullary activity have been tentatively linked to coronary heart disease, and those associated with increased pituitary-adrenal cortical function have been even more tentatively linked to impaired immune system function and possibly cancers.

The second criticism is that the physiological approach does not allow for individual differences in the way people respond to stress factors. People are treated as passive vehicles for the translation of environmental stimuli into physiological responses. They largely ignore the interactions between the person and their various environments, in particular the psychosocial and organisational contexts of work stress. Over time the Swedes have come to recognise the importance of psychological measures, focusing particularly on the variable of controllability. In laboratory experiments and field studies they have been able to consistently show that perceived control is related to stress hormone secretion. Their most famous study related to groups of blue collar workers in a saw mill, where the most stressed groups in terms of physical symptoms and stress hormone levels were engaged in intensive and repetitive machine based work over which little control could be exercised (Frankenhaeuser 1981, ref. no. 72).

2.2.1.1   Demands-control model

The Stockholm Schools' ideas on controllability as a key factor in modifying the experience of stress have been taken up by the American Robert Karasek. In his model of work stress 'demands' and 'constraints' are presumed varying properties of jobs and environments. Psychological strain arises not from a single aspect of the work environment but from the joint effects of the demands of the work situation and the range of decision-making freedom available to the worker in meeting those demands. Job demands such as heavy workload, interpersonal conflict, time pressure, etc place the individual in a motivated or energised state. Constraints on the alternative actions to deal with the demands may inhibit the conversion of this potential energy into the energy of action. If no action can be taken, or if the individual cannot take the appropriate action because of lack of decision-making authority, the unreleased energy may manifest itself internally as mental strain. In Karasek's model stress sources such as heavy workload present in the environment are referred to as job demands. The degree of decision-making freedom or decision latitude available to the worker in meeting the job demands is called 'job control' or 'discretion'. Decision latitude is assessed by combining the scores of subscales measuring skill discretion (the worker's ability to use judgement and to assert control over the use of skills within the work process) and decision authority (the worker's freedom to make decisions about task performance). Distress arising from a combination of high demands and low decision latitude is referred to as job strain. Karasek's model contains two basic predictions. Strain is predicted to increase as job demands increase relative to decreasing decision latitude. Secondly, personal growth and development are predicted to occur when the challenges of the situation are matched by the individual's skill or control in meeting the challenge. When demands and decision latitude are both high, the job is defined as 'active' and will lead to personal growth and development. Jobs at the opposite extreme are defined as 'passive' and are said to induce a reduction in overall activity and well-being (Karasek, 1979, ref. no. 76).

2.2.1.2   Methodological critique

The job demands-control model has been criticised on several grounds. The central claim of the model concerns the interaction of high demands and low decision latitude to produce job strain. In most demands–control studies, consistent support was found for additive rather than interactional effects (Melamed, Kushnir and Meir, 1991, ref. no. 81; Payne and Fletcher, 1983, ref. no. 78; Warr, 1990, ref. no. 80; Fletcher and Jones, 1993, ref. no. 83). For the benefit of non-statisticians, additive effects are caused by two or more stress factors working independently of each other to produce strain. When they occur together, they produce a cumulative effect. In interactional effects, two stress factors work in combination. One factor would not cause distress on its own, without the presence of the other. The most pronounced adverse additive effects in the aforementioned demands–control studies were usually reported under conditions of high demands and low control. Failure to find interactional effects could be due to inadequate measurement of the concepts of demands and control. Ganster and Fusilier (1989, ref. no. 277), in a detailed discussion, criticised the model because the concept of job discretion combined control with the arguably different concept of skill variety. Job demands are viewed by the model as the externally determined amount of effort which the job requires. Measures of job demands in the research literature are often simplistic constructions of very few items assessing high stimulation, overload and total effort required at work (Reed *et al*, 1989, ref. no. 79). There are many sources of job stress besides workload, ranging from conflict with colleagues, through insecurity, to poor communication. These adverse job characteristics tend to be excluded from the measurement of demands.

The model has been widely applied to the prediction of the prevalence rates of coronary heart disease (CHD) in both the USA and Sweden. For example, Alfredsson and colleagues (1982, ref. no. 77) assessed the characteristics of 118 jobs by interviews with a sample of 3876 men. An analysis of job characteristics that distinguished the low from the high CHD jobs showed that low control combined with high demand or rushed work tempo was a significant predictor. However the model's power of prediction of heart disease has been criticised by Ganster and Fusilier (1989, ref. no. 277) because tests have been largely based on an occupation level of analysis. The problem with such analyses is that it is not possible to rule out confounding by socioeconomic status, health behaviour or variability of job characteristics within occupations. That is, the high prevalence of CHD within certain occupational groups may be due to the social class, educational level or unhealthy lifestyle of the workers rather than to adverse job characteristics. A final criticsm of the Karasek model was raised by Warr (1990, ref. no. 80). He suggests that his vitamin model of stress would predict that discretion and job demand have a curvilinear relationship with well-being, such that the middle range would be most beneficial, with adverse health outcomes at both high and low levels of the job characteristics. That is, too much or too little responsibility and too many or too few challenges are equally damaging. Warr found his prediction supported, but found no evidence of the interaction effect predicted by Karasek's model. However, Fletcher and Jones (1993, ref. no. 83) found little evidence to support the hypothesis of a curvilincar relationship, with the exception of job and life satisfaction for men. They suggest that job features may need to be very extreme to give rise to curvilinearity in respect of anxiety and depression.

2.2.2   The Michigan School and Person – Environment Fit

The person–environment fit model of stress was developed at the University of Michigan Institute for Social Research in the 1960s. Two kinds of fit, or 'misfit' are proposed: the fit between a person's values and the environmental supplies available to fulfil those values and the fit between the individual's resources (their skills and abilities) and the organisation's demands on them (French, Caplan and Van Harrison, 1982, ref. no. 89). The P–E fit model postulates that a central source of strain, and ultimately ill-health, is a sufficiently large degree of misfit stress between individual and job. In the context of the model, values represent a person's conscious desires and needs including preferences, interests, motives and goals. Supplies refer to organisational resources and attributes of the work environment that may meet an individual's needs and include for example social support, promotion, job security, and good working conditions such as low noise levels and cleanliness. Most research based on supplies–values fit proposes that strain increases as supplies fall short of values, i.e. as organisational resources fail to meet employees' needs. Demands–abilities fit refers to the match between work demands and a person's abilities. Abilities include the skills, time, knowledge and energy that a person can draw upon to meet work demands. Demands refer to work requirements which can be objective, e.g. assembly line speed or length of working day, or social, e.g. fulfilling colleagues' expectations or fitting in with the team. In either case, only demands that a person perceives can elicit stress. The mechanism underlying demands–abilities fit is the comparison of perceived work demands to the person's abilities to meet those demands. Most theories hased on demands–abilities fit predict that excess demands increase strain (Edwards, 1996, ref no. 93).

While there is a general agreement that strain arises when demands exceed abilities or supplies fall short of values, researchers are more equivocal about the effects of excess supplies or abilities. One approach is to consider the effects of excess supplies or abilities on a given aspect of supplies–values fit or demands–abilities fit over time (Harrison, 1978 ref. no. 88 and Edwards, 1996, ref. no. 93). This approach allows the identification of four distinct processes. The first, labelled conservation by Edwards, occurs when excess resources are retained to meet future needs, for example when surplus income is saved for a rainy day. Similarly excess abilities may reduce strain if they can be conserved to meet future demands. For example, spare time may enable a worker to plan ahead to make future demands more manageable. The second process, called carryover, occurs when excess resources in one area can be used to meet needs in another area, as when excess autonomy enables a person to bring about desired changes at work. In both carryover and conservation, strain decreases as resources and abilities to meet needs and demands increase and continues to decrease as resources and abilities exceed needs and demands. The other two processes, called depletion and interference by Edwards, occur when excess resources and abilities increase strain. Depletion occurs when excess resources or abilities hinder the fulfilment of needs or demands. For example, excess support from a supervisor in one crisis may preclude support on later occasions, or poor work scheduling may cause employees to alternate between underload and overload, with slack time being paid for by later periods of extreme exertion. Interference occurs when excess resources in one area prevent the fulfilment of needs in another area, as when excess of contact with co-workers inhibits an employee's desire for privacy. Excess abilities may also cause interference, as when developing specialised skills above and beyond what the job requires may prevent an employee from learning other more relevant skills. Both interference and depletion show a curvilinear relationship with strain, which is at its lowest when demands/needs and resources/ abilities are in balance. Finally, the relationship between resources and strain will be essentially flat when excess resources do neither harm nor good once an acceptable level has been attained. Resources of this kind include job security and working conditions such as cleanliness or low noise levels. Similarly abilities such as excess motor co-ordination or manual dexterity may be irrelevant to many jobs and so will not affect strain.

The processes off carryover and interference can also occur in relationships between supplies–values and demands–abilities fit. For example, excess staff resources may enable a manager to delegate work, thus reducing demands on his/her time. Excess abilities may produce spare time which can be spent in leisure pursuits or with family, thus reducing strain.

2.2.2.1   *Methodological critique*

In spite of the intuitive appeal of the theory, studies of P–E fit are plagued with theoretical and methodological problems which render their results largely inconclusive (Edwards and Cooper, 1990, ref. no. 91). Major difficulties identified are as follows:

- Though supplies–values fit and demands–abilities fit are distinct versions of Person-Environment fit both in terms of their underlying processes and outcomes, empirical research has often minimised or entirely overlooked these distinctions. This has stalled investigation of the processes and outcomes that purport to distinguish supplies–values and demands–abilities fit, and has in some cases produced studies which claim to test one version of fit but actually test another.

- Research into P–E fit presents three basic forms of fit: discrepancy (where the characteristics of the job and the person deviate, resulting in square pegs in round holes), interactive (where strain is produced when certain personal characteristics combine with certain attributes of the work environment), and proportional (focusing on the proportion of personal needs/abilities that is fulfilled by the work environment). The three forms are distinct both mathematically and theoretically but have been considered interchangeable by some researchers. This has generated statistical tests that do not correspond to stated hypotheses and has encouraged inappropriate generalisations from one study to another.

- Methodological problems include imprecise and non-comprehensive measurement of P–E fit dimensions and use of inappropriate analytical techniques for assessing the effects of fit.

Taken together, these problems have produced research studies which overlook the distinct mechanisms associated with different versions of P–E fit, consider a limited range of fit dimensions and employ statistical tests which do not correspond to stated hypotheses. As a result, we have not yet amassed a sound body of empirical evidence that adequately addresses the basic propositions of the P–E fit approach to stress.

2.2.3   Transactional stress model of appraisal and coping

The problem with both the psychobiological model and the P–E fit model is that they play down differences between individuals' psychological preferences, response patterns and coping styles. A rather different model, originally proposed by an American psychologist, Richard Lazarus, in the 1960s, prioritises individuals' beliefs, feelings and wishes rather than their work environments or physiology. Stress is not directly given by the environment but depends on how an individual appraises or perceives the situation. For a situation to be stressful, there must, first, be something important to the person at stake in the outcome, such as danger to the health or well-being of a loved one, threat to self-esteem, or potential frustration of personal goals. Secondly, psychological stress only occurs when the person has evaluated the situation and concluded that external or internal demands tax or exceed his or her resources (Lazarus, 1966, ref. no. 94). Stress depends on the balance of power, as judged subjectively, between the environmental demands, constraints and resources and the ability of the person to manage them. The process through which the person evaluates whether a particular situation is relevant to his or her well-being, and if so, in what ways, is called cognitive appraisal. In primary appraisal, the person evaluates whether he/she has anything at stake in the encounter. A situation may be appraised as irrelevant, benign/positive or stressful. When a situation is appraised as stressful, the stress may be further appraised as being concerned with harm/loss threat, or challenge. Harm refers to damage which has already occurred, such as the loss of a job, a poor performance appraisal, or disapproval by management or one's peers. Threat refers to a harm which has not yet happened, but is anticipated in the future. Challenge refers to a condition of high demand where the emphasis is on overcoming the obstacles, mastering the demands and growing as a person. Challenge is classed as a stress appraisal because the person must mobilise to cope with the obstacles in order to produce the positive outcome, and because to experience challenge, there must be some risk of harm. Since personal agendas (e.g. goals and beliefs) vary from person to person, and even within the person from moment to moment, and since the environment is often quite complex and ambiguous, people attend selectively to what is happening and evaluate it in different ways. This results in great variation in the appraisals that different people make in the same situation. A sound theory of psychological stress must be capable of increasing understanding of variations in the ways in which individuals appraise and respond to their environment.

Once a situation has been assessed, the person then decides what if anything can be done to avert threat, overcome harm or loss or to improve the prospects of benefit.

This process Lazarus called secondary appraisal. Various coping options are evaluated, such as altering the situation, accepting it, seeking more information, or holding back from acting impulsively or in a counter-productive way.

2.2.3.1   Coping

Coping is defined by Lazarus as a person's ongoing cognitive and behavioural efforts to manage specific external and/or internal demands that are appraised as taxing or exceeding the resources of the person (Lazarus, 1993, ref. no. 110). Lazarus' view of coping is process oriented, in that his research focuses on what a person actually thinks and does in a specific stressful encounter, and how coping methods change as the episode unfolds. For example, in a quasi-experimental study of students facing a college examination, Folkman and Lazarus (1985, ref. no. 98) found that coping patterns changed dramatically over the examination period. An examination is not a unitary event but involves a series of stages. The stages consist of a period of warning of the imminence of the examination, a waiting period between sitting the examination and the results being announced, and a period after the results are announced. With respect to coping, seeking information and social support occurred quite frequently in the anticipatory stage, but dropped off sharply in later stages. Distancing (dissociation or detachment) was frequently employed in as a coping strategy while waiting for the results, but was infrequently used during other stages. Coping in transactional research is also viewed as contextual or situation specific, that is influenced by a person's appraisal of what is at stake in the encounter and of the resources available for managing it. Folkman and colleagues (1986, ref. no. 99) found in a study of community-residing adults that people sought less social support in encounters that involved a threat to self-esteem than they did in encounters where this concern was low. In encounters appraised as changeable, subjects used more confrontive coping (arguing and pleading), planful problem solving, and acceptance of responsibility (self-blame), but when situations were appraised as having to be accepted they turned to distancing and escape-avoidance strategies. Finally, research in this tradition makes no prior assumptions about what constitutes good or bad coping: coping is defined simply as a person's efforts to manage demands, whether or not these are successful. Whether a coping behaviour is good or bad, successful or unsuccessful, depends on the particular persons, the specific type of encounter, and the outcome variables being studied, e.g. morale, health complaints, or social functioning. Thus Ashford (1988, ref. no. 102) found in a study of stress during an organisational transition that the most effective coping response was sharing worries and concerns about the future. On the other hand, those seeking direct feedback and fuller information actually experienced more stress following the transition. Ashford hypothesised that by seeking direct feedback employees might learn things they would rather not know, or learn that no-one in the organisation was sure what would happen.

2.2.3.2   Coping style

Coping can also be studied as a stable trait rather than a behaviour (Norman and others, 1995, ref. no. 115; Miller, Brady and Summerton, 1988, ref. no. 103). This dispositional method seeks to obtain information about an individual's typical coping patterns regardless of situational context. Dispositional studies of coping have been dogged by measurement problems as there is little agreement between studies as to the method of assessing coping consistency. Differences in indices used, the number of situations examined and the types and classifications of events included may have contributed to discrepancies in results reported (Parkes, 1994, ref. no. 112).

2.2.2.3   Coping resources

Employee responses to stress or coping behaviours are determined by the amount and quality of resources which the employee can draw upon when faced with a stressful situation at work. Researchers typically distinguish between personal and social resources. In relation to personal resources, self-esteem and internal locus of control (Callan, Terry and Schweitzer, 1994, ref. no. 113; Terry, Tonge and Callan, 1995, ref. no. 117) have been shown to have direct effects on the well-being of employees. Having a positive self-image may allow people to cope more effectively with the ill effects of stress and such people may have a longer history of successful coping. Internal locus of control refers to the extent to which individuals perceive they have control over any given situation. Internally oriented persons believe their decisions and actions will influence what happens to them; externally oriented persons believe rewards and punishments are beyond their control and trust to luck or fate. An internal locus of control encourages the appraisal of events as more controllable, and such persons tend to use more problem-focused coping strategies. By solving the problem, they succeed in eliminating the source of stress. However, coping resources can also include characteristics of the social and organisational environment that facilitate effective coping behaviour. Social support at work can decrease emotional upset associated with a problematic situation or help an employee deal with, or solve, the problem being faced. For example, supervisors and co-workers can provide help and advice or assist in accomplishing a task. Heaney and her colleagues found in a study of workers in an automobile factory that employees who perceived their co-workers and supervisors to be supportive were more likely to mobilise that support when faced with workplace stress instead of trying to cope alone. Thus employees who made use of the abilities of their co-workers and supervisors were less constrained by the limitations of their own resources (Heaney *et al*, 1995, ref. no. 120). On the other hand, social support may not always be beneficial. Terry, Callan and Sartori (1996, ref. no. 122) found in a study of employee response to an organisational merger that subjects high in colleague support rated the event as more stressful and used higher levels of escapism than their more isolated colleagues. They hypothesise that this may be because discussion of the change with colleagues bred anxiety.

2.2.3.4   Coping strategies

Coping strategies fall into two categories. Problem-focused coping strategies actively confront and attempt to solve the problem causing distress. Emotion-focused coping, on the other hand is used to manage the emotional distress caused by the situation. The global categories of problem/emotion focused coping are made up of numerous subdimensions:

- First, coping can be cognitive (mental strategies) or behavioural (taking action). For example, emotion-focused coping can take a cognitive form as in trying to see the positive side of things or can be behavioural as in exercising more or smoking more.

- Secondly, there is a clear distinction between control-oriented coping methods and escape/avoidance methods. Control strategies show a proactive, take charge approach, eg making a plan of action, while escape strategies consist of staying clear of the person or situation or trying not to get concerned about it. Again, each can focus on the problem or on the emotional reactions.

- Thirdly, coping methods can be social or solitary. One can seek social or informational support from others, or one can remind oneself that work isn't everything.

2.2.3.5   Coping and individual differences

A number of studies have demonstrated significant associations between personality traits and coping behaviours. In a study by Bolger (1990, ref. no. 104), 50 premedical students reported their coping efforts at 35 days before, 10 days before and 17 days after an important examination. They also provided daily reports of anxiety for 35 days surrounding the examination. Results showed that trait anxiety or neuroticism (the disposition to show anxiety across diverse situations) led people to cope ineffectively, and that this ineffective coping led, in turn, to increases in distress. Ineffective coping behaviours, specifically wishful thinking and self-blame, mediated, or explained over half of the effect of neuroticism on state anxiety. Neuroticism was related to wishful thinking and self-blame only under conditions of stress and these coping behaviours in turn led to increases in anxiety under stress. Similarly, in a study by Havlovic and Keenan, (1995, ref. no. 116) results of a survey of 135 past graduates of continuing management education programmes at a Midwestern university in the US showed that Type A behaviour, job tenure and managerial experience were significantly associated with coping response patterns. Type A individuals are characterised by strong work commitment, a sense of time urgency and competitiveness. Type A persons in this study used more control oriented coping methods, but did not employ help seeking strategies. Similarly, in a study of young professional engineers by Newton and Keenan (1985, ref. no. 97), Type A individuals were move likely to react to stress by exhibiting helplessness and expressing feelings of resentment and frustration towards others.

2.2.3.6   Coping measurement

There are many different ways of measuring coping, including standardised coping inventories, interviewing protocols, observational techniques and personality or defence mechanism inventories. The most popular way of describing coping is in terms of either specific methods of coping or specific focuses of coping efforts. Typically this approach involves the development off a classified inventory of coping items which categorises coping efforts according to the method used or the focus of the responses. Latack and Havlovic (1992, ref. no. 109) have produced a helpful evaluation framework for coping measures to aid researchers in choosing or developing instruments applicable to job stress. Coping measures should:

- Reflect a clear conceptual definition of coping.

- Be comprehensive in that they include coverage of the two main recognised coping dimensions: focus of coping (the target towards which the coping response is directed) and method of coping.

- Be specific, in that they tap coping behaviour rather than the related concepts of coping resources or coping style. The best known coping taxonomy is the 'Ways of Coping Checklist' (WCCL) developed by Lazarus and his colleagues. The WCCL consists of 67 items that describe a broad range of cognitive and behavioural coping responses. Embedded in it is the distinction between coping efforts focused on solving the problem and those focused on managing the emotional reactions to the problem. Most commonly respondents describe their coping responses to a problem situation simply by indicating how often each way of coping was used on a scale of 0 to 3. Ratings for the 67 items are then factor analysed so that distinct but more general coping strategies can be identified. The factors emerging represent both problem-focused and emotion-focused strategies such as:

- Active problem solving. Represents deliberate problem-focused efforts to alter the situation with items such as 'came up with a couple of different solutions to the problem'.

- Escapism. An emotion-focused strategy related to wishful thinking and behavioural efforts to escape or avoid the situation through drinking, smoking or drug use.

- Self-blame. Self-punishing strategies represented by items such as 'Realised I had brought the situation on myself.'

- Positive reappraisal. Describes efforts to create positive meaning by focusing on personal growth, e.g. 'Changed or grew as a person in a good way.'

In many studies, coping strategies identified through the WCCL or some other coping inventory are then used to predict situational outcomes (e.g. Folkman et al, 1986, ref. no. 99); burnout (e.g. Leiter, 1991, ref. no. 106); health complaints (e.g. Beehr, Johnson and Nieva, 1995, ref. no. 118); and psychological ill-health (e.g. Terry, Tonge and Callan, 1995, ref. no. 117). Coping inventories are easy to use, little training is required for administrators, they can be used with large samples and include lists of items which assess use of both problem- and emotion-focused strategies. However, findings based on these quantitative measures, which simply count how many times given strategies are used, are often inconsistent and contradictory. Oakland and Ostell (1996, ref. no. 124) suggest that a particular coping strategy cannot be labelled as 'effective' or 'ineffective' without reference to the context in which it is used. Different coping strategies can have different outcomes in different situations, or the same coping strategies can be used by different people in the same type of situation with different outcomes. The most we can deduce from any study using coping inventories is that some forms of coping such as planful problem solving or positive reappraisal will have positive effects on certain outcomes in certain circumstances involving certain individuals and that other strategies such as wishful thinking or information seeking will have deleterious effects in some populations in some contexts (Ashford, 1988, ref. no. 102). The root of the problem lies in the fact that standard coping measures give a static picture of what is essentially a dynamic relationship between the individual and the situation. Oakland and Ostell suggest using more qualititative measures. Coping with many problem situations involves seeking advice, help, information or emotional support. Measures need to take account not only whether and how often external advice, etc was sought, but how useful that advice, etc was in resolving the problem. Similarly, typical quantitative coping checklists only yield information about how often a particular coping strategy was used. Results from Oakland's studies of headteachers, however, show that it is not how often a strategy is used that is crucial, but whether it worked. Finally, coping is a dynamic process and people may have to revise strategies in the light of others' response, learn technical skills in order to cope effectively, and deal with the fact that sometimes attempts to cope create more problems.

O'Driscoll and Cooper (1994, ref. no. 114) argue that while many investigators have elicited specific job stressors from individuals, and others have examined actual coping behaviours, research on the stress–coping relationship has not simultaneously explored both specific stressors and actual responses to those stressors. There has been little effort to link specific coping responses to actual sources of stress. They propose a method based on Critical Incident Analysis (CIA) which entails asking individuals to describe stressful incidents in terms of three elements: (i) the circumstances in which the stress occurred, (ii) their responses in the situation, along with the responses of other people, and (iii) the consequences of both their own and other peoples' behaviour. They argue that this approach has three advantages:

- Ensuring validity of information about individuals' responses in specific situations.

- Ensuring a more accurate portrayal of the specific behaviours which people employ in response to stressful events. Existing coping inventories contain no mechanism for checking whether strategies listed are those which individuals actually use (Cox and Ferguson, 1991, ref. no. 107).

- Enabling a closer examination of outcomes of situationally-specific coping responses. Rather than asking general questions about effectiveness, CIA probes the specific consequences of behaviours for individuals, together with their evaluation of the outcomes of those behaviours.

2.2.3.7   Application of the transactional model

Although the transactional model of work stress has been widely accepted by researchers at the conceptual level, at the empirical level work-related stress research is still largely influenced and guided by definitions that focus on the stressor-strain relationship, thus emphasising the different components of the transaction rather than the transaction itself. Research efforts have continued to focus on the interaction between work demands and different psychological and physical health outcomes, without paying due attention to the two mediational processes of appraisal and coping (Dewe, 1991, ref. no. 108).

2.2.4   Work stress in perspective

Of course work-related problems are not the only sources of stress in peoples' lives. Many other life events exert pressure and produce strains in individuals. Obvious candidates include bereavements, marriage, divorce, financial problems, difficulties with children and serious injury. Many attempts have been made to identify and determine the relative importance of such stressful life events.

One such attempt is represented by the PERI Life Events Scale. To construct this scale Dohrenwend *et al* (1982, ref. no. 53) constructed a list of 102 objectively verifiable life events. These were then classified according to 11 life domains: school, work, love and marriage, having children, family, residence, crime and legal matters, finances, social activities, health and miscellaneous. Subjects were then asked to rate events against marriage which was given on arbitrary rating of 500. Subjects were grouped according to criteria such as age, sex and ethnic background, and mean sub group ratings were calculated for each event. The highest ranked event overall was 'child died' with a rating of 1036 and the lowest 'acquired pet' at 163. The highest ranked work-related stress factor was 'suffered business loss or failure' at 510. Demoted and promoted at work ranked 379 and 374 respectively. These findings suggest that work-related stressors are not trivial and are among those which have the greatest perceived impact.

There is also strong evidence that work stress can 'spill over' into home and social life, and vice versa. It is nonsensical to believe that work and nonwork activities are unrelated in their psychological and health effects. The interaction between the work and nonwork domains is explored in detail in Chapter 3.

2.3 Bibliography

2.3.1 General overviews and handbooks

(52)
STRESS at work
C L Cooper and R Payne (editors)
Chichester: Wiley, 1978. 293p.

Useful early introduction to the field covering sources of stress in both blue and white-collar jobs, the part that individual differences in personality play in the stress process, the interaction between the stressors and the person and finally what can be done to arrest the pathological consequences of physical and psychological strain.

DSC Shelfmark: 88/02225

(53)
PSYCHIATRIC Epidemiology Research Interview Life Events Scale
B S Dohrenwend *et al*
In Handbook of stress: theoretical and clinical aspects edited by L Goldberger and S Breznitz. New York: Free Press, 1982. p.332–363.

DSC Shelfmark: lost

(54)
ORGANIZATIONAL stress and preventive management
J C Quick and J D Quick
New York: McGraw-Hill, 1984. 346p.

Book provides a good introduction to the field of organisational stress and reviews a range of practical ways of managing such problems in the work setting.

DSC Shelfmark: 84/04935

(55)
CAUSES, coping and consequences of stress at work
C L Cooper and R Payne (editors)
Chichester: Wiley, 1988. 418p.

Papers by well-known researchers cover topics such as epidemiology of stress, individual differences and coping, effect of computers on office workers, industrial relations and stress at work, physiological studies, approaches to interventions in the work setting, and methodological issues.

DSC Shelfmark: 88/19899

(56)

UNDERSTANDING stress: a psychological perspective for health professionals

V J Sutherland and C L Cooper

London: Chapman and Hall, 1990. 307p.

(Psychology and health series; 5)

Explains the sources of stress, the health impacts of stress and its organisational costs, followed by a discussion of how health professionals can manage stress by adapting their own approaches to work and the workplace.

DSC Shelfmark: 6946.535327 (Lost)

(57)

STRESS in organizations

R L Kahn and P Byosiere

In Handbook of industrial and organizational psychology. 2nd.. ed. edited by M D Dunnette and L M Hough. Palo Alto, Calif.: Consulting Psychologists Press, 1992. p.571-650.

Compares eight models of the stress process which have been influential in research and discusses empirical findings since 1976 in terms of an elaboration of the Michigan model (Person-Environment Fit) proposed by the authors. Concludes with a critical evaluation of current approaches to stress management and a set of proposals for improvement in the field.

DSC Shelfmark: q1/05980 (Vol. 1)

q2/13841 (Vol. 2)

q3/18540 (Vol. 3)

(58)

STRESS and coping

P Shipley and V Orlans

London: External Advisory Service, University of London, 1993. 73p.

Explains key approaches to the definition, diagnosis and measurement of stress, followed by a discussion of its social and corporate costs. Finally examines organisational intervention strategies for stress management. This is a very useful and accessible general introduction to the area.

DSC Shelfmark: Not found

(59)
STRESS and research and stress management: putting theory to work
T Cox
Sudbury: HSE Books, 1993. 117p.
(HSE contract report; no.61/ 1993)

Review commissioned by the Health and Safety Executive to provide an overview, within the conceptual framework implied by current health and safety legislation, of the scientific literature relating to the nature and health effects of work stress and to the nature and effectiveness of stress management programmes.

DSC Shelfmark: 4335.321000

(60)
MANAGING pressure for peak performance: the positive approach to stress
S Williams
London: Kogan Page, 1994. 150p.

Popular approach giving psychological procedures for controlling and managing pressure. Covers management of behaviour, achieving a healthy lifestyle, communication skills, and management of mood and organisational pressures.

DSC Shelfmark: Not found

(61)
OCCUPATIONAL stress: a handbook
R Crandall and P L Perrewé (editors)
Washington, DC: Taylor & Francis, 1995. 307p.

Handbook brings together renowned scholars in the field who cover theoretical approaches to work stress, model testing, coping, burnout and stress management interventions.

DSC Shelfmark: 95/21400

(62)
ORGANIZATIONAL risk factors for job stress
S L Sauter and L R Murphy (editors)
Washington, DC: American Psychological Association, 1995. 400p.

Investigates the changing structure of work in our society and presents empirical studies that examine organisational factors which appear to promote or decrease job stress. Covers organisational culture and climate, the job demands-control model, electronic performance monitoring and stress in high risk occupations such as nursing and fire fighting.

DSC Shelfmark: q95/28608

(63)

PSYCHOLOGICAL stress in the workplace

T A Beehr

London: Routledge, 1995. 258p.

Takes the organisational psychology approach to work stress. Begins with a definition and model of work stress, followed by a description of its causes and organisational and individual outcomes. Finally discusses research on the treatment of organisational stress, with special attention to social support.

DSC Shelfmark: 95/01653

(64)

THRIVE on stress: how to make it work to your advantage

R Sharpe

London: Souvenir Press, 1995. 338p.

Offers scientifically based procedures to enable you to control and use the stressors in your life, analyse your own pressures, and determine the level at which you function most healthily and effectively. Most importantly, shows how to maintain your personal optimum pressure level.

DSC Shelfmark: Not found

(65)

HANDBOOK of stress, medicine and health

C L Cooper (editor)

Boca Raton, Fla.: CRC Press, 1996. 388p.

Examines links between stress and health generally, the links between life events, control, coping and ill-health, the role of personality in illness, the role of social support in moderating ill health, and prevention and treatment of stress related illnesses.

DSC Shelfmark: 95/34903

(66)

HANDBOOK of work and health psychology

M J Schabracq, J A M Winnubst and C L Cooper (editors)

Chichester: Wiley, 1996. 496p.

Major handbook covering the theory of the links between work, stress and health, diagnosis of individual stress and psychosocial work hazards, interventions for a wide range of problems, and preventive programmes for health promotion and counselling at work.

DSC Shelfmark: 96/10410

(67)
TOWARDS a phenomenological framework for the study of work and organizational stress
M J Schabracq and C L Cooper
Human relations, vol.51, 1998, p.625-648

Analyses situations in terms of individual options for action, that is What one can (is able), will (wants to), may (is allowed to) and must (has to) do. Stressors are divided into those which primarily affect the task and those that disturb the immediate environment of the task. These stressors can be described as too much or too little of a number of variables, of which only the medium range is conducive to well-being.

DSC Shelfmark: 4336.400000

2.3.2   Physiological model

(68)
THE STRESS of life. Rev. ed.
H Selye
New York: McGraw-Hill, 1978. 515p.

Seminal work, presenting Selye's theories of the 'stress response' and general adaptation syndrome. Explains the three stages of the general adaptation syndrome: the alarm stage, an integrated call to arms which mobilises the biochemical resources of the organism; the resistance stage, in which the organism begins to adapt to the stressful stimuli, and the exhaustion stage, where, following prolonged exposure to the stressor, there is a reversion to the earlier symptoms of alarm, and, if the stressor persists, the ultimate result for the organism is death. Also explains how to overcome the harmful effects of stress and how to use it to one's own advantage.

DSC Shelfmark: 87/20669

(69)
PSYCHOBIOLOGICAL aspects of life stress
M Frankenhaeuser
In coping and health edited by S Levine and H Ursin. New York: Plenum, 1980, p.203-223
(NATO conference series III, Human factors; vol.12)

Proposes that the effectiveness of psychosocial factors in arousing the sympathetic adrenal-medullary and pituitary-adrenal cortical systems is determined by the person's cognitive appraisal of the balance between environmental threat and his or her personal coping resources. Assumes that the neuroendocrine responses to the psychosocial environment reflect the emotional impact of that environment on the individual.

DSC Shelfmark: 6033.653000

(70)
SHORT-TERM catecholamine response to psychological stress
J E Dimsdale and J Moss
Psychosomatic medicine, vol.42, 1980, p.493–497.

Article considers the transient reactivity of plasma catecholamines to a familiar potent stressor, public speaking. Plasma epinephrine levels differ significantly between the initial moments of public speaking and the middle of public speaking. These differences are large enough to affect the conclusions reached in comparing public speaking values with baseline values. It is therefore vital to ensure that blood samples are obtained consistently vis-à-vis the stress immersion experience.

DSC Shelfmark: 6946.555000

(71)
PLASMA catecholamines in stress and exercise
J E Dimsdale and J Moss
Journal of the American Medical Association, vol.243, 1980, p.340–342.

Studied nine young physicians as they went about their normal hospital activities. Results showed that epinephrine secretion was highest during public speaking and norepinephrine secretion highest during physical exercise. While physical exercise induced a response of the sympathetic nervous system, psychological stress induced primarily an adrenal response.

DSC Shelfmark: 4689.000000

(72)
COPING with stress at work
M Frankenhaeuser
International journal of health services, vol.11, 1981, p.491–510.

Attempts to integrate the concepts and methods of social psychology and psychobiology within a common frame to improve understanding of work stress. Examples are given from a multidisciplinary research programme concerned with the dynamics of stressful person-environment transactions viewed from a psychological and biological perspective. Consideration is given to coping and adaptation in workers exposed to conditions of underload, overload and lack of control. On the basis of results it is suggested that a moderately varied flow of stimuli and events, psychologically meaningful work and the exercise of personal control are key components of a healthy environment.

DSC Shelfmark: 4542.278000

(73)
EFFECTS of simulated repetitive work on urinary catecholamine excretion
S Cox *et al*
Ergonomics, vol.25, 1982, p.1129-1141.

An experimental study was conducted to investigate the effects of short-cycle repetitive work on catecholamine excretion rates. Results showed a clear elevation in both adrenaline and noradrenaline excretion rates associated with the two repetitive tasks, button loading and sorting compared to minding, the nonrepetitive task. Excretion rates were affected by method of payment, time of day and pacing requirement. These three factors interacted in producing their effects. Suggestions are made regarding the psychological and physical mechanisms underpinning these effects.

DSC Shelfmark: 3808.500000

(74)
THE ROLE of the adrenals in the psychophysiology of stress
T Cox and S Cox
Current issues in clinical psychology, vol.3, 1985, p.175-190.

Examines the role and control of activity of two particular neuroendocrine systems, the sympathetic-adrenal medullary system and the pituitary-adrenal cortical system, in the psychophysiology of stress. Suggests that situations which give rise to anxiety may increase sympathetic-adrenal medullary activity, while situations associated with depression or helplessness may increase pituitary-adrenal cortical activity. Anxiety-producing situations may elicit escape behaviour, while depression and helplessness may be elicited by loss of status or control. Psychosocial factors associated with increased sympathetic-adrenal medullary activity have been tentatively linked to coronary heart disease, and those associated with increased pituitary-adrenal cortical function even more tentatively linked to impaired immune-system function and possibly cancers.

DSC Shelfmark: 3499.058000

(75)
STRESS and strategy
S Fisher
London: Lawrence Erlbaum, 1986. 272p.

Explores the association between stress and control, reflecting the idea that responses to stress are likely to be strategic and designed to achieve control in different ways. A cognitive model of illness is developed, which assumes that the characteristics of strategies specified in terms of modes of control determine the features of arousal pathology via hormone routes and thus influence the risk of illness.

DSC Shelfmark: 86/15503

2.3.2   Karasek's Demands–Control model

(76)
JOB demands, job decision latitude and mental strain: implications for job redesign
R A Karasek
Administrative science quarterly, vol.24, 1979, p.285–306.

Reports tests of the job demands-decision latitude model with data from national surveys of workers in the US and Sweden. Found that decision latitude was a modest predictor of pill consumption, depression and job satisfaction. Concluded that job demands and decision latitude interacted to predict exhaustion, job dissatisfaction and life dissatisfaction in the US data and depression in the Swedish data.

DSC Shelfmark: 0696.517000

(77)
MYOCARDIAL infarction risk and psychosocial work environment: an analysis of the male Swedish working force
L Alfredsson, R Karasek and T Theorell
Social science and medicine, vol.16, 1982, p.463–467.

All cases of myocardial infarction in men below the age of 65 living in the greater Stockholm area during the years 1974-1976 were identified in the official registries of hospitalisations and deaths. For each case, two controls without infarction (in younger age groups four) matched for age, area of residence and sex were selected randomly from the parish registers. For each case and control, information was available regarding occupation. The psychosocial characteristics of each occupation were imputed from the results of a nationwide interview survey of 3876 working men in 1977. Shift work and monotony were associated with significant excess risk. Hectic work was not associated with excess risk in itself, but in combination with variables associated with low decision latitude it was associated with significant excess risk.

DSC Shelfmark: 8318.157000

(78)
JOB demands, supports and constraints as predictors of psychological strain among schoolteachers
R Payne and B Fletcher
Journal of vocational behaviour, vol.22, 1983, p.136–147.

Proposes a model which assumes that stress is a function of the balance of job demands, social support and job constraints. The model is tested on a homogenous professional group of workers because a previous study had suggested that models of this kind are powerful enough to detect differences in psychological strain when unskilled workers are compared with managers, but not when managers are compared with managers. The results show modest support for the model, but confirm that the percentage of variance accounted for by these sorts of measures is very low.

DSC Shelfmark: 5072.510000

(79)
OCCUPATIONAL strain and the incidence of coronary heart disease
D M Reed *et al*
American journal of epidemiology, vol.129, 1989, p.495-502.

The hypothesis that men in high strain occupations have an increased risk of coronary heart disease was tested during an 18-year follow-up study from 1965-1983 of a cohort of 8,006 men of Japanese ancestry in Hawaii. There were no significant associations between the incidence of coronary heart disease and the individual job components of high psychological demands and low job control or for the high strain interaction of these characteristics. There were also no significant associations among the various job characteristics and the major risk factors for coronary heart disease in this cohort. The inconsistency of these results with those of other studies may be due to methodologic differences of using men whose usual and current occupations were the same in this study compared with using only current occupation in other studies.

DSC Shelfmark: 0824.600000

(80)
DECISION latitude, job demands and employee well-being
P B Warr
Work and stress, vol.4, 1990, p.285-294.

The analyses make clear that there is a significant non-linear component in the relationship between job characteristics and well-being. No evidence was found of a synergistic interaction between job demands and decision latitude. Employees' job demands and decision latitude were each more closely associated with job-related anxiety-contentment and depression-enthusiasm respectively.

DSC Shelfmark: 9348.102000

(81)
ATTENUATING the impact of job demands: additive and interactive effects of perceived control and social support
S Melamed, T Kushnir and E I Meir
Journal of vocational behavior, vol.39, 1991, p.40-53.

Study investigated the combined additive and interactive effects of psychosocial resources (perceived control and social support) in reducing the adverse impacts of job demands. Results among 267 female social workers indicate that perceived control and social support exert an additive effect in attenuating the impact of job demands. The lowest burnout level and the highest job satisfaction were found under conditions of low stress, i.e. low demands, high perceived control and high social support. The opposite occurred under high stress, i.e. high demands, low perceived control and low social support. No evidence of an interactive (moderating) effect was found.

DSC Shelfmark: 5072.510000

(82)

WORK-LOAD, perceived control and psychological distress in Type A/B industrial workers

T Kushnir and S Melamed

Journal of organizational behavior, vol.12, 1991, p.155–168.

The effects of workload and perceived control on the psychological well-being of Type A and Type B industrial workers were studied using Karasek's Job Demands-Control model. Type As were not more stressed than Type Bs under conditions of low workload or low perceived control. Type As were adversely affected by high load while Type Bs were not. High strain jobs combining high load and low personal control proved stressful for Type As only.

DSC Shelfmark: 5027.066000

(83)

A REFUTATION of Karasek's demand–discretion model of occupational stress with a range of dependent measures

B C Fletcher and F Jones

Journal of organizational behavior, vol.14, 1993, p.319–330.

Study examined the ability of Karasek's demand-discretion model to predict raised blood pressure, anxiety, depression, job and life satisfaction in a large heterogeneous sample of over 3000 people. Results showed that demands and discretion do separately predict psychological strain, job and life satisfaction although they account for a very small percentage of the variance. There was no evidence of interactive effects. The model also failed to predict casual blood pressure. Observed relationships were in the opposite direction to that predicted. Social support accounted for additional variance over and above job demand and discretion for psychological strain, job and life satisfaction.

DSC Shelfmark: 5027.066000

(84)

THE RELATIONSHIP between job experiences and psychological distress: a structural equation approach

R C Barnett and R T Brennan

Journal of organizational behavior, vol.16, 1995, p.259–276.

Using structural equations, study estimates the relationship between employees' experiences of seven job conditions (skill discretion, decision authority, schedule control, job demands, pay adequacy, job security and relations with supervisor) to psychological distress (depression and anxiety). Skill discretion and job demands only were related to psychological distress in the random sample of 504 white full-timed employed men and women in dual earner couples. The magnitude of the relationships did not differ between men and women.

DSC Shelfmark: 5027.066000

(85)
CONSTRUCT validity of the demand–control model: a double cross-validation approach
P J G Schreurs and T W Taris
Work and stress, vol.12, 1998, p.66–84

Confirmatory factor analysis of data from two samples demonstrated that a three-factor model (with factors skill discretion, decision authority and psychological job demands) fitted the data best. In a second study using the same data, the authors examined how these three factors were related to a range of work-related and health-related strain outcomes. No interaction effect was found, but results did show main effects of the three factors.

DSC Shelfmark: 9348.102000

(86)
JOB characteristics and employee well-being: a test of Warr's Vitamin Model in health care workers using structural equation modelling
J de Jonge and W B Schaufeli
Journal of organizational behavior, vol.19, 1998, p.387–407.

Investigated Warr's Vitamin Model with a representative sample of 1437 Dutch health care workers. Tested the hypothesis that three job characteristics (job demands, job autonomy and social support) are curvilinearly related to three indications of employee well-being (job satisfaction, job-related anxiety, and emotional exhaustion). Except for the relationship between job autonomy and emotional exhaustion, relationships followed the predicted U-shaped or inverted U-shaped curvilinear pattern.

DSC Shelfmark: 5027.066000

(87)
MODELLING occupational stress and health: the impact of the demand-control model on academic research and on workplace practice
F Jones *et al*
Stress medicine, vol.14, 1998, p.231–236.

Argues that research has been constrained by a limited focus on demands and control. These dimensions of work are too general to produce results which can be applied to specific situations at a time when work environments are rapidly changing and practical guidance is needed for interventions based on clear research findings about health risks. There is a tension between the need to reduce the relevant factors in the psychosocial environment to a 'parsimonious set of theoretically meaningful dimensions' and the need for a deeper knowledge of relationships between very specific aspects of work and health outcomes which would give guidelines for job design interventions.

DSC Shelfmark: 8474.129500

2.3.4   Person-environment fit model

(88)
PERSON-environment fit and job stress
R van Harrison
In Stress at work edited by C L Cooper and R Payne
Chichester: Wiley, 1978. p.175-205.

Presents a general theory of the interrelationship between the person and the environment, followed by a more detailed consideration of the relationship between stress and the degree of fit between the person and the environment. The theory is used to predict relationships between strain and person-environment (P-E) fit. The next section presents data relevant to the theoretical predictions and the findings are used to evaluate the usefulness of the theory. Finally, suggestions for reducing job stress arising from the theory are presented.

DSC Shelfmark: 88/02225

(89)
THE MECHANISMS of job stress and strain
J R P French, R D Caplan and R van Harrison
Chichester: Wiley, 1982. 160p.

Presents the person-environment fit model of job stress, which postulates that where there is a poor fit between the characteristics of a person and the related characteristics of his/her job, employee well-being will be reduced.

DSC Shelfmark: 82/26936

(90)
PERSON-environment fit: past, present and future
R D Caplan
In Stress research: issues for the eighties edited by C L Cooper. Chichester: Wiley 1983. p.35-78.

Proposes an elaboration of the person-environment fit model of stress to include the concepts of retrospected and nonretrospected past fit, and future, anticipated fit. Presents hypothetical examples of data to demonstrate how joint consideration of P-E fit in the past, present and future time frames may increase the explanatory and predictive power of the theory.

DSC Shelfmark: 83/09503

(91)

THE PERSON-environment fit approach to stress: recurring problems and some suggested solutions

J R Edwards and C L Cooper

Journal of organizational behavior, vol.11, 1990, p.293–307.

Current research into the person-environment fit approach to stress is plagued with theoretical and methodological problems which render results inconclusive. Article highlights the problems and proposes some solutions.

DSC Shelfmark: 5027.066000

(92)

JOB demands and worker health: three-dimensional reexamination of the relationship between person-environment fit and strain

J R Edwards and R van Harrison

Journal of applied psychology, vol.78, 1993, p.628–648.

Study clarifies and refines the results reported by French, Caplan and van Harrison (1982) regarding the relationship between Person-Environment fit and strain. The original results were often ambiguous because of the use of fit measures that collapsed E and P into a single score. The present re-analysis of the data used a procedure which avoided the problems of fit measures and preserved the inherently three-dimensional relationship between environment, person and strain. The procedure resolved the ambiguities in the original results and showed that the relationship between environment, person and strain was often more complex than could be shown by the fit measures used by French and colleagues.

DSC Shelfmark: 4947.000000

(93)

AN EXAMINATION of competing versions of the person-environment fit approach to stress

J R Edwards

Academy of Management journal, vol.39, 1996, p.292–339.

Study examined two versions of the person-environment fit model of job stress: environmental supplies and employee values fit (S-V fit) and environmental demands and employee abilities fit (D-A fit). For S-V fit, job dissatisfaction increased as supplies deviated from values and was also higher when supplies and values were both low than when both were high. Tension was positively related to supplies and negatively related to values. For D-A fit, job dissatisfaction decreased as demands and abilities increased. Tension was positively related to demands and negatively related to abilities.

DSC Shelfmark: 0570.587000

2.3.5 Transactional model of stress and coping

(94)
PSYCHOLOGICAL stress and the coping process
R S Lazarus
New York: McGraw–Hill, 1966. 466p.

Seminal work presenting Lazarus' transactional model of stress in which psychological stress is seen as arising from recognition or appraisal of a threat of impending harm. Coping refers to strategies for dealing with the threat.

DSC Shelfmark: Not found

(95)
THE STRUCTURE of coping
L I Pearlin and C Schooler
Journal of health and social behavior, vol.19, March 1978, p.2-21.

Describe coping in terms of (a) problem-focused behaviours, (b) emotion-focused behaviours and (c) reappraisal.

DSC Shelfmark: 4996.730000

(96)
THE STRESS and coping paradigm
R S Lazarus
In Models for clinical psychopathology edited by C Eisdorfer and others. New York: Spectrum, 1981, p.177-214.

Gives an overview of the transactional model of stress and coping. Psychological stress is viewed as referring to demands (or conflicts among them) that tax or exceed available resources (internal and external) as appraised by the person involved. The function of coping is to change the situation for the better either by changing one's own offending action or by changing the threatening environment or to manage the subjective and somatic components of the stress-related emotions themselves so that they do not get out of hand and do not damage or destroy morale and social functioning.

DSC Shelfmark: 81/25585

(97)
COPING with work–related stress
T J Newton and A Keenan
Human relations, vol.38, 1985, p.107-126.

Study examined the coping behaviour of a sample of young professional engineers in response to stressful incidents at work. Results showed that certain types of coping strategies were behavioural correlates of particular individual characteristics. In addition, both the way in which stress was appraised and the nature of the work environment in which it occurred predicted choice of coping behaviours.

DSC Shelfmark: 4336.400000

(98)
IF it changes it must be a process: study of emotion and coping during three stages of a college examination
S Folkman and R S Lazarus.
Journal of personality and social psychology, vol.48, 1985, p.150–170.

Emotion and coping were studied at three stages of a mid-term college examination: the anticipation stage before the exam, the waiting stage after the exam but before results were announced, and after results were announced. There were significant changes in emotions and coping across the three stages. Different forms of coping were salient during the anticipation and waiting stages, with problem-focused coping and emphasising the positive more prominent during the former and distancing during the latter.

DSC Shelfmark: 5030.901000

(99)
DYNAMICS of a stressful encounter: cognitive appraisal, coping and encounter outcomes
S Folkman *et al*
Journal of personality and social psychology, vol.50, 1986, p.992–1003.

Study examined the functional relations among cognitive appraisal and coping processes and their short term outcomes within stressful encounters. Used an intraindividual approach to compare each person with himself across 5 stressful encounters. Results showed that variability in coping was at least partially a function of people's judgements about what was at stake (primary appraisal) and what they view as the options for coping (secondary appraisal). Coping was also differentially related to satisfactory and unsatisfactory encounter outcomes.

DSC Shelfmark: 5030.901000

(100)
STRESS, coping and problem solving
T Cox
Work and stress, vol.1, 1987, p.5–14.

Defines stress as a psychological state derived from a person's appraisal of their ability to cope with the demands made of them. Then examines the concept of coping and its role in stress theory. Contrasts two approaches to the study of coping with work stress: the classification of all possible coping strategies as opposed to investigation of the process of coping in terms of problem solving.

DSC Shelfmark: 9348.102000

(101)

TRANSACTIONAL theory and research on emotions and coping

R S Lazarus and S Folkman

European journal of personality, vol.1, 1987, p.141-169.

Examines the fundamental premises of the cognitive-relational theory of emotion and coping and assesses progress in examining them through a 10-year programme of empirical research.

DSC Shelfmark: 3829.733800

(102)

INDIVIDUAL strategies for coping with stress during organizational transitions

S J Ashford

Journal of applied behavioral science, vol.24, 1988, p.19-36.

Study examined coping mechanisms used by a sample of employees of the Bell Telephone System who had to cope with the company's transition to an unregulated entity. Results suggested that uncertainty across several domains and the perceived disruption caused by the organisational transition were associated with increased stress, both while anticipating the change and six months after it had occurred. Of the coping behaviours studied, sharing worries and concerns appeared to be the most effective buffering response, while active attempts to structure the situation by obtaining information either failed to affect or actually increased stress levels. Feelings of personal control and the ability to tolerate ambiguity were also linked with improved stress levels.

DSC Shelfmark: 4940.500000

(103)

STYLES of coping with threat: implications for health

S M Miller, D S Brady and J Summerton

Journal of personality and social psychology, vol.54, 1988, p.142-148.

Study explored individual differences in health-seeking behaviour and health status in a primary care population. Overall, high monitors (those who typically scan for threat relevant information) came to the doctor for more benign medical conditions, but showed equivalent psychological and physical distress, as well as greater preferences for information and intervention than do low monitors (those who typically ignore threat relevant information), while preferring to assume a less active role in their own care.

DSC Shelfmark: 5030.901000

(104)

COPING as a personality process: a prospective study

N Bolger

Journal of personality and social psychology, vol.59, 1990, p.525-537.

Goals of the study were (a) to examine the emergence of a major personality disposition, neuroticism, in patterns of coping over time and (b) to test whether coping mediated the influence of neuroticism on psychological distress and on performance under stress. Fifty premedical students reported their coping efforts 35 days before, 10 days before, and 17 days after a medical school entrance examination. They provided daily reports of anxiety for 35 days surrounding the examination. Results showed that ineffective coping modes, specifically wishful thinking and self-blame, explained over half the effects of neuroticism on anxiety. Neither neuroticism nor specific coping efforts influenced examination performance.

DSC Shelfmark: 5030.901000

(105)

STRESS, Type A, coping and psychological and physical symptoms: a multi-sample test of alternative models

J R Edwards, A J Baglioni and C L Cooper

Human relations, vol.43, 1990, p.919-956.

Article discusses and empirically evaluates seven alternative conceptual models specifying the interrelationships among stress, personality, coping and psychological and physical symptoms using data from 1468 adults in four occupations. Of the seven models, the direct effects model, the mediated effects model and the mediating mediated effects model received most support. Results failed to support four models which incorporated interactive effects.

DSC Shelfmark: 4336.400000

(106)

COPING patterns as predictors of burnout: the function of control and escapist coping patterns

M P Leiter

Journal of organizational behavior, vol.12, 1991, p.123-144.

A sample of 177 workers in a mental hospital provided information regarding coping patterns, burnout and organisational commitment as well as various demands and resources of the work environment. Results showed that use of control coping reduced emotional exhaustion and gave an increased sense of personal accomplishment. Workers who used escapist coping strategies experienced greater levels of emotional exhaustion.

DSC Shelfmark: 5027.066000

(107)
INDIVIDUAL differences, stress and coping
T Cox and E Ferguson
In Personality and stress: individual differences in the stress process edited by C L Cooper and R Payne. Wiley, 1991, p.7-30.

Explores the roles of personality hardiness and locus of control as mediators and moderators of stress and coping. Questions the role played by personality hardiness both as a mediator and a moderator, but finds evidence that locus of control acts in a way that is consistent with the moderation hypothesis. Coping is treated both as a source of individual differences and as an outcome of other such differences. Its architecture and measurement are discussed in the context of the transactional model of stress.

DSC Shelfmark: 91/20462

(108)
PRIMARY appraisal, secondary appraisal and coping: their role in stressful work encounters
P Dewe
Journal of occupational psychology, vol.64, 1991, p.331-351.

Study explored the ways in which individuals cognitively appraise and cope with stressful encounters. Each respondent was asked to write about the most stressful event he/she had experienced during the last month. Respondents were then asked to focus on the event and to use it as the basis for answering other sections of the questionnaire. Results establish the significant role played by appraisals and coping, and point to a number of definitional, methodological and measurement issues that require further research and analysis if the transactional approach to the study of work stress is to be fully realised.

DSC Shelfmark: 5026.120000

(109)
COPING with job stress: a conceptual evaluation framework for coping measures
J C Latack and S J Havlovic
Journal of organizational behavior, vol.13, 1992, p.479-508.

Aims to provide a mechanism for imposing meaning on the large body of research on coping, a set of criteria for choosing among existing coping measures, and a conceptual blueprint for developing new measures or for adapting existing measures specifically to job stress. Offers a conceptual framework which serves to evaluate the extent to which coping measures are comprehensive (covering focus and method of coping) and specific (tapping coping behaviours rather than coping effectiveness, coping style and coping resources).

DSC Shelfmark: 5027.066000

(110)
COPING theory and research: past, present and future
R S Lazarus
Psychosomatic medicine, vol.55, 1993, p.234-247.

Contrasts two approaches to coping: one emphasises style, treating coping as a personality characteristic; while the other emphasises process, in which efforts to manage stress change over time, and are shaped by the adaptational context out of which the stress is generated.

DSC Shelfmark: 6946.555000

(111)
INDIVIDUAL strategies for coping with stress at work: a review
P Dewe, T Cox and E Ferguson
Work and stress, vol.7, 1993, p.5-15.

Reviews 17 papers representative of the coping literature. Review focuses on the methodologies used and related conceptual issues, although the question of utility of the findings is also discussed. Identifies four issues which should be considered in future research.

DSC Shelfmark: 9348.102000

(112)
PERSONALITY and coping as moderators of work stress processes: models, methods and measures
K R Parkes
Work and stress, vol.8, 1994, p.110-129.

Article reviews the role of the personality variables hardiness, locus of control, Type A personality, optimism and neuroticism as moderators of the stress/strain relationship. Vulnerability/resilience and person-environment fit models of the moderator effect are presented. Associations between personality and coping, inventories for the assessment of coping and the dimensions of coping behaviour are then considered. The implications of structural and transactional models of stress for coping are discussed with reference to situational versus dispositional approaches and other psychometric issues.

DSC Shelfmark: 9348.102000

(113)
COPING resources, coping strategies and adjustment to organizational change: direct or buffering effects?
V J Callan, D J Terry and R Schweitzer
Work and stress, vol.8, 1994, p.372-383.

A sample of 100 lawyers completed a structured self-administered questionnaire that measured their personal and social resources, use of problem-focused and emotion-focused coping strategies, and appraisals of the stressfulness of the situation. Lower levels of anxiety were directly linked to judgements of lower levels of organisational change, greater self-confidence, greater internality of control beliefs and less use of emotion-focused coping. Lower levels of depression were also directly linked to judgements of lower levels of organisational change, greater use of resources and less appraised stress.

DSC Shelfmark: 9348.102000

(114)
COPING with work-related stress: a critique of existing measures and proposal for alternative methodology
M P O'Driscoll and C L Cooper
Journal of occupational and organizational psychology, vol.67, 1994, p.343-354.

Proposes an approach which enables a mapping of coping behaviours onto sources of stress experienced by individuals at work through the use of Critical Incident Analysis (CIA). This entails asking individuals to describe stressful transactions in terms of three elements: (i) the antecedents or circumstances in which the stress occurred, (ii) their responses in that situation, along with the responses of other people, and (iii) the consequences of their own and other individuals' behaviour. The methodology links specific coping responses which individuals exhibit to the actual source of the stress.

DSC Shelfmark: 5026.082000

(115)
ATTRIBUTIONS, cognitions and coping styles: teleworkers' reactions to work-related problems
P Norman *et al*
Journal of applied social psychology, vol.25, 1995, p.117-128.

Tested the hypothesis that teleworkers making optimistic attributions and cognitions about work-related problems would be more likely to engage in problem-focused coping strategies and to report better psychological and job related outcomes. Results showed that cognitions about the consequences of such problems, but not attributions regarding their causes, were predictive of psychological and job related well-being. A tendency to engage in self-blame was related to the use of emotion-focused coping strategies, which in turn were linked to negative outcomes.

DSC Shelfmark: 4947.080000

(116)
COPING with work stress: the influence of individual differences
S J Havlovic and J P Keenan
In Occupational stress: a handbook edited by R Crandall and P L Perrewé.
Washington, DC: Taylor and Francis, 1995. p.179-192.

In a cross-sectional study, authors examine the relationship between the common work stressors of role conflict and role ambiguity and the coping behaviour of a sample of managers. Individual differences (Type A behaviour, gender, job tenure and managerial experience) are also considered in the examination of coping activities used. Male and female managers did not exhibit different coping behaviours. Type As used more control-orientated coping methods, but help seeking behaviours were not employed. Those with greater managerial experience used increased positive thinking, but those with longer job tenure relied more on escaping the situation than on using proactive coping behaviours.

DSC Shelfmark: 95/21400

(117)
EMPLOYEE adjustment to stress: the role of coping resources, situational factors and coping responses
D J Terry, L Tonge and V J Callan
Anxiety, stress and coping, vol.8, 1995, p.1–24.

A sample of 153 male and female employees in a public sector department provided data about a recent stressful event at work. Relations among employees' coping resources (self-esteem, internal-external locus of control, neuroticism and social support), appraisals of the event (appraised stress, self-efficacy and situational control beliefs), coping strategies (problem- and emotion-focused coping) and levels of adjustment (psychological well-being and job satisfaction) were explored. Results showed that use of problem-focused coping had, in general, positive relationships with measures of adjustment, while emotion-focused coping was, in general, not helpful. There was also evidence that coping resources had both direct and indirect (through situational appraisals and coping responses) effects on employee adjustment.

DSC Shelfmark: 1566.612000

(118)
OCCUPATIONAL stress: coping of police and their spouses
T A Beehr, L B Johnson and R Nieva
Journal of organizational behavior, vol.16, 1995, p.3–25.

One hundred and seventy-seven police officers and their spouses from a large city police department and a suburban county department in the same US state completed separate questionnaires regarding stress and coping. Police and spouses reported using four coping strategies: problem-focused, emotion-focused, religiosity and rugged individualism. Results showed that problem-focused coping reduced police officers' health complaints, emotional exhaustion, depersonalisation and thoughts of suicide. Problem-focused coping among spouses reduced divorce potential. Emotion-focused coping among police was helpful in relation to every strain except drinking. Emotion-focused coping among spouses reduced divorce potential. Religiosity among police officers was unrelated to any strains but reduced spouses' drinking and experienced stress. Rugged individualism among police was related to drinking.

DSC Shelfmark: 5027.066000

(119)

PSYCHOLOGICAL stress in the workplace

R S Lazarus

In Occupational stress: a handbook edited by R Crandall and P L Perrewé.
Washington, DC.: Taylor & Francis, 1995, p.3-14.

Presents the transactional model of stress. It is argued that a transaction between a person and the environment is only stressful when it is evaluated by the person as a harm or threat. Coping is then defined as the cognitive and behavioural efforts a person makes to manage demands that tax his/her personal resources.

DSC Shelfmark: 95/21400

(120)

THE RELATIONSHIP of organizational and social coping resources to employee coping behaviour: a longitudinal analysis

C A Heaney *et al*

Work and stress, vol.9, 1995, p.416-431.

Study investigated the role of supportive work relationships and of participation in, and influence on decision-making, in determining coping behaviour of employees in a manufacturing plant. Results showed that perceiving oneself to have influence over decision-making at work predicted increases in active, problem-solving coping attempts and decreases in resignation to work stressors. Workers who perceived their colleagues and supervisors as supportive were more likely to mobilise that support to alleviate worksite stress.

DSC Shelfmark: 9348.102000

(121)

A CRITICAL incident analysis of stress-coping behaviours at work

M P O'Driscoll and C L Cooper

Stress medicine, vol.12, 1996, p.123-128.

Study aimed to demonstrate the application of critical incident analysis (CIA) as a technique for eliciting stress-coping behaviours of employees in their work settings. Advantages and limitations of CIA for exploring coping with job stress are highlighted.

DSC Shelfmark: 8474.129500

(122)

EMPLOYEE adjustment to an organizational merger: stress, coping and intergroup differences

D J Terry, V J Callan and G Sartori

Stress medicine, vol.12, 1996, p.105-222.

Tested a stress and coping model of adjustment to organisational change. Data were collected from 662 fleet staff (mainly pilots) of a newly merged airline. Evidence was found linking event characteristics, situational appraisals, coping responses and coping resources to levels of adjustment. On an intergroup level, the research also compared the situational appraisals, coping responses and adjustment of the employees of the two pre-merger companies. The employees of the domestic airline had more positive reactions to the merger than those of the international airline, presumably because the merger offered them opportunities to improve their social identity.

DSC Shelfmark: 8474.129500

(123)
THE INTERACTIONAL context of problem-, emotion-, and relationship-focused coping: the role of the big five personality factors
T B O'Brien and A DeLongis
Journal of personality, vol.64, 1996, p.775–813.

Data collected by self-report questionnaire from a sample of 270 undergraduates showed that coping responses differed depending on whether the stressor was work-related or interpersonal. Work stressors were primarily associated with problem-focused coping and interpersonal stressors with relationship-focused coping (empathic responding). Dimensions of personality derived from the five-factor model (neuroticism, extraversion, openness to experience, agreeableness and conscientiousness) had important associations with different coping responses. Results suggest that a model of coping that considers both work-related and interpersonal dimensions of stressful situations, includes relationship-focused coping, and considers personality and situational factors in tandem, is needed to increase the predictive power of current models.

DSC Shelfmark: 5030.900000

(124)
MEASURING coping: a review and critique
S Oakland and A Ostell
Human relations, vol.49, 1996, p.133–155.

The most popular method of measuring coping is currently the quantitative, methods-foci approach developed by Lazarus and his colleagues. Following a critical review of studies using this approach, and citing qualitative data on coping drawn from a study of head teachers, paper argues that these widely used measures need refining. Qualitative measures of the efficacy of coping and the adequacy of external resources need to be incorporated.

DSC Shelfmark: 4336.400000

(125)

BUSSY business: how urban bus drivers cope with time pressure, passengers and traffic safety

T F Meijman and M A J Kompier

Journal of occupational health psychology, vol.3, 1998, p.109-121.

Bus drivers are exposed to conflicting demands of adhering to schedule, providing service to passengers and driving safely. Data from 4 interrelated studies explore the ways in which drivers cope with these demands. Results showed that favouring adherence to the schedule over and above traffic safety and passenger comfort was associated with higher risks of impaired health and well-being. Too many passengers in combination with too tight a time schedule might force the bus driver into a situation of high time pressure and too little recovery or spare time at work. High time pressure and little spare time were related to psychophysiological stress reactions during work.

DSC Shelfmark: 5026.095000

(126)

FIFTY years of the research and theory of R S Lazarus: an analysis of historical and perennial issues

R S Lazarus

Mahwah, N J: Erlbaum, 1998. 425p.

Compilation of theoretical articles and papers describing the author's empirical research into stress, emotion and coping from the late 1940s to the present. New interstitial text discussions explain what was taking place at the time the research was conducted, how the field responded, and what happened to issues tackled during the ensuing years.

DSC Shelfmark: 98/10245

3 Psychosocial Hazards in the Workplace

3.1 Introduction

Work hazards can be broadly divided into two categories: physical and psychosocial hazards. Physical hazards in the workplace have been the traditional area of concern of health and safety professionals. They include exposure to dangerous machinery, chemical spillages, high noise levels, extremes of heat and cold, etc. Psychosocial hazards are defined by Cox (1993, ref. no. 59) as 'aspects of job content, work organisation and management, and of environmental, social, and organisational conditions which carry the potential for psychological and physical harm'. It is the literature on psychosocial hazards which is reviewed here.

There is a reasonable consensus among experts about which psychosocial characteristics of work can be considered to be stressful and to carry the potential for harm. These include workload and work pace, work schedule, career security factors, role in the organisation, interpersonal relations, job content and design, and external factors such as family problems and personality which may impinge on the workplace (Sauter, Murphy and Hurrell, 1990, ref. no. 563; Cox, 1993, ref. no. 59; Quick, Murphy and Hurrell, 1992, ref. no. 561). Beyond these traditional sources of stress, changing work environments have seen the emergence of new risk factors. In post-industrial economies such as the UK, the manufacturing sector has declined and been replaced by the service and information industries as the predominant forms of work. The past two decades have seen the development of the long hours culture and reduction of leisure time following downsizing and delayering, the more widespread use of flexible work practices such as part-time and contract working, and the proliferation of information technology. New stress factors which have emerged as a result of these developments include the threat of violence from disgruntled clients or colleagues and the intrusive use of computers for monitoring workers.

Recent research has also pointed to the significance of macroscopic aspects of the organisational environment, such as culture and climate, as determinants both of organisational effectiveness and worker well-being. However, work to explore the role of these global organisational features in the stress process in relation to micro-organisational factors such as task design and interpersonal relationships is only just beginning.

The following sections highlight psychosocial hazards in the work environment which are experienced as stressful and carry potential for harm to both the individual and the organisation.

3.2   Working hours

Researchers at Demos, the independent think tank, (1995, ref. no. 136) have compiled the following statistics about time pressures on the British worker:

- 44% of British workers report coming home exhausted (*International Social Attitudes* 1994, p.105.)
- The average lunch hour now lasts thirty minutes. (*The Independent on Sunday*, 29 January 1995).
- One in three British men now work a six to seven day week (*Labour Force Survey*, 1990/91).
- Full–time British employees work a longer week than any other country in the EU (*Labour Force Survey* 1990/91).
- 86% of women workers say they never have enough time to get things done.
- Over 70% of British workers want to work 40 hours or less, though only 31% actually do (NOP poll for the TUC, March 1995).

The prevalence of long working hours in the UK is confirmed by a 3i European Enterprise Centre survey which found that 47% of the British workforce works over 40 hours per week and only 9% works less than 36 hours (1997, ref. no. 143). Similarly a survey by WFD for *Management Today* portrays a workforce where only 4 out of 10 are reasonably sure that their work/life balance is about right, and where many managers appear to be sacrificing their personal life, and that of those close to them, to their work. A majority of managers emerged as working long, not always justifiable, hours under increasingly higher levels of pressure, and admitted that in many cases they were pushing staff too hard, (1998, ref. no. 144). The upshot of all this is, unsurprisingly, very high levels of stress and feelings of time pressure (Demos, 1995, ref. no. 136). In extreme cases excessive hours can be a killer. *The Observer* (1994, ref. no. 135) has reported the case of a junior hospital doctor, Alan Massie, who died in Warrington District Hospital in 1994 at the end of an 86 working week. The Japanese, who work longer hours than people in the US or UK, experience karoshi (death from overwork). This is a documented ailment in which people develop illnesses and die from high stress and the pressures of overtime. Karoshi was officially registered as a fatal illness in 1989, and in 1990 the Labour Ministry received 777 claims for compensation (Uehata, 1991, ref. no. 132).

The long hours culture also appears to be leading to the emergence of a class of money rich/time poor people who do not have the time to enjoy the fruits of their labour. Ray Pahl, Professor of Sociology at Essex University, cites research based on the British Household Panel Survey which demonstrates that the highest paid 20% work about 10 hours longer per week than do the worst paid (1996, ref. no. 139). Martin and Mason (1998, ref. no. 147) point to a polarisation of society into full time core workers who are money-rich but time poor and groups who have time on their hands but no money, such as the unemployed, part-time workers and poorer pensioners. The increasing inequality of time and money in the UK in recent years has led to growing dissatisfaction with life at both ends of the working scale.

The culture of workaholism can lead to perverse behaviour as reported by Professor Hochschild of the University of California. A survey of 130 US workers over three years revealed that 30% preferred to spend time at their workplaces rather than at home, (1997, ref. no. 142). At work people feel empowered, make decisions, and have a social life. At home they are confronted by a range of unexciting domestic duties and demanding children and spouses.

Scientific investigation of the effects of long hours has tended to concentrate on military work and performance. Long hours of work, from extended work days of 12 hours to sustained working over several days with sleep loss, has been shown to increase fatigue (Krueger, 1989, ref. no. 128). Performance can be severely compromised by accumulation of sleep debt (Haslam, 1982, ref. no. 127). The upper limit of human performance working intensively and continuously is 2-3 days (Haslam, 1982, ref. no. 127). Outside the military sphere, Spurgeon and Harrington have reviewed the effects of long hours on junior hospital doctors. They conclude that a number of studies have shown that a significant proportion of newly qualified doctors develop some degree of psychological ill-health (1989, ref. no. 129).

A recent meta-analysis of 19 studies supplemented by a quantitative analysis of a further 12 by Sparkes and her colleagues (1997, ref. no. 140) investigated the relationship between long working hours and health. Results indicated a small but significant positive mean correlation between poor physical and psychological health and hours of work. However, the relationship between working hours and health is complex and can be influenced by many other factors. For example, the adverse health impact of long hours may be greater for jobs which require extended periods of concentration and attention such as long-distance driving (Raggatt, 1991, ref. no. 134) or repetitive work (Morgenstern *et al*, 1991, ref. no. 131). Several studies have highlighted the importance of 'choice' or 'control' in this context. A person who works long hours or shifts by choice is likely to suffer far less adverse health consequences than those who have no control over their work schedule. An individual's lifestyle is also an important factor. It is generally agreed that smoking and drinking contribute to the development of a number of serious illnesses such as heart disease, liver problems and cancers. Working long hours *per see* may not directly affect health but could lead to an increase in such behaviour, eventually resulting in ill-health. Raggatt (1991, ref. no. 134), for example, found that use of stimulants and sleep disturbance were related to negative health outcomes for long-distance coach drivers. Finally, health problems which arise from the poor working conditions such as noise levels, poor ventilation, inadequate lighting, heat and vibration can be made worse by long working hours.

Sparkes and her colleagues conclude that much more research is needed to clarify the work hours–health relationship. Questions which need to be addressed include the direct effects of working hours on health, the effects of factors, such as age and working conditions, which exacerbate or ameliorate the health impacts of long hours, and the distinctions that may occur between jobs.

3.3   Shiftwork

To begin with a matter of definition, 'shiftworker' in the scientific literature refers to an individual, some of whose work is done at night and 'night-worker' refers to a shiftworker when working at night as well as to someone who is a permanent night-worker.

The human being is not a naturally nocturnal creature. Activity is usually concentrated in the daylight hours, with the night being given over to rest. This pattern of activity is enforced by an in-built body clock whose primary purpose is to enforce regular cycles of sleep and diurnal activity in our behaviour. Night work involves patterns of behaviour which are essentially unnatural. Clearly a pattern of behaviour can be unnatural without being harmful. Indeed, many of the activities of modern life such as living in air-conditioned rooms or travelling in cars can be termed unnatural. The harm that such activities cause arises not from their unnaturalness but from the inability of human beings to adjust to them. Similarly shiftwork is an unnatural activity which under some circumstances can lead to problems and eventually to harm.

Problems caused by shiftwork fall into four categories: health problems, sleep loss, domestic and social disruption and performance problems.

3.3.1　Health problems

There is now considerable evidence in the literature that shiftwork is associated with increased risk of cardiovascular disease. Studies conducted by Knutsson and his colleagues show the incidence to be, on average, about 40% higher in shiftworkers than day-workers. Risk appears to increase progressively with the number of years spent shiftworking (Knutsson *et al*, 1986, ref. no. 152). There is also general agreement that shiftworkers are more prone to gastrointestinal disturbances than day-workers, with 30–50% of shiftworkers being affected. This can arise from a variety of possible causes, including altered or irregular meal times, poor diet and increased smoking and drinking. Finally, there seems to be a greater tendency towards general malaise – including anxiety and depression – in shiftworkers than in dayworkers. The cause for this is unknown but may be associated with poorer working conditions and disruption of social life due to night work, which may exacerbate any difficulties arising from physiological factors such as disturbance of biorhythms.

3.3.2　Sleep loss

Shiftworkers commonly complain of fatigue. This arises because of the decreased amount of sleep which night-workers are able, or choose, to take. Average figures indicate that there is a loss of about two hours sleep per day during night work. The operation of the in-built body clock means that normally sleep is easiest to initiate in the late evening and during the night, with a further preferred time in the early part of the afternoon. Sleep is most difficult to initiate in the hours before noon. Waking up, by contrast, is most likely to occur in the morning, late afternoon and early evening. This means that the night-worker's attempts to sleep in the morning and stay asleep for a satisfactory length of time are in direct opposition to the effects of the body clock.

3.3.3   Domestic and social disruption

Human beings are social creatures and may not be able to cope with the disruption of normal patterns of domestic and social life which arise from shiftwork. As a spouse, the shiftworker will have roles as sexual partner, social companion and protector/caregiver. All three roles are compromised by shiftwork. As a parent, work on an afternoon/evening shift may mean that an individual will not see his/her children for days on end during school terms. On the other hand, child care and household management responsibilities may erode sleep time, especially for women. In addition to disrupted family life, the shiftworker may also suffer from social isolation from day-working friends and community organisations that operate on the assumption that evenings and weekends will be free for meetings and activities.

3.3.4   Performance

Not surprisingly, circadian fluctuations in physiology are reflected in equivalent fluctuations in mood and performance. People's ability to perform most tasks is thought to be at its lowest ebb in the early hours of the morning. Studies have also shown that individuals are more fatigued during the night-shift than during the day, and that fatigue reaches its maximum in the early hours of the morning. There is general agreement in the literature of shiftworking that:

- Errors and general performance show rhythmic changes with the night-shift being the worst.
- The position of the night-shift would be improved if work breaks were feasible, and the work was interesting.
- The position is worsened if boring and repetitive tasks are involved, if sleep loss has occurred or if length of time on duty is increased.

3.3.5   Shiftwork tolerance

Research has shown that some individuals appear better able to cope with shiftwork than others. Harma, (1993, ref. no. 164) suggests that commitment to shiftwork may be the most important factor affecting shiftwork tolerance. Workers who have freely chosen to work shifts may be more willing to schedule their lives, and especially their sleeping habits, to working unusual hours. For the committed, skills and coping mechanisms promoting adjustment to shiftwork are available, including correct sleeping habits, good eating and drinking regimes and physical exercise. Olsson, Kandolin and Kauppinen-Toropainen (1990, ref. no. 157) found in a study of nurses and paper mill workers that for all groups active cognitive coping styles were associated with less stress and fewer health complaints. Active cognitive coping included seeking social support, prioritisation of tasks, and good time-use planning.

Other individual differences affecting shiftwork tolerance identified by Harma include:-

- Ageing, which has been found to increase the adverse effects of shiftwork.
- Flexibility of sleeping habits i.e. ability to sleep at odd times, which is related to better long term tolerance of shiftwork.
- Physical fitness, which appears to reduce sleepiness, probably due to improved sleep quality.
- Morningness/eveningness, where morning people are more alert in the morning than evening people. Morning peoples' biorhythms do not adjust so readily to shiftwork and their sleeping habits tend to be more rigid.

3.4 Interpersonal relationships

Research suggests that responsibility for budgets or material property is not as stressful as responsibility for the well-being of others, especially in a human services context (Cherniss, 1980 ref. no. 175). In the early 1970s H J Freudenberger, a psychiatrist, was employed in an alternative health care agency in the United States. He noticed that many of the volunteers with whom he was working experienced a gradual emotional depletion and a loss of motivation and commitment. The process took about a year and was accompanied by a variety of mental and physical symptoms. Freudenberger christened this particular state of mental exhaustion 'burnout', borrowing a term colloquially used to refer to the effects of chronic drug abuse (Freudenberger, 1974, ref. no. 174).

Freudenberger had obviously touched a raw nerve, as in the next five years there was a flood of writing about 'burnout'. Traditionally the major cause of burnout has been the emotionally demanding interpersonal relationships of professional caregivers with their recipients. By definition, these relationships are asymmetric. Professionals in the human services provide care, support, attention, comfort and assistance to their clients, patients and pupils, whereas the recipient is supposed to receive. Nevertheless, professionals do look for some rewards from their efforts: for example, they expect recipients of their care to show gratitude, or to make a real effort to get well. However, these expectations are seldom fulfilled because recipients are in need of help and take the efforts of the professional for granted. In addition, recipients may be unco-operative and unwilling to follow advice or guidelines and therefore improve only slowly. Eventually the strains in this asymmetric relationship may result in the depletion of the caregiver's emotional resources, the core symptom of burnout.

The most influential and widely accepted definition of burnout comes from Maslach and Jackson (1986, ref. no. 194). They define it as an inappropriate response to chronic emotional stress characterised by:-

•   Emotional exhaustion including the feeling of having nothing to offer to others.
•   Depersonalisation, including negative, distant and insensitive attitudes to the recipient of the service.
•   Reduced personal accomplishment, including feelings of inadequacy for the daily task which arise from the perception that demands are greater than the capacity to meet them.

Burnout can lead to a deterioration in the quality of the service provided, appears to be a factor in job turnover, absenteeism and low morale and seems to be related to various self-reported indicators of personal dysfunction, including physical exhaustion, insomnia, increased use of alcohol and drugs, and marital and family problems.

Cherniss (1980, ref. no. 175) offers a different definition of the phenomenon. For him, burnout refers to a process in which the professional's attitudes change in negative ways in response to job strain. These attitudinal changes include loss of concern for the client; increasing discouragement, fatalism and pessimism about one's work; decline in motivation, effort and involvement in work; apathy and negativism; frequent irritability and anger with clients and colleagues; a tendency to rationalise failure by blaming clients or 'the system'; and resistance to change, growing rigidity and loss of creativity. Physical and behavioural consequences of burnout include chronic fatigue; frequent colds, flu, headaches and gastrointestinal symptoms; sleeplessness; loss of self-esteem; and marital and family conflict.

An alternative way of defining burnout represents it as a unique way of coping with the strain of interacting with other people at work. Leiter (1988, ref. no. 176) examined the relationship between social involvement with co-workers and psychological burnout among human services workers. The results indicated that psychological burnout was higher for workers who communicated extensively with co-workers about work but had relatively few informal supportive communications with them. This school of theory and research contends that social interactions are the critical stressors. Leiter and Maslach (1988, ref. no. 177) found that nurses, when asked to identify sources of stress in their jobs, cited interactions with co-workers ten times more often than interactions with patients.

Burnout can be thought of as arising from strained interpersonal relationships at work, but its effects can also be mitigated by an effective collegial support network. Corrigan, Holmes and Luchins (1995, ref. no. 187) found that satisfaction with support systems diminished the effects of burnout, which manifested themselves in frequency of illness and poor job attitudes. Similarly Huebner (1994, ref. no. 185) found support from supervisors, spouse, friends or co-workers to be the most influential contributor to school psychologists' well-being.

Strained interpersonal relations with colleagues and difficulties with clients are obviously not the only causes of burnout. As long ago as the early 1980s, Cherniss saw burnout as in part an organisational problem arising from strain caused by bureaucratic interference and loss of professional autonomy (Cherniss, 1980, ref. no. 175). Leiter also considered burnout to be a function of organisational environments. In 'The Dream Denied', he argues that the conflict between professional ideals and the reality of what is achievable within organisational constraints accelerates the development of the syndrome (Leiter, 1991, ref. no. 179). Winnubst (1993, ref. no. 181) analyses the relationship between organisational structure, social support and burnout. He argues that particular organisational structures produce particular organisational cultures. For instance, a machine bureaucracy that is characterised by standardisation of work and formalisation tends to reinforce perfectionism and conformity. Hierarchy and authority play an important role and most communication is vertical. In this organisational culture burnout is caused by emotional drain due to routine, monotony and lack of control. On the other hand, a professional bureaucracy that is characterised by standardisation of skill and little formalisation tends to reinforce creativity and autonomy. Team work and guidance are important principles and communication is horizontal as well as vertical. In this culture, burnout is caused by the relatively loose structure and the resulting continuous struggle with other people leading to role problems, domain fights, etc.

There is a growing interest in the more recent literature in the influence of personality on the development of burnout. In particular the personality trait of neuroticism or negative affectivity is thought to be an influential antecedent of the human stress process and burnout. Individuals high in negative affectivity tend to look on the black side of life and to be prone to anxiety. When responding to questionnaires, they tend to exaggerate both the intensity of stress at work and its ill effects on themselves. The association of stress factors with strains such as poor mental and physical health thus may be inflated by over-reporting due to negative affectivity. Deary and his colleagues in a study of 333 consultant doctors found most of the dimensions of a five factor model of personality were related to aspects of a doctors' professional activity. For example, neuroticism had strong associations with many aspects of job-related stress and feelings of poor job achievement, while extraversion and conscientiousness made independent contributions to feelings of positive job achievement. Agreeableness was associated with less tendency to dehumanise patients. Neuroticism was found to lead to use of emotion-focused coping strategies and a tendency to view organisational change as threatening. This led in turn to feelings of being under stress which resulted in burnout (Deary et al, 1996, ref. no. 196). Rowe, in her study of a sample of 448 health care professionals, found strong support for the hypothesis that particular dimensions of temperament impact on the burnout process and that certain personality traits make individuals more resilient (Rowe, 1997, ref. no. 200). Similarly Elliott and his colleagues found in a study of nurses in physical rehabilitation units that individuals with higher burnout scores were distinguished by their difficulties in tolerating stress and use of emotion-focused coping strategies. Interestingly, interpersonal conflict on the job was the most frequently reported source of stress among these participants (Elliott et al, 1996, ref. no. 197).

No consensus exists in the literature about the relationships among the three elements of burnout as defined and measured by the Maslach Burnout Inventory (MBI). In exploring factors associated with burnout, researchers have generally analysed the effects and antecedents of emotional exhaustion, depersonalisation and reduced personal accomplishment separately. Golembiewski and his colleagues suggest that depersonalisation is the earliest symptom of burnout and leads to reduced accomplishment, which is followed by emotional exhaustion (Golembiewski et al, 1996, ref. no. 192). Leiter, on the other hand, regards depersonalisation as occurring after the onset of emotional exhaustion. Demanding aspects of the work environment (workload, personal conflict, hassles) aggravate exhaustion, which in turn contributes to increased depersonalisation, while the presence of resources (social support, opportunities for learning new skills) enhances personal accomplishment (Leiter, 1993, ref. no. 180). Koeske and Koeske (1989 & 1993, ref. nos. 178 & 182) propose limiting the concept of burnout to emotional exhaustion alone, with depersonalisation and personal accomplishment playing subsidiary roles. Depersonalisation is seen as one possible outcome of persistent emotional exhaustion, while personal accomplishment is important for its moderating effects.

The vast majority of empirical work on burnout consists of correlational studies which collect self-report data (mostly employing the Maslach Burnout Inventory) at one point in time from a non-representative sample. Some of the correlations between burnout and different variables may be an artifact of reliance on a single method or the use of a specialised group. Such studies do not permit a test of causal hypotheses, even though causal links are usually presumed and discussed. In cross-sectional studies of this kind it is not possible to tell if the work stress factors are causing the symptoms of burnout, or if the burnout is causing the individual to perceive his/her work environment as stressful. Finally, subjective assessments of certain variables may not accord with their objective reality. Thus, a supervisor might offer helpful advice which is perceived as condescending by an employee who then reports lack of supervisor support. Given these limitations, one must be cautious about interpreting empirical data unless sophisticated statistical techniques such as path analysis or structural equation modelling have been used and/or the self-reports have been cross-checked against some objective measures such as absence records or physiological tests.

3.5   Violence and bullying

Violence and bullying in the workplace can be divided into two categories:

*   Violence and bullying between employees.
*   Violence between employees and clients.

Workplace bullying by management is commonly defined as the abuse of power by the bully, and includes verbal and/or physical intimidation, ostracism, or, conversely, excessive supervision, constant criticism, impossible deadlines, changing objectives without discussion, and taking credit for the victims idea's. Bullies are conceived as being insecure and inadequate individuals who cannot relinquish control. Four kinds of management bullying can be identified:

- Situational bullies who react badly to pressure.
- Punishing bullies who use bullying to motivate staff.
- Pathological bullies with sadistic tendencies.
- Role playing bullies who feel that the culture of the organisation requires them to act in this way.

Bullying causes damage to both psychological and physical health. Its effects include loss of self-confidence and self-esteem, anxiety, depression and panic attacks, and the development of stress related illnesses such as migraine, irritable bowel syndrome, raised blood pressure, inability to sleep and loss of appetite. Organisational outcomes include increased sickness absence and staff turnover and falling morale and performance levels.

The most advanced academic research on adult bullying is found in Scandinavia and is matched by a strong public awareness which led to the establishment of laws against bullying in Sweden in 1993 and Norway in 1994. The Scandinavian research has tended to focus on the relationship between bullying and the quality of the work environment. High occurrence of bullying is associated with leadership style, work control and conflicting demands. Insufficient work control and high levels of conflicting demands are seen as precursors to bullying, with the manager responsible for them being seen as the bully. Lack of leadership is seen as needing to exist for bullying to be accepted (Einarsen, Raknes and Matthiesen, 1994, ref. no. 208; Ashforth, 1994, ref. no. 209).

The phenomenon of 'mobbing' or bullying of workers by their peers rather than by management is explored by Leymann (1990, ref. no. 204). It involves a group of employees 'ganging up' on a colleague and subjecting him/her to a campaign of psychological harassment. The harassment can take the form of:

- Destruction of the victim's reputation through rumour mongering, slander and ridicule.
- Social isolation of the victim.
- Constant criticism.
- Violence or threats of violence.

Such a reign of psychological terror can lead to a deterioration in the victim's work performance and his/her eventual expulsion from the workplace. Health consequences include depression, hyperactivity, compulsive behaviour, suicides and psychosomatic illnesses.

Surveys conducted by trade unions indicate a high prevalence of workplace bullying:

* 38% of all calls to the TUC's bad bosses hotline in December 1997 were from people who claimed to have been bullied at work (TUC, 1998, ref. no. 215).

* A survey by local MSF representatives in 1995 of ca. 140,000 union members showed that 30% of respondents considered bullying to be a significant problem (MSF, 1995, ref. no. 210).

* A study of union members by UNISON in 1997 showed that 66% had either witnessed or experienced bullying at work (TUC, 1998, ref. no. 215).

In the academic literature, Rayner (1997, ref. no. 211) reports results of a survey of 1137 part-time students at Staffordshire University showing that half of the sample claimed to have been bullied during their working lives.

The extent of the problem of workplace violence is very difficult to estimate due to the fact that in most countries statistics on violence at work are not collected as a separate category and research in this area is in its infancy. Existing statistical evidence of patterns and trends has been most recently summarised by Chappell and Di Martino (1998, ref. no. 230). They cite the second European Survey on Working Conditions carried out in 1996 as the most recent indicator of the prevalence of workplace violence in Europe. Findings, based on interviews with 15,800 workers throughout the EU, show that 4% of employees (6 million) had been subjected to physical violence. The highest incidence of violence was in service industries (public administration with 6% and retail industry with 5%). They also quote a number of other useful statistical indicators, including:

* An increase of 73% in the number of reported robberies of financial institutions in the Nordic countries between 1988 and 1992.

* A survey by the UK Health and Safety Executive in which 30% of staff interviewed said they were verbally abused or threatened more than once a week.

A snapshot of the extent of violence in the workplace is given by the results of an Institute for Personnel Development telephone survey conducted in 1995 and reported in 'People Management' 25 July 1995, p.29. The survey shows that overall

11% of workers had observed workplace violence between employees in the previous year. Some 7.2% of male workers and 2% of women reported personal experience of workplace violence and 40% of victims were subjected to violence on more than 5 occasions in the previous year.

Results of a systematic study of the problem in Finland confirm that work–related violence is on the increase. Findings show that reported incidents of violence at work rose from 16% of all violent incidents in 1980 to 23% in 1988. The range of occupations affected extended from jobs traditionally associated with workplace violence (prison officers, police officers, retail shop employees) to include social workers, teachers, clerical workers and doctors and nurses (Heiskanen *et al*, 1991, ref. no. 216).

The escalation of violence in the workplace in the US is seen as being associated with the job insecurity and overwork arising from the corporate restructuring and downsizing of the 1980s and 1990s. Displaced workers have difficulty in finding another job of similar rank and status and are forced into low-paid, part-time and often insecure employment. Survivors are exposed to overwork and conflicting demands, and are caught up in a long hours culture. At the same time, stabilising social institutions such as the family, church, school and community are breaking down and violence is glamorised by the media. The degradation of labour associated with the scientific management of technological change and coupled with the undermining of existing forms of social control produces stress and frustration which can trigger assaultative violence (Kinney, 1995, ref. no. 218; Capozzoli and McVey 1996, ref. no. 224; Baxter and Margavio, 1996, ref. no. 222).

3.6   Work–non-work conflict

People do not work in a vacuum; behaviour on the job is often influenced by experiences and in other areas of life. Research has tended to focus on the interaction between work and family life. This is justified on the grounds that family life is generally the most important aspect of a person's life and contributes heavily, along with job satisfaction, to general life satisfaction. Unlike most of the literature on work-related stress, women rather than men tend to be the predominant subjects. This is justified on the grounds that, because women traditionally have primary responsibility for child care, elder care and household management, they are more likely to experience conflict between the demands of work and family.

The relationship between an employed person's life at work and life outside work can be analysed in terms of various different connections between the two domains:

- Role processes analyse the distribution of an individual's time, energy and talents between social roles, for example paid worker and spouse. Stress arises either from interrole conflict or role overload. Interrole conflict arises when the demands of work and family life are incompatible as, for example, when the requirement to attend a school concert conflicts with the need to work late to meet a deadline. A role overload model postulates that the two domains of work and family/social life compete for limited personal resources and that an individual can easily become overburdened by a combination of demands. In this perspective, evenings spent caring for a sick relative may leave the employee fatigued and distracted the next day at work. In contrast, a role accumulation model suggests that the combination of multiple roles is positively beneficial to the individual through increased opportunities for social interaction and personal development and the raising of self-esteem.

- Spillover processes describe the effects family events can have on the employed person's emotional well-being, and so on motivation and job performance. For example, a parent who is worried about childcare arrangements may be distracted at work and more prone to errors. Spillover is a two way process in that experiences at work intrude into family life as much as experiences are conveyed from the family to work. The classic example would be the way in which a man who has had a bad day in the office comes home, behaves like a bear with a sore head, and takes out his frustration on his wife and children.

- Socialisation processes suggest that values, skills and attitudes learned at home influence behaviour at work. Thus a supervisor's ability to be supportive may arise from learning patience and understanding as a parent. However, not all behaviours that work well in a family setting function well at work. For example, family systems theory suggests that a high level of bonding amongst family members is an effective response to stress, yet detachment or disengagement has been found to be an effective coping mechanism in the workplace.

The relationship between job stress and family system variables is circular and reciprocal. Occupational experiences can affect the family as much as family experiences affect work. This can make empirical findings difficult to interpret.

For example, a statistically significant association between marital satisfaction and job satisfaction can be interpreted as support for opposite causal propositions. One can either assert that a high level of job satisfaction leads to greater marital satisfaction or that marital happiness leads to greater satisfaction at work.

Spillover, role processes and socialisation can each result in a positive or a negative outcome. To cite a common example, a person socialised in team sports has an advantage in jobs that emphasise team working, but a person socialised in a caring role may be able to cope better than others in jobs requiring interpersonal skills. When considered out of context, it is often impossible to tell how a particular family event will affect job adjustment.

3.7   Role ambiguity and role conflict

Role ambiguity is defined by Beehr (1995 ref. no. 63) as 'deficient or uncertain information in the environment regarding the role behaviours expected of the focal person'. Translated into lay terms this means that role ambiguity arises when a worker has inadequate information about his/her work role. It manifests itself as confusion about objectives, a lack of clarity about what is expected of the person and general uncertainty about the scope of the job (Cox, 1993, ref. no. 59). Ambiguity can arise when role senders, e.g. supervisors, do not communicate adequate information about what is expected, communicate information that is unclear or confusing, do not make clear to the job incumbent what activities or behaviours will enable the incumbent to fulfil their expectations of him/her, or do not make clear the consequences of failure or success in meeting goals. A shining example of the first quoted by Quick and Quick (1984 ref. no. 54) is when a worker joining the distribution department of a large retailer was told to 'do what that guy does' and given no further information. The problem of unclear or confusing information is most likely to arise in work environments where technical terms or jargon are prevalent, such as hospitals. The third problem of uncertainty about appropriate behaviours happens when people are set objectives without guidance or how to fulfil them, though this can be considered to be part of normal managerial life. The final problem of lack of clarity about consequences is exemplified by the position of a salesman who is unclear about the consequences of meeting a target (a bonus?), exceeding a target (a bigger bonus? or no bonus because the original target was too low?) or failing to meet the target (a commission penalty or no consequence at all because the target was too high?).

Early work by Beehr shows role ambiguity associated as a stress factor with job dissatisfaction, life dissatisfaction, low self-esteem and depressed mood. (Beehr 1976 ref. no. 254). These findings are confirmed in studies by Margolis, Kroes and Quinn (1974 ref. no. 252), French and Caplan (1970 ref. no. 250) and Kahn *et al* (1964 ref. no. 249) where role ambiguity is associated with job dissatisfaction, tension, feelings of futility and lack of self-confidence.

Role conflict is defined by Beehr (1995 ref. no. 63) as 'the existence of two or more sets of demands or expectations on the focal person such that compliance with one would make it more difficult or impossible to comply with others'. Intrasender role conflict occurs when a single person in the work environment (usually the boss) communicates conflicting or incompatible expectations. For example, a worker may be asked to increase productivity while adhering to the letter of the company's safety procedures, and may come to feel that the first cannot be achieved without compromising the second. Intersender role conflict occurs when two or more role senders communicate conflicting expectations. This is not uncommon in matrix forms of organisation where an individual will have a functional manager and a project manager. The expectations of the two managers may be somewhat different leaving the individual caught in the middle. Person–role conflict occurs when there is an incompatibility between the individuals values or beliefs and the requirements of various role senders. This form of conflict may arise amongst military personnel unable to carry out orders which violate their ethical systems. Interrole conflict arises when the requirements of one role conflict with the requirements of a second role occupied by the same person. Everyone occupies more than one role in life and multiple roles increase the chances of this type of conflict. Expectations accompanying one's roles as a patriotic citizen, a member of a religion, a member of a family and a holder of a job can easily be in conflict (Kahn *et al* 1964, ref. no. 249; French and Caplan, 1970, ref. no. 250; Shirom *et al*, 1973, ref. no. 251).

Role conflict does not necessarily lead to role stress. The worker may not realise that conflicting expectations about him/her exist, or, even if he/she does perceive a conflict, the perception of role conflict still may not be stressful. For example, he/she simply may not care about others' expectations. Role conflict in the workplace is likely to lead to distress in situations where either the role sender has power of over the worker or the worker attaches importance to fulfilling the role sender's expectations. In organisational terms, person A has power over person B to the extent that person B needs person A for the attainment of desired goals. The measure of person A's power is the amount of resistance from B he/she can expect to overcome. The role sender's importance is defined as the worker's experienced desire to meet a particular role sender's expectations. Regardless of the balance of power between them, how much does the worker want to live up to the role sender's image of him? (Siegall and Cummings, 1995, ref. no. 269; Kahn *et al*, 1964, ref. no. 249).

Jones (1993, ref. no. 266) argues that role conflict can have a positive rather than a negative outcome for individuals and organisations. Her year-long qualitative study of child welfare administrators showed that in spite of a public presentation of self that indicated they were under extreme stress and placed in impossible situations, they in fact enjoyed the challenge, and were forced through their daily confrontation with conflicting roles to become more flexible, to be open to different points of view and to expand their sources of information.

Negative outcomes of role conflict have been identified as reduced organisational commitment, job involvement and work satisfaction (Fisher and Gitelson, 1983, ref. no. 256). Kahn and his colleagues in their seminal work (1964, ref. no. 249) associate role conflict with increased tension and anxiety, reduced job satisfaction and the undermining of trust and confidence in supervisors, colleagues and the organisation as a whole. These in turn lead to a breakdown in communication and inter-personal relationships and a withdrawal of co-operation by the worker. Bedeian and Armenakis (1981, ref. no. 255) propose a model of role stress which predicts that role conflict and role ambiguity will directly increase job tension, reduce job satisfaction and increase turnover intentions. Results generally supported the model's fit, although several paths were not consistently significant. Attempts to replicate these results, however, have not been markedly successful (Lang, Wittig-Berman and Rizkalla, 1992, ref. no.261; Klenke-Hamel and Mathieu, 1990, ref. no. 259; Netemeyer, Johnston and Burton, 1990, ref. no. 260). There is also some evidence in the literature that role stressors are associated with burnout in the human services. Manlove (1994, ref. no. 267) found significant relationships between role conflict and ambiguity and burnout among child care workers. Starnaman and Miller (1992, ref. no. 264), in a study of teachers, also found that both role stressors had an impact on burnout. In their study role conflict was related to emotional exhaustion and role ambiguity to reduced personal accomplishment. Both role stressors predicted depersonalisation. On the other hand Burke and Greenglass (1993, ref. no. 265) found levels of role conflict unrelated to burnout in their study of 833 teachers.

Much effort in role stress research has been devoted to the study of moderators which either increase or decrease the effect of the stress factors on the strain outcomes. Kahn and his colleagues (1964, ref. no. 249) hypothesised three categories of contextual variables or moderators: personality factors, inter-personal relations and organisational factors. Research has however been plagued by a failure to find moderators and an inability to replicate results. Fisher and Gitelson in their 1983 meta-analysis (ref. no. 256) found little support for job type as a moderator. They stated that 'the results of the moderator analysis are neither strong nor particularly enlightening' but went on to declare a potential 'need to pursue further moderator research'. On the other hand Jackson and Schuler in their larger 1985 meta-analysis differed with Fisher and Gitelson, finding that their results suggested that most of the relationships describing the potential causes and consequences of role ambiguity and role conflict were likely to be influenced by moderator variables (ref. no. 257).

In a promising fresh approach, Fried and his colleagues (1998, ref. no. 271) began to look for interactions between role conflict and ambiguity. Results supported the hypothesis that simultaneous increases in role conflict and ambiguity would lead to evidence of strain, in this case poor job performance. It is argued that employees who are exposed to a single threatening stressor may be able to use their experience and personal resources to cope successfully. However, they may find it more difficult to function effectively in an environment where a number of role stressors are present concurrently.

3.8   Control in the workplace

Frese (1989, ref. no. 281) identifies various theoretical models of stress, control and well-being. The most parsimonious model of how control affects well-being is one that proposes a direct main effect of control on well-being. Work-related stress is associated with impaired well-being but control at work is seen as a countering force which positively promotes well-being. Frese has suggested that the main–effect model is based on the human need for control, and argues that if this need is not satisfied negative consequences will occur. Certainly there is a wealth of evidence in the literature that autonomy, a construct akin to control, is strongly and consistently related to various facets of job satisfaction (Kelloway and Barling, 1991, ref. no. 284; Loher et al, 1985, ref. no. 274; Spector, 1986, ref. no. 276).

Perhaps the most widely cited model of stress and control is the job demands-decision latitude model developed by Karasek and his colleagues. To recap from chapter 2, the central proposition of this model is that worker well-being is determined by the interaction of job demands and decision latitude. The strain experienced by the worker is expected to be high when demands are high and decision latitude is low. When demands are high but accompanied by high levels of decision latitude, the theory predicts that new behaviour patterns will be acquired and that the job is 'active'. 'Active' jobs will have regenerative effects on workers and can actually improve their well-being. Karasek (1979, ref. no. 76) reported tests of his theory with data from national surveys of workers from the United States and Sweden. He concluded that high job demands and low decision latitude interacted to predict exhaustion, job dissatisfaction and life dissatisfaction in the US data and depression in the Swedish data.

Karasek and his colleagues subsequently invested considerable effort in establishing a link between cardiovascular disease and job strain arising from the interaction of high job demands and low job control. Many of these studies were done using datasets not designed to test the model. For example, in one sample data taken from the US Health Examination Survey were linked to survey data from the Quality of Employment Survey to test for prevalence of heart disease in 'high strain' occupational groups. In this type of general survey data, items reflecting control over various workplace conditions (e.g. pacing or schedule) are combined with items reflecting skill utilisation or job complexity. Results are thus likely to reflect the influence of more general job complexity or job scope factors (Karasek and Theorell, 1990, ref. no. 282; Karasek, 1989, ref. no. 278). Thus despite the popularity of the interactive model, supporting evidence for it has been relatively weak (Ganster and Fusilier, 1989, ref. no. 277). Problematic aspects of the research include confounding worker control with other aspects of job design (e.g. skill variety), the conduct of analyses at the occupational rather than the individual level and the failure to test specifically for an interaction between job demands and decision latitude.

Later results based on workplace surveys or physiological measurements (or a combination of both) continue to be contradictory, some supporting the model and some not. To take some examples, Landsbergis et his colleagues (1992, ref. no. 288) tested Karasek's model among 297 healthy men aged 30-60 years in different worksites, and found it supported by various psychological outcome measures. Men in active jobs reported the highest level of Type A behaviour, job involvement and positive attributional style. Men in low strain jobs reported lowest job dissatisfaction and trait anxiety. Men in high strain jobs had the highest dissatisfaction. Low social support was associated with greater symptomology. On the other hand when Greenlund and colleagues (1995, ref. no. 457) tested the hypothesis that high job demands, low decision latitude and job strain are associated with increased levels of cardiovascular disease risk factors in a sample of 2665 black and white working men and women aged 18-30, they found few associations to support the model. Similarly Tyler and Cushway (1998, ref. no. 298) found no interaction effect between measures of job demands and discretion in a sample of English health care staff after controlling for age, gender and negative affectivity.

Wall and his colleagues (1996, ref. no. 293) tested Karasek's model in a heterogeneous sample of 1451 manufacturing employees using a narrowly focused measure of job control and a purely descriptive measure of job demands with no evaluative component. Results supported the model and the interaction between demands and control was as predicted. Demands were found to be associated with decreased job satisfaction where employees reported low and very low levels of control, but there was little or no effect of demands on job satisfaction at moderate and high levels of control. For depression there was an equivalent pattern. Parallel analyses using a broad measure of decision latitude encompassing a wide range of job properties including control, task variety and learning opportunities did not show an equivalent effect. Based on these results Wall and his colleagues suggest that lack of empirical support for the model in other studies may arise from too broad a definition of decision latitude, when the original theory proposes that it is control that is the crucial factor. Similarly Sargent and Terry (1998, ref. no. 295), using a sample of university administrative staff, found that the adverse effects of job demands were buffered by high levels of task control, but not by more peripheral aspects of work control such as decision authority and control over scheduling.

However, Carayon (1993, ref. no. 292) in a longitudinal test of the model in a homogenous sample of 122 office workers over time found no evidence of an interactional effect of decision latitude and workload on worker strain. Decision latitude and workload had an additive effect on worker strain in only one of 16 instances. In this study decision latitude was defined as including control and skill utilisation which were measured separately. Control was associated with tension-anxiety and depression at the first measurement but not at the second, and to physical health symptoms at the second but not at the first. Skill utilisation was related to none of the strain indicators except to tension-anxiety at the second measurement. Carayon concludes that Karasek's model may be verifiable in heterogeneous populations only, but doubt is cast on this deduction by the results of Sargent and Terry's study, which found interactive effects with a homogeneous sample.

The two factor demands–control model may in the final analysis be too simple to grasp the complexity of interaction between people and their work environment. Worker strain may be determined by a range of factors in the work environment such as work organisation, physical and social environment and technology, and by the interactions among all these factors.

3.9   Monotonous work

Warr (1992, ref. no. 286) points out that from lack of decision latitude flow other sources of unacceptable stress such as lack of task variety and underutilisation of skills. Jobs involving repetitive work and the underutilisation of skills are just as stressful as those which demand too much of the incumbent. For example Lundberg and colleagues (1989, ref. no. 280) found in a study of assembly line workers that repetitive work induced a significant elevation in almost all psychological and physiological measurements. In this case catecholamine elevation was associated with feelings of time prssure and pressure by job demands, while cortisol elevation was associated with irritation, tenseness and tiredness. Exposure to monotonous work leads to boredom, which leads in turn to reduced efficiency and poor job performance. When monotonous tasks involve repetitive motor activity, impairment can take the form of occasional slow reactions that either increase output variability or lead to timing errors. Tracking performance tends to deteriorate during continuous manual control tasks due to transient attention lapses. Finally, fault or target detection performance has been found to deteriorate over time in task, or to remain stable at a very low level of efficiency. Performance can be improved in all cases by short pauses in the work routine (O'Hanlon, 1981, ref. no. 273).

Boredom not only leads to poor performance, but it can also have serious health consequences, including increased incidence of cardiovascular disease, gastritis and peripheral neurological disorders (O'Hanlon, 1981, ref. no. 273). There is also a voluminous literature associating repetitive work with musculoskeletal problems including work-related upper limb disorders. A full discussion and references are included in chapter 5.

Ganster and Fusilier (1989, ref. no. 277) point out that over 100 studies had been conducted by 1989 to assess the effect of external control of work pace on various worker outcomes including error rates and efficiency, physiological responses and psychological stress. Pacing is an objectively measureable aspect of the work environment and researchers have the potential to assess the impact of this kind of control on various worker outcomes while investigating the effects of worker control perceptions. Generally the weight of results of experimental and survey research suggests that workers on externally paced jobs suffer higher levels of subjective stress and associated mental and physical symptoms than do workers on self-paced jobs. However, what is not clear is whether perceived control is the essential intervening variable or whether the stress arises from other aspects of paced work such as short cycle time, repetitious tasks, and high work pressure or production demands. It may be that control over pacing becomes important only when other demands imposed by repetition, cycle time or work pressures create a threatening situation.

3.10 Job insecurity

Job insecurity came to prominence as a modern stress factor as companies responded to economic stringency in the 1980s and 1990s by drastically cutting staff for a 'lean and mean' operation. At the same time a combination of mergers, acquisitions and technological change rendered many jobs superfluous. Companies no longer have a tacit or contractual understanding with their employees that promises a secure job and steady advancement up the career ladder in exchange for loyal and dedicated service. This transformation of the old paternalistic relationship between companies and their employees is judged by most observers to reflect a major structural change in business organisation. For the forseeable future, then, employees can no longer assume that their jobs are 'for life' but must now confront chronic and on-going job insecurity.

The prevalence of job insecurity has been hotly debated in the literature. Some commentators such as David Smith (1997, ref. no. 321) dismiss generalised job insecurity as a myth, claiming that it is largely confined to the young, the old and the unskilled. Insecurity affects poorly paid, unskilled workers at least twice as much as white-collar professionals. Burchell (1998, ref. no. 324) finds from an analysis of a dataset of transitions between jobs created from the Social Change and Economic Life Initiative dataset that the more skilled and advantaged incumbents were protected from job insecurity during the 1980s. On the other hand findings of surveys conducted by the Centre for Micro-Social Change at Essex University during 1990-92 confirmed a striking rise in insecurity of employment, with growing unemployment, movement into casual part-time jobs and enforced self-employment, particularly amongst older men (Buck *et al*,1994, ref. no. 311).

Similarly the key findings of a longitudinal study of 800 managers over 13 years from 1980 to 1992 by Kerr Inkson showed that managers were changing jobs more often, that sideways or downwards moves amongst managers were increasing, that upward managerial moves were declining, and that managers were increasingly subjected to changes imposed unilaterally by employers (1992, ref. no. 308).

Whatever the objective reality of the threat of job loss, the psychological impact on the individual arises from his/her evaluation or perception of the situation as dangerous. Objectively, the average job tenure of men has not decreased much since the mid 1970s and there has been no decline at all for women. Unemployment is now at a much lower level than during the 1980s. Yet results of a 1997 survey of 2467 people in employment aged between 20 and 60 compared with results of an even larger survey of 4047 people in the same age group conducted in 1986 showed that perceptions of job and employment insecurity had increased sharply among those in highly paid occupations such as managers and professionals. Among those in occupations not so highly paid, feelings of job insecurity did not alter all that much, while perceptions of employment insecurity went down a little if anything (Felstead, Burchell and Green, 1998, ref. no. 323). Job insecurity is connected by Burchell and his colleagues with one's perceptions of the likelihood of losing one's present job, while employment insecurity is connected with perceived likelihood of being able to find another job in case of redundancy. Thus it is the eye of the beholder, rather than the objective characteristics of the situation, that determine whether the circumstances are appraised as threatening or not. Employees exposed to the same threatening signals will therefore experience different degrees of job and employment insecurity.

Job insecurity is defined by Klandermans, Van Vuuren and Jacobson (1991, ref. no. 305) as a function of the perceived probability and the perceived severity of losing one's job. That is, the more likely it is that a person will lose his or her job, and/or the more severe the consequences of that loss, the stronger his or her feelings of job insecurity will be. However perceived susceptibility to job loss in the face of the same threatening cues varies widely from person to person. For example, some people may perceive themselves as susceptible to job loss because their performance is below standard, while others are convinced they are indispensable to the organisation. In general, the perceived probability of job loss is influenced by characteristics of the person such as age, health, seniority, etc., personality characteristics such as natural tendencies towards optimism or pessimism, and the organisational/industrial relations climate. The perceived severity of job loss is affected by the value of various job features such as income, career progression, status, self-esteem, etc., the likelihood of losing these features, and the employees dependence on his or her present job. Employees who feel that they could easily get another job at a similar salary will be less alarmed at the prospect of redundancy than those who feel that they have few alternatives.

For many people job insecurity has a detrimental effect on their psychological well-being. It is related to impaired mental health, reduced job satisfaction and reduced organisational commitment. Its behavioural consequences reveal that an insecure workforce has few positive implications for the organisation either. Some employees respond by actively seeking other jobs so that the most able and well-qualified jump ship, with obvious harmful consequences to the organisation. Others are likely to withdraw psychologically, if not physically, reducing their intended level of contribution to the minimum necessary to avoid being fired. Insecurity also tends to reduce the loyalty or commitment that employees feel towards their organisation. Companies may find that they have created a breed of hard-nosed employees prepared to look elsewhere to further their careers if their current employer is not meeting their expectations. This erosion of commitment following experience of job insecurity and redundancy is illustrated by a longitudinal study by Hallier and Lyon (1996, ref. no. 316) of middle managers threatened by redundancy. Managers made redundant and subsequently re-employed felt their previous employers had broken their psychological contract with them. In consequence, the men commonly withdrew particular aspects of commitment in their new jobs. This included intentions to quit, reduced work effort, maximising opportunities to gain additional skills, more time devoted to outside commitments and a rejection of senior management objectives where these conflicted with personal commitments.

A further body of research into job insecurity and redundancies looks at their effect on the attitudes of survivors. Brockner and his colleagues, combining a laboratory experiment with field research, found that survivors responded with reduced performance levels and reduced organisational commitment when they felt that laid-off co-workers had been treated unfairly, or when they identified strongly with them (Brockner et al, 1987, ref. no. 301). Brockner, Davey and Carter (1985, ref. no. 300) demonstrated in a laboratory experiment that survivors of lay-offs experienced guilt and remorse about their co-worker's dismissal, which acted as a spur to increased productivity. In order to reduce their remorse or guilt over their co-workers dismissal, workers increased their level of output. Finally, Brockner and his colleagues (1992, ref. no. 309) found that survivors' level of work effort was low both when they themselves did not feel personally threatened, and when they felt very insecure through a certainty of further redundancies to come due to circumstances beyond their and their employers' control. Work effort increased with moderate levels of job insecurity which were high enough to overcome complacency but not so high as to cause despair and helplessness.

Finally, as the economy pulls out of recession and the threat of redundancy recedes, does the British worker feel more secure? There is evidence that the feel-good factor began to return to the workplace during 1997 in reports from the Institute for Personnel and Development (IPD) and the Conference Board, the business research organisation. According to a 1997 IPD survey almost all employees believed they were treated fairly at work, more than three-quarters trusted their organisations to keep their promises and similar numbers were proud to tell people who they worked for. Only a minority – albeit a significant one of 25% – expressed worries about job security (Guest and Conway, 1997, ref. no. 319). The Conference Board research showed that for the well-qualified employee security is not necessarily top of the wish list. Interesting work, good communication and opportunities for development ranked more highly, (1997, ref. no. 320).

3.11 Bibliography

3.11.1 Long working hours

(127)
SLEEP loss, recovery sleep and military performance
D R Haslam
Ergonomics, vol.25, 1982, p.163-178.

Ten trained infantrymen completed a 9-day tactical defense exercise combining 90 hours of continuous activity with 144 hours of limited sleep. Results showed that tasks with a vigilance and cognitive element began to deteriorate after one night without sleep. After 90 hours without sleep, a block of 4 hours sleep had a marked beneficial effect on performance. After a total of 12 hours sleep over 3 days (72 hours), performance had recovered from 50 to 88 per cent of control values. 30 hours of rest, of which an average of 19 hours were spent asleep, eliminated any remaining decrement.

DSC Shelfmark: 3808.500000

(128)
SUSTAINED work, fatigue, sleep loss and performance: a review of the issues
G P Krueger
Work and stress, vol.3, 1989, p.129-141.

Reviews factors associated with sustained work which affect the psychological and physiological condition of the worker and moderate job performance. Decrements in sustained performance are reported as a function of fatigue, especially after or during one or more nights of complete sleep loss or longer periods of reduced sleep. Sleep loss appears to result in reduced reaction time, decreased vigilance, perceptual and cognitive disorders and changes in affect.

DSC Shelfmark: 9348.102000

(129)
WORK performance and health of junior hospital doctors: a review of the literature
A Spurgeon and J M Harrington,
Work and stress, vol.3, 1989, p.117-128

Concern has been expressed over many years about long working hours and consequent sleep loss experienced by junior hospital doctors. A number of studies have shown that a significant proportion of junior doctors develop some degree of mental ill-health. Even among doctors who cope adequately with other stressful aspects of the work, there are likely to be effects on performance resulting from sleep loss.

DSC Shelfmark: 9348.102000

(130)
STRUCTURAL changes, ill-health and mortality in Sweden, 1963-1983.
B Starrin *et al*
International journal of health services, vol.20, 1990, p.27-42.

Found an association between the suicide rate and both overemployment in the form of an increase in overtime worked and underemployment in the form of an increase in unemployment. A relative increase in the mortality rate for cardiovascular disease was found to be related to increases in both unemployment and overtime worked in women only.

DSC Shelfmark: 4542.278000

(131)
A CROSS-SECTIONAL study of hand/wrist symptoms in female grocery checkers
H Morgenstern *et al*
American journal of industrial medicine, vol.20, 1991, p.209-218.

Prevalence of symptoms of carpal tunnel syndrome in female grocery checkers was positively associated with age, average work hours per week, years worked as a checker and use of diuretics. The estimated effect of years worked as a checker was greater for younger than older women, in whom the association reversed, suggesting a selective loss of symptomatic workers.

DSC Shelfmark: 0826.750000

(132)

LONG working hours and occupational stress-related cardiovascular attacks among middle-aged workers in Japan

T Uehata

Journal of human ergology, vol.20, 1991, p.147-153.

Reports case study of 203 Karoshi victims who suffered cardiovascular attacks and for whom workers' compensation was claimed. Two-thirds of them proved to have been working more than 60 hours per week, more than 50 hours overtime per month or more than half of their fixed holidays before the attack. These long hours were complicated by other work stressors such as career problems, excessive business trips and organisational changes. The various work stressors brought about unhealthy behaviours such as smoking, drinking, lack of exercise and poor dietary habits. The resulting cardiovascular attacks were triggered by minor work-related troubles or events.

DSC Shelfmark: 5003.414000

(133)

THE OVERWORKED American: the unexpected decline of leisure

J B Schor

New York: Basic Books, 1991. 247p.

Presents estimates showing that work-time has been steadily increasing since the 1960s. According to these estimates the average employed person worked 163 hours per year longer in 1987 than in 1969. The increase in employed women's hours is greater at 305 hours over the same period. This increase is caused by two factors: increased hours worked per week and increased weeks worked per year. Over the same period, greater use of technological aids in the household has not significantly reduced the amount of time spent on domestic work.

DSC Shelfmark: 92/04093

(134)

WORK stress among long-distance coach drivers: a survey and correlational study

P T F Raggatt

Journal of organizational behavior, vol.12, 1991, p.565-579.

Paper presents findings from an Australian survey of working conditions, coping behaviours and stress among 93 long-distance coach drivers. Results suggest that long driving hours are the best predictors of maladaptive behaviours such as stimulant use and sleep disturbance. The maladaptive behaviours in turn predict stress symptoms such as doctor visits and symptom reports.

DSC Shelfmark: 5027.066000

(135)
JUNIOR hospital doctor drops dead after 86 hour week
J Jones
Observer, 10 April 1994.

Report of death of junior doctor Alan Massie in Warrington District Hospital at the end of an 86 hour working week. He had worked 7 of the previous 8 days including two unbroken spells of 27 hours and one of 24 hours.

DSC Shelfmark: not found

(136)
THE TIME squeeze
Demos quarterly, issue 5, 1995. 56p.

Highlights the growing imbalance between unemployment for some and overwork for others; poor management of public spaces and transport, which has forced up time required to get to work, care for children and even to shop; and severe stress for millions, particularly women, trying to juggle conflicting responsibilities. Argues for government policies to support greater autonomy and flexibility around work, leisure and leave, to sustain sabbaticals and parental leave, and to encourage better use of time in work and leisure.

DSC Shelfmark: 3550.630600

(137)
EFFECTS of long work hours on life-style, stress and quality of life among intermediate Japanese managers
S Maruyama and K Morimoto
Scandinavian journal of work environment and health, vol.22, 1996, p.353-359.

Questionnaires were sent concerning work hours, life-style, subjective stress and quality of life to 3870 heads of division or section and 2666 foremen in 110 firms in Japan. Men who worked long hours generally had a more unhealthy life style. Long hours were associated with sleep loss, irregular mealtimes, and use of stimulants. The frequency of high subjective stress was 2.51 times greater for the divisional or section heads and 2.35 times higher for the foreman who worked long hours than among those who worked relatively shorter hours.

DSC Shelfmark: 8087.568000

(138)
INDIVIDUAL and nomothetic models of job stress: an examination of work hours, cohesion and well-being
P D Bliese and R R Halverson
Journal of applied social psychology, vol.26, 1996, p.1171-1189.

Job stress can be studied both at the level of individual perception and by examining consistencies in how groups of individuals appraise their work environment. Current study examined linkages between work hours, vertical cohesion, horizontal cohesion and psychological well-being from both an individual and group perspective using survey data collected from 7382 US Army enlisted personnel. Results showed that respondents from the same work group agreed about perceptions of the work climate. Both individual and group perspectives were useful in describing the relationship between cohesion and psychological well-being, but relationship between work hours and well-being was best modelled from a group perspective.

DSC Shelfmark: 4947.080000

(139)
OUR time-less lives
R Pahl

Times higher education supplement, August 30, 1996, p.15.

Focuses on time pressures caused as both men and women attempt to juggle work and family responsibilities in a world where both partners are likely to be in employment.

DSC Shelfmark: 8853.700000

(140)
THE EFFECTS of hours of work on health: a meta-analytic review
K Sparks *et al*

Journal of occupational and organizational psychology, vol.70, 1997, p.391–408.

A quantitative and qualitative review of existing literature on working hours and health was carried out. Results of the meta-analyses carried out on 21 studies indicated small, but significant, positive mean correlations between overall health symptoms, physiological and psychological health symptoms and hours of work. Qualitative analysis of a further twelve studies also produced evidence of a positive relationship between long hours and ill-health. Various factors which may moderate the relationship between long hours and ill-health are discussed.

DSC Shelfmark: 5026.082000

(141)
FINDING time: how corporations, individuals and families can benefit from new work practices
L A Perlow

Ithaca, NY: ILR Press, 1997. 156p.

Author spent 9 months studying the work practices of a team of software engineers at a Fortune 500 corporation. Describes workers caught in a chronic sense of crisis, pelted by interruptions and too busy to help colleagues. This work culture deprives employees of private time and also adversely affects profits.

DSC Shelfmark: 98/05581

(142)
THE TIME bind
A R Hochschild
New York: Metropolitan Books, 1997. 316p.

Reports results of a three year study of 130 US workers which showed people prefer the office to the home. Many are eager to get in to the office early, leave late and put in extra hours at weekends to the neglect of their children and family life. This is attributed to the success of modern management techniques in making workers feel valued. At work, people are empowered, make decisions and have a social life, whereas home life is associated with unrewarding domestic chores performed under time constraints.

DSC Shelfmark: 97/19074

(143)
WORKING in Europe
P Burns and O Whitehouse
Milton Keynes: 3i European Enterprise Centre, 1997. 7p.
(Special report; 22)

Reports results of a postal survey of over 8000 SMEs (under 500 employees) carried out in Nov.–Dec. 1996 covering Britain, France, Germany, Italy and Spain. Results show that the British workforce works the longest hours and takes the least holiday.

DSC Shelfmark: Not found

(144)
THE GREAT work/life debate 1998: the definitive report
WFD in association with Management Today
London, 1998. 31p.

Sample of 5,501 general subscribers to Management Today completed a questionnaire distributed as part of the standard mailing for the February 1998 edition of the journal. Results provide insight into individual experiences and patterns of responsibility at work and at home, the perceived difficulties of balancing these two aspects of life and respondents views on the extent to which the organisation has a responsibility in these matters.

DSC Shelfmark: Not found

(145)
LIBERATE lunchtime now!
Robinsons Fruit and Barley
London: Red Consultancy, 1998. 4p.

Press release reports results of a survey carried out for Robinsons Fruit and Barley which shows that only 2.3% of respondents take one hour or more per day for lunch and 25% have no lunch breaks at all. The average time out of the office for lunch is now only 40 minutes.

DSC Shelfmark: Not found

(146)
THE QUALITY of working life: 1998 survey of managers' changing experiences
L Worrall and C L Cooper
London: Institute of Management, 1998. 96p.

Managers acknowledge the adverse effects of long hours on their health, morale, productivity and family lives, but many still feel compelled to work in excess of their contracted hours. Results showed that 44% of managers always work over their contracted hours, and 78% regularly work more than 40 hours per week. There is strong evidence that organisations exploit the goodwill of their staff, and that staff feel they have insufficient time and resources to do their jobs effectively.

DSC Shelfmark: 98/03797

(147)
TRANSFORMING the future: rethinking free time and work
W H Martin and S Mason
Sudbury: Leisure Consultants, 1998. 155p.

Proposes encouragement of greater flexibility in working lives so that individuals have greater control over when, and how much, they are in paid work. There should be public campaigns to provide information about the positive use of free time, and transport and planning policies which encourage more use of free time in the local neighbourhood and the sustainable use of free time.

DSC Shelfmark: Not found

3.11.2 Shiftwork

(148)
SHIFTWORK and performance
S Folkard and T H Monk
Human factors, vol.21, 1979, p.483–492.

The level of performance efficiency on a night shift would seem to depend primarily on three factors: task demands, the type of shift system (and hence the potential for short and long-term adjustment) and individual differences between shiftworkers in how their biorhythms adjust to nightwork. For perceptual-motor tasks involving little memory load, better nightshift performance may be achieved by the use of permanent shift systems that maximise both short- and long-term adjustment. In contrast, cognitive tasks involving a high memory load may be performed better during the night on a rapidly rotating shift system.

DSC Shelfmark: 4336.075000

(149)
WORK schedules and sleep
T Åkerstedt
Experientia, vol.40, 1984, p.417–422.

Paper reviews the effects of work schedules on sleep and fatigue. Available data demonstrate that work schedules interfering with conventional sleep hours are associated with disturbed sleep. The main reason for disturbed daytime sleep is the influence of a circadian 'arousing' factor which starts its upswing at the time when the shiftworker is going to bed after the night shift.

DSC Shelfmark: 3837.000000

(150)
SHIFTWORK and the length and quality of sleep
M Frese and C Harwich
Journal of occupational medicine, vol.26, 1984, p.561–566.

Results of survey of German chemical workers shows that night and morning shifts lead to shortened sleeping hours but that overall length of sleep is not different for shift and non-shiftworkers. On the other hand, length of sleep is related only weakly to quality of sleep. Sleep disturbance and problems are predicted by shiftwork v non-shiftwork, psychological stress, a noisy sleeping room, and drinking more coffee during the night shift.

DSC Shelfmark: 5026.100000

(151)
SHIFT work
T H Monk and D I Tepas
In Job stress and blue collar work edited by C L Cooper and M J Smith.
Chichester: Wiley, 1985, p.65–84.

Argues that shiftwork is unnatural and runs counter to the in-built biological clock which determines sleep-wake rhythms in human beings. Shiftwork can disturb sleep patterns, lead to domestic and social disruption and exacerbate the effects of certain diseases. The harmful effects of shiftworking tend to get worse with age.

DSC Shelfmark: 86/03860

(152)
INCREASED risk of ischaemic heart disease in shift workers
A Knutsson *et al*
The Lancet, 12 July 1986, p.89–92.

504 papermill workers were followed up for 15 years and the incidence of ischaemic heart disease in shiftworkers was compared with that in day workers. Results indicate an association between shiftwork and increased risk of ischaemic heart disease at least during the first two

decades of shiftworking. The association is independent of age and smoking habits. Relative risk of IHD fell after 20 years of exposure to shift work, probably due to the pronounced positive selection that had taken place in this group.

DSC Shelfmark: 5146.000000

(153)
CARDIOVASCULAR diseases and the work environment: a critical review of the epidemiologic literature on nonchemical factors
T S Kristensen
Scandinavian journal of work, environment and health, vol.15, 1989, p.165–176.

The better quality studies in this field consistently find a modestly higher incidence of CVD among shiftworkers (and dropouts).

DSC Shelfmark: 8087.568000

(154)
THE EFFECT of shift work on gastrointestinal (GI) function: a review
K J Vener, S Szabo and J G Moore
Chronobiologia, vol.16, 1989, p.421–439.

Paper reviews literature related to the central nervous system control and integration of circadian rhythms and published work on the association of shiftwork and gastrointestinal symptoms/disease. The two literature bases are then integrated to develop a theoretical framework to explain altered physiological states which produce the gastrointestinal symptoms or diseases that are related to shiftwork, notably ulcer disease.

DSC Shelfmark: 3188.300000

(155)
EXTENDED workdays: effects of 8-hour and 12-hour rotating shift schedules on performance, subjective alertness, sleep patterns and psychological variables
R R Rosa, M J Colligan, and P Lewis.
Work and stress, vol.3, 1989, p.21–32.

A newly instituted 3-4 day/12-hour rotating shift system was compared with a previous 5-7 day/8-hour schedule using standard measures of performance and alertness, and a questionnaire on sleep patterns and other personal habits. After 7 months adaptation to the new schedule, there were decrements in the laboratory-type tests of performance/alertness which could be attributed to the extra 4 hours of work per day. There were also reductions in sleep and disruption of social life. On the other hand, increases in stress were attenuated by the shorter work week.

DSC Shelfmark: 9348.102000

(156)

CIRCADIAN performance rhythmns: some practical and theoretical implications

S Folkard

Philosophical transactions of the Royal Society of London, Series B, vol.327, 1990, p.543-553.

Reduced productivity and safety at night appear to be due to shiftworkers' relatively normally phased body temperature clocks. As a consequence they will be trying to work when many of their performance capabilities are at a low ebb, when they are relatively unable to resist sleep, and when they may have accrued a cumulative sleep debt. The latter problem can be minimised by the use of rapidly rotating shift systems that involve a maximum of 2 or 3 successive night shifts. Such systems may also be more beneficial for memory loaded jobs.

DSC Shelfmark: 6464.000000

(157)

STRESS and coping strategies of three-shift workers

K Olsson, I Kandolin and K Kauppinen-Toropainen

Le travail humain, tome 33, 1990, p.175-188.

Study monitored stress and coping strategies of three-shift workers in a paper mill and a hospital in Finland. Nurses working an irregular three shift system reported more mental and physical occupational strain than the paper workers in regular shifts. All shiftworkers used active physical coping styles. The nurses reported more active cognitive coping strategies than the paperworkers. All subjects used passive relaxation to recover from stress. The nurses and the female paperworkers used more passive somatising methods of coping.

DSC Shelfmark: 9027.300000

(158)

THE RESPONSE of day and night nurses to their work schedules

J Barton and S Folkard

Journal of occupational psychology, vol.64, 1991, p.207-218.

Survey results do not support the existing literature concerning the detrimental effects of night work. This may be due to the fact that nurses in the study had freely chosen to work either the night or the day shift on a permanent basis. Permanent night nurses who had freely chosen to work the schedule reported fewer health problems than nurses on a rotating shift system who had not specifically chosen to work at night. Freedom to choose particular hours of work appears to have implications for the degree to which subsequent problems are experienced as a result of shiftwork.

DSC Shelfmark: 5026.120000

(159)
WORKING hours and fatigue of Japanese flight attendants (FA)
Y Ono *et al*
Journal of human ergology, vol.20, 1991, p.155-164.

Study aimed to clarify the problems of working conditions of Japanese flight attendants focusing on working hours and their relation to fatigue symptoms. On international flights, night and early morning work, long flight hours and large time differences were suspected of jointly causing fatigue symptoms through disturbance of the biological rhythms of the flight attendants. On domestic flights, early starts and late debriefings, combined with a highly irregular flight attendant time schedule, were considered to contribute significantly to high fatigue complaints.

DSC Shelfmark: 5003.414000

(160)
THE healthy-worker effect: self-selection amongst Swedish shift workers
A Knutsson and T Åkerstedt
Work and stress, vol.6, 1992, p.163-167.

Study cohort comprised 53 male applicants for blue-collar jobs at a papermill. All subjects completed a questionnaire on their medical history, current symptoms, smoking habits, residence, relevant family history and sleeping habits one week before employment commenced. Results showed that applicants for shiftwork had a less rigid sleep pattern than those who applied for day work. Results suggest a self-selection into shiftwork of individuals with sleep behaviours that enable them to withstand odd work hours.

DSC Shelfmark: 9348.102000

(161)
HOUSE staff = shift workers: editorial
A J Scott
Journal of occupational medicine, vol.34, 1992, p.1161-1163.

Comments on the effects of sleep deprivation on the work performance of junior hospital doctors in the US.

DSC Shelfmark: 5026.100000

(162)
SHIFTWORK, health and safety: an overview of the scientific literature 1978-1990
J M Waterhouse, S M Folkard and D S Minors
London: HMSO, 1992. 31p.
(HSE contract research report; no.31/1992).

Literature review suggests that there is strong evidence for a link between shiftwork and cardiovascular disease and gastrointestinal disorders. There is also evidence for a greater tendency to general malaise including anxiety and depression in shiftworkers than in day workers. Individuals differ in their tolerance of shiftwork, the moderating variables being age, personality, mode of social life, and medical condition. Finally explores the complex relationship between shiftwork and safety, including the effects of fatigue, length of shift and rhythmic changes.

DSC Shelfmark: 4335.321000

(163)
DOES individual choice determine shift system acceptability?
J Barton *et al*
Ergonomics, vol.36, 1993, p.93-99.

A survey of 1082 nurses and midwives was used to examine the relationship between individual control of hours of work and tolerance of shiftwork. Results showed that nurses who chose to work on a regular night shift and those working on a flexible rotating shift system where individual preferences could be taken into account experienced less negative health consequences, sleep disturbances and social and domestic disruption than those working on irregular rotating systems where individuals had no control over shift sequencing.

DSC Shelfmark: 3808.500000

(164)
INDIVIDUAL differences in tolerance to shiftwork: a review
M Härmä
Ergonomics, vol.36, 1993, p.101-109.

Most research in this field concentrates on the relationship between circadian regulation and shiftwork tolerance. However, surprisingly little strong evidence exists on the relationship of individual circadian rhythms to shift work tolerance in different shift schedules. Tolerance of shiftwork is increased by physical fitness and flexibility of sleeping habits. Shiftworkers can use different coping mechanisms by trying to schedule their lives around the requirement to work unusual hours.

DSC Shelfmark: 3808.500000

(165)
PERFORMANCE and alertness on 8-h and 12-h rotating shifts at a natural gas utility
R R Rosa and M H Bonnet
Ergonomics, vol.36, 1993, p.1177-1193.

An 8-h/5-7 day shift schedule was compared with a newly instituted 12-h/2-4 day schedule. Workers completed a performance/alertness test battery and a questionnaire on sleep patterns and other personal habits 2-4 times a week on all shifts. After 10 months adaptation to the

12-h shift schedule, analyses of measures suggested lowered alertness attributable to the extra 4-h on the extended shift. There were also reductions in sleep across the work week which were most apparent on the 12-h night shift.

DSC Shelfmark: 3808.500000

(166)
INCREASED injuries on the night shift
L Smith, S Folkard and C J M Poole
The Lancet, vol.344, 1994, p.1137-1139.

Analysed 4645 injury incidents reported for a year on a rotating three shift system in a large engineering company where the accident risk appeared to be constant. The relative risk of sustaining an injury was 1.23 higher on the night shift than on the morning shift, which showed the lowest incidence. For self-paced work the risk of more serious injury on the night shift compared with the morning shift was 1.82.

DSC Shelfmark: 5146.000000

(167)
SHIFT work and health: a critical review of the literature on working hours
J M Harrington
Annals of the Academy of Medicine Singapore, vol.23, 1994, p.699-705.

Literature review demonstrates that the link between shift work and cardiovascular disease has strengthened over the years and that the association with gastrointestinal disease remains strong. Optimal hours for the working week cannot be formulated on existing scientific evidence, but it does appear that working weeks in excess of 48-56 hours are harmful.

DSC Shelfmark: 1018.300000

(168)
EXTENDED workshifts and excessive fatigue
R R Rosa
Journal of sleep research, vol.4, suppl.2, 1995, p.51-56.

Research demonstrating increased fatigue with long workshifts and a lack of substantial research on factors which may modulate fatigue means that schedules requiring long workshifts should be instituted with caution. Fatigue is likely to be higher during the final 4 hours of a 12 hour shift because the fatigue from extra work hours combines with the circadian low-point in arousal to produce the highest subjective sleepiness and fatigue, and the lowest efficiency in performance. To combat this, breaks should be liberally distributed throughout the shift and job rotation used to reduce the boredom of repetitive or monotonous tasks.

DSC Shelfmark: 5064.680000

(169)

TWELVE hour shifts: editorial

M Wallace and K M Greenwood

Work and stress, vol.9, 1995, p.105–108.

Warns that extended shifts may be inappropriate in jobs which are physically or mentally too demanding, too monotonous or require vigilance and alertness. Work environments which are too hot or too cold, noisy or dusty need particular caution. Commonly observed benefits of extended shifts include improved sleep quality and restedness, a reduction in digestive discomfort, and improved family and social life. Problems identified are fatigue associated with the nature of the work and uneven distribution of recovery days and difficulty in maintaining communication between management and shift crews.

DSC Shelfmark: 9348.102000

(170)

HEALTH, well–being and burnout of ICU nurses on 12- and 8-h shifts

I Iska-Golec *et al*

Work and stress, vol.10, 1996, p.251-256.

The 12-h shift nurses experienced more chronic fatigue, cognitive anxiety, sleep disturbance and emotional exhaustion than their 8-h shift colleagues. On the other hand they reported less social and domestic disruption. The 12-h shift nurses showed worse indices of health, well-being and burnout than the 8-h shift nurses. It is suggested this may be associated with their longer daily exposure to stress at work. Job satisfaction seems to be independent of shift duration.

DSC Shelfmark: 9348.102000

(171)

SOCIAL tolerance of working time scheduling in nursing

A Büssing

Work and stress, vol.10, 1996, p.238-250.

Results of a study of 297 nurses in a German general hospital show the dominance of social and health-related factors over economic and practical aspects of working time schedules as desired by the nurses independent of gender. Nurses working on a regular day-time schedule felt less depersonalisation, exhaustion and tedium, as well as more satisfaction with their work, than nurses working on non-standard shiftwork schedules or working permanently at night. Autonomy proved to have a moderating function for highly demanding work situations characteristic of non-standard working time schedules with respect to 7 out of 12 important indicators of stress, burnout and well-being at the workplace.

DSC Shelfmark: 9348.102000

(172)
DOES 'hardiness' predict adaptation to shiftwork?
P Bohle
Work and stress, vol.11, 1997, p.369–376.

Longitudinal study examined whether the dimensions of hardiness (commitment, control and challenge) predicted psychological symptoms and dissatisfaction with shiftwork in a sample of 36 nurses. Findings failed to support the proposition that the three hardiness dimensions provide resources for resisting the stress associated with rapid rotation shiftwork. Even the commitment dimension showed little potential to predict shiftwork tolerance.

DSC Shelfmark: 9348.102000

(173)
MODELS of shiftwork and health: an examination of the influence of stress on shiftwork theory
E Taylor, R B Briner and S Folkard
Human factors, vol.39, 1997, p.67–82.

Paper argues that models of shiftwork and health are predominantly hypothetical, are broad conceptually, and are becoming increasingly so by encompassing more variables and a greater number of interrelationships among them. In part this is because stress theory has influenced conceptualisations of the relationship between shiftwork and health, which in turn has influenced practice.

DSC Shelfmark: 4336.075000

3.11.3 Interpersonal relationships and burnout

(174)
STAFF burnout
H J Freudenberger
Journal of social issues, vol.30, 1974, p.159–165.

Seminal article which first described the signs and symptoms of burnout in free clinic workers. Burned out workers are physically exhausted, irritable, suspicious, rigid, stubborn and inflexible. Long hours are spent at work with little being accomplished.

DSC Shelfmark: 5064.755000

(175)
PROFESSIONAL burnout in human service organizations
C Cherniss
New York: Praeger, 1980. 295p.

Analyses sources of strain affecting new professionals entering the human services and shows how failure to cope effectively leads to a decline in idealism and psychological withdrawal. Goes on to consider the impact of the work setting, work-home conflicts and career orientation on the problem of burnout. Finally covers the role of training and workplace interventions in reducing burnout.

DSC Shelfmark: Not found

(176)
BURNOUT as a function of communication patterns: a study of a multidisciplinary mental health team
M P Leiter
Group and organization studies, vol.13, 1988, p.111–128.

Explored a model predicting burnout among 34 human service workers in terms of their social involvement with co-workers and job satisfaction. Results were consistent with a model that depicts co-worker interactions as both aggravating and alleviating burnout. Levels of burnout were higher for workers who communicated regularly about work but maintained relatively few informal, supportive relationships with co-workers. A large number of contacts with co-workers on work matters was related to higher feelings of accomplishment, but may contribute to higher emotional exhaustion as well. Informal contact with co-workers was related to higher levels of personal accomplishment as well as to increased job satisfaction.

DSC Shelfmark: 4220.174000

(177)
THE IMPACT of interpersonal environment on burnout and organizational commitment
M P Leiter and C Maslach
Journal of organizational behavior, vol.9, 1988, p.297–308.

Assessed positive and negative contacts on the job and investigated their contributions to burnout and organisational commitment. Data were gathered from 52 nurses and support staff in a small private hospital. High burnout was related to diminished organisational commitment. Results supported the hypothesis that stressful interactions with supervisors increased workers' feelings of emotional exhaustion, that high levels of exhaustion led to depersonalisation, unless workers had frequent supportive contact with co-workers and that as depersonalisation persisted, workers' feelings of personal accomplishment diminished, although supportive interpersonal contact with co-workers may have helped to decelerate this.

DSC Shelfmark: 5027.066000

(178)
CONSTRUCT validity of the Maslach Burnout Inventory: a critical review and reconceptualization
G F Koeske and R D Koeske
Journal of applied behavioral science, vol.25, 1989, p.131–144.

Proposes an alternate model of burnout which views emotional exhaustion as its essential component and as an indicator of strain arising from the demands of work and the resulting stress. Depersonalisation is viewed as one possible outcome of persistent exhaustion which is not buffered by other variables, e.g. social support. Personal accomplishment may play a moderator role, as when a sense of accomplishment with clients protects exhausted workers from experiencing depersonalisation.

DSC Shelfmark: 4940.500000

(179)
THE DREAM denied: professional burnout and the constraints of human service organisations
M Leiter
Canadian psychology, vol.32, 1991, p.547–558.

Presents a conceptual model of burnout as a function of the organisational environments of human service organisations. The conflict of professional role expectations with administrative policies accelerates the development of the syndrome. This perspective places secondary importance on client demands as a determinant of burnout.

DSC Shelfmark: 3044.105000

(180)
BURNOUT as a developmental process: consideration of models
M P Leiter
In Professional burnout: recent developments in theory and research edited by W B Schaufeli, C Maslach and T Marek. Washington, DC: Taylor & Francis, 1993. p.237–250.

Places burnout in a time perspective and regards it as a developmental process. Emotional exhaustion is seen as resulting from a demanding work environment, which in turn contributes to increased depersonalisation. Accordingly, depersonalisation is seen as a coping response, which occurs after emotional resources have been depleted. Reduced personal accomplishment develops in parallel with, but separately from, emotional exhaustion and depersonalisation.

DSC Shelfmark: 93/11843

(181)

ORGANIZATIONAL structure, social support and burnout

J Winnubst

In Professional burnout: recent developments in theory and research edited by W B Schaufeli, C Maslach and T Marek. Washington, DC: Taylor & Francis, 1993, p.151–175.

Analyses the relationship between organisational structure, social support and burnout. Argues that particular organisational structures produce particular organisational cultures. Social support systems are closely linked to the organisational regime. The antecedents of burnout differ depending on the organisational structure and the institutionalisation of social support.

DSC Shelfmark: 93/11843

(182)

A PRELIMINARY test of a stress–strain–outcome model for reconceptualizing the burnout phenomenon

G F Koeske and R D Koeske

Journal of social service research, vol.17, 1993, p.107–135.

Proposes the reconceptualisation of burnout so that emotional exhaustion is equated with strain and hypothesised to mediate the stress–outcome relationship. Personal accomplishment in conjunction with social support, is conceived as moderating or buffering the stress–exhaustion and exhaustion–outcome relationships. Depersonalisation of clients is eliminated from the model to reduce the complexity of the interrelationships.

DSC Shelfmark: 5064.913000

(183)

PROFESSIONAL burnout: recent developments in theory and research

W B Schaufeli, C. Maslach and T. Marek (editors)

Washington, DC: Taylor & Francis, 1993. 299p.

Offers a state-of-the-art analysis of burnout presenting interpersonal, individual and organisational approaches to the phenomenon, followed by consideration of methodological issues.

DSC Shelfmark: 93/11843

(184)

A REVIEW and an integration of research on job burnout

C L Cordes and T W Dougherty

Academy of Management review, vol.18, 1993, p.621–656.

Concludes that burnout is a unique type of stress syndrome which includes perceptions of emotional exhaustion, a dehumanisation of clients in one's work, and perceptions of diminished personal accomplishment. It has been clearly distinguished empirically and conceptually from other forms of stress, and can be measured in a reliable and valid fashion.

DSC Shelfmark: 0570.587600

(185)
RELATIONSHIPS among demographics, social support, job satisfaction and burnout among school psychologists
E S Huebner
School psychology international, vol.15, 1994, p.181-186.

Study explored the relationship between demographics, social support, global job satisfaction and burnout using school psychologists as subjects. Social support, especially from supervisors, was found to be related to depersonalisation reactions, over and above the contribution of demographics. Social support also contributed to job satisfaction.

DSC Shelfmark: 8092.926300

(186)
BEYOND burnout: helping nurses, therapists and lawyers recover from stress and disillusionment
C Cherniss
New York: Routledge, 1995. 234p.

Describes a ten year follow-up of a group of professionals originally studied in their first year of practice. Addresses the question of why some of the professionals were able to overcome or avoid early career burnout. Highlights the importance of doing fulfilling work for sustained commitment and caring, and the utility of working in settings that provide both support and autonomy for recovery from burnout. Notes personal characteristics that enabled some to sustain commitment and caring for more than a decade.

DSC Shelfmark: 96/20429

(187)
BURNOUT and collegial support in state psychiatric hospital staff
P W Corrigan, E P Holmes and D Luchins
Journal of clinical psychology, vol.51, 1995, p.703-710.

Forty-seven employees of a US state psychiatric hospital completed measures of burnout, collegial support, prolonged anxiety, physical health and job attitude. Results showed burnout positively correlated with anxiety, frequency of illness and contrary job attitudes, and negatively with level of satisfaction with collegial support network. Partial correlations showed that satisfaction with support systems diminished the effects of burnout on frequency of illness and job attitudes.

DSC Shelfmark: 4958.690000

(188)

BURNOUT, self and supervisor-related job performance and absenteeism among nurses

P A Parker and J A Kalik

Journal of behavioral medicine, vol.18, 1995, p.581-599.

Analysis indicates that levels of work support and job stress were both significant predictors of burnout. Higher burnout levels were associated with poorer self-rated and supervisor-rated performance, more sick leave and more reported absences for mental health reasons. Results are also consistent with the notion that emotional exhaustion may serve as a mediator between social support and self-reported job performance, absences for mental health reasons and intentions to quit. Data consisted of supervisor-rated job performance and employee absence records as well as self-report measures.

DSC Shelfmark: 4951.262000

(189)

A LONGITUDINAL examination of the Cherniss model of psychological burnout

R J Burke and E Greenglass

Social science and medicine, vol.40, 1995, p.1357-1363.

Tested the Cherniss model psychological burnout as a process through a longitudinal study of a sample of teachers. Questionnaires were administered at one year intervals to 362 respondents. Results showed a significant direct relationship of work setting characteristics to burnout measures, and a significant indirect relationship of work setting characteristics to burnout measures through experienced sources of stress.

DSC Shelfmark: 8318.157000

(190)

A LONGITUDINAL study of psychological burnout in teachers

R J Burke and E R Greenglass

Human relations, vol.48, 1995, p.187-202.

Antecedents of psychological burnout include individual and situational characteristics, work stressors and measures of social support. Consequences emphasised satisfaction, emotional and physical well-being variables. Participants in the study were 362 school based educators, teachers and administrators. Respondents completed questionnaires sent to them at their schools at two points in time, one year apart.

DSC Shelfmark: 4336.400000

(191)

BURNOUT among mental health workers: a review and a research agenda

M P Leiter and P L Harvie

International journal of social psychiatry, vol.42, 1996, p.90–101.

Results of a literature review show that burnout is most evident in work situations that inhibit mental health workers' capacity to realise their values through their work. Problems arise through excessive demands associated with case loads or personal conflicts that interfere with opportunities to attend to the needs of service recipients. Difficulties are exacerbated by lack of social support at work and at home. Active coping styles and a general sense of positive affectivity enhance workers' resolve to remain firm in their values while encountering difficulties at work, while social anxiety, escape coping and lack of confidence weaken that resolve.

DSC Shelfmark: 4542.560000

(192)

GLOBAL burnout: a worldwide pandemic explored by the phase model

R T Golembiewski *et al*

Greenwich, Conn.: Jai Press, 1996. 315p.

Presents the phase model of burnout which both posits and then assesses the relative potencies of the three proposed contributors to burnout (emotional exhaustion, depersonalisation and reduced personal accomplishment).

DSC Shelfmark: 5915.843000

(193)

INEQUITY among human service professionals: measurement and relation to burnout

D van Dierendonck, W B Schaufeli and B P Buunk

Basic and applied social psychology, vol.18, 1996, p.429-451.

Study investigated the relation between burnout and inequity as experienced by human service professionals through surveys of 112 therapists working with inmates in a forensic psychiatric centre and 189 staff members of an institute for care of the mentally disabled. Results showed that the majority of professionals thought that they invested more in their relationships with recipients and the organisation than they received in return. In both samples inequity in the relation with the recipients seemed to be curvilinearly related to burnout, especially to emotional exhaustion. Surprisingly, professionals who felt they received more from their clients than they gave experienced more burnout than colleagues who gave more than they received.

DSC Shelfmark: 1863.913300

117

(194)

MASLACH Burnout Inventory manual. 3rd ed.

C Maslach, S E Jackson and M P Leiter

Palo Alto, Calif: Consulting Psychologists Press, 1996. 52p

Most widely used instrument for measuring burnout.

DSC Shelfmark: q97/15058

See also: Maslach Burnout Inventory: manual by C Maslach and S E Jackson. 2nd ed. Palo Alto, Calif: Consulting Psychologists Press, 1986. 34p.

DSC Shelfmark: Not found

(195)

A META-ANALYTIC examination of the correlates of the three dimensions of job burnout

R T Lee and B E Ashforth

Journal of applied psychology, vol.81, 1996, p.123-133.

The findings of previous research are empirically integrated through meta-analysis. Thus, structural relations among burnout syndromes as well as antecedents and outcomes can be examined within the context of a causal model. Results indicate that emotional exhaustion and depersonalisation are strongly associated with turnover intentions and organisational commitment but are weakly associated with control coping. In contrast, personal accomplishment is strongly associated with control coping. Outcomes which stem from emotional exhaustion and reflect the desire to withdraw may be offset by outcomes that stem from personal accomplishment and reflect the desire to seek control.

DSC Shelfmark: 4947.000000

(196)

MODELS of job-related stress and personal achievement among consultant doctors

I J Deary *et al*

British journal of psychology, vol.87, 1996, p.3-29.

The antecedents and outcomes of feelings of job-related stress and personal achievement were studied in a large sample of consultant doctors working in Scotland. In a sample of 333 doctors it was found that a tendency to use emotion-oriented coping strategies and negative appraisals of organisational changes mediated the effect of the personality dimension neuroticism on reported job stress. Job stress levels predicted the degree of burnout experienced by doctors.

DSC Shelfmark: 2321.000000

(197)

OCCUPATIONAL burnout, tolerance for stress and coping among nurses in rehabilitation units

T K Elliott *et al*

Rehabilitation psychology, vol.41, 1996, p.267–283.

The relation of problem-solving confidence, perceived tolerance and situation-specific coping efforts to occupational burnout were studied among nurses in physical rehabilitation units. Consistent with predictions, confidence in one's ability to handle problems and perceived tolerance for stress were significantly predictive of lower burnout scores. Emotion-focused coping was significantly associated with higher burnout scores. Some coping efforts (e.g. taking time off from work, confronting a supervisor), could be construed as symptoms of burnout.

DSC Shelfmark: 7350.290000

(198)

PREDICTING teacher burnout over time: effects of work stress, social support and self-doubts on burnout and its consequences

R J Burke, E R Greenglass and R Schwarzer

Anxiety, stress and coping, vol.9, 1996, p.261–275.

Longitudinal study examined antecedents and consequences of burnout among 362 teachers and school administrators. Antecedents included red tape, disruptive students and lack of supervisor support. Consequences of burnout included heart symptoms and depressed mood. Burnout served as a mediator between the predictors and emotional and physical health outcomes.

DSC Shelfmark: 1566.612000

(199)

A STRUCTURAL equation model of burnout and job exit among child protective services workers

B Drake and G N Yadama

Social work research, vol.20, 1996, p.179–187.

Study tested the hypotheses that (1) workers who are emotionally exhausted will become more depersonalised, (2) emotionally exhausted workers will be more likely to leave their jobs, (3) depersonalised workers will be more likely to leave their jobs, (4) personal accomplishment will have broad effects, decreasing emotional exhaustion, depersonalisation and job exit. Data obtained from self-report questionnaires completed by 177 child protective services workers generally supported the model with only the relationships between depersonalisation and job exit and personal accomplishment and job exit being non-significant.

DSC Shelfmark: 8318.229800

(200)

HARDINESS, stress, temperament, coping and burnout in health professionals

M M Rowe

American journal of health behavior, vol.21, 1997, p.163–171.

Study examined the relationships among hardiness, temperament, coping and burnout in a sample of 448 health care professionals. Results showed that demographic variables did not affect burnout. Stress and a lack of control best predicted emotional exhaustion, stress and a lack of good coping predicted depersonalisation, and a lack of challenge and commitment and ineffective coping predicted lack of personal accomplishment. Personality hardiness was found not to mediate or buffer the stress–strain connection. However, results strongly supported the hypothesis that particular dimensions of temperament impact on the burnout process and that certain temperament types sustain more resilient individuals.

DSC Shelfmark: 0824.700000

(201)

Patterns of burnout among managers and professionals: a comparison of models

C L Cordes, T W Dougherty and M Blum

Journal of organizational behavior, vol.18, 1997, p.685–701

Paper compares the differing temporal sequences of the burnout components proposed by Maslach and Golembiewski, using responses from 354 human resources professionals. Results support Maslach's hypothesis that emotional exhaustion leads to depersonalisation, which leads in turn to lack of professional accomplishment. Investigation of the relationship between several stress factors and the components of burnout revealed significant associations between (a) role overload and emotional exhaustion, (b) undeserved punishment and depersonalisation, and (c) lack of deserved rewards and low personal accomplishment.

DSC Shelfmark: 5027.066000

(202)

PREDICTING burnout with a hassle-based measure of role demands

D Zohar

Journal of organizational behavior, vol.18, 1997, p.101–115.

A hassle scale relating to role conflict, ambiguity and overload was tested on a sample of 145 Canadian hospital nurses and their partners who completed self-report questionnaires. The incremental prediction of burnout afforded by the new scale compared with other role stressor scales was tested using hierarchical multiple regression. Results supported a balance model of burnout, specifying that exhaustion is an outcome of daily demand level on the one hand and recovery availability on the other.

DSC Shelfmark: 5027.066000

(203)

A STUDY of coping: successful recovery from severe burnout and other reactions to severe work–related stress

D Bernier

Work and stress, vol. 12, 1998, p.50–65

Reports a qualitative study of the situational determinants of coping with severe reactions to work-related stress, including burnout. Comparative analysis of the accounts of 20 human service workers and 16 other professionals led to the identification of a common process involving six consecutive stages: admitting the problem, distancing from work, restoring health, questioning values, exploring work possibilities and making objective changes. The ultimate strategy used by most subjects was to change their working conditions. The recovery process was long, lasting from one to two years.

DSC Shelfmark: 9348.102000

3.11.4 Bullying

(204)

MOBBING and psychological terror at workplaces

H Leymann

Violence and victims, vol.5, 1990, p.119–126.

Proposes a phased model of the phenomenon of 'mobbing', which involves employees ganging up on a target employee and subjecting him or her to psychological harassment. The phases of mobbing are: (1) an original triggering incident, often a work conflict, (2) mobbing and stigmatising, involving an assault on the victim's reputation, isolation of the victim, continual criticism, violence or threats of violence and giving the victim either no work or humiliating and meaningless tasks, (3) formal disciplinary action, (4) explusion from working life. Psychosomatic and psychiatric effects of this treatment include depression, hyperactivity, suicide and psychosomatic illness.

DSC Shelfmark: 9237.751000

(205)

ABUSE in the workplace: management remedies and bottom line impact

E S Bassman

Westport, Conn.: Quorum Books, 1992. 206p.

Covers both bullying of employees by managers and institutional abuse of the workforce through overwork, privacy invasion and screening testing. Explores the organisational costs of employee abuse and offers guidance on constructive corporate response.

DSC Shelfmark: 94/03546

(206)

BULLYING at work: how to confront and overcome it

A Adams

London: Virago, 1992. 195p.

Through personal accounts the author explores the demoralising and often isolating experience of bullying facing countless men and women at work every day. Plots the destructive forces eroding people's professional lives, and provides an insight into why things can go badly wrong. The final sections on self-help offer practical advice and organisational guidance on combating bullying.

DSC Shelfmark: 93/14347

(207)

SEXUAL harassment: violence against women in the workplace

L F Fitzgerald

American psychologist, vol.48, 1993, p.1070-1076.

Article provides a brief review of the prevalence and consequences of sexual harassment and outlines social policy implications for research, legislation and primary prevention. Data suggest that 50% of working women will be harassed at some point during their working lives. Consequences include job loss, decreased morale and absenteeism, decreased job satisfaction, and damage to interpersonal relationships at work, as well as negative effects on psychological and physical health.

DSC Shelfmark: 0853.400000

(208)

BULLYING and harassment at work and their relationships to work environment quality: an exploratory study

S Einarsen, B J Raknes and S B Matthiesen

European work and organizational psychologist, vol.4, 1994, p.381-401.

Data were collected by postal questionnaire from 2215 employed people who were either trade union members or representatives of the Norwegian Employers Federation. Results showed that low levels of control at work and poor social climate, particularly the experience of role conflict, were most strongly associated with bullying. Different work conditions were associated with bullying in different organisations. Only role conflict was associated with bullying in all subsamples.

DSC Shelfmark: 3830.370850

(209)
PETTY tyranny in organizations
B Ashforth
Human relations, vol. 47, 1994, p.755–778.

Preliminary research suggests that a petty tyrant is an individual who acts in an arbitrary and self-aggrandizing manner, belittles subordinates, shows lack of consideration, discourages initiative and metes out undeserved punishment. Argues that tyrannical behaviour arises from a combination of the tyrant's own beliefs and personality traits and a deficient organisational culture. Effects of petty tyranny on subordinates include poor performance, high frustration, work alienation, loss of self-esteem and stress.

DSC Shelfmark: 4336.400000

(210)
HOW big is the problem of bullying at work? Report of a survey of MSF workplace representatives on their experience and impressions of bullying at work
[London]: [MSF], 1995. [6p].

Surveyed local MSF representatives in workplaces employing ca. 140,000 people. 30% of respondents considered bullying a significant problem, 29% said it had got worse over the past five years and 48% said their managers 'hadn't really thought about it'. A worrying 17% considered their companies encouraged a bullying management style and 78% said their organisations had no policy for dealing with it.

DSC Shelfmark: Not found

(211)
THE INCIDENCE of workplace bullying
C Rayner
Journal of community and applied social psychology, vol.7, 1997, p.199–208.

Reports results of a survey of 1137 part-time students at Staffordshire University carried out in 1994. Approximately half the sample reported they had been bullied during their working lives. Apart from the sex of the bully, there was no significant differences in the bullying experience between men and women. Many people reported being bullied in groups, which is contrary to current anecdotal evidence.

DSC Shelfmark: 4961.693000

(212)

PERSONAL standards in professional relationships: limiting interpersonal harrassment

B A Thomas-Peter

Journal of community and applied social psychology, vol.7, 1997, p.233-239.

Suggests three criteria for identifying abusive behaviour: that it is avoidable, that it damages the psychological contract between employer and employee, and that it would be likely to be appraised as unacceptable by an objective observer. Goes on to give illustrative examples of interpersonal abusive actions and outlines a strategy to inhibit them based on 'reasonable expectations' of one person's behaviour towards another. Interpersonal harrassment will be limited by translating these expectations into interpersonal commitments.

DSC Shelfmark: 4961.693000

(213)

A SUMMARY review of literature relating to workplace bullying

C Rayner and H Hoel

Journal of community and applied social psychology, vol.7, 1997, p.181-191.

Defines bullying behaviours in the workplace as falling into the categories of threat to professional status, threat to personal standing, isolation, overwork and destabilisation. Comment on bullying in the UK and US tends to be anecdotal, with most serious scientific research emanating from Scandinavia. This has focused on the relationships between bullying and the quality of the work environment. Insufficient work control and high levels of role conflict are seen as precursors to bullying.

DSC Shelfmark: 4961.693000

(214)

BULLYING at work: a psychoanalytic perspective

N Crawford

Journal of community and applied social psychology, vol.7, 1997, p.219-225.

Places workplace bullying on a spectrum which covers workplace homicide, violence at work, sexual harassment and the harnessing of aggressive instincts into effective work. Thought is given to which behaviours should be classified as bullying and to the responsibility of individuals and organisations to understand and manage it.

DSC Shelfmark: 4961.69300

(215)

BEAT bullying at work: a guide for trade union representatives and personnel managers

London: TUC, 1998. 28p.

Defines bullying behaviour, describes its effects using case studies, and advises unions and employers how to tackle it. Includes a note of the legal position and a list of useful contacts.

DSC Shelfmark: 4961.693000

3.11.5 Violence

(216)
ACCIDENTS and violence 1988
M Heiskanen *et al*
Helsinki: Central Statistical Office of Finland, 1991.
(Publication; no.108).

DSC Shelfmark : Not found

(217)
WORKPLACE violence: an issue of the nineties
P R Johnson and J Indvik
Public personnel management, vol.23, 1994, p.515–523.

Workplace violence arises in a climate of hopelessness about economic conditions, downsizings, mergers and acquisitions and increased pressure to work harder and more quickly. Breach of the psychological contract between employer and employees causes the latter to feel powerless and to strike out in an explosive manner. Recommendations on prevention of workplace violence include the development of a crisis management plan, employee empowerment and the building up and maintenance of employee self-esteem, and the use of an Employee Assistance Program.

DSC Shelfmark: 6967.890000

(218)
VIOLENCE at work: how to make your company safer for employees and customers
J A Kinney
Englewood Cliffs, N J: Prentice-Hall, 1995. 254p.

Identifies causes of the escalation in workplace violence as job insecurity arising from downsizing and business process re-engineering, exposure to role overload, conflicts and ambiguity, the breakdown of stabilising institutions such as the family, church, school and community, and the glamorisation of violence by the media. The final chapters describe the options available to employers for addressing violence, with a special focus on threat management.

DSC Shelfmark: 95/32546

(219)
VIOLENCE at work: the brutal truths
S Crabbe and O Aikin
People management, 25 July 1995, p.25-29.

Article looks at how Midland Bank deals with allegations of intimidation, bullying and physical violence among its employees, and then counsels the victims. The employers' legal duty to provide a safe working environment is also explained.

DSC Shelfmark: 6422.876650

(220)
WORKPLACE assault: an emerging job stressor
R J Driscoll, K A Worthington and J J Hurrell
Consulting psychology journal: practice and research, vol.47, 1995, p.205-212.

Article examines the psychological effects of workplace assault on some 5,000 public service employees. Workers who were assaulted were more likely to report depression, anxiety and low job satisfaction than their non-assaulted co-workers. Evidence for a moderating effect of work-based social support on the relationship between assault and depression is noted.

DSC Shelfmark: 3424.011000

(221)
WORKPLACE violence in Europe: it is time to act
R Wynne and N Clarkin
Work and stress, vol.9, 1995, p.377-379.

Highlights existing evidence that violence between employees and clients is a growing problem and calls for more research into its extent. Recommends a comprehensive approach to all aspects of workplace violence which would include preventive, reactive and treatment-oriented strategies.

DSC Shelfmark: 9348.102000

(222)
ASSAULTIVE violence in the US Post Office
V Baxter and A Margavio
Work and occupations, vol.23, 1996, p.277-296.

It is proposed that the degradation of labour under conditions of rapid technological and organisational change causes a form of social disorganisation that provides the external conditions for outbreaks of assaultive violence. Employees are objectified, pressured and intimidated by the authoritarian nature of scientific management. Resultant frustration and alienation weaken employee integration and commitment to the organisation and undermine traditional forms of social control. When the experience of work degrades a person's identity or sense of self-control, especially in the uncertain context of rapid change, it can trigger assaultive violence.

DSC Shelfmark: 9348.075000

(223)
CORRELATES and consequences of workplace violence
J W Budd, R D Arvey and P Lawless
Journal of occupational health psychology, vol.1, 1996, p.197-210.

A random telephone survey was used to interview 598 employees about instances of physical violence or threats of physical harm in the workplace. Data suggest that the risk of experiencing physical violence or threats of violence is quite low, with only 8.7% of respondents reporting incidents within the previous 12 months. Demographic and workplace characteristics were analysed as correlates of these forms of violence. The only at risk category identified was employees who worked night-time hours. However, the consequences of experiencing violence are clear and include intention to quit, distress, reduced productivity, lowered job satisfaction and increased intention to bring a weapon to work.

DSC Shelfmark: 5026.095000

(224)
MANAGING violence in the workplace
T K Capozzoli and R S McVey
Delray Beach, Fla: St. Lucie Press, 1996. 138p.

Identifies causes of workplace violence as job insecurity, long hours, performance appraisals, general job stress, personality conflicts, mental illness, and substance abuse. The final chapter discusses strategies for the management and prevention of violence.

DSC Shelfmark: 96/26600

(225)
VIOLENCE on the job: identifying risks and developing solutions
G R VandenBos and E Q Bulatao (editors)
Washington, DC: American Psychological Association, 1996. 438p.

Analyses the problem of workplace violence from a US perspective and describes violence prevention and response programmes. Includes programmes instituted in advance of corporate downsizing, programmes designed to respond to violence in health-care settings, and the employee assistance programme used by the US Postal Service. Discusses links between alcohol abuse and violence, interaction between job stress and violence, and risks for violence against individuals in specific occupations such as social workers.

DSC Shelfmark: q97/23260

(226)

WORK-related violence: is national reporting good enough?

D Beale, T Cox and P Leather

Work and stress, vol.10, 1996, p.99–103.

Relatively few statistics on incidence of workplace violence are collected at national level in Europe. In the UK the 1995 revision of the Reporting of Injuries, Diseases and Dangerous Occurrences Regulations (RIDDOR) means that certain violent incidents now have to be reported on a national basis. However, as the regulations only require certain major incidents to be reported, the authors recommend that employers develop, keep and use their own internal records of a wider range of violent incidents, which could then be used to inform risk assessment and risk management.

DSC Shelfmark: 9348.102000

(227)

WORKPLACE violence and workplace aggression: evidence of their relative frequency and potential causes

R A Baron and J H Neuman

Aggressive behavior, vol.22, 1996, p.161–173.

Data from a survey of 178 currently employed individuals provided support for hypotheses that verbal and passive forms of aggression are more common in workplaces than physical and active forms and that organisational changes such as increased workforce diversity, changes in management, pay cuts and freezes, and increased use of part-timers are related to the perceived frequency of both witnessed and experienced aggression.

DSC Shelfmark: 0736.285000

(228)

EFFECTS of exposure to occupational violence and the mediating impact of fear

P Leather, D Beale and C Lawrence

Work and stress, vol.11, 1997, p.329–340.

The threat or reality of violence, whatever its form, is a significant source of chronic and/or acute stress for many employees. Violence-related stress has a negative impact on organisational functioning as well as upon individual health and well-being. Organisations need a clear understanding of the role of fear in mediating the relationship between exposure to violence and negative organisational and individual outcomes.

DSC Shelfmark: 9348.102000

(229)

EXPOSURE to occupational violence and the buffering effects of intra-organisational support

P Leather *et al*

Work and stress, vol. 12, 1998, p.161-178.

Investigates the effects of exposure to various forms of workplace violence on the work attitudes and general well-being of a sample of UK public house licensees. Results show a consistent interaction between exposure to such violence and the availability of intra-organisational support in determining the size of any negative effects upon individual well-being, job satisfaction and organisational commitment. The stress of exposure to all forms of work-related violence, including intimidation, verbal abuse and threat, is buffered by perceived support from within the organisation, but not by support from family and friends.

DSC Shelfmark: 9348.102000

(230)

VIOLENCE at work

D Chappell and V Di Martino

Geneva: International Labour Organization, 1998. 165p.

Report is intended to provide a basis for understanding the nature of workplace violence and to suggest strategies for prevention. Part 1 offers an analysis of existing data showing patterns and trends in workplace violence, the occupations most affected, vulnerable situations and groups, and the costs of violence to individuals and organisations. Part 2 examines different responses to violence at work and identifies the best solutions. Part 3 considers the key lessons to be drawn and suggests specific and practical action based on successful experience.

DSC Shelfmark: Not found

3.11.6 Work-non-work conflict

(231)

WORK stressors and wife abuse

J Barling and A Rosenbaum

Journal of applied psychology, vol.71, 1986, p.346-348.

To assess whether work experiences and stressors are associated with wife abuse separate groups of satisfied, distressed nonabusive and distressed abusive husbands completed questionnaires on work involvement, organisational commitment, job satisfaction and work stress. The results of multivariate analysis of variance suggested an association between work-related variables and wife abuse. Subsequent univariate analysis of variance showed that the occurrence of stressful work events and their negative impact were related to wife abuse.

DSC Shelfmark: 4947.000000

(232)

OUTCOMES of work-family conflict among married male and female professionals

A G Bedeian *et al*

Journal of management, vol.14, 1988, p.475–491.

Mailed questionnaire data from a US national sample of 423 male and 335 female accounting professionals are drawn on to evaluate a model of the process by which job stress and parental demands interact to influence job, marital and life satisfaction. Results revealed only minor sex differences. The relationship between parental demands and life satisfaction was mediated by satisfaction with child care arrangements for women but not for men.

DSC Shelfmark: 5011.100000

(233)

EMPLOYMENT, stress and family functioning

J Barling

Chichester: Wiley, 1990. 286p.

Assesses the effects of both work and unemployment on family functioning. The central theme of the book is that it is people's positive and negative experiences of employment or unemployment that explain the effects of work on the family. Major topics covered are: the effects of men's and women's employment on marital functioning; the effects of maternal and paternal employment on children and the effects of unemployment on both marital functioning and children. The effects of family functioning on employment are also considered.

DSC Shelfmark: 90/05168

(234)

WORK and non-work issues in the management of occupational careers in the 1990s

R S Bhagat and D L Ford

Prevention in human services, vol.8, 1990, p.99–112.

Literature review suggests that personal stressors may affect work performance and career progress as well as health and well-being. Three organisational strategies for preventing distress arising from home-work conflict are presented: provision of opportunities for home-based work, training in coping strategies, and changes in organisational culture to allow for greater work/nonwork role integration.

DSC Shelfmark: 6612.773000

(235)
PHYSICAL symptoms and the interplay of work and family roles
R C Barnett, H Davidson and N L Marshall
Health psychology, vol.10, 1991, p.94–101.

Investigated the relationship between work and physical health symptoms in women, through data gathered from a stratified random sample of 403 nurses and social workers. Study focused on job rewards and concerns and the impact of family roles on the relationship between job rewards, concerns and physical health.

DSC Shelfmark: 4275.105200

(236)
A COMMUNITY study of dual-role stress and coping in working mothers
P Shipley and M Coats
Work and stress, vol.6, 1992, p.49–63.

A pilot study of dual-role stress and coping was conducted through analysis of interview data collected from 45 women with dependent children at home living in North London. Evidence of dual role stress was found, but many women obtained important benefits from work. Both the quality of the job and of domestic support were important for stress management. Child-care problems were reported by most women, with low-income single women suffering the highest levels of financial, child-care and work stress.

DSC Shelfmark: 9348.102000

(237)
JOB stress, psychosocial strain and physical health problems in women employed full-time outside the home and homemakers
B K Houston, D S Cates and K E Kelly
Women and health, vol.19, 1992, p.1–26.

Job related stress and lack of social support were investigated via questionnaire among 95 homemakers and 91 working women in Lawrence, Kansas. Quantitative overload was associated with more tension and health problems for both groups and more marital dissatisfaction for homemakers. Under-utilisation of skills for both groups caused more tension and poorer marital relations. Both groups' marital relations and tension levels were improved by social support.

DSC Shelfmark: 9343.260000

(238)

ROLE stressors, social support and well-being among two-career couples

S Parasuraman, J H Greenhaus and C S Granrose

Journal of organizational behavior, vol.13, 1992, p.339-356.

A sample of 119 dual career couples in the eastern US were surveyed on work role stressors, family conflict, work-family conflict, well-being and social support. Neither stress nor social support appeared to cross over between work and family domains. Partners may minimise stress by strictly compartmentalising work and family life.

DSC Shelfmark: 5027.066000

(239)

AN EMPIRICAL study of occupational stress transmission in working couples

F Jones and B Fletcher

Human relations, vol.46, 1993, p.881-903.

The extent and direction of occupational stress transmission in working couples was measured with 60 English and Welsh couples who completed a questionnaire on work demands, constraints and supports, and their impacts on home life. Results show that work-related discussions were frequent among couples, and that both partners had accurate perceptions of the other's job. Correlational analysis showed that stress was transmitted from males to females, especially for high strain jobs, but not from females to males.

DSC Shelfmark: 4336.400000

(240)

MOVING beyond traditional predictors of job involvement: exploring the impact of work-family conflict and overload

C A Thompson and G Blau

Journal of social behavior and personality, vol.8, 1993, p.635-646.

Postal survey data obtained from a sample of 234 employees from diverse organisations are used to investigate whether work/family conflict and role overload account for additional variance in job involvement beyond variables normally studied, e.g. demographics. Results suggest that the extent to which work interferes with family life and incompatibility between parent and work roles are significant predictors of the level of job involvement.

DSC Shelfmark: 5064.751500

(241)

JOB stress in a changing workforce: investigating gender, diversity and family issues

G P Keita and J J Hurrell (editors)

Washington, DC: American Psychological Association, 1994. 345p.

Examines how economic and demographic trends affect stress among workers, providing data from national and international studies. The first major section focuses on workforce diversity and investigates how gender, ethnocultural background and age relate to job stress. The second major section focuses on work and family, revealing how such issues as child care and marital functioning affect, and are affected by, job stress.

DSC Shelfmark: 95/22921

(242)
ROLE overload and health: the married mother in the waged labour force
N C Facione
Health care for women international, vol.15, 1994, p.157-167.

An increasing number of women hold multiple roles, each of which pose significant time and labour demands. An attempt is made to identify the risks to women's health associated with these increased demands.

DSC Shelfmark: 4274.950600

(243)
SHORT-term and long-term processes linking job stressors to father-child interaction
R L Repetti
Social development, vol.3, 1994, p.1-15.

Data from a small sample of air traffic controllers was used to explore the association between two job stressors, task overload and negative social interactions, and two dimensions of parent-child interaction, emotional tone and level of parental involvement. Results suggest that parental withdrawal may be a way of fathers coping, in the short term, with overloads at work. Poor social relations at work may lead, in both long and short term, to a spillover of negative feelings into home life.

DSC Shelfmark: 8318.079100

(244)
THE CONSEQUENCES of caring: exploring the links between women's job and family emotion work
A S Wharton and R J Erickson
Sociological quarterly, vol.36, 1995, p.273-296.

Surveyed 555 female employees of a Catholic teaching hospital through a questionnaire measuring work and family situations, social-psychological dimensions and demographic characteristics. Results showed that performance of family emotion work had negative consequences for job-related well-being. This was not so much at risk from the performance of emotional labour on the job.

DSC Shelfmark: 8319.630000

133

(245)

CROSSOVER of stress, strain and resources from one spouse to another

M Westman and D Etzion

Journal of organizational behavior, vol.16, 1995, p.169–181.

Questionnaires measuring level of burnout, job stress, work support, family support and sense of control were filled out by 101 male military officers and their wives. Findings showed that an individual's burnout affects his/her spouse's burnout after his/her own job stress and resistance resources were controlled for. Burnout crossover was evident in both directions, i.e. from husband to wife and wife to husband. Sense of control was negatively related to stress and burnout. Mutually supportive interrelationships were found between the spouses' sense of control, but not in the area of family support.

DSC Shelfmark: 5027.066000

(246)

BALANCING employment and fatherhood: a systems perspective

J O Berry and J M Rao

Journal of family issues, vol.18, 1997, p.386–402.

Devised a measure of work-family stress experienced by employed men in dual-earner families and explored contributions from various system levels to this in 3 studies. Results indicate that all system levels examined (the individual, the family and the workplace microsystem) contributed to stress experienced with the greatest contribution coming from the family.

DSC Shelfmark: 4983.690000

(247)

ANTECEDENTS and outcomes of work-family conflict among employed women and men in Finland

U Kinnunen and S Mauno

Human relations, vol.51, 1998, p.157–177

Data were obtained by questionnaire from 501 employees working in four organisations. Interference from family to work (family-work conflict) was less prevalent than interference from work to family (work-family conflict) among both sexes. Family-work conflict was best explained by family domain variables (eg number of children living at home) for both sexes. Work-family conflict was associated with work domain variables (eg full-time job, poor leadership) among women and high education and high number of children living at home among men. Family-work conflict adversely affected home life and work-family conflict had negative impacts, in particular, on well-being at work.

DSC Shelfmark: 4336.400000

(248)

OCCUPATIONAL stress and family life: a comparison of male and female doctors

V Swanson, K G Power and R J Simpson

Journal of occupational and organizational psychology, vol.71, 1998, p.237–260.

Study examined the relationship between occupational stress and home life among doctors in Scotland, comparing male and female general practitioners and specialist consultants. Increasing domestic role demands were related to higher levels of stress for both male and female doctors. Increased domestic role complexity was significantly related to 'work to home' stress for both sexes. Role complexity was related to reduced occupational workload for females only, and to increased domestic workload for both male and female doctors. General practitioners were found to record greater stress in the home/work interface than consultants.

DSC Shelfmark: 5026.082000

3.11.7 Role conflict and ambiguity

(249)

ORGANIZATIONAL stress: studies in role conflict and ambiguity

R L Kahn *et al*

New York: Wiley. 1964. 470p.

Proposes a role episode model in which a focal person and role senders (collectively constituting a role set) interact cyclically within a context influenced by organisational factors (e.g. size of organisation), personality factors (e.g. motives, values and fears) and interpersonal relations factors (e.g. power to influence others). A seminal and very influential work written in an accessible style with lots of illustrative examples.

DSC Shelfmark: not found

(250)

PSYCHOSOCIAL factors in coronary heart disease

J R P French and R D Caplan

Industrial medicine, vol.39, 1970, p.383–397.

Presents a model which hypothesises that development of coronary heart disease (CHD) is associated with risk factors such as smoking, blood pressure, cholesterol, serum uric acid and glucose. Changes in the risk factors may be precipitated by work-related stressors such as objective and subjective overload and responsibility for people. Different occupations may be characterised by different patterns of stress. Personality may influence heart disease via occupational choice, and may also change risk factors through mediating and moderating effects on the stressor-strain relationship. Significant relationships were discovered between types of job stress and risk factors. Different occupational groups showed different patterns of job stress and levels of risk factors. Further research is required to pin down causal paths.

DSC Shelfmark: 4542.304000

(251)

JOB stresses and risk factors in coronary heart disease among five occupational categories in Kibbutzim

A Shirom *et al*

Social science and medicine, vol.7, 1973, p.875–892.

Relationships between a cluster of job stressors (role overload, intrarole conflict and interrole conflict) and CHD risk factors in 5 occupational categories were studied in a sample of 762 adult male kibbutz workers in Israel. The associations of the job stressors with the risk factors were shown to increase progressively in strength from white collar workers to craftsmen, factory workers and agricultural workers.

DSC Shelfmark: 8318.157000

(252)

JOB stress: an unlisted occupational hazard

B L Margolis, W H Kroes and R P Quinn

Journal of occupational medicine, vol.16, 1974, p.659–661.

Data from the 1972/73 Quality of Employment Survey were analysed. The scores on 6 specific job stress indices (role ambiguity, underutilisation, overload, resource inadequacy, insecurity and non-participation) were averaged to form overall job stress scores. Scores on 10 indicators of strain (physical health, escapist drinking, depressed mood, self-esteem, life satisfaction, job satisfaction, motivation to work, intention to quit, frequency of suggestions to employer and absenteeism) were related to overall job stress. Results indicate that increased stress was associated with poorer mental and physical health. Correlations were also obtained between each of the job stressors and each of the strain measures. Underutilisation and non-participation were significantly correlated with all 10 strain indicators, whereas overload was only related to 5 of the 10 and role ambiguity to 6 of the 10.

DSC Shelfmark: 5026.100000

(253)

EFFECTS of work load, role ambiguity, and Type A personality on anxiety, depression and heart rate

R D Caplan and K W Jones

Journal of applied psychology, vol.60, 1975, p.713–719.

Type A personality was studied as a moderator of the effects of quantitative workload and role ambiguity on anxiety, depression, resentment and heart rate among 73 male users of a university computer system that was approaching a 23-day shutdown. Role ambiguity was positively associated with anxiety, depression and resentment; subjective workload was positively associated only with anxiety. Anxiety was positively correlated to heart rate. The relationship between workload and anxiety was greatest for Type A persons.

DSC Shelfmark: 4947.000000

(254)

PERCEIVED situational moderators of the relationship between subjective role ambiguity and role strain
T A Beehr
Journal of applied psychology, vol.61, 1976, p.35–40.

Searched for situational moderators in the relationship between role ambiguity and life dissatisfaction, job dissatisfaction, low self-esteem and depressed mood. Three situational characteristics were thought to moderate the relationship: group cohesiveness, supervisor support and autonomy. Results showed that the relationship between role ambiguity and low self-esteem is weaker for persons in cohesive groups than for those in non-cohesive groups. Job dissatisfaction and life dissatisfaction tend to be correlated more strongly with role ambiguity in high-cohesive groups than low-cohesive groups. Autonomy proved to be the strongest and most consistent moderator of the relationship between role ambiguity and role strain.

DSC Shelfmark: 4947.000000

(255)

A PATH-analytic study of the consequences of role conflict and ambiguity
A G Bedeian and A A Armenakis
Academy of Management journal, vol. 24, 1981, p.417–424.

Data from 202 hospital staff showed that role conflict and ambiguity were both associated with high levels of job-induced stress.

DSC shelfmark: 0570.587000

(256)

A META-analysis of the correlates of role conflict and ambiguity
C D Fisher and R Gitelson
Journal of applied psychology, vol. 68, 1983, p.320–333.

Meta-analysis procedures were applied to the results of 43 previous studies of the antecedents and consequences of role conflict and ambiguity. Inconsistencies between the results of some studies could be ascribed to methodological problems. In other cases, conflicting results may indicate the presence of moderator variables.

DSC Shelfmark: 4947.000000

(257)

A META-analysis and conceptual critique of research on role conflict and role ambiguity in work settings

S E Jackson and R S Schuler

Organizational behavior and human decision processes, vol. 36, 1985, p.16-78.

Study analysed 29 correlates of role ambiguity and role conflict. These correlates included ten organizational context variables, five individual characteristics, ten affective reactions and four behavioural reactions. Meta-analysis procedures were also used to measure the strength and consistency of the relationship found between each of the 29 correlates and role conflict and ambiguity.

DSC Shelfmark: 6290.749000

(258)

'BURNOUT', absence and turnover amongst British nursing staff

H Firth and P Britton

Journal of occupational psychology, vol.62, 1989, p.55-59.

Based on longitudinal inventory and questionnaire data collected over two years from qualified nursing staff in long-stay settings in GB, 'burnout' variables, role ambiguity and perceived support from their supervisor were assessed and absence through sickness and job turnover were measured. Results provide evidence that emotional exhaustion and perceived lack of support both influence motivation to attend work and feelings of depression, and hence longer periods of absence, whereas ambiguity about limits of authority leads staff to avoid particular situations, thereby influencing short absences.

DSC Shelfmark: 5026.120000

(259)

ROLE strains, tension and job satisfaction influences on employees' propensity to leave: a multi-sample replication and extension

K E Klenke-Hamel and J E Mathieu

Human relations, vol.43, 1990, p.791-807.

Tested the Bedeian and Armenakis model of the effects of role ambiguity and role conflict with four independent samples. A path analysis showed inconsistent results for both overall fit and predicted individual linkages.

DSC Shelfmark: 4336.400000

(260)

ANALYSIS of role conflict and role ambiguity in a structural equations framework

R G Netemeyer, M W Johnston and S Burton

Journal of applied psychology, vol.75, 1990, p.148-157.

Used structural equation modelling to test the Bedeian and Armenakis model of the effects of role ambiguity and role conflict on data from outside salespersons. Analysed a latent variable model with estimates of measurement error and a single indicator model without error estimates. Both methods showed inadequate overall fit.

DSC Shelfmark: 4947.000000

(261)
THE INFLUENCES of role stress, physical symptoms and job satisfaction on turnover intentions: a two-sample test of a modified Bedeian and Armenakis model

D Lang, U Wittig-Berman and A Rizkalla
Journal of social behavior and personality, vol.7, 1992, p.555-562.

Purpose of the study was to test a trimmed version of the B&A model using physical symptoms as a measure of job tension and including realistic error estimates. Two independent samples were used: data collected from full-time employed evening MBA students as part of a larger study and published data from university employees. For both datasets, the paths from role ambiguity to job satisfaction and from job satisfaction to turnover intentions were the most highly significant. However several predicted linkages failed to reach significance in one or both samples, including the paths from role conflict to job satisfaction, role ambiguity to physical symptoms and physical symptoms to job satisfaction.

DSC Shelfmark: 5064.751500

(262)
ORGANIZATIONAL exit pressures and role stress: impact on mental health

K H Price and R Hooijberg
Journal of organizational behavior, vol.13, 1992, p.641-651.

Hypotheses regarding role stress, chronic burden and two forms of vulnerability to mental health symptoms were tested in a longitudinal sample of 590 caregivers working in group homes for the mentally ill. In addition, an organisational exit pressure hypothesis is offered. Results suggest that role ambiguity has a direct impact on anxiety and depression net of baseline symptom levels. In addition, exit pressures have an impact on somatisation over and above baseline symptom levels, providing some support for the direct effects of exit pressures. Results also suggest that exit pressures can combine with role ambiguity to exacerbate psychological distress.

DSC Shelfmark: 5027.066000

(263)
SOCIAL support under conditions of organizational ambiguity
I P Erera
Human relations, vol.45, 1992, p.247-264.

Study examines how supervisors in departments of social services perceive characteristics of social support from their supervisor, peers and subordinates. It also explores the effects of organisational ambiguity on each of these support sources. Only subordinates were perceived as supportive, providing emotional and approval support. Supervisors were regarded as withholding approval, emotional, tangible and informational support. Peers were accused of withholding emotional support. Relationships between units were characterised by competitiveness, suspicion and mistrust. It is argued that relationships with all these support sources were determined by confusion arising from ambiguous policies.

DSC Shelfmark: 4336.400000

(264)
A TEST of a causal model of communication and burnout in the teaching profession
S M Starnaman and K I Miller
Communication education, vol.41, 1992, p.40-53.

The causal model developed in this paper indicates that teachers' workload and support from their principal influenced perceptions of role conflict and ambiguity. These role stressors, in turn, influenced perceptions of burnout, job satisfaction and occupational commitment.

DSC Shelfmark: 3359.830000

(265)
WORK stress, role conflict, social support and psychological burnout among teachers
R J Burke and E Greenglass
Psychological reports, vol.73, 1993, p.371-380.

Data were collected from 833 school teachers using questionnaires completed anonymously. Demographic characteristics, work stressors, role conflict and social support were investigated as predictors of psychological burnout. Individual demographic characteristics were only weakly related to burnout. Work stressors were consistently and strongly related to burnout. Levels of role conflict and social support were unrelated to burnout measures. Two work stressors in particular (lack of stimulation and narrow range of interpersonal contacts) were fairly consistently associated with increased burnout.

DSC Shelfmark: 6946.525000

(266)
ROLE conflict: cause of burnout or energizer?
M L Jones
Social work, vol.38, 1993, p.136-141.

A year-long study of public child welfare administrators examined the effects of role conflict on their attitudes and performance. Results showed that the subjects experienced professional role conflict and organisational goal conflict. However they had all developed specific, effective skills for responding to role conflict. In fact role conflict encouraged a flexible approach to work and the challenge of seeking resolution of the various conflicts released energy and prevented boredom. The process of articulating conflicts and coming to some resolution of them also resulted in clarification of their own sense of role and mission.

DSC Shelfmark: 8318.221100

(267)
CONFLICT and ambiguity over work roles: the impact on child care work burnout
E E Manlove
Early education and development, vol.5, 1994. p.41-55.

Subjects included 188 child care workers from licensed child care centres in rural areas of Pennsylvania who completed questionnaires. Significant relationships were found between both role conflict and role ambiguity and all three facets of burnout (depersonalisation, emotional exhaustion and low personal accomplishment). Social support was found to moderate the effect of both role stressors on perceived emotional exhaustion and depersonalisation, but not personal accomplishment.

DSC Shelfmark: 3642.964800

(268)
JOB stressors, job involvement and employee health: a test of identity theory
M R Frone, M Russell and M L Cooper
Journal of occupational and organizational psychology, vol.68, 1995, p.1-11.

Study tested the moderating influence of job involvement on the relationships of work pressure, lack of autonomy and role ambiguity to depression, physical health and heavy alcohol use. Data were obtained from household interviews with a random sample of 795 employed adults. High levels of job involvement exacerbated the relationships between role ambiguity and physical health, role ambiguity and heavy alcohol use and work pressure and heavy alcohol use.

DSC Shelfmark: 5026.082000

(269)
STRESS and organizational role conflict
M Siegall and L L Cummings
Genetic, social and general psychology monographs, vol.121, 1995, p.65-95.

Argues that role conflict will generate role stress where strain exists within the focal person's social network. This strain occurs when the role sender is perceived as possessing a high degree of power over the focal person and when the expectations of the sender are important to the focal person. Role stress will produce role distress as a function of several individual personality characteristics such as intolerance for ambiguity, need for dependence, high need for affiliation and low risk propensity. Role distress produces coping attempts that in turn depend on a number of individual or situational moderators: access to source of stress, perceived costs of coping, perceived ability to affect the source of stress, etc.

DSC Shelfmark: 4111.916000

(270)
ROLE stress–mental health relations in Japanese bank workers: a moderating effect of social support
N Iwata and K Suzuki
Applied psychology: an international review, vol.46, 1997, p.207-218.

Self-report data were collected by questionnaire from a sample of Japanese bank workers. Hierarchical moderated multiple regression analyses revealed that role overload had the largest association with mental health status. Effects of social support differed according to type of role stress, support provider, and sex and job status.

DSC Shelfmark: Not found

(271)
THE INTERACTIVE effect of role conflict and role ambiguity on job performance
Y Fried *et al*
Journal of occupational and organizational psychology, vol.71, 1998, p.19-27.

Study investigated the combined effects of role conflict and ambiguity on performance in a sample of 359 blue-collar workers in an Israeli industrial organisation. Results supported the hypothesis that simultaneous increases in role conflict and ambiguity would be associated with poorer job performance.

DSC Shelfmark: 5026.082000

(272)
A LONGITUDINAL study of workload, health and well–being among male and female urban bus drivers

L W Rydstedt, G Johansson and G W Evans
Journal of occupational and organizational psychology, vol.71, 1998, p.35-45.

Investigated health consequences of occupational stress among male and female urban bus drivers in a longitudinal study over 18 months. Increased workload, modelled in terms of role overload and conflicting demands on the driver, was associated with exhaustion, difficulties in unwinding after work, and problems in coping with demands at home. Workload was also related to increased health symptoms, but not to drug use. No gender differences nor any interaction between gender and occupational stress factors were found. Controlling for negative affectivity did not change the pattern or significance of relationships between workload demand and outcome measures in this study.

DSC Shelfmark: 5026.082000

3.11.8 Job control

(273)
BOREDOM: practical consequences and a theory
J F O'Hanlon
Acta psychologica, vol.49, 1981, p.53-82.

Physical factors which cause boredom are complex, but always include exposure to constant or repetitious sensory stimulation. Two underlying physiological factors are identified: the process, initiated by monotony, of inhibiting cortical arousal (habituation) and a compensating process aimed at restoring arousal to an optimal level for task performance (effort). Performance inefficiency accompanies boredom, as does general dissatisfaction with the setting in which the boredom occurs.

DSC Shelfmark: 0661.490000

(274)
A META-ANALYSIS of the relation of job characteristics to job satisfaction
B T Loher *et al*
Journal of applied psychology, vol.70, 1985, p.280-289.

Purpose of the study was to determine the strength of the relationship between job characteristics (skill variety, task identity, task significance, autonomy and feedback) and job satisfaction, and whether the relationship between job characteristics and job satisfaction is moderated by growth need strength. The correlation between the job characteristics index and job satisfaction is moderate, about .39. The hypothesis that growth need strength acts as a moderator of the relationship between job characteristics and satisfaction is confirmed.

DSC Shelfmark: 4947.000000

(275)

REPETITIVE WORK: occupational stress and health

T Cox

In Job stress and blue collar work, edited by C L Cooper and M J Smith. Chichester: Wiley, 1985. p.85–109.

Describes evolution of industrial repetitive work and attempts an analysis of its stressful aspects. Validates the assessment of repetitive work as stressful against data from a variety of field studies. Two types of evidence are considered: data from studies of workers' perceptions of their jobs which confirm the assessment, and data on effects of repetitive work on suboptimum health, overt illness and disability.

DSC Shelfmark: 86/03860

(276)

PERCEIVED control by employees: a meta-analysis of studies concerning autonomy and participation at work

P E Spector

Human relations, vol.39, 1986, p.1005–1116.

A meta-analysis was conducted of studies relating perceived control variables to 19 employee outcome variables. For all studies combined it was found that high levels of perceived control were associated with high levels of job satisfaction, commitment, involvement, performance and motivation, and low levels of physical symptoms, emotional distress, role stress, absenteeism, intent to quit and turnover.

DSC Shelfmark: 4336.400000

(277)

CONTROL in the workplace

D C Ganster and M R Fusilier

International review of industrial and organisational psychology, 1989, p.235–280.

Surveys literature on control theory in organisational settings, including participation in decision-making, job design research, machine pacing and job decision latitude. The impact of individual difference variables (locus of control and Type A behaviour) on employee perceptions of control is also covered. Literature touching on the effect of organisational changes such as the introduction of quality circles and flexitime on control beliefs is also analysed.

DSC Shelfmark: 4547.325000

(278)
CONTROL in the workplace and its health-related aspects
R Karasek

In Job control and worker health, edited by S L Sauter, J J Hurrell and C L Cooper. Chichester: Wiley, 1989 p.129-159.

Describes the evolution of the job demands-decision latitude model of job strain and the findings linking job control, cardiovascular disease and other illnesses. The first test based on Swedish Level of Living Survey data showed that in the highest strain group 20% of the men reported CHD symptoms in 1974. In the most leisurely group none of the subjects described CHD symptoms. Further studies are based on job characteristics 'estimated' from occupational titles. The US 'estimates' are based on the Quality of Employment Survey and are linked to CHD data in the Health Examination Survey and the Health and Nutrition Examination Survey. Analyses showed that CHD was more prevalent in high strain group than in other men in all but one case (age group 45-54 in the HES). Effects of job change were studied through a survey of workers in Sweden's Federation of White Collar Unions. Increases in job control were associated with a significant relative risk reduction for 11 out of 12 illnesses for males.

DSC Shelfmark: 89/23682

(279)
JOB control and worker health
S J Sauter, J J Hurrell, and C L Cooper (editors)
Chichester: Wiley, 1989. 311p.

Represents a major attempt to review and appraise the research linking job control to health. Documents what is known about the influence of job control on worker well-being and addresses the theoretical bases and mechanisms of this influence. Examines the implications of modern work practice for worker control and worker health.

DSC Shelfmark: 89/23682

(280)
PSYCHOLOGICAL and physiological stress responses during repetitive work at an assembly line
U Lundberg *et al*
Work and stress, vol.3, 1989, p.143-153.

Examined the association between psychological and physiological stress responses in 20 male workers aged 19-25 years at an assembly line. Work induced a significant elevation in almost all psychological and physiological measurements.

DSC Shelfmark: 9348.102000

(281)

THEORETICAL models of control and health

M Frese

In Job control and worker health edited by S L Sauter, J J Hurrell and C L Cooper. Chichester: Wiley, 1989. p.107–127.

Explores conceptual issues of control at work and mechanisms of control effects on health. Identifies 5 mechanisms:(1) stressor reduction; (2) fitting stressful environment to psychological prerequisites of the person; (3) safety signal; (4) persistence in coping; (5) need for control.

DSC Shelfmark: 89/23682

(282)

HEALTHY work: stress, productivity and the reconstruction of working life

R Karasek and T Theorell

New York: Basic Books, 1990. 381p.

Based on a ten year study of nearly 5,000 workers, this book postulates a connection between work-related illness and workers' lack of participation in the design and outcome of their labours. Analyses are based on Karasek's model of job strain arising from the interaction of high job demands and low decision latitude leading to a number of negative health outcomes, especially cardiovascular disease.

DSC Shelfmark: 90/23252

(283)

LOWER health risk with increased job control among white collar workers

R Karasek

Journal of organizational behavior, vol.11, 1990, p.171–185.

Investigated associations between increased job control and health status among 4,881 male and 3,623 female white-collar, full-time workers. 1,937 subjects had undergone a company-initiated job reorganisation during previous years. Subjects who had input into the job reorganisation process and obtained increased task control as a result had lower levels of illness symptoms. Coronary heart disease was lower in circumstances of increased job control for males. Absenteeism and depression were lower; however smoking was significantly higher for women.

DSC Shelfmark: 5027.066000

(284)

JOB characteristics, role stress and mental health

E K Kelloway and J Barling

Journal of occupational psychology, vol.64, 1991, p.291-304.

Tests the hypothesis that individual perceptions of job characteristics (autonomy, task variety, task identity, feedback from job and feedback from co-workers) and role stressors give rise to job related affective well-being (or lack of it) and perceptions of competence at work. In turn, these context specific reactions predict context free mental health. Confirmatory path analysis of responses from 720 hospital employees shows that all but 4 of the 20 hypothesised effects were significant in the expected direction, and that the model is a good fit for the data.

DSC Shelfmark: 5026.120000

(285)

EMPLOYEE stress in jobs with and without electronic performance monitoring

M J Smith *et al*

Applied ergonomics, vol.23, 1992, p.17-27.

Examined critical job design elements that could influence worker stress in an electronic monitoring context. Results indicate that employees of telecommunications companies who had their performance electronically monitored perceived their working conditions as more stressful and reported higher levels of boredom, tension, anxiety, depression, health complaints and fatigue. It is postulated that these effects may relate to changes in job design due to EPM.

DSC Shelfmark: 1572.500000

(286)

JOB features and excessive stress

P Warr

In Prevention of mental ill health at work: a conference edited by R Jenkins and N Coney. London: HMSO, 1992, p.40-49.

Focuses on low job discretion as a major cause of employee stress. From low job discretion flow restricted use of skills and lack of job variety. Conversely, if employees are given some control over their work, they must possess and use the necessary skills, and can introduce some variety into what they do. They can also tackle unavoidable demands in ways and at times most acceptable to them. The combination of lack of job discretion, lack of job variety and low use of skills means that it is often employees at the bottom of an organisation who report most stress symptoms in terms of depression and less active involvement in life.

DSC Shelfmark: OP-92/h

(287)

MODERATING effect of decision latitude on stress–strain relationship: does organizational level matter?

M Westman

Journal of organizational behavior, vol.13, 1992, p.713-722.

Tested the hypothesis that decision latitude and role stressors have a differential effect on strain in a group of clerical bank employees as compared to their managers. Results supported the hypothesis that the moderating effect of decision latitude on the job stress–psychological strain relationship tends to be specific to the lower echelons of employees.

DSC Shelfmark: 5027.066000

(288)

THE PATTERNING of psychological attributes and distress by 'job strain' and social support in a sample of working men

P A Landsbergis *et al*

Journal of behavioral medicine, vol.15, 1992, p.379-405.

Tested Karasek's job strain model amongst 297 healthy men at various work sites controlling for demographic variables. The job strain model was supported by various psychological outcome measures. Subjects in low strain jobs had the lowest job dissatisfaction and trait anxiety. Subjects in high strain jobs had the highest job dissatisfaction. Low social support was associated with greater symptomology.

DSC Shelfmark: 4951.262000

(289)

STRESS, computer-based work monitoring and measurement systems: a conceptual overview

B C Amick and M J Smith

Applied ergonomics, vol.23, 1992, p.6-16.

In work environments where EPM is in use, control and coordination functions are allocated to the computer. Some work arrangements in EPM systems provoke stress responses in employees that can result in short term illness and potentially long term changes in health status. Information enriched work environments could improve job resources and social resources to manage job demands and reduce potentially damaging stress responses.

DSC Shelfmark: 1572.500000

(290)

EFFECT of electronic performance monitoring on job design and worker stress: review of the literature and conceptual model

P Carayon

Human factors, vol.35, 1993, p.385-395.

Model proposed hypothesises that EPM has direct and indirect effects on worker stress. The indirect effects result from job design. The effects of EPM on 3 job design characteristics (job demands, job control and social support) are examined in more detail.

DSC Shelfmark: 4336.075000

(291)
JOB design and job stress in office workers
P Carayon
Ergonomics, vol.36, 1993, p.463-477.

Proposes job control to be a primary cause of job stress outcomes. The effects of perceived demands, job content and career/future concerns were hypothesised to influence stress outcomes only to the extent of their influence on job control. This was tested in 170 government office employees who completed a self-administered questionnaire. Job control was not a crucial determinant of stress outcomes. Job demands and career/future concerns were consistent determinants of stress outcomes. Job content, demands and career/future concerns did not influence stress outcomes through job control.

DSC Shelfmark: 3808.500000

(292)
A LONGITUDINAL test of Karasek's job strain model among office workers
P Carayon
Work and stress, vol.7, 1993, p.299-314.

Karasek's job strain model was tested in a sample of 122 office workers. The interaction of job control and workload and of skill utilisation and workload and their relationship to various indicators of strain were examined. The results indicated that there was neither a multiplicative nor additive effect of job control/skill utilisation and workload on worker strain.

DSC Shelfmark: 9348.102000

(293)
THE DEMANDS-CONTROL model of job strain: a more specific test
T D Wall *et al*
Journal of occupational and organizational psychology, vol.69, 1996, p.153-66.

Used focused measures of demands and control with a sample of manufacturing employees, and found evidence of a predicted interaction effect. Parallel measures using decision latitude rather than job control did not show an equivalent effect.

DSC Shelfmark: 5026.082000

(294)

ACTIVE coping and need for control as moderators of the job demand-control model: effects on burnout

A E de Rijk *et al*

Journal of occupational and organizational psychology, vol.71, 1998, p.1-18.

The study tested the job demand-control model with burnout as the strain outcome in a homogeneous sample of 367 Dutch nurses from 18 intensive care units. In addition two individual characteristics, active coping and need for control, were included as potential moderators of the demands-control interaction. The demands-control interaction posited by Karasek's model could not be demonstrated. However, active coping style was shown to moderate an interaction between job demands and job control. For nurses low in active coping skills, enhanced job control actually increased the strain produced by high job demands.

DSC Shelfmark: 5026.082000

(295)

THE EFFECTS of work control and job demands on employee adjustment and work performance

L D Sargent and D J Terry

Journal of occupational and organizational psychology, vol.71, 1998, p.219-236.

Study tested the hypothesis that high levels of control over task-related aspects of the job would protect the person against high levels of work demands. It was also expected that levels of work control would exert main effects on level of employee adjustment. Methodological improvements over previous research included the use of both self-reported adjustment measures and supervisor ratings of work performance as outcome variables, and the assessment of outcome and predictor measures at different points in time. Results showed some support for the hypothesis that effects of job demands would be buffered by high levels of task control, but not by more peripheral aspects of work control such as decision authority and control of scheduling. There were also significant direct effects of task control on job satisfaction.

DSC Shelfmark: 5026.082000

(296)

FACILITATING and inhibiting effects of job control and social support on stress outcomes and role behavior: a contingency model.

J Schaubroeck and L S Fink

Journal of organizational behavior, vol.19, 1998, p.167-195.

Data were collected by self-report survey from 214 employees of a large US insurance company. Results showed that supervisor consideration was positively related to subordinate job performance, conscientiousness and extra-role behaviour among staff perceiving low job control. The relationship between supervisor consideration and performance and extra-role behaviour was negative among subordinates perceiving high levels of job control. Increasing worker control appears to aid in stress coping, but only if existing social support is high or if it can be increased concomitantly. Increased support appears to enhance performance only when control is low. Thus there is a conflict between the desired outcomes of performance and well-being.

DSC Shelfmark: 5027.066000

(297)

RELATIONSHIP of job strain and iso-strain to health status in a cohort of women in the United States

B C Amick *et al*

Scandinavian journal of work, environment and health, vol.24, 1998, p.54–61

Data were collected by self-report questionnaire from 33,689 women. Results showed that, when compared to active work, high strain work (high job demands and low job control) was associated with lower vitality, poorer mental health, higher pain and increased risks of both physical and emotional role limitations. Iso-strain work (high strain and low work-related social support) increased the risks further.

DSC Shelfmark: 8087.568000

(298)

STRESS and well-being in health-care staff: the role of negative affectivity, perceptions of job demand and discretion

P Tyler and D Cushway

Stress medicine, vol.14, 1998, p.99–102

Study investigated the relationship between job stress factors, coping strategies, job satisfaction and well-being in the light of Karasek's demands-discretion model. Data were collected by self-report survey from volunteer staff in the Surgical and Mental Health Directorates of an English hospital district. After controlling for age, gender and negative affectivity, no interaction effect was found between measures of job demands and discretion for either job satisfaction or psychological distress. Both job dissatisfaction and psychological distress were associated with lack of resources, while perception of the job as demanding was associated with workload. Controlling for negative affectivity had a stronger influence on the measures of distress than on job dissatisfaction.

DSC Shelfmark: 8474.129500

3.11.9 Job insecurity

(299)
JOB insecurity: towards conceptual clarity
L Greenhalgh and Z Rosenblatt
Academy of Management review, vol.9, 1984, p.438-448.

Presents a model of job insecurity in which an employee perceives a threat to his/her continued employment from environmental cues such as formal organisational communications and rumours. The perceived severity of the threat is moderated by individual personality traits and level of dependence on continuation of the present job. Reactions to job insecurity include reduced work effort, propensity to leave, resistance to change, all of which lead to reduced organisational effectiveness as productivity falls, and adaptability decreases and staff turnover increases.

DSC Shelfmark: 0570.587600

(300)
LAYOFFS, self-esteem and survivor guilt: motivational, affective and attitudinal consequences
J Brockner, J Davy and C Carter
Organizational behavior and human decision processes, vol.36, 1985, p.224-244.

Laboratory study exploring the effect of layoffs on the subsequent productivity of 'survivors'. The quantity but not the quality of the workers' task performance was enhanced by the dismissal of their fellow subjects, as predicted. The participants level of self-esteem proved to be an important moderator variable in that only the productivity of the low SEs was significantly affected by the layoff manipulation.

DSC Shelfmark: 6290.749000

(301)
SURVIVORS' reactions to layoffs: we get by with a little help from our friends
J Brockner *et al*
Administrative science quarterly, vol.32, 1987, p.526-541.

Used a combination of a laboratory study and field research to investigate survivors' reactions to layoffs within a justice theory framework. Survivors reacted most negatively when they identified with layoff victims who were perceived to have been inadequately compensated. The negative reaction took the form of reduced work performance in the lab study and lowered organisational commitment in the field study.

DSC Shelfmark: 0696.517000

(302)

CONTENT, causes and consequences of job insecurity: a theory-based measure and substantive test

S J Ashford, C Lee and P Bobko

Academy of Management journal, vol.32, 1989, p.803–829.

Authors developed a new job insecurity measure based on recent theory, and then used the measure to test several substantive hypotheses about the antecedents and consequences of job insecurity. Results support the argument that perceived lack of predictability and control may induce perceptions of job insecurity. Outcomes of job insecurity included declines in commitment to, and trust in, an organization and a rise in intentions to quit. Job security was not related to either health complaints or performance.

DSC Shelfmark: 0570.587000

(303)

SURVIVOR sense making and reactions to organizational decline: effects of individual differences

L Greenhalgh and T D Jick

Management communication quarterly, vol.2, 1989, p.305–327.

In the objective environment of a declining organization, staff will see different degrees of risk to their jobs in response to the same objective predicament. There are individual differences in the perceptual and cognitive processes involved in sense making, so that different responses to environmental stimuli can be partly explained in terms of personality variables. The effects of personality variables are greater in situations perceived as ambiguous, such as workforce shrinkage processes arising from mergers and acquisitions or downsizing.

DSC Shelfmark: 5359.013900

(304)

JOB insecurity in managers: antecedents and consequences

E Roskies and C Louis-Guerin

Journal of organizational behavior, vol.11, 1990, p.345–359.

This study examines perceptions of, and reactions to, insecurity as a chronic, ambiguous threat. Managers insecure about their jobs showed poorer health, and the level of distress rose proportionately with the level of insecurity. Insecurity was also related to negative work attitudes and behaviour, with insecure managers reporting decreased work effort, trust, career satisfaction and career optimism. However, only a small minority of managers were worried about imminent job loss, with substantially more anxious about a deterioration in working conditions and long term security.

DSC Shelfmark: 5027.066000

(305)
EMPLOYEES and job insecurity
B Klandermans, T van Vuuren and D Jacobson
In Job insecurity: coping with jobs at risk by J Hartley and others.
London: Sage, 1991. p.40-64.

Conceptualises job insecurity as a function of the perceived probability and the perceived severity of job loss.

DSC Shelfmark: 91/07908

(306)
JOB insecurity: coping with jobs at risk
J Hartley *et al*
London: Sage, 1991. 228p.

Defines job insecurity as a 'perceived powerlessness to maintain desired continuity in a threatened job situation'. Based on this definition, the authors tackle the issues surrounding job insecurity at three levels: the individual employee, union-management relations and business organisation. At each level the authors provided one chapter devoted to theoretical questions before considering the results of their own and others studies in the light of these models.

DSC Shelfmark: 91/07908

(307)
TOWARDS a theoretical distinction between the stress components of the job insecurity and job loss experiences
D Jacobson
Research in the sociology of organizations, vol.9, 1991, p.1-19.

Job insecurity is defined and distinctions from job loss are presented relating to the nature of the transition into job insecurity and job loss respectively, the relative social visibility of each state, the extent to which they are governed by clear role expectations, the contrasting environmental sources of stress, and the different nature of the crises involved for the individual. It is concluded that stressful perceptions of job insecurity are influenced by threat appraisal, counteractive resources and seriousness of the consequences of job loss.

DSC Shelfmark: 7770.733000

(308)
ARE career ladders disappearing?
K Inkson and T Coe
London: Institute of Management, [1992]. 6p.

Research investigated all the job changes experienced over 13 years from 1980 to 1992 by a sample of more than 800 managers who were members of the Institute of Management.

Findings show that managers are changing jobs more often, sideways or downward moves are increasing, upward moves are declining and managers are increasingly subject to changes imposed by their employer.

DSC Shelfmark: q93/21184

(309)
LAYOFFS, job insecurity and survivors' work effort: evidence of an inverted-U relationship
J Brockner *et al*
Academy of Management journal, vol.35, 1992, p.413-425.

Results of a field study demonstrated that moderate levels of job insecurity associated with a layoff led to a greater increase in work effort than did low job insecurity and very high job insecurity. Survivors economic need to work moderated these effects.

DSC Shelfmark: 0570.587000

(310)
COPING with job insecurity: how does personality make a difference?
E Roskies, C Louis-Guerin and C Fournier
Journal of organizational behavior, vol.14, 1993, p.617-630.

Reports an investigation of the role of personality disposition (positive and negative) in understanding the impact of job insecurity. Findings show that there is a strong beneficial impact of positive personality disposition on mental health, an effect that is as strong as the damaging impact of negative affectivity. Thus personality disposition may cushion as well as aggravate the impact of occupational stress.

DSC Shelfmark: 5027.066000

(311)
CHANGING households: the BHPS 1990 to 1992
N Buck *et al* (editors)
Colchester: ESRC Research Centre on Micro-social Change, University of Essex, 1994. 312p.

Book presents the first findings from the British Household Panel Survey. The 10,000 members of the panel, randomly selected from throughout Great Britain, are interviewed annually about their work, income, health, attitudes, household living arrangements, housing and consumption. Each chapter of the book examines a different aspect of change in people's lives based on the findings of the first two years of the study. Topics covered include housing, income, employment, family and work, household finances, consumption, health, political beliefs and household transitions.

DSC Shelfmark: 94/27217

(312)

CHRONIC job insecurity among automobile workers: effects on job satisfaction and health

C A Heaney, B A Israel and J S House

Social science and medicine, vol.38, 1994, p.1431-1437.

Longitudinal survey data from 207 automobile manufacturing workers indicates that long term job insecurity acts as a chronic stressor whose effects become more potent as the time of exposure increases. Extended periods of job insecurity decrease job satisfaction and increase physical symptomology.

DSC Shelfmark: 8318.157000

(313)

THE EFFECTS of labour market position, job insecurity and unemployment on psychological health

B Burchell

In Social change and the experience of unemployment edited by D Gallie, C Marsh and C Vogler. Oxford: OUP, 1994. p.188-212.

Presents evidence that people in insecure employment at the disadvantaged end of the labour market suffer approximately the same level of psychological disadvantage as the unemployed themselves.

DSC Shelfmark: 94/09652

(314)

HEALTH effects of anticipation of job change and non-employment: longitudinal data from the Whitehall II Study

J E Ferrie *et al*

British medical journal, vol.311, 1995, p.1264-1269.

The Whitehall II study began in 1985 and involves 10308 staff working in 20 civil service departments in London. Found that workers who thought they were at risk of job loss suffered more symptoms and reported more health problems than colleagues who believed themselves secure. The changes in physical health were greater for men, while women suffered more psychological symptoms. The health problems could not be linked to behaviours such as smoking, drinking or lack of exercise.

DSC Shelfmark: 2330.000000

(315)

FEELING insecure?

P Gregg and J Wadsworth

Employment audit, issue 2, 1996, p.17-25

Concludes that less legal protection from dismissal, rising job instability (particularly for men) and a growing income penalty attached to job loss are at the root of widespread public anxiety about job insecurity.

DSC Shelfmark: 3737.213700

(316)
JOB insecurity and employee commitment: managers' reactions to the threat and outcomes of redundancy selection
J Hallier and P Lyon
British journal of management, vol.7, 1996, p.107-123.

Examines changes in the work attachments of long-service managers under threat of redundancy. Over a 12 month period, interviews were conducted with 42 middle managers who had been warned of the threat of redundancy. Initially most of the managers experienced significant threats to their views of themselves and their employers. However, the organisational attachment of reprieved managers was quickly re-established, while those demoted or re-employed by other companies became less trusting of their employers and reported reduced job effort and lowered organisational commitment.

DSC Shelfmark: 2311.180000

(317)
THE STATE of the psychological contract in employment
D Guest *et al*
London: Institute of Personnel and Development, 1996. 40p.
(Issues in people management; no.16).

Shows the return of the feel-good factor to the workplace, with two out of three working people out of 1000 questioned saying they were not worried about being made redundant. Four out of five felt they were being fairly treated at work and three out of five expected to be with the same employer in five years time. Nearly 90% were proud to tell people who they worked for and more than one in five said they preferred work to home.

DSC Shelfmark: 4584.312500

(318)
THE 1997 Ashridge management index
Ashridge: Ashridge Research, 1997.

Notes the emergence of a new breed of 'mercenary' manager prepared to move to the highest bidder following the wave of insecurity that overtook managers during the corporate downsizings of the early 1990s.

DSC Shelfmark: Not found

(319)

EMPLOYEE motivation and the psychological contract

D E Guest and N Conway

London: Institute of Personnel and Development, 1997. 60p

(Issues in people management; no.21).

Report of a survey of a random sample of 1000 people in employment interviewed in July 1997 by Harris Research. Results show that almost all employees believe they are fairly treated at work, more than three-quarters trust their organisations and similar numbers are proud to tell people who they work for. Job insecurity is no longer the issue it was: a minority of respondents (albeit a significant one of 25%) expressed worries about job security.

DSC Shelfmark: 4584.312500

(320)

IMPLEMENTING the new employment contract

HR executive review, vol.4, no.4, 1997. 18p

Explores the changing psychological contract between companies and their staff. The old paternalistic relationship has disappeared and assurances of help to improve employability have replaced pledges of employment for life. Employees themselves now rank interesting work, good communication and opportunities for development above job security.

DSC Shelfmark: 4335.266700

(321)

JOB insecurity vs labour market flexibility

D Smith

London: Social Market Foundation, 1997. 38p.

Argues against the existence of widespread insecurity in Britain in the 1990s. Insecurity is confined to the unskilled, young and over 50s. Also challenges the idea that there is a causal relationship between flexible working practices and job insecurity. Labour market flexibility is seen as playing a minor role in creating temporary insecurity.

DSC Shelfmark: 3461.117000

(322)

MODERATING effects of work-based support on the relationship between job insecurity and its consequences

V K G Lim

Work and stress, vol.11, 1997, p.251-266.

Study examined the buffering effects of support provided by work colleagues and supervisor on the relationship between job insecurity and (1) job satisfaction and (2) non-compliant job behaviours. Data were collected by questionnaire from the alumni of a large university in the

USA. Results suggest that support from others at the workplace can contribute significantly in buffering individuals against job dissatisfaction and non-compliant job behaviours when their job security is at stake.

DSC Shelfmark: 9348.102000

(323)
INSECURITY at work: is job insecurity really much worse now than before?
A Felstead, B Burchell and F Green
New economy, vol.5, 1998, p.180–184.

A survey of 2467 employed people aged 20–60 was conducted in 1997 and results compared to those from a 1986 survey of 4047 employed people in the same age bracket. Results showed that fear of job loss had increased substantially among those in highly paid occupations such as managers and professionals. Among less highly paid occupations, perceptions of job insecurity had not altered much. Job insecurity had therefore not fallen in line with the decline in overall unemployment between 1986 and 1997.

DSC Shelfmark: 6083.670500

(324)
THE UNEQUAL distribution of job insecurity
B Burchell
Cambridge: ESRC Centre for Business Research, 1998. 41p.
(Working paper; no.88).

Findings based on analysis of 6,111 job histories from the Social Change & Economic Life Initiative dataset show that job insecurity is concentrated among manual workers who are 60% more likely to move into unstable jobs than professionals. Paper also points out that job insecurity can cause serious psychological problems, marital breakdowns and reduced life expectancy, and reports the existence of 'Survivor Syndrome', among those left after redundancy. Among survivors researchers have found lowered morale, decreased motivation, loyalty and commitment and increased stress, anger and bitterness.

DSC Shelfmark: 9349.2269

4   Stress and Personality: Individual Differences in the Stress Process

4.1   Individual difference in the stress process

In 1988 Payne suggested that individual differences in personality might be involved in the stress process in at least five different ways. He presented these in the form of a series of questions which he argued could be asked of every personality trait separately:

- Do individual differences play a role in causing people to choose jobs which differ in stressfulness?

- How do individual differences relate to the development of symptoms of psychological strain such as depression and anxiety?

- How do individual differences relate to perceptions of stress in the environment?

- Do they act as moderators of the stress–strain relationship?

- Do they affect the way people cope with stress?

In practice, personality differences have been investigated as mediators of stress perception and appraisal, or, as moderators or buffers of the stress-strain relationship. The distinction between individual differences as mediators of stress perception/appraisal and as moderators of the stress–strain relationship has important methodological implications. However some researchers do not appear to appreciate the distinction between the two positions, and have used the terms interchangeably, both with each other and with a variety of other words such as buffer, vulnerability factor or modifier. This can be very confusing for the reader, and some clarification is required. Conceptually, a mediator variable is one that is responsible for the transmission of an effect, but does not alter the nature of the effect. Mediator variables, for example, offer some explanation as to how external physical events take on psychological meaning, and are perceived as harmful or threatening. On the other hand, a moderator variable is one whose presence alters the strength of the relationship between a stress factor such as overwork and a strain outcome such as health complaints or absenteeism. In other words, the moderator variable will either reduce or increase the impact of the stress factor and ameliorate or exacerbate the strain outcome.

Beyond the categories of involvement suggested by Payne, individual differences have also been studied as confounding or nuisance variables, artificially inflating associations between self-report measures of stress factors and strains. Negative affectivity or trait anxiety has come under particular suspicion in this regard. In a study of managerial and professional personnel, Brief and colleagues (1988, ref. no. 361) found that negative affectivity explained much of the relationship of self-reported job and personal stress to job dissatisfaction, health complaints at work, life dissatisfaction and depressive symptoms. It is hypothesised that people high in negative affectivity tend to look on the black side of life and may exaggerate both the levels of stress in their workplace and the severity of the health complaints or psychological distress they experience as a result. This tendency to exaggerate when completing survey questionnaires will artificially strengthen the relationship between stress factors and strains. The results of this and related studies have called into question a large proportion of psychological stress research, which rests upon the associations between self-reports of stress factors and self-reports of strains. However, the proverbial baby should not be thrown away with the bath water, since, although controlling statistically for negative affectivity has been shown to weaken the associations between stress factors and strains, such associations often remain statistically significant. For example, in a study of mostly professional and white collar workers, Chen and Spector (1991, ref. no. 364) examined the relation of a variety of work-related stressors, such as role ambiguity, role conflict and interpersonal conflict with other workers, to job strains, such as job satisfaction, anger and health symptoms. They found that associations changed relatively little when negative affectivity was controlled. Similarly, Schonfeld's longitudinal study of 250 new women teachers found that before and after employment changes in depressive symptoms, job satisfaction, and motivation were related to objective difficulties in the workplace rather than to negative affectivity as a personality trait. The findings were consistent with Chen and Spector in suggesting that negative affectivity does not overly distort the relationship of some work–environment measures to depressive symptoms, job satisfaction and motivation (Schonfeld, 1996, ref. no. 371). Finally, analysis of inconsistent findings suggests that some types of stress factors and some types of strain outcomes are particularly susceptible to contamination. Questionnaires measuring life stress generally require subjects to make subjective judgements about how stress factors have affected their health, happiness and well-being. When answering these questions people are prone to lapses of memory and to attribution errors. That is, they wrongly attribute having a stomach upset to stress arising from a family row, rather than to a surfeit of little green apples. In work stress research, questionnaires are more objective, asking subjects to note the presence or absence of some feature such as tight deadlines or excessive workloads (Schonfeld, 1996, ref. no. 371; Schaubroeck, Ganster and Fox, 1992, ref. no. 366). There is therefore less risk of false reporting. Similarly, negative affectivity appears to cause people to exaggerate the severity and frequency of health complaints more than the level of job dissatisfaction they experience (Chen and Spector, 1991, ref. no. 364; Schaubroeck and Ganster, 1991, ref. no. 365; Schaubroeck, Ganster and Fox, 1992, ref. no. 366). This may indicate that different types of strain outcomes are differently influenced by negative affectivity, or observed differences may be a methodological artefact due to the way the questions are phrased. Questions in the job satisfaction surveys are phrased so as to encourage an upbeat response.

Finally, individual differences may have a direct effect on self-reported strains, irrespective of the presence of environmental stress factors. Thus people who are high in negative affectivity also score consistently highly on self-report symptom scales such as the General Health Questionnaire regardless of whether or not they are under stress. This has led to some debate as to whether these individuals actually experience poorer health, or merely report greater distress. In contrast, reports of numerous studies have shown that internal locus of control is related to a number of desirable outcomes, including better physical health, higher levels of achievement, lower anxiety and depression and higher self-esteem (Koeske and Kirk, 1995, ref. no. 359). An internal locus of control has been characterised as involving taking responsibility for one's behaviour, attributing outcomes to effort and skill, rather than chance, task difficulty, system constraints or powerful others, and a sense of personal control.

4.2   Popular personality variables

Many individual differences have been explored as potentially influencing the stress process in one or other of these ways. Four particular personality traits are reviewed here: hardiness, locus of control, Type A behaviour pattern and negative affectivity.

4.2.1 Hardiness

Hardiness has been defined as a personality construct composed of three characteristics: control, which refers to a belief in one's ability to influence events; commitment, which refers to an approach to life marked by curiosity and a sense of meaningfulness; and challenge, which refers to an expectation that change is normal and stimulates development. The concept was first advanced by Kobasa and her colleagues in an effort to explain why some executives experienced debilitating illness in the face of stressful life events while others did not. Results from a growing body of research suggest that personality hardiness may exert a protective effect against physical illness and psychological distress in the face of work and life stressors (Hills and Norvell, 1991, ref. no. 342; Pierce and Molloy, 1990, ref. no 341: Kobasa, Maddi and Puccetti, 1982, ref. no. 335; Rush, Schoel and Barnard, 1995, ref. no. 345). High hardy individuals may experience less physical illness and psychological distress because they perceive stressful life and work events as more controllable and positive than people low in hardiness. This may lead on to healthy coping responses, such as adoption of a healthy lifestyle, or building up strong social support networks, which reduce the ill effects of stress on health and well-being. Although Kobasa and her colleagues have offered numerous studies supporting the positive effects of hardiness on health status, some studies have failed to replicate the predicted association. Criticisms of the hardiness construct and measures have emerged, of which three are mentioned here.

First, the construct may be multidimensional. Kobasa originally conceived hardiness as consisting of three components in a single inseparable constellation, not three independent aspects. When the separate components of hardiness were tested by Hull and colleagues and by Roth only control and commitment appear related to well-being (Hull, Van Treuren and Virnelli, 1987, ref. no. 337; Roth et al, 1989, ref. no. 338). On the other hand, Contrada (1989, ref. no 339) in his study of hardiness, Type A behaviour and cardiovascular reactivity to psychological stress, found that the challenge component of hardiness was uniquely associated with diastolic blood pressure responsiveness to a laboratory stressor. These results do not support Kobasa's view that the personality construct hardiness consists of 'inextricably intertwined aspects that bear a considerable resemblance to each other'.

Secondly, hardiness may be confused with negative affectivity. Reviews of the hardiness literature by Funk (1992, ref. no. 343) and Hull and colleagues (1987, ref. no. 337) have concluded that, in general, questionnaires intended to measure hardiness may actually be measuring negative affectivity. Those low on hardiness may report more illness because the measure might actually be tapping into negative affectivity, and individuals high in negative affect tend to report more illness. On the other hand, Hills and Norvell (1991, ref. no. 342) found in their study of 234 male highway patrol officers that low hardiness added to the likelihood of people reporting lots of health complaints, over and above how prone they were to anxiety and how many daily hassles they perceived.

Finally, criticisms have been made of the validity of the hardiness measures. During the early years of hardiness research, as many as 19 different questionnaires were used to assess the construct. An inventory of 71 items, the Unabridged Hardiness Scale (UHS) became the most widely used measure of Kobasa's original hardiness dimensions of commitment, control and challenge. Second generation measures followed in 1982 in the shape of a 20 item Abridged Hardiness Scale and a 36 item Revised Hardiness Scale. New third generation scales have since been developed: the 30 item Personal Views Survey (PVS), the 45 item Dispositional Resilience Scale (DRS) and the 30 item Cognitive Hardiness Scale (CHS). The PVS and DRS share similar formats and item contents to the original Kobasa scales and provide separate measures of the three hardiness dimensions. The CHS was rationally derived from the three hardiness dimensions, but provides only a global measure of the hardiness construct. The diversity of measures of this personality construct makes the body of hardiness research difficult to interpret. Differences in health outcomes across hardiness studies may be due to the questionaires being used rather than to a true hardiness effect (Greene and Nowack, 1995, ref. no. 344 ; Funk 1992, ref. no. 343).

4.2.2   Locus of control

The construct locus of control is rooted in social learning theory, which maintains that behaviour in a given situation is determined by expectancy and reinforcement value. People can be differentiated on the basis of their 'generalised expectancy' concerning internal and external control of life events and outcomes. If an individual perceives outcomes to be the result of his/her own actions (ie has an internal orientation), then good or bad outcomes will strengthen or weaken behaviour patterns. If, on the other hand, an individual believes that outcomes and life events are externally controlled by chance, fate or powerful others, then good or bad outcomes will not change his/her behaviour.

In the empirical literature on work-related stress, external locus of control is consistently associated with self-reports of ill-health and distress. Externals have been shown to report more burnout (St Yves et al, 1989, ref. no. 353); higher levels of perceived stress (Cooper, Kirkaldy and Brown, 1994, ref. no. 331); less job satisfaction (Spector and O'Connell, 1994, ref. no. 330): greater anger, frustration and hostility (Newton and Keenan, 1990, ref. no. 355), and higher levels of anxiety (Parkes, 1991, ref. no. 356). Internal locus of control, in contrast, is associated with a number of highly desirable behaviours and attributes, including higher job motivation and better performance (Spector, 1982, ref. no. 347); higher job satisfaction (Koeske and Kirk, 1995, ref. no. 359; Kirkaldy et al, 1993, ref. no. 329) and psychological well-being (Kirkaldy et al, 1993, ref. no. 329; Daniels and Guppy, 1992, ref. no. 358).

However, in spite of the apparent consistency of the findings, these results are difficult to interpret. Most of the studies are cross-sectional in nature the direction of causality therefore cannot be inferred. Associations may be due to the influence of an underlying trait, such as our old friend negative affectivity. Distortion due to negative affectivity may artificially inflate associations between, say, external locus of control and self-reports of ill-health. Most studies have assessed stress by means of self-report questionnaires. Self-report data can be unreliable, especially in the work-setting where motivations may exist to either exaggerate or under-report stress levels. It is therefore desirable to supplement self-report data with objective measures of either the stress factors or the strain outcomes or both. Interestingly, in a study where strain was measured both by self-report data and salivary cortisol output, the three personality traits studied (negative affect, Type A behaviour and locus of control) showed different patterns of relation to stress when assessed by the different measures (Walsh et al, 1997, ref. no. 333).

Some doubts have also been raised as to the stability of locus of control beliefs. There is some evidence that locus of control beliefs can change over time or in response to life events. The instrument of choice for measuring locus of control beliefs has been the Rotter External-Internal Scale first published in 1966. Rotter determined average levels of internality and externality using a population of students at the Ohio State University. During the winter of 1980, a sample of 298 students of introductory psychology completed the I-E scale. The distribution of internal-external scores was different from the original data provided by Rotter's research at the same institution 15 years earlier. Results showed a general trend towards more external orientation in college students. It is possible that these changed scores reflect social changes, and a general feeling that individuals are at the mercy of political and economic forces which allow them less control over their lives (Cellini and Kantorowski, 1982, ref. no. 348).

A considerable body of research has sought to examine and define the interrelationships among stress factors, psychological and physical symptoms, personality factors (in this case, locus of control) and other resources such as social support. All of these factors are known to be important and to work in combination, but there is considerable disagreement as to the precise relationships between them. A number of studies have examined the moderating effects of locus of control on the job stressor/strain outcome relationship. In general, the underlying premise is that individuals who define stress factors as controllable will be more likely to try and cope with them using a problem solving approach and thereby experience fewer ill effects. Thus Fusilier, Ganster and Mayes (1987, ref. no. 349) found that externals who believed themsleves at the mercy of 'powerful others' experienced greater increases in physical health problems when exposed to role conflict than did people low on this orientation. The authors hypothesised that, unlike internals, these externals might not take active steps to resolve their role conflict. Newton and Keenan, (1990, ref. no. 355), on the other hand, found in their study of a sample of young British graduate engineers, that increases in role conflict and quantitative workload were associated with greater increases in strain among internals. Externals appeared more sensitive to role ambiguity and environmental frustration. If you believe in external control, in an ambiguous environment 'your fate is unknown' because you do not know what is expected of you and you will feel especially threatened. Finally, Parkes (1991, ref. no. 356) in both a cross-sectional study of civil servants and a longitudinal study of teachers found that externals who perceived their work to be high in demands and low in discretion showed higher levels of psychological distress than internals under the same conditions. Externals appeared to find particular difficulty in copying with work situations where demands and discretion were not balanced. However, inconsistent results have been reported. Batlis (1980, ref. no. 346), for example, found no evidence for a moderating effect of locus of control on the relationship between role stress and job satisfaction in a sample of supermarket department managers. Daniels and Guppy (1992, ref. no. 358) found no evidence of a stress-moderating effect of control beliefs. However, internal locus of control was found to have a direct effect on psychological well-being. That is, people with an internal orientation enjoyed better psychological health, regardless of whether they were under stress or not.

The moderator studies reviewed above have treated locus of control as an independent, stable trait, and have not considered the potential influence of other personality characteristics and resources such as social support. In contrast, Dolan and his colleagues, in a study of hospital employees, examined the relationship between two sources of job demands, three psychological symptoms (anxiety, depression and irritation), four personality types and three areas of social support.

The personality types were (a) high striver-achiever/high internal; (b) high striver-achiever/high external; (c) low striver-achiever/high internal; (d) low striver-achiever/high external. Striver-achiever in the authors' definition is an approximation of Type A personality. Type A individuals are characterised by ambitiousness, aggressiveness, competitiveness, impatience, potential for hostility and a hard driving nature. Results suggested that the effects of social support varied significantly depending on the source of job demands, the worker's personality and the psychological symptom manifested (Dolan, van Ameringen and Arsenault, 1992, ref. no. 328). Thus for instance high striver-achiever, high internal individuals are formal, and dominant, action-oriented leaders who experience the need for social support as a sign of weakness, and therefore a threat to their proper identity. Kirkaldy, Furnham and Cooper (1994, ref. no. 332) have explored interactions between Type A behaviour and locus of control and their associations with health and job satisfaction among German police managers. Results showed that the internal A Types had the lowest stress and greatest satisfaction scores. External A types seemed hostile, competitive, and dominant but felt threatened and unable to control the forces surrounding them. However, results of a similar study of British police managers by the same authors found, that, although locus of control was a clear and constant predictor of job related stress, satisfaction and health, Type A personality had no effect on strain outcomes, either directly or in combination with control orientation. One explanation of this lies in the fact that total, as opposed to subscale, scores of Type A were used. It may be that only certain components of Type A, notably aggressiveness, influence work-related behaviour. (Kirkaldy *et al*, 1993, ref. no. 329).

4.2.3   Negative affectivity

Negative affectivity is defined as the tendency for a person to experience a variety of negative emotions across time and situations. Negative affectivity subsumes a broad range of unpleasant mood states, including anger, scorn, disgust, guilt, fearfulness and depression. It can be measured either as a state (ie transient fluctuations in mood) or as trait (i.e. stable individual differences in general affective level). The trait of negative affectivity represents a predisposition to experience the corresponding state mood. Individuals high in negative affectivity are more likely to experience significant levels of distress and dissatisfaction at all times and in any given situation, even in the absence of any overt stress. They are more introspective and tend to dwell on their failures and shortcomings. They are inclined to focus on the negative side both of themselves and the world in general. In a work context, negative affectivity may manifest itself in job dissatisfaction, high levels of perceived job stressors, and high levels of perceived job strains. The trait negative affectivity construct has also been called neuroticism, trait anxiety and general maladjustment in the literature (Watson and Pennebaker, 1989, ref. no. 362).

Most recent research, particularly in the USA, has focused on the role of negative affectivity as a potential confounding variable or nuisance factor in stressor-strain relations. Persons high in negative affectivity consistently report higher levels of physical symptoms of ailments such as headaches, stomach pains and chest pains. This may be because they experience poorer objective health, or because they perceive, overreact to, and/or complain about minor physical problems. Research data received by Watson and Pennebaker (1989, ref. no. 362) showed that negative affectivity to be unrelated to an array of objective health indicators including frequency of illness, visits to doctors, sick absence from work or school, or to any objective evidence of risk of serious illness. Thus, although negative affectivity is related to complaints of ill-health, its links with actual disease are unproven. Similarly, there will be a tendency for persons high in negative affectivity to report greater dissatisfaction and more job-related distress than persons low in negative affectivity, even in the absence of any objective source of stress. This over-reporting may artificially inflate the associations between self-reports of stress factors and strain outcomes (Brief et al, 1988, ref. no. 361). These findings have generated much debate and called into question the validity of a large proportion of the psychological stress research, which rests on associations of self-reported stressors and strains.

A number of later studies have tested the hypothesis that negative affectivity spuriously inflates relationships between self-reported stressors and self-reported strain outcomes. Chen and Spector (1991, ref. no. 364) found that associations between job related stressors including role ambiguity and conflict and interpersonal conflict at work and job strains including job dissatisfaction, state anger and health symptoms changed relatively little when negative affectivity was controlled. In a longitudinal study of a cohort of college graduates, Spector and

O'Connell (1994, ref. no. 330) found that negative affectivity was significantly associated with role ambiguity, role conflict, and interpersonal conflict, but not with lack of autonomy or heavy workload. It was also associated with the strains of work anxiety and physical health complaints, but not with job dissatisfaction or frustration. These results only partially support the hypothesis that people high in negative affectivity will respond more negatively than people low in negative affectivity to most questionnaires about job stressors and strains. Moyle (1995, ref. no. 369) in a study of employed adults from three different work groups, also found that negative affectivity was not strongly associated with all measures of work stress factors, and therefore, could not generally account for observed associations between work stress measures and strain. When negative affectivity was statistically controlled, work stressor-strain outcome associations were only substantially reduced for the prediction of physical symptoms, and in no case were they reduced to zero. There was no evidence of negative affectivity distorting the relationship between job satisfaction and work stress factors. These findings are in keeping with Watson and Pennebaker's view that health complaints reflect negative affectivity. Similarly, Schonfeld (1996, ref. no. 371) found in a longitudinal study of new women teachers that changes in depressive symptoms, expected job satisfaction and motivation after one term in employment were related to adverse working conditions, not negative affectivity, and underlined the potency of difficulties encountered by teachers. In keeping with the view that health complaints reflect negative affectivity, the relationships of two measures of work stress factors to post employment physical symptoms were weakened when pre-employment physical symptoms were controlled. Finally, a study by Schaubroeck, Ganster and Fox (1992, ref. no. 366) of fire-fighters and police officers found that negative affectivity had no relationship with six objective stress indicators measured with multiple physiological readings. Furthermore, significant positive effects of lack of workload variability on adrenaline were unaffected by the presence of either neuroticism or trait anxiety in the analysis. Latent variable structural equations analysis, however, found that estimating negative affectivity reduced the relationships between perceived work stressors and depression and physical symptoms. Negative affectivity had no relationship with job dissatisfaction. This may reflect the way in which the questions on job satisfaction were phrased, or their content.

It has also been suggested that the self-report questionnaires used to measure stress factors, negative affectivity and physical and psychological strains partially overlap. This means that the questionaires may be measuring the same thing under different names. This would of course artificially inflate the associations between the variables. Brett and colleagues (1990, ref. no. 363) observed that stress factors that

169

were judged to be contaminated by over-reporting due to negative affectivity correlated with self-reported stress symptoms over time, but that stressor items not contaminated by negative affectivity did not so correlate. On the other hand Schaubroeck, Ganster and Fox (1992, ref. no. 366) found no evidence that negative affectivity was a contaminant of stress reports in terms of measuring the same phenomenon under two different names.

To sum up, the weight of empirical evidence suggests that:

- Negative affectivity is not a causal factor in objective ill-health.

- However, it probably leads to the over-reporting of health symptoms.

- Negative affectivity is not strongly associated with all measures of stress factors, and therefore does not generally distort the relationship between all stressors and all strains.

4.2.4   Type A behaviour pattern

Interest in the concept of the Type A behaviour pattern (TABP) has been fuelled by the reported links between it and increased risk of heart disease. Making the link between Type A behaviour and heart disease is usually attributed to the cardiologists Friedman and Rosenman (1974, ref. no. 372). Although this link has not been consistently observed, the concept continues to generate serious interest among researchers. The Type A individual is characterised by feelings of time urgency, impatience, aggressiveness, and competitiveness. In a work environment Type A behaviour will manifest itself in constantly working long hours to meet deadlines and under conditions of overload, taking work home in the evenings and at week-ends, cutting short holidays, constantly competing with themselves and others, driving themselves to meet high, often unrealistic, standards, and feeling frustrated with the work situation, misunderstood by superiors, and irritable with work efforts of subordinates (Brief, Rude and Rabinowitz, 1983, ref. no. 374). The Type B person is characterised by the absence of these characteristics.

Two major early prospective studies, the Western Collaborative Group Study (WCGS) and the Framingham Heart Study support the existence of a relationship between Type A Behaviour Pattern and increased risk of cardiovascular disease independent of traditional biomedical risk. In the Framingham Study, respondents were followed for the development of coronary heart disease (CHD) over an eight year period. Women who developed CHD scored significantly higher on the

Framingham Type A behaviour, suppressed hostility, tension and anxiety symptoms scales than women remaining free of CHD. Men exhibiting Framingham Type A behaviour, work overload, suppressed hostility, and frequent job promotions were at increased risk of developing CHD, especially in the age group 55-64 years. The association was found only among white collar workers and was independent of standard coronary risk factors (Haynes, Feinleib and Kannel, 1980, ref. no. 373). However, the strength of the observed relation of Type A behaviour and disease has decreased in more recent research, as shown in a meta-analysis by Booth-Kewley and Friedman (1987, ref. no. 378). In addition, UK research summarised by Sutherland and Cooper (1990, ref. no. 56) does not replicate the original findings. The studies reported by Sutherland and Cooper all used the Bortner Scale to measure Type A behaviour, and the samples included all socioeconomic groups. Use of different scales to measure Type A behaviour, differences in the structure of the populations studied and different study designs may account for the inconsistent results. Booth-Kewley and Friedman reported that relations between Type A and disease found in prospective studies were much smaller than those found in cross-sectional studies. This was the case for the two most popular measures of Type A, the Structured Interview and the Jenkins Activity Scale. The point that changing methodologies will produce inconsistent results is neatly illustrated in a recent review of the literature on psychosocial influences on blood pressure by Carels, Sherwood and Blumenthal (1998, ref. no. 395). Early studies examining ambulatory blood pressure and heart rate often showed no difference between Type As and Type Bs. These studies often had few participants and tested vague hypotheses. Later studies that found differences between Type As and Type Bs had larger samples and greater methodologic sophistication. Differences were found to occur during specific activities (e.g. talking), in response to specific stress factors, (e.g. ambient noise) and/or in conjunction with other personality factors (e.g. dependency).

Type A behaviour may work in combination with other personality factors to predict coronary proneness. Booth-Kewley and Friedman found in their meta-analysis that depression was also related to cardiovascular disease and that this relation was of comparable strength to that of Type A behaviour as measured by the Structured Interview (the best predictor of the relationship between Type A and CHD). Anxiety also appeared to be slightly related to coronary-proneness, whereas extraversion was not. Overall, the picture of the coronary-prone person emerging from the review was not that of the workaholic, hurried impatient individual but that of a person with one or more negative emotions: someone who is depressed, aggressively competitive, easily frustrated, anxious, angry or some combination.

The Type A Behaviour Pattern is a multidimensional construct and not all of its components are associated with the development of CHD. Of the personality factors underlying the global Type A Behaviour Pattern, hostility has the strongest relationship with disease outcomes. Ganster and his colleagues (1991, ref. no. 388) found that hostility was reliably related to both reactivity to challenging stimuli and recovery from them. They hypothesise that because persons scoring high in hostility tend to both hyperreact to a challenging stimulus and to recover less quickly, hostility may well be an important contributor to cardiovascular disorders. The weight of empirical research suggests that hostility predicts heart disease independently of other traditional Type A characteristics (Booth–Kewley and Friedman, 1987, ref. no. 378; Sutherland and Cooper, 1990, ref. no. 56; Burns, Hutt and Weidner, 1993, ref. no. 391; Ganster et al, 1991, ref. no. 388; Carels, Sherwood and Blumenthal, 1998, ref. no. 395). Hostility itself is a multidimensional construct with two components: covert and overt hostility. Aggression and anger turned inwards are strongly associated with negative affectivity. Aggression and anger turned outwards on other people is associated with need for power but not with negative affectivity. Of the two forms, overt hostility has been found more toxic in its effects on coronary disease (Schaubroeck and Ganster, 1991, ref. no. 365).

Type A behaviour pattern has been measured by a plethora of different instruments, the most popular of which have been reviewed by J R Edwards (1991, ref. no. 387). The most widely used instruments are the Structured Interview, the Jenkins Activity Survey, the Framingham Scale and the Bortner Scale. The strength of the relationship between Type A behaviour and CHD appears to depend on method of measurement, with the structured interview producing the strongest association. Edwards concludes that the four instruments have yet to demonstrate adequate validity. He recommends abandoning these global TABP measures in favour of separate measures of the various TABP components. This would allow researchers to model and measure the relationships and interactions of the various components, increasing understanding of the determinants, nature and consequences of TABP. In a comparison of the three self-report measures of TABP, the Jenkins Activity Survey, the Bortner Scale and the Framingham Scale, Edwards, Baglioni and Cooper (1990, ref. no. 384) found that the scales:

- Measure different underlying constructs, reflecting different aspects of the TABP.

- Measure multiple dimensions or components of the TABP. Some of these components of the TABP are included in all the scales; others may be unique to one scale.
- Are prone to measurement error.

These measures cannot be used interchangeably as indicators of the TABP, hindering the generalisation and accumulation of findings across studies. The measures need to be substantially modified, or preferably replaced with measures of the specific TABP components.

In a work context Type A Behaviour is hypothesised to function in 4 different ways:

- Type A persons may choose to work in challenging and highly pressurised jobs.

- Due to their aggressiveness, impatience and competitiveness Type As may not form supportive relationships with colleagues.

- Type A individuals may perceive the work environment as more stressful than Type Bs.

- Type A Behaviour Pattern may exacerbate the relationship between stress factors and strain outcomes, because Type As are more vulnerable to the damaging effects of stress.

A number of organisational studies provide relevant, but ambiguous data regarding the prevalence of Type A across occupations and job types. Haynes, Feinleib and Kannel (1980, ref. no. 373) found that working women scored higher on the Type A scale than housewives, suggesting that Type A women are more apt to be employed. Whether this represents a higher exposure to stressors, depends on whether one thinks that paid employment is more stressful than house work. Similarly Boyd (1984, ref. no. 375) examined Type A scores of small business owners using the Jenkins Activity Survey. He found that 82% of his sample of 368 chief executives of small business were classified as Type As, and that this exceeded percentages reported by managers in larger firms. Again, one must make some assumptions about the inherent stressfulness of being a small business owner before one can use these data to support a self-selection hypothesis. Finally Ganster, Sime and Mayes (1989, ref. no. 383), found in a multiple occupation study that 66% of extreme Type As worked in low-stress occupations and 34% worked in high-stress occupations. Of the extreme Type Bs, 42% were in low-stress occupations and 58% in high-stress occupations. These data argue against the hypothesis that Type A individuals deliberately choose to work in inherently high-stress occupations.

There is some evidence in the more recent research literature that Type A individuals do respond differently from Type Bs to social support. Hagihara and his colleagues (1997, ref. no. 393) found in a study of 560 Japanese white collar workers that social support from management increased mental strain among Type A workers under conditions of heavy workload. The researchers speculated that this effect arose because social support could be perceived as distracting the worker from total concentration on his job. Dolan and his colleagues (1992, ref. no. 328) reported in a study of 807 hospital employees that certain personality types might not even seek social support. High striver-achiever, high internal individuals, for example, might perceive the need for social support as a sign of weakness and a menace to their proper identity. High striver-achiever, high external types might be reluctant to exhibit strain in front of colleagues in case it might be interpreted as a sign of weakness and might tend to export complaints to family and friends. Lack of support from family and friends might contribute to enhancement of strain in the face of increased workload and responsibilities.

There is considerable support in the research literature for the hypothesis that Type A individuals appraise their work environment differently to Type Bs. Hagihara and his colleagues found, for example, that among Japanese white collar workers long working hours and social support from management were significant predictors of mental strain for type A individuals while work requiring new knowledge and performance appraisal by management were significant predictors among Type Bs (Hagihara *et al*, 1997, ref. no. 393). Van den Berg and Schalk (1997, ref. no. 394) found in a study of Dutch office workers that Type A individuals appeared to experience more subjective work overload than Type Bs. That is, they tended to perceive their tasks as more demanding, even when they were objectively the same. The authors recommend that Type As should be trained to perceive their tasks in a more realistic fashion. Ganster, Sime and Mayes (1989, ref. no. 383) in their study of almost 700 employees representing 26 different occupations found that the Type A dimensions of competitiveness and hostility appeared to be related to the experience of role conflict, role ambiguity and responsibility without authority. Stress factors associated with work demands (workload, work variability) tended to be associated with Type A dimensions related to behavioural intensity (rapid and accelerating speech, speed and impatience). When an occupational stress rating based on the US Dept of Labor's Dictionary of Occupational Titles was used to exclude objective stress from the analysis, the associations remained the same. This somewhat suggests that Type As may be appraising their work environment differently to Type Bs. Finally, in their prospective study of college graduates, Spector and O'Connell (1994, ref. no. 330) found that two components of Type A had different relationships to perceived stress factors. High impatience-irritability employees reported higher levels of constraints and interpersonal conflicts, perhaps reflecting that through impatience they perceive more impediments, and through irritability they get into conflicts with others. On the other hand, achievement striving correlated with workload, indicating that Type As are actually working harder than Type Bs, or at least that they perceive that they are.

The moderating or buffering hypothesis postulates that Type A employees with high job stress will be more seriously affected than Type B employees in similar situations. The research literature is divided in its support for this hypothesis. Jamal (1990, ref. no. 385), in a study of Canadian nurses, found that Type A nurses experienced more serious adverse consequences of job stress than Type B nurses. Psychosomatic health problems and turnover motivation were the two outcomes more seriously affected by the interaction of job stressors and Type A behaviour. Similarly, in a replication of a 1984 study, Rhodewalt and his colleagues found that Type A individuals reported more job stress under lower levels of perceived control and that perceptions of elevated job stress led Type As to report higher levels of psychological disturbance and physical symptoms than Type Bs. Given similar objective situational demands, Type As were more likely to suffer strain than Type Bs. Type As functioning in a work environment over which they felt they had only moderate control were the most stressed and displayed the most psychological distress and physical symptoms (Rhodewalt et al, 1991, ref. no. 390). On the other hand, Kushnir and Melamed (1991, ref. no. 82) found that, while perceived control exerted a direct effect, it did not interact with Type A personality to increase reported levels of distress. The job control aspect tapped in this study was the perceived freedom to make decisions concerning job performance. Since controllability is multidimensional, it could be that other aspects are especially important for Type As.

It is clear that not all components of the Type A personality are toxic. For example, Kivimäki and his colleagues found in a study of industrial managers that the ambition–energy component of Type A was activated by an abundance of development possibilities experienced at work. This perception of development possibilities led in turn to a decrease in psychological and physiological strain symptoms in managers (Kivimäki, Kalimo and Julkunen, 1996, ref. no. 392). Results of a study of 568 occupationally diverse workers by Ganster and his colleagues showed the speed, impatience and competitiveness components of the Type A Behaviour Pattern to be fairly benign and to bear no relationship to coronary or other illness proclivity (Ganster et al, 1991, ref. no. 388). Finally, results of a longitudinal study of British graduate engineers showed that Type Bs and not Type As reported greater strain with elevated job demands (role conflict, role ambiguity, high workload, and organisational frustration) (Newton and Keenan, 1990 ref. no. 355). In contrast, Melamed and Kushnir in a study of 3562 male Israeli factory workers found that Type As were stressed under conditions of overload which Type Bs found stimulating and challenging (1991, ref. no. 82). Inconsistent results such as these may be due to differences in the social context, the psychometric instruments used, or the statistical methodology employed for analysis.

4.3   Bibliography

4.3.1   Individual differences in the stress process

(325)
INDIVIDUAL differences in the study of occupational stress
R Payne
In Causes, coping and consequences of stress at work edited by C L Cooper and R Payne. Chichester: Wiley, 1988. p.209-231.

Reviews the role of negative affectivity, Type A Behaviour Pattern and locus of control in the stress process. Explores how these variables relate to the development of illness and perception of stress in the environment as well as asking whether they act as moderators of the stress–strain relationship and whether they affect the way people cope with stress.

DSC Shelfmark: 88/19899

(326)
PERSONALITY characteristics as moderators of the relationship between stress and disorder
S Cohen and J R Edwards
In Advances in the investigation of psychological stress edited by R W J Neufeld. New York: Wiley, 1989. p.235-283.

Review of studies investigating stress and a personal resource presumed to act as a stress buffer published up to Jan. 1986. Concludes that research has provided suggestive evidence that a number of specific personality resources may influence the appraisal and/or coping process. However, statistical and conceptual problems, a lack of consistency in results and inadequate numbers of replications make much of the evidence difficult to interpret.

DSC Shelfmark: 89/08277

(327)
PERSONALITY and stress: individual differences in the stress process
C L Cooper and R Payne (editors)
Chichester: Wiley, 1991. 289p.

Book explores the relationship between certain personality characteristics and stress. It examines the role of personality and individual differences in the stress process, highlighting their relation to coping and health behaviour. Includes consideration of Type A behaviour, neuroticism, locus of control, hardiness, cognitive style and cognitive ability and other individual difference factors such as sex, age, gender, and social class.

DSC Shelfmark: 91/20462

(328)
PERSONALITY, social support and workers' stress
S L Dolan, M R van Ameringen and A Arsenault
Relations industrielles, vol. 47, 1992, p.125-139.

The primary objective of the study was to test the moderating effect of social support on the relationship between perceived stress factors and strain symptoms whatever the personality type. A secondary objective was to explore how this moderating effect varied from one personality type to another. Data were collected by questionnaire from a sample of 807 hospital workers. Data were obtained regarding two sources of job demands (intrinsic and extrinsic), three psychological strains (anxiety, depression and irritation), four categories of personality and three areas of social support (superiors, colleagues, family and friends). Results suggest that the effects of social support vary significantly depending upon the source of job demands, personality type and the psychological symptom manifested.

DSC Shelfmark: 7352.075000

(329)
PERSONALITY, job satisfaction and well-being among public sector (police) managers
B D Kirkaldy *et al*
European review of applied psychology, vol. 43, 1993, p.241-248.

Study examined over 530 British superintendent police officers' reaction to stress. They were categorised into four groups: Type A internal and external and Type B internal and external locus of control. Locus of control emerged as a clear and consistent predictor of job related stress, satisfaction and health, with internals displaying the lowest stress and greatest satisfaction scores and the best mental and physical health scores. Type A/B failed to yield any significant differences either as a main effect or in interaction.

DSC Shelfmark: 3829.942000

(330)

THE CONTRIBUTION of personality traits, negative affectivity, locus of control and Type A to the subsequent reports of job stressors and job strains

P E Spector and B J O'Connell

Journal of occupational and organizational psychology, vol. 67, 1994, p. 1–11

Personality variables (negative affectivity, locus of control and two components of Type A behaviour) were assessed in a cohort of final year undergraduates and then used one year later to predict reports of job stressors (autonomy, role ambiguity, role conflict, workload, constraints and interpersonal conflict) and job strains (job satisfaction, work anxiety, frustration and health symptoms). For all variables except work frustration, personality was a significant predictor.

DSC Shelfmark: 5026.082000

(331)

A MODEL of job stress and physical health: the role of individual differences

C L Cooper, B D Kirkaldy and J Brown

Personality and individual differences, vol. 16, 1994, p.653–655.

A total of over 500 senior British police officers (ranked superintendent or above) completed the Occupational Stress Indicator together with a biographic and demographic inventory. Results show that Type A behaviour has both a direct effect on physical and psychosomatic health and an indirect effect through the job stressors. Neither the locus of control nor coping factors have a direct effect on health, but are indirectly related through perception of the job stressors and job satisfaction.

DSC Shelfmark: 6428.010500

(332)

POLICE personality, job satisfaction and health

B D Kirkaldy, A Furnham and C L Cooper

Studia psychologia, vol. 36, 1994, p.55–63.

Study examined over 90 senior German police managers categorised into Type A internal and external and Type B internal and external locus of control. It compared the four groups' experience of work stress, job satisfaction and general health. Individuals with high levels of Type A behaviour coupled with high internal locus of control expressed least stress and most satisfaction. Personality was not as clearly linked to physical or psychological health.

DSC Shelfmark: 8482.347000

(333)

NEUROTICISM, locus of control, Type A behaviour pattern and occupational stress

J J Walsh *et al*

Work and stress, vol.11, 1997, p.148–159.

Stress in lecturers employed by a computer training organisation was assessed by self-report and measurement of salivary cortisol output during lecturing and non-lecturing weeks. The three dimensions of individual differences (neuroticism, Type A behaviour and locus of control) showed different patterns of relation to stress levels when assessed through self-report measures and cortisol output. Self-reported stress was found to be more closely related to neuroticism than to Type A behaviour or locus of control. Cortisol output appeared to be unrelated to neuroticism but related, albeit in a complex manner, to Type A behaviour, and, to a lesser extent, to locus of control.

DSC Shelfmark: 9348.102000

4.3.2   Hardiness

(334)
THE HARDY personality: towards a social psychology of stress and health
S C Kobasa
In Social psychology of health and illness edited by G S Sanders and J Suls.
Hillsdale, N J: Erlbaum, 1982. p.3–32.

Describes the three dimensions of the hardy personality: commitment, control and challenge. Reports research supporting the hypothesis that hardiness acts as a stress resistance resource, buffering the relationship between stressful life events and illness.

DSC Shelfmark: 82/29835

(335)
PERSONALITY and exercise as buffers in the stress–illness relationship
S C Kobasa, S R Maddi and M C Puccetti
Journal of behavioral medicine, vol. 5, 1982, p.391–404.

Study examined the roles of hardiness and exercise in protecting health. Data were collected by questionnaire from a sample of 137 male middle- and upper- level managers. Results were consistent with the hypothesis that personality hardiness has its effect through activities which directly transform events, thereby reducing their stressfulness, whereas exercise buffers stress by decreasing the organismic strain produced by stressful events. The buffering effects seemed additive in that persons who both were hardy and exercised were the healthiest.

DSC Shelfmark: 4951.262000

(336)
TYPE A and hardiness
S C Kobasa, S R Maddi and M A Zola
Journal of behavioral medicine, vol. 6, 1983, p.41–51.

Self-report questionnaires were completed by 140 middle- and upper- level male executives. Under highly stressful life events, male executives who were high in Type A and low in hardiness tended towards higher health complaint scores than any other executives. Findings also confirm the buffering effects of hardiness but suggest that Type A behaviour by itself has little direct effect on general health/illness status.

DSC Shelfmark: 4951.262000

(337)
HARDINESS and health: a critique and alternative approach
J G Hull, K R Van Treuren and S Virnelli
Journal of personality and social psychology, vol. 53, 1987, p.518-530.

On the basis of their own study and a review of earlier literature, the authors offer an alternative definition of hardiness variables. Firstly, hardiness does not appear to be a unitary concept. Commitment and control appear to have independent effects on health, whereas challenge is unrelated. Secondly, there is no evidence of buffering effects of hardiness in addition to direct effects. Thirdly, composite hardiness should not be measured because it obscures the independent contribution of its subcomponents. Commitment should be measured using the short form developed by Kobasa and Maddi. Control should be measured using Rotter's Locus of Control Scale.

DSC Shelfmark: 5030.901000

(338)
LIFE events, fitness, hardiness and health: a simultaneous analysis of proposed stress-resistance effects
D L Roth *et al*
Journal of personality and social psychology, vol. 57, 1989, p.136-142.

Results of a study of 373 undergraduate psychology students suggested that the commitment component of hardiness was the most important in terms of independent association with health. Challenge was found to be virtually unrelated to any measure, including the other two hardiness components, (commitment and control).

DSC Shelfmark: 5030.901000.

(339)
TYPE A behavior, personality hardiness and cardiovascular responses to stress
R J Contrada
Journal of personality and social psychology, vol. 57, 1989, p.895-903.

Type A behaviour and hardiness were examined as predictors of cardiovascular responses to stress in 68 male undergraduates. Systolic and diastolic blood pressure and heart rate were monitored while subjects performed a difficult mirror-tracing task. Type A assessments based on the Structured Interview, but not the Jenkins Activity Survey, showed a modest but reliable association with cardiovascular reactivity. Hardiness was associated with significantly reduced DBP responsiveness. The stress dampening effects of hardiness were largely due to the challenge component. A combination of high hardiness with Type B behaviour classification was associated with the lowest DBP reactivity.

DSC Shelfmark: 5030.901000

(340)
HARDINESS and social support
P H Blaney and R J Ganellan
In Social Support: an interactional view edited by B R Sarason, I G Sarason and G R Pierce.
New York: Wiley, 1990, p.297-318.

Reviews research on the direct and moderating effects of hardiness and social support on well-being. Research on the moderating effects of both constructs has produced inconsistent results and is inconclusive. However, an interesting picture occurs with the coping-style correlates of control and hardiness. Hardiness is associated with self-blame and self-isolation coping, whereas control is associated with support seeking.

DSC Shelfmark: 90/13986

(341)
PSYCHOLOGICAL and biographical differences between secondary school teachers experiencing high and low levels of burnout
C M B Pierce and G N Molloy
British journal of educational psychology, vol. 60, 1990, p.37-51.

A total of 750 teachers from 16 government and non-government schools from areas of contrasted socio-economic status responded to a questionnaire designed to investigate correlates of burnout among teachers in secondary schools in Victoria, Australia. Results showed that hardiness and role stress are the most significant predictors of the three aspects of burnout. Teacher biographical characteristics (sex, age, marital status, teaching experience, level of education and parental status) are less significant predictors of burnout than work pattern variables (school type, position in school) and psychological variables (role stress, hardiness, social support, pupil control ideology).

DSC Shelfmark: 2307.650000

(342)

AN EXAMINATION of hardiness and neuroticism as potential moderators of stress outcomes

H Hills and N Norvell

Behavioral medicine, vol. 17, 1991, p.31–38.

Study of a random sample of 234 male highway patrol officers examined the relationship of stress measures (perception of stress, report of daily hassles, and items unique to police work) to strain outcomes (burnout, reports of physical symptoms and job dissatisfaction). The two hypothesised moderator variables, hardiness and negative affectivity, in fact exerted clearer main or direct than moderating effects on strain outcomes.

DSC Shelfmark: 1877.560000

(343)

HARDINESS: a review of theory and research

S C Funk

Health psychology, vol. 11, 1992, p.335–345.

Concludes on the basis of a literature review that hardiness research has been hampered by several fundamental short-comings: measurement problems, the failure to adequately test hardiness theory, the failure to find predicted results and the neuroticism confound. Recommends that researchers adopt a standard hardiness scale, and use interactive tests to examine buffering effects, or, techniques such as path analysis to examine mediated effects. Concludes there is no evidence to support the hypothesis that hardiness buffers stress and that both old and new hardiness scales inadvertently measure neuroticism.

DSC Shelfmark: 4275.105200

(344)

HASSLES, hardiness and absenteeism: results of a 3-year longitudinal study

R L Greene and K M Nowack

Work and stress, vol. 9, 1995, p.448–462.

In a three-year longitudinal study of 228 full-time employees, the association between hassles, two measures of personality hardiness, absenteeism verified from medical personnel records and self-reported hospitalisation due to illness and injury was investigated. Hassles, but not personality hardiness, significantly contributed to predictions of absenteeism after controlling for relevant demographic variables and psychological well-being. The alternative measure of hardiness, but not any of the original Kobasa personality scales, predicted self-reported hospitalisation for illness or injury. Little evidence for the predictive validity of the Kobasa personality hardiness components, or composite hardiness score, existed for either absenteeism or self-reported hospitalisation in this study.

DSC Shelfmark: 9348.102000

(345)

PSYCHOLOGICAL resiliency in the public sector: 'hardiness' and pressure for change

M C Rush, W A Schoel and S M Barnard

Journal of vocational behaviour, vol. 46, 1995, p.17-39.

A structural model of hardiness was investigated which is consistent with the direct and mediated effects of hardiness as applied to the immediate, specific work experiences associated with pressure for change was investigated. Self-report data were supplied by a sample of 325 senior employees of state agencies in Tennessee. Results showed that hardiness directly reduced stress and increased satisfaction. Results of the structural analysis indicated that the indirect effect of hardiness on stress was mediated solely by an increased use of control coping, which in turn reduced stress.

DSC Shelfmark: 5072.510000

4.3.3   Locus of control

(346)

JOB involvement and locus of control as moderators of role-perception/individual outcome relationships

N C Batlis

Psychological reports, vol. 46, 1980, p.111-119.

Study investigated locus of control and job involvement as moderators of the relationships between role ambiguity, role conflict and three individual outcome variables: job satisfaction, job-related anxiety and propensity to quit. Self-report data were obtained from a sample of 111 supermarket departmental managers. Neither job involvement nor locus of control proved to be a viable moderator of role perception/individual outcome correlations.

DSC Shelfmark: 6946.525000

(347)

BEHAVIOR in organizations as a function of employee's locus of control

P E Spector

Psychological bulletin, vol. 91, 1982, p.482-497.

The results of the research reviewed suggest that locus of control is related to motivation, supervisory style, compliance with authority and ability to handle complex information. Internals respond to incentive systems, prefer participative supervision, demonstrate initiative and tend to take personal action on the job. Externals seem unresponsive to incentives and prefer directive supervision.

DSC Shelfmark: 6946.300000

(348)

INTERNAL-external locus of control: new normative data

J V Cellini and L A Kantorowski

Psychological reports, vol. 51, 1982, p.231-235.

Rotter's Internal-External Locus of Control Scale was administered to a sample of 298 students during Winter 1980. Scores were compared to original normative data produced by Rotter in 1966 on the basis of a similar sample of students from the same institution. Results show that students are becoming more external in their orientation.

DSC Shelfmark: 6946.525000

(349)

EFFECTS of social support, role stress and locus of control on health

M R Fusilier, D C Ganster and B T Mayes

Journal of management, vol. 13, 1987, p.517-528.

The hypothesis that the buffering effect of social support would prevail for individuals with an internal locus of control, but not for those with an external locus of control was examined in a study of 312 police officers and firefighters. A multidimensional measure of locus of control was used and both long term outcomes (depression and health complaints) and a short term strain response (epinephrine secretion) were measured. Results showed that social support had ameliorative effects on depression and health complaints. The two-way interaction effects suggested that social support may buffer the effects of job stress on health complaints and externals may respond more strongly to job stress than internals. The three-way interaction effects showed that internals with low social support exhibited the strongest relationship between role ambiguity and health complaints. High social support exacerbated the relationship between role conflict and epinephrine for internals but not for externals.

DSC Shelfmark: 5011.100000

(350)

LOCUS of control as a potential moderator of the turnover process

G J Blau

Journal of occupational psychology, vol. 60, 1987, p.21-29.

Using a sample of 119 nurses, this longitudinal study found that locus of control interacted with satisfaction with pay and promotion prospects to affect intentions to quit and actual turnover. Internals dissatisfied with pay and promotion prospects are more likely than externals to think about leaving and to leave. Internals were more likely to actually leave once they had formed the intention to do so than externals.

DSC Shelfmark: 5026.120000

(351)

RELATIONSHIPS of organizational frustration with reported behavioural reactions: the moderating effect of locus of control

P L Storms and P E Spector

Journal of occupational psychology, vol. 60, 1987, p.227-234.

Data were collected by questionnaire from 160 employees from all levels of a community mental health facility. Results showed that measures of organisational frustration were positively related to perceived frustration, and perceived frustration to counterproductive behaviour (aggression, sabotage and withdrawal). Support for locus of control as a moderator was strongest for sabotage. Frustrated external subjects tended to engage in sabotage; frustrated internals were not likely to display this behaviour.

DSC Shelfmark: 5026.120000

(352)

PERCEPTIONS of social support, receipt of supportive behaviors and locus of control as moderators of the effects of chronic stress

R C Cummins

American journal of community psychology, vol. 16, 1988, p.685-700.

Study extended the approach of investigating the joint role of social support and locus of control in moderating the effects of stress by using a proximal measure of stress and by examining two dimensions of social support (received support and perceived availability of support). Participants were 112 individuals enrolled in evening classes in business administration. Individuals high in internal locus of control experienced a positive stress buffering effect of received social support. The same internals also reported a negative buffering effect for reassurance of support. Significant main effects of social attachment and social integration in the whole sample suggest that feelings of emotional closeness are important to a sense of well-being regardless of the individual's perception of locus of control.

DSC Shelfmark: 0824.070000

(353)

EXTERNALITY and burnout among dentists

A. St-Yves *et al*

Psychological reports, vol. 65, 1989, p.755-758.

Study investigated the relationship between burnout and locus of control in a sample of 82 dentists. Correlations were found between external locus of control and higher levels of emotional exhaustion and lower personal accomplishment.

DSC Shelfmark: 6946.525000

(354)

LOCUS of control and social support: clarifiers of the relationship between job stress and job satisfaction

R Cummins

Journal of applied social psychology, vol. 19, 1989, p.772-788.

Study investigated the joint role of social support and locus of control in moderating the relationship of job stress to job satisfaction. Data were collected by self-report questionnaire from a sample of 96 employed adults enrolled in evening classes in business administration. Results suggest that the kind of support relevant to an individual's job satisfaction depends on the individual's locus of control orientation. Social support may buffer the effects of job stress only for a particular subgroup of individuals (internals on LOC) and only when it focuses on substantive (work) issues.

DSC Shelfmark: 4947.080000

(355)

THE MODERATING effect of the Type A behavior pattern and locus of control upon the relationship between change in job demands and change in psychological strain

T J Newton and A Keenan

Human relations, vol. 43, 1990, p.1229-1255.

Examines the moderating effect of Type A Behaviour Pattern (TABP) and locus of control on the relationship between changes in job demands and changes in psychological strain across time in a sample of young British engineers. Results showed significant moderating effects for both TABP and locus of control. As job demands increased, Type As experienced less psychological strain than Type Bs. With locus of control, outcomes varied dependent on the type of job demand.

DSC Shelfmark: 4336.400000

(356)

LOCUS of control as moderator: an explanation for additive versus interactive findings in the demand-discretion model of work stress?

K R Parkes

British journal of psychology, vol. 82, 1991, p.291-312.

In a sample of civil servants, regression analyses demonstrated a three-way interaction between locus of control, job demands, and discretion for affective distress but not for absenteeism. In longitudinal data from student teachers, a similar three-way interaction was observed. In this case the result applied to anxiety as an outcome, but not to social dysfunction. In each study, the form of the three-way interaction was such that demand and discretion combined interactively to predict outcomes for externals, whereas for internals, additive findings were obtained.

DSC Shelfmark: 2321.000000

(357)
STRESS and mental strain in hospital work: exploring the relationship beyond personality

A Arsenault, S L Dolan and M R van Ameringen

Journal of organizational behavior, vol. 12, 1991, p.483–498.

Study focuses on the relationship between job stressors and mental strain in hospital work, adjusting for differences in two personality traits (locus of control and striver-achiever). Questionnaires were obtained from 760 full-time employees. Results showed locus of control to be a strong correlate of mental strain. The striver-achiever trait was associated with workload problems but not with mental strain. After adjustment for differences in personality traits, role stress and professional latitude were most strongly related to mental strain. High levels of role stress and low levels of professional latitude interacted significantly to increase mental strain.

DSC Shelfmark: 5027.066000

(358)
THE DIMENSIONALITY and well-being related correlates of work locus of control

K Daniels and A Guppy

European work and organizational psychologist, vol. 2, 1992, p.319-330.

The multidimensionality of work-specific locus of control is explored by subjecting Spector's work locus of control scale to principal components analysis. Using samples of 221 university staff and 399 accountants, a two-dimensional structure was uncovered: external agents control and personal control. In the university sample, external agents control did not correlate with workload and managerial stressors, but did correlate with role stressors. For the accountants, personal control exhibited stronger correlations with the measures of well-being, social support, stressors and work autonomy that external agents control.

DSC Shelfmark: 3830.370850

(359)
DIRECT and buffering effects of internal locus of control among mental health professionals

G F Koeske and S A Kirk

Journal of social service research, vol. 20, no.3/4, 1995, p.1-28.

In a study of Pennsylvania clinical social workers and New York State mental health professionals, internality was consistently associated with favourable qualities such as job satisfaction, life satisfaction and psychological well-being. For a group of care managers of severely mentally ill patients, internality consistently buffered the impact of emotional exhaustion and negative job attitudes on intention to quit the job and overall life satisfaction.

DSC Shelfmark: 5064.913000

(360)

A STRUCTURAL equations model of stress, locus of control, social support, psychiatric symptoms and propensity to leave a job

M A Rahim and C Psenicka

Journal of social psychology, vol. 136, 1996, p.69-84.

Data were collected on job stress, locus of control, social support, psychiatric symptoms and propensity to leave and the moderating effects of locus of control and social support were examined using LISRAEL. Results show that role overload and role insufficiency increased psychiatric symptoms and that role ambiguity and role conflict increased propensity to leave a job. Overall, the moderating effects of locus of control on the relationships of stress factors to psychiatric symptoms and propensity to leave were significant, but similar moderating effects for social support were not.

DSC Shelfmark: 5064.800000

4.3.4   Negative affectivity

(361)

SHOULD negative affectivity remain an unmeasured variable in the study of job stress

A P Brief *et al*

Journal of applied psychology, vol. 73, 1988, p.193-198.

Tested the hypothesis that negative affectivity would spuriously inflate relationships between self-reported stress and strain in a sample of 497 managers and professionals. Findings confirmed pre-existing zero-order relationships between various stress and strain indices, demonstrated that NA is significantly related to these stress and strain measures, and indicated that contamination by NA inflates the correlations between stressors and strains.

DSC Shelfmark: 4947.000000

(362)

HEALTH complaints, stress and distress: exploring the central role of negative affectivity

D Watson and J W Pennebaker

Psychological review, vol. 96, 1989, p.234-254.

Argues that self-report health measures reflect a pervasive personality trait of negative affectivity (NA); self-report stress scales also contain a substantial NA component. Although NA is correlated with health complaints, it is not strongly or consistently related to actual, objective illness, and thus will act as a general nuisance factor in health research. Because stress and health self-report measures both contain a significant NA component, correlations between such measures are likely to over-estimate the true association between stress and health.

DSC Shelfmark: 6946.530000

(363)
NEGATIVE affectivity and the reporting of stressful life events
J F Brett *et al*
Health psychology, vol. 9, 1990, p.57-68.

Found that NA-contaminated events were correlated significantly with indicators of well-being. Uncontaminated events were not significantly correlated with any of the three indicators of well-being. Results suggest that prior correlations of self-reported stressful life events with reduced well-being are considerably inflated. NA appears to contaminate the reporting of life-events by causing people to interpret them more negatively, and also to raise the level of self-reported health complaints.

DSC Shelfmark: 4275.105200

(364)
NEGATIVE affectivity as the underlying cause of correlations between stressors and strains
P Y Chen and P E Spector
Journal of applied psychology, vol. 76, 1991, p.398-407.

Study was undertaken to explore the role of negative affectivity (NA) in explaining relations between self-reported stressors and strains. Little evidence was found to support the idea that NA accounts for a large amount of the relation between chronic work stressors and affective strains (job satisfaction, anger and frustration). Relations between stressors and physical strains (physical symptoms and doctor visits) were quite small and in some case almost entirely attributable to NA.

DSC Shelfmark: 4947.000000

(365)
THE ROLE of negative affectivity in work-related stress
J Schaubroeck and D C Ganster
Journal of social behavior and personality, vol. 6, 1991, p.319-330.

Some research findings suggest that trait negative affectivity may lead to over-reporting of stressors and strains in the workplace. Paper critically reviews the literature on this issue. The use of confirmatory factor analysis to test for the presence of bias in self-report data caused by negative affectivity is advocated. Further research is also required into the role of trait negative affectivity in the etiology of stress disorders.

DSC Shelfmark: 5064.751500

(366)

DISPOSITIONAL affect and work–related stress

J Schaubroeck, D C Ganster and M L Fox

Journal of applied psychology, vol. 77, 1992, p.322-335.

Negative affectivity has been asserted to be a factor which spuriously inflates relationships between self-reported stressors and self-reported strain outcomes. This hypothesis was tested with conventional questionnaires and physiological measures on a sample of 311 firefighters and police officers. Confirmatory factor analysis showed that negative affectivity did not measure a factor in common with measures of subjective strain. Latent-variable structural equation analyses, however, showed that estimating the effects of negative affectivity on strain significantly attenuated the effects of work stressors. It had no correlation with physiological stress outcomes. In the light of these findings it is recommended that outcome measures should be assessed independently of the respondent where possible, and that where self-report instruments are used they should contain a minimum of reference to internal subjective states.

DSC Shelfmark: 4947.000000

(367)

THE ROLE of negative affectivity in understanding relations between self–reports of stressors and strains: a comment on the applied psychology literature

M J Burke, A P Brief and J M George

Journal of applied psychology, vol. 78, 1993, p.402-412.

Reanalyses of four data sets confirmed the hypothesis that negative affectivity (NA) spuriously inflates the correlations between self-reported stressors and strains. When self-reports are used researchers should also include a measure of negative affectivity so that they can explore the effects of this variable on the self-reports and the relationships among them. The use of more objective measures of stressors and strains is recommended.

DSC Shelfmark: 4947.000000

(368)

NEGATIVE affectivity, emotional distress and the cognitive appraisal of occupational stress

T R Elliott, J M Chartrand and S W Harkins

Journal of vocational behaviour, vol. 45, 1994, p.185-201.

Study examined the mediating effects of trait negative affectivity (TNA) and trait positive affectivity (TPA) on the relation of cognitive appraisal to emotional distress associated with occupational stress in samples of teachers and journalists. Appraisals of perceived interference of the stress factor, ability to tolerate discorrespondence imposed by the stress factor and the degree of perceived control were culled from each participant. Results from separate multiple regression analyses indicated that TNA did not completely explain the appraisal-distress relation for either sample. Appraisals of interference, tolerance and control were associated with distress as expected. Both cognitive processes and TNA contributed to the negative emotional reactions to occupational stress.

DSC Shelfmark: 5072.510000

(369)
THE ROLE of negative affectivity in the stress process: tests of alternative models
P Moyle
Journal of organizational behavior, vol. 16, 1995, p.647-668.

Self-report data were obtained from 21 employees of small businesses, 36 bank employees and 86 employees of a business consultancy firm. In terms of symptom report, negative affectivity was found to have direct effects on strain, to act as a partial confound, and to play a significant role as a vulnerability (moderating) factor. In contrast, for the prediction of job satisfaction, the influence of negative affectivity was found to be mediated through perceptions of the work environment.

DSC Shelfmark: 5027.066000

(370)
THE IMPACT of negative affectivity on stressor-strain relations: a replication and extension
S M Jex and P E Spector
Work and stress, vol. 10, 1996, p.36-45.

Results from two samples of university employees showed that partialling out trait anxiety, dispositional optimism or both reduced the magnitude of stressor-strain correlations very little. It does not appear that stressor-strain correlations can be attributed to negative affectivity.

DSC Shelfmark: 9348.102000

(371)
RELATION of negative affectivity to self-reports of job stressors and psychological outcomes
I S Schonfeld
Journal of occupational health psychology, vol. 1, 1996, p.397-412.

A sample of 250 new women teachers participated in a longitudinal study of the influence of negative affectivity on the relation of self-report work environment measures to psychological outcomes. Three 'neutrally-worded' work environment measures were specially constructed to minimise confounding with NA. Pre- to post- employment changes in depressive symptoms, job satisfaction and motivation were related to adversity in the workplace. The size of each correlation and regression coefficient linking the episodic and ongoing stressor scales to post-employment depression, job satisfaction and motivation was largely unchanged when pre-employment symptoms were controlled. The findings support the view that NA does not overly distort the relation of some work-environment measures to depressive symptoms, job satisfaction and motivation.

DSC Shelfmark: 5026.095000

4.3.5   Type A behaviour pattern

(372)
TYPE A behavior and your heart
M Friedman and R H Rosenman
London: Wildwood House, 1974. 276p.

Authors postulate that coronary heart disease is of behavioural origin and is particularly associated with the behaviour pattern classified as Type A. This behaviour type is characterised by excessive competitive drive, aggressiveness, impatience and a harrying sense of time urgency.

DSC Shelfmark: Not found

(373)
THE RELATIONSHIP of psychosocial factors to coronary heart disease in the Framingham Study. III. Eight year incidence of coronary heart disease
S G Haynes, M Feinleib and W B Kannel
American journal of epidemiology, vol.111, 1980, p.37-58.

An extensive psychosocial questionnaire was administered to 1674 coronary free individuals participating in the Framingham Heart Study between 1965 and 1967. The respondents were followed for the development of coronary heart disease (CHD) over an eight year period. Results suggested that Type A behaviour and suppressed hostility might be involved in the pathogenesis of CHD in both men and women.

DSC Shelfmark: 0824.600000

(374)
IMPACT of Type A behaviour pattern on subjective work load and depression
A P Brief, D E Rude and S Rabinowitz
Journal of occupational behaviour, vol. 4, 1983, p.157-164.

A sample of 162 high school basketball coaches were administered a battery of tests that assessed behaviour patterns, subjective quantitative work load, dissatisfaction and depression.

Results showed that Type A subjects perceived exposure to greater levels of job stressors than Type B subjects. Among Type A subjects, a strong positive relationship between subjective work load and dissatisfaction was detected. This was not found for Type B subjects.

DSC Shelfmark: 5026.085000

(375)
TYPE A behaviour, financial performance and organizational growth in small business firms
D P Boyd
Journal of occupational psychology, vol. 57, 1984, p.137–140.

Eight hundred randomly selected subjects were sent the Jenkins Activity Survey (JAS) and a biodata questionnaire. A total of 368 Chief Executive Officers responded, representing a response rate of 46%. Of these, 82% were classified as Type A.

DSC Shelfmark: 5026.120000

(376)
COMPONENTS of Type A, hostility and anger-in: relationship to angiographic findings
T M Dembroski *et al*
Psychosomatic medicine, vol. 47, 1985, p.219-231.

Findings suggest that hostility, in conjunction with acquired coping mechanisms such as anger suppression (anger–in) may lie at the foundation of coronary-prone behaviour, and that other attributes contained in the conceptual and operational definition of the Type A Behaviour Pattern may be relatively benign correlates of these traits.

DSC Shelfmark: 6946.555000

(377)
TYPE A behavior and occupational stress
D C Ganster
Journal of organizational behavior management, vol. 8, 1986, p.61–84.

Research reviewed supports the hypothesis that Type A individuals are hyper-reactive to subjective work stressors. However, examination of objective stressors is rare. Hyper-responsivity of Type A persons to challenging stimuli has been widely observed in the laboratory, but field studies have not yet convincingly replicated these results.

DSC Shelfmark: 5027.068000

(378)
PSYCHOLOGICAL predictors of heart disease: a quantitative review
S Booth-Kewley and H S Friedman
Psychological bulletin, vol. 101, 1987, p.343-362.

Reports results of a meta-analysis performed to integrate and organise the results of studies that investigated certain personality variables in relation to coronary heart disease (CHD). Personality variables included were anger, hostility, aggression, depression, extroversion, anxiety and Type A. Strongest associations with CHD were found for Type A and depression, but anger, hostility, aggression and anxiety also related reliably to CHD. The Structured Interview diagnosis of Type A was shown to be clearly superior to the Jenkins Activity Survey as a predictor of CHD. The Type A-CHD relation was smaller in prospective than cross-sectional studies and smaller in recent than in less recent studies.

DSC Shelfmark: 6946.300000

(379)
COMPONENTS of hostility and the severity of coronary artery disease
A W Siegman, T M Dembroski and N Ringel
Psychosomatic medicine, vol. 49, 1987, p.127-135.

Study examined the relationship of two dimensions of hostility, experienced anger associated with neuroticism and expressed anger, to severity of coronary artery disease. For patients 60 years and younger results were significant, showing that expressed anger was positively related to severity of disease, whereas experienced anger was inversely associated with extent of disease. Individuals high in neurotic hostility feel resentment at their life situation, believe they have been frequently mistreated and suspect the motives of most other people. Persons high in expressive hostility often display or express anger and annoyance, and are capable of physical violence if pushed.

DSC Shelfmark: 6946.555000

(380)
HISTORICAL and current developments in coronary-prone behavior
T M Dembroski and S M Czajkowski
In: In search of coronary-prone behavior: beyond Type A edited by A. W. Siegman and T M Dembroski. Hillsdale, N J: Erlbaum, 1989. p.21-37.

Explains that with the utility of the global Type A Behaviour Pattern as a tool for identifying individuals at risk for CHD currently being called into question, investigation of the role of hostility in CHD development and occurrence represents the most promising strategy for clarifying the evolving concept of the coronary-prone personality.

DSC Shelfmark: 89/06781

(381)
IN search of coronary prone behavior: beyond Type A
A W Siegman and T M Dembroski
Hillsdale, N J: Erlbaum, 1989. 244p.

Describes research which examines whether some of the components of the multidimensional Type A behaviour pattern are related to clinical manifestations of coronary heart disease. There is mounting evidence that the hostility component of the TABP confers risk for CHD. Research is currently under way to determine whether some facets of hostility confer more risk than others.

DSC Shelfmark: 89/06781

(382)
THE RELATIONSHIP between the Type A behavior pattern and physiological responsivity: a quantitative review
T J Harbin
Psychophysiology, vol. 26, 1989, p.110–119.

Results of a meta-analysis indicate that Type As respond to cognitive and psychomotor stimulus situations with greater heart rate and systolic blood pressure responses, that this relationship is not evident in females, that the relationship is more evident for some cognitive tasks than for others, and that the strength of the relationship depends on the instrument used to assess Type A behaviour.

DSC Shelfmark: 6946.552000

(383)
TYPE A behavior in the work setting: a review and some new data
D C Ganster, W E Sime and B T Mayes
In: In search of coronary prone behavior: beyond Type A edited by A W Siegman and T M Dembroski. Hillsdale, N J: Erlbaum, 1989, p.169–194.

Provides an overview of early field research which has examined the Type A Behaviour Pattern (TABP) in the context of work stress. Concludes that support for the hypothesis that TABP moderates the stress-strain relationship is relatively common with respect to responses to perceived stressors. Empirical support for causal relationships between Type A and objective stressors is very weak. There is no evidence that Type A individuals choose to work in more stressful occupations. Existing field studies yield little insight as to whether Type A individuals, through their behaviour, partially determine their exposure to stressors, or whether prolonged exposure to such stressors encourages the development of the pattern.

DSC Shelfmark: 89/06781

(384)

EXAMINING the relationships among self-report measures of the Type A behavior pattern: the effects of dimensionality, measurement error, and differences in underlying constructs

J R Edwards, A J Baglioni, and C L Cooper

Journal of applied psychology, vol. 75, 1990, p.440-454.

The most popular self-report measures of the Type A Behaviour Pattern (TABP) are the Bortner Scale, the Framingham Scale, and the Jenkins Activity Survey (JAS). Low correlations among these measures are attributable to a combination of differences in underlying constructs, measurement error and multidimensionality. These factors not only lower the correlations among the measures, but also suggest serious flaws in their psychometric properties. The measures need to be substantially modified or replaced with measures of specific TABP dimensions.

DSC Shelfmark: 4947.000000

(385)

RELATIONSHIP of job stress, and Type A behavior to employees' job satisfaction, organizational commitment, psychosomatic health problems and turnover motivation

M Jamal

Human relations, vol. 43, 1990, p.727-738.

In a study of 215 nurses working in a large Canadian hospital, job stressors (role ambiguity, overload, conflict and resource inadequacy) were significantly related to the four outcome variables. Type-A behaviour pattern was found to be independently related to role ambiguity, conflict, resource inadequacy, and psychosomatic health problems. In addition Type A behaviour was found to be an important moderator of stress-outcome relations.

DSC Shelfmark: 4336.400000

(386)

TYPE A behavior pattern: a personal overview

R H Rosenman

Journal of social behavior and personality, vol. 5, 1990, p.1-24.

Reviews evidence for a link between Type A behaviour and its components (hostility and competitiveness) and cardiovascular heart disease (CHD).

DSC Shelfmark: 5064: 751500

(387)

MEASUREMENT of Type A behavior pattern: an assessment of criterion-oriented validity, content validity and construct validity

J R Edwards

In Personality and stress: individual differences in the stress process edited by C L Cooper and R Payne. Chichester: Wiley, 1991, p.151-179.

Evidence for criterion-oriented validity is fairly strong for the Structured Interview (SI), mixed for the Jenkins Activity Survey (JAS) and Bortner scale, and limited but supportive for the Framingham scale. None of the measures reviewed evidenced adequate content validity, and evidence for construct validity varied depending on the psychometric property under consideration.

DSC Shelfmark: 91/20462

(388)

THE NOMOLOGICAL validity of the Type A personality among employed adults

D C Ganster *et al*

Journal of applied psychology monograph, vol. 76, 1991, p.143-168.

The Structured Interview (SI) and a battery of personality trait, physical health and strain measures were administered to an occupationally diverse sample of 568 workers. Subjects were also monitored for physiological reactivity to, and recovery from, the SI and a subsequent Stroop Colour-Word Conflict Task. A confirmatory factor analysis demonstrated that SI scores can be factored into three distinct dimensions (Hostility, Speech Characteristics and Answer Content). Only the Hostility dimension was significantly related to physiological reactivity and recovery.

DSC Shelfmark: 4947.005000

(389)

THE RELATIONSHIP between stress and coping among Type As

E R Greenglass and R J Burke

Journal of social behavior and personality, vol. 6, 1991, p.361-373.

Study was designed to examine the relationship between Type A, coping, and work stress, and various psychosomatic outcomes in a sample of female and male teaching personnel. Data were collected by mail-out questionnaire. Results showed that certain coping forms (internal control and preventive coping) appeared to be acting as buffers or moderators of the negative outcomes of work stress, in this case anxiety and depression. This effect was observed in Type As and not in Type Bs.

DSC Shelfmark: 5064.751500

(390)

STRESS and distress as a function of Jenkins Activity Survey-defined Type A behavior and control over the work environment

F Rhodewalt *et al*

Basic and applied social psychology, vol. 12, 1991, p.211-226.

Study aimed to identify factors in the work situation which lead Type A individuals to perceive their job as stressful. A sample of 336 male school principals (categorized as Type A or Type B by the Jenkins Activity Survey) completed questionnaires assessing their degree of control in their work environment, perceived job stress and physical and psychological well-being. A path mediation analysis indicated that Type A individuals reported more job stress under lower levels of perceived control, and that higher job stress levels subsequently led to greater incidence of physical and psychological symptoms, especially for Type As.

DSC Shelfmark: 1863.913300

(391)

EFFECTS of demand and decision-latitude on cardiovascular reactivity among coronary-prone women and men

J W Burns, J Hutt and G Weidner

Behavioral medicine, vol. 19, 1993, p.122-128.

Evaluation of the degree to which individual differences in Type A behaviour and hostility may interact with factors of demand and decision latitude to explain variance in cardiovascular reactivity. Results showed that conditions of low demand/high decision latitude (ie. low strain) appeared to be related to minimal diastolic blood pressure increases only among Type B subjects. Hostility did not emerge as a moderator but was found to be independently related to systolic blood pressure changes among men, regardless of levels of demand and decision latitude.

DSC Shelfmark: 1877.560000

(392)

COMPONENTS of Type A behavior pattern and occupational stressor-strain relationship: testing different models in a sample of industrial managers

M Kivimäki, R Kalimo, and J Julkunen

Behavioral medicine, vol. 22, 1996, p.67-76.

Study explored the roles of the impatience-irritability and ambition-energy components of Type A behaviour pattern in the occupational stress-strain relationship. A sample of 659 industrial managers was used to determine whether the TABP components affected strain independently of perceived stressors, or by moderating the effects of perceived stressors, or whether perceived stressors provoked TABP components, which in turn influenced the number of strain symptoms. The impatience-irritability component consistently increased numbers of psychological and physiological symptoms regardless of perceived occupational stressors. The ambition-energy component, on the other hand, was activated by an abundance of development possibilities experienced at work. This in turn partly explained a decrease in perceived levels of psychological and physiological symptoms.

DSC Shelfmark: 1877.560000

(393)
TYPE A and Type B behaviors, work stressors and social support at work
A Hagihara *et al*
Preventive medicine, vol. 26, 1997, p.486-494.

Study used signal detection analysis to identify respective aspects of work perceived as stressful by Type A and B workers. Interactions of social support at work and stressor variables among Type A and B workers were also evaluated. Except for one significant predictor (being unable to learn new things at work), the perceived causes of mental stress were quite different for Type A and B workers. Specifically, social support from management was a cause of mental stress for certain groups of Type A workers.

DSC Shelfmark: 6612.790000

(394)
TYPE A behavior, well-being, work overload and role-related stress in information work
P T van den Berg and R Schalk
Journal of social behavior and personality, vol. 12, 1997, p.175-187.

Self-report data were gathered by questionnaire from a sample of 893 employees holding office jobs in a large insurance company, a library, and a staffing organisation. Path analysis showed that work overload partially mediated the relationship between Type A behaviour and well-being, in that Type As perceived their tasks as more demanding, or made them more demanding, than Type Bs. The hypothesis that Type As are more vulnerable to the damaging effects of work overload than Type Bs was not supported.

DSC Shelfmark: 5064.751500

(395)
PSYCHOSOCIAL influences on blood pressure during daily life
R A Carels, A Sherwood and J A Blumenthal
International journal of psychophysiology, vol. 20, 1998, p.117-124.

Article reviews psychosocial research relating ambulatory blood pressure (ABP) to psychological factors (e.g. Type A behaviour, anger/hostility) and environmental factors (e.g. job strain). Psychological factors and environmental factors alone and in interaction with each other appear to substantially influence ABP.

DSC Shelfmark: 4542.506500

5   Stress Costs and Consequences

5.1   Introduction

The experience of stress can alter the way in which individuals feel, think and behave and can also produce changes in physiological functioning. Many of these changes simply represent mild health symptoms such as headaches or indigestion and modest subclinical levels of anxiety or depressed mood. Although distressing at the time, they are easily reversible and cause no permanent damage. However, for some workers, and under some circumstances, they may translate into poor performance at work, serious psychological and social problems and poor physical health.

The following sections summarise the possible effects of stress on physical and psychological health and well-being. We then look at behavioural outcomes of stress such as smoking and substance use which may effect health. Finally we examine the organisational costs of stress-related ill-health in terms of sickness absence, poor performance and legal liability.

5.2   Stress and health outcomes

The relationship between stress and ill-health is contentious due to continuing difficulties in establishing the link between exposure to the stress factors and the development of diseases. Ganster and Schaubroeck in their incisive review (1991, ref no. 404) show that, although the general notion that prolonged exposure to stressful job demands can lead to a variety of pathological outcomes receives support from a broad literature in behavioural medicine and epidemiology, close inspection of the research into the effects of specific work-related stressors fails to produce a satisfying picture of how, or even whether, certain work experiences lead to physical or mental disorders. They identify methodological weakness in all four of the main types of study used by researchers attempting to determine the extent of association between stress exposures at work and serious health outcomes.

Studies at the occupational level of analysis examine how prevalence of diseases and mortality rates vary between occupations or jobs which are categorised as stressful or non-stressful. Occupational variation can be measured either through the use of fairly objective occupational classifications (e.g. retail sales person) and the relation of these to aggregate health data. Alternatively, data about job characteristics can be collected using self-report surveys and then aggregated to occupational status as in the work of Karasek and his colleagues (1981, ref. no. 438; 1989, ref. no. 278; 1990, ref. no. 282). In this occupational literature, weak results are so common and alternative interpretations of findings so pervasive that is not possible to glean conclusions concerning the role work stressors in causing disease (Reed *et al*, 1989, ref. no. 79; Pieper, La Croix and Karasek, 1989, ref. no. 442; Albright *et al*, 1992, ref. no. 449; Colligan *et al*, 1977, ref. no. 491).

Studies using self-reports for both stressors and health status are the most common in the literature. They obtain measures of perceived workplace stressors such as role conflict, role ambiguity, lack of control, etc and evaluate strength of their association with self-reported strains such as depression, anxiety and physical health complaints. The limitations of this kind of study are many. Apparent associations may be statistical artefacts arising from methodological errors. Many of these studies are cross-sectional and causality cannot be proven, although the implicit assumption is that the stressor causes the strain. However, results may be interpreted the other way round. For example, a person who is dissatisfied with his/her job may perceive the work environment as riddled with stressors such as overwork, difficult colleagues, unreasonable deadlines, etc. Apparent associations between subjective stressors and self-reported health outcomes may also reflect nothing more than the influence of a third factor. We have already seen that the personality trait of Negative Affectivity has recently been receiving much attention in this regard. Put simply, this means that a person who is a natural pessimist will be prone to view the work environment as more stressful than a natural optimist, regardless of objective reality. Finally Kasl (1986, ref. no. 399) points out that survey questions about workplace stressors (eg. to what extent do conflicting demands from different people at work cause stress in your job?) may contain so much conceptual overlap with questions about outcomes (e.g. how much work-related tension do you experience on your job?) that their correlation reveals little of theoretical or practical significance.

Studies using self-reported stressors and objective outcomes are a methodological improvement on total dependence on self-report data. Objective outcome measures are most commonly physiological measurements that are interpreted either as indicators of stress based arousal or as precursors of disease. The problem with studies in this category is that overall they have not shown a consistent relationship between self-reports of stress factors and physiological indicators of disease (Greenlund *et al*, 1995, ref. no. 457; Albright *et al*, 1992, ref. no. 449, etc.).

Studies using objective assessments of job stressors attempt to link objective work demands to either subjective or objective indicators of a stress response. An early classic study of this kind by Friedman, Rosenman and Carroll (1958, ref. no. 437) revealed that tax accountants' levels of serum cholesterol rose as the tax deadline approached and returned to normal after this busy period. One of the most comprehensive studies of this kind was undertaken by Rose and his colleagues (1987, ref. no. 401). This 5 year longitudinal study of air traffic controllers comprehensively measured objective work demands, subjects' appraisals of demands, job attitudes, physiological indicators of strain and changes in physical and mental health. Overall, studies of this type present a believable picture of how individuals respond emotionally and physiologically to periods of acute high workloads or events in which performance is critical. It is not clear, however, what implications there are in these short term responses for the development of disease.

5.3   Pathways to disease

Physical ill-health has been associated with stress through self-report data and statistical analysis of prevalence by occupation, yet the psychophysiological pathways that connect stress to disease largely remain to be specified. Very little is known about the precise mechanisms whereby stress increases health risks. This is partly because the ill effects of stress on health remained hidden for a long time, and partly because our knowledge of the causes of many diseases is still limited. Stress and disease are interrelated via a complex interplay of physiological and psychological processes, and it is impossible to describe their associations simply in terms of cause and effect. Models specifying the manner by which stress may directly or indirectly influence the development of medical disorders commonly assume that changes in bodily functioning under acute or chronic stress may, in conjunction with pre-existing risk factors, trigger pathophysiological processes. These, in turn, may cause changes in the body's regulatory mechanisms, lead to tissue damage, provoke the development of malignant processes, or suppress the immune system (Gaillard and Wientjes, 1994, ref. no. 405). Sutherland and Cooper (1990, ref. no. 56) based on Krantz, Grunberg and Baum (1985, ref. no. 398) suggest the following possible pathways and mechanisms:

•   Hormonal and chemical defence mechanisms are triggered in response to stress, as part of the "fight or flight" mechanism. The sympathetic division of the autonomic nervous system mobilises the body for action. Sympathetic activity causes the blood vessels of the skin to constrict, the muscle blood vessels to dilate and sweat to be secreted. The adrenal medulla (the inner portion of the adrenal gland) is triggered to increase the secretion of adrenalin and noradrenalin. Adrenalin is a powerful cardiac stimulant that accelerates the heart rate and increases cardiac output. Exposure to stress also increases the production of cortisol from the adrenal cortex (the outer portion of the adrenal gland). Cortisol, the most active steroid of the glucocorticoid group, influences carbohydrate and protein metabolism. The synthesis of the carbohydrate glycogen in the liver is promoted and the production of glucose from protein is encouraged by the glucocorticoids, raising the blood sugar level. Overall, the process enhances one's level of arousal because the cognitive, neurological, cardiovascular and muscular systems are stimulated as the body prepares for an emergency in response to a sudden shock. The heart rate is increased, glucose stored as glycogen in the liver is released for energy, blood supplies are redirected from the skin to the brain and skeletal muscles and the secretion of sweat increases.

- It is suggested that modern man is denied the natural dissipation of these physiological changes in fighting or running and that therefore our natural response to stress may ultimately cause harm. Enduring threatening or adverse conditions may lead to a state of chronic stress. Chronic stress is characterised by emotional vulnerability, persistent negative emotions, elevated hormonal base levels, hyper-activity of the autonomic nervous system so that the body never relaxes, and tendencies to experience psychosomatic symptoms. Over time this state of affairs may cause illness due to the wear-and-tear on tissues, in particular the target organ. (Zegans, 1982, ref. no. 397). Chronic stress may play a part in the development of diseases in several ways. Firstly, chronic stress responses may not necessarily directly trigger the disease process, but may promote an already-existing pathology. Secondly, pathological processes may be triggered in the physiological system in which a particular individual shows greatest reactivity. Thirdly, it is suggested that the physiological responses may be dependent on coping style. Active or aggressive coping styles may be associated with qualitatively and quantitatively different modes of physiological responses from defensive or palliative coping styles.

- Stress may lead to health impairing habits or behaviours. If it is not possible to remove the source of stress, the individual may resort to the use of palliatives. The negative impact of stress may be reduced by escapist eating, drinking alcohol or use of drugs such as tobacco, which are risk factors for certain kinds of diseases.

- The stress of illness may cause behaviour which influences the course of the disease. Therefore, the way in which a patient perceives and copes with the stress of illness is the mechanism that influences the disease. A fighting spirit, for example, may increase the survival times of cancer patients.

5.4   Gastrointestinal disorders

Since the beginning of the century gastrointestinal disorders, especially peptic ulcer, have been considered to be archetypal examples of stress-related diseases. However, the discovery in 1983 of *Helicobacter pylori* in gastric mucosa and the demonstration that it is present in the gastric mucosa of 85% to 100% of patients suffering from duodenal ulcer has revolutionised thinking about the likely causation of the disease, and its redefinition as an infectious disorder. Given the widespread occurrence of infection with *H. pylori* in both first and third world populations, only a very few actually develop duodenal ulcers. Other factors have to be operative to determine why ulcers develop in certain people. This deduction is reinforced by the knowledge that a small percentage of chronic duodenal ulcer patients are neither infected with *H. pylori* nor have been exposed to agents such as alcohol and cigarettes which may trigger the development or activation of the condition. The epidemiological, clinical and genetic evidence suggests that the effects of stress may be decisive in determining who develops a duodenal ulcer (Melmed and Gelpin, 1996, ref. no. 412).

There is good evidence that work patterns contribute to the development of gastrointestinal disorders. Irregular meals are related to gastrointestinal disorders, especially peptic ulceration, and many blue collar workers and professionals in the human services are required to work various shift patterns including night working which encourage skipping meals and making do with snacks. Vener, Szabo and Moore (1989, ref. no. 154) hypothesise that shiftwork may lead to ulcer disease in the following way. Altered sleep patterns produce marked changes in adrenal secretary patterns, digestive enzyme secretion, feeding patterns and gastrointestinal motility. It is possible to conceive of shiftwork as producing a "stress like" state, due to the continual process of disruption of the biorhythms which most often operates in shiftworkers. In those individuals who are susceptible, ulcer disease occurs. In 1979 House and his colleagues (ref. no. 408) reported a link between work stress – particularly stressful relations with others – and ulcers after eliminating seven possible alternative explanations. House's study showed that effects of work stress could be buffered by a supportive supervisor. Low levels of reported supervisor support were related to the occurrence of ulcers, angina pectoris, itch and rash.

The role of stressful life events in the development of duodenal ulcer was investigated by Gilligan and his colleagues (1987, ref. no. 409) using a semi-structured face to face interviewing technique in a group of 66 ulcer patients and a matched physically healthy control group. The results showed no difference in the frequency of stressful life events between patients and controls. However, the investigation of chronic difficulties showed, in all instances except one, that the duodenal ulcer patients experienced more chronic difficulties than paired matched controls. The authors argue that chronic difficulties produce chronic emotional arousal (anxiety or depression) and this is associated with chronic changes in the autonomic nervous system and the immune system that might be linked to duodenal ulcer disease in some way.

Psychological stress is also implicated in disorders of gastrointestinal motility (unconscious or involuntary movement). Gastrointestinal motility is controlled directly by the enteric nervous system (ENS). This is a complex network of intrinsic neurons that regulate the motor activity of the esophagus, stomach, small intestine and colon. Stressors may influence the central nervous system to select dysfunctional motility patterns for implementation by the ENS. Experimental stress in humans can affect gastric emptying, small intestinal motility and colonic motility. The most consistently documented alteration in gastrointestinal motility associated with experimental stress in humans is increased contractile activity of the colon. Altered colonic and small intestinal contractions have also been found in functional bowel diseases such as irritable bowel syndrome. Evidence has been put forward that some components of the gastrointestinal response to stress may be mediated by extrapituitary actions of corticotrophin-releasing factor (CRF). Identification of CRF as a critical link in the effect of psychological stress factors on gastrointestinal motility provides opportunities to understand one of the most typical responses of the body to stress (Burks, 1991, ref. no. 410).

5.5 Diabetes

Diabetes mellitus is defined as the existence of abnormally high glucose in the blood stream and is a disorder of carbohydrate metabolism due mainly to insulin deficiency. It is in this context that stress and the stress-related stimulation of blood sugar are implicated in its onset. There is some evidence that stress is associated with an increase in blood glucose in non–diabetic subjects, and that the removal of the stress facilitates return to normal (Wales, 1995, ref. no. 418). However, the evidence that stress actually causes the clinical syndrome of diabetes is weaker and equivocal. Criticism has been levelled at the research methodology used in laboratory designs in terms of use of unrepresentative samples, the mixing of Type I (juvenile-onset) and Type II (mature onset) patients, the lack of certainty that the experimental stressor condition was actually perceived as stressful by the subjects, the fact that blood glucose level might not be the best measure of the impact of stress, the lack of attention paid to circadian rhythms, and the high degree of individual variation that exists in patients and controls (Shillitoe, 1988, ref. no. 416) Although there is little scientific evidence that stress can cause diabetes *de novo*, there is more support for the concept that stress may precipitate clinical diabetes in a person who is predisposed to the condition. Some support for this is found in a study of Pima Indians who have a strong genetic predisposition to non–insulin dependent diabetes. A 10-minute mental arithmetic test induced an increase in blood glucose levels in the Pima Indians but not in the control group of white subjects (Surwit, 1990, ref. no. 417).

Another line of research has been to investigate the effects of environmental stress agents such as major life events and/or daily hassles on diabetes. Findings indicate that it is necessary to distinguish between positive and negative experiences. That is, stress agents producing happiness tend to send the blood glucose down, whilst factors producing feelings of worry, sadness and frustration are associated with increased blood glucose. Both Cox and his colleagues (1984, ref. no. 414) and Hanson and Pichert (1986, ref. no. 415) found that blood glucose level is associated with the number of reported hassles, even when the effects of diet, exercise, insulin and food intake are excluded from the analysis.

5.6   Musculoskeletal disorders

It is generally agreed that back pain and other musculoskeletal disorders have many causes. Heavy physical work, motor vehicle driving and prolonged standing are generally accepted as risk factors for back trouble. Ergonomic factors such as lifting in bent or twisted postures also have an impact on low back pain. Repetitive strain or static work load, eg. sitting for long periods in constrained postures, may contribute to occupational disorders of the neck, shoulders and upper limbs. However, exposure to a particular set of working conditions may cause discomfort or pain for some individuals but not for others. The perceived pain and ability to work despite it also varies from person to person. It is generally accepted that work-related physical load in relation to individual functional capacity can only partially explain the high prevalence of musculoskeletal disease. Walsh and his colleagues estimate (1989, ref. no. 419) that only 20% of back symptoms can be explained by physical load. Recently the potential significance of psychosocial factors as contributory causes of musculoskeletal disorders has received increasing attention. Analysis of their role in the development of musculoskeletal disorders may contribute to the understanding and reduction of work-related musculoskeletal disease and disability (Vender, Kasdan and Trappa, 1995, ref. no. 430).

Psychosocial factors at work may directly influence the mechanical load through changes in posture, movement and exerted forces. For example, time pressure may increase hurried movements with poor posture. Alternatively, pressures such as high job demands, low control and lack of social support, together with personal capacity to cope with such factors, may increase work-related stress. This increase in stress may increase muscle tension, which may lead to the development of musculoskeletal symptoms through some as yet unknown physiological mechanism, e.g. hormonal path. It may also increase an individual's awareness of musculoskeletal symptoms or reduce his/her capacity to cope with them. Thus musculoskeletal symptoms due to heavy physical work may be prolonged or intensified.

Studies on the role of psychosocial factors in the development of musculoskeletal disorders suffer from many of the same limitations as the generality of published investigations of the link between stress factors and ill health:

- Many of the studies are cross-sectional, so that cause and effect cannot be established with certainty. Psychosocial factors may contribute to the development of musculoskeletal disorders, or existing Musculoskeletal problems may sharpen the perception of unsatisfactory working conditions.

- Few studies conduct a physical examination to confirm the objective existence of musculoskeletal problems. Most rely on self-reports. When both the stress factors and health outcomes are based on self-reports, an apparent relationship can arise from general dissatisfaction and a readiness to report complaints. It can be hypothesised that psychosocial factors, stress symptoms and individual characteristics are more strongly related to complaints about unspecified aches and pains than to clinically diagnosed disorders such as slipped disc (Skov, Borg and Ørhede, 1996, ref. no. 431).

- In assessing the importance of psychosocial factors in the development of musculoskeletal symptoms, it is important to take into account the effects of physical load. Many studies fail to do this. Those which do take physical load into account mostly rely on self-reports for its assessment. Some occupations, such as health care, are both physically and emotionally demanding. In these cases it is difficult to disentangle the effects of physical load from those of emotional distress.

When the reported data in a representative sample of studies is combined, the weight of the evidence supports the conclusion that monotonous work, time pressure and perceived high work load are each associated with musculoskeletal trouble. Several studies also highlight the importance of social relations at work in the development of musculoskeletal disorders. Leino and Hänninen (1995, ref. no. 428) found that dissatisfaction with social relationships at work predicted an increase in musculoskeletal disease. Ahlberg-Hultén, Theorell and Sigala (1995, ref. no. 429) showed that symptoms of the neck and shoulders were associated with social support at work – the lower the support score, the more severe the symptoms. The importance of job control to workers health is again highlighted, in that one of the most consistent findings in the literature reviewed is the association of low job control/intellectual discretion with the incidence of musculoskeletal problems (Houtman *et al*, 1994, ref. no. 426; Leino and Hänninen, 1995, ref. no. 428; Skov, Borg and Ørhede, 1996, ref. no. 431, etc.).

Theorell and his colleagues (1991, ref. no. 421) propose muscle tension as a pathway from psychosocially adverse working conditions to symptoms of the musculoskeletal system. In their study, strong relationships were observed between muscle tension and emotional states, psychological demands and lack of possibility to talk at work. Muscle tension in turn was related to back, neck or shoulder symptoms. No information was presented about any direct associations between stress symptoms and symptoms of the back, neck or shoulders, although self-reported stress symptoms were found to relate to self-reported muscle tension.

Ursin and his colleagues (Ursin, 1993, ref. no. 423) suggest that chronic muscle pain develops in muscles that perform prolonged static or repetitive monotonous contractions. This type of contraction may be a consequence of physical work, may be related to posture or may be part of psychological activation of the system due to anxiety. Pain itself tends to increase the tension and a vicious circle is set up producing more pain.

208

It is clear that the relationship of psychosocial factors at work to the development of disorders of the musculoskeletal system is not well understood. It is important for future research to assess the psychosocial factors at work through observation or with neutral questions. The workers' perception of these factors, and self-reported stress and stress symptoms need to be combined with objective measurement of physical load and confirmation of the actual presence of musculoskeletal symptoms and signs through physical examination (Bongers *et al*, 1993, ref. no. 424).

5.7   Cardiovascular disease

Epidemiological studies have identified several risk factors for cardiovascular disease (CVD), including genetic influences, high blood pressure, high serum cholesterol levels, high lipoproteins in the blood, cigarette smoking, obesity, glucose intolerance and lack of exercise. Several research traditions have also implicated psychosocial stress as a potential risk factor. Models focus either on personal characteristics such as Type A behaviour or hostility or on environmental stressors such as low socioeconomic status, unemployment, social isolation, or occupational stress. The literature on the link between occupational stress and cardiovascular disease has been dominated by Karasek's job demands–control or "job strain" model. Karasek defines job strain as occurring in jobs characterised by high "psychological workload demands" combined with low decision latitude. Decision latitude is defined as the combination of decision-making authority at work and use of skills on the job. High strain jobs are hypothesised to result in biological arousal, which leads to elevated levels of hormones such adrenalin and noradrenalin and to raised blood pressure, which in turn contribute to the ultimate development of CVD. In addition, job strain may promote unhealthy coping behaviours, such as smoking, which also contribute to CVD. Karasek's ideas are explained in more detail in Chapter 2.

Most, but not all, published studies which have tested the job demands–control model have found a significant positive relationship between job strain and CVD. Early studies relied upon available national databases in Sweden or the US to link job characteristics with CVD. More recent studies have tended to focus on CVD risk factors such as elevated blood pressure in smaller-scale surveys in which individual level exposure and outcome data were collected. Positive associations have been reported in both blue-collar and white-collar workers, in both men and women, and among cross-sectional, case control and cohort studies. Although the weight of the evidence does seem to support Karasek's model, methodological threats to the validity of the studies have been identified, including:

- Low response rates to surveys leading to unrepresentative samples.

- Testing of the model at an occupation level of analysis, where certain types of job are classified as inherently stressful. The problem here is that it is not possible to rule out confounding by socioeconomic status, health behaviour or variability of job characteristics within occupations. That is, high prevalence of CHD within certain occupational groups may be due to the social class, educational level or unhealthy lifestyle of the workers, rather than to adverse job characteristics.

- The fact that workers may leave certain jobs due to ill health. There is evidence of older workers leaving high strain jobs. In Sweden, among individuals whose job characteristics did not change over six years, prospective job strain/heart disease associations were stronger than in the full population. If workers leaving high strain jobs are also leaving the workforce because of illness, and only employees in good health are left behind, then samples drawn from the working population will be unrepresentative and this will lead to an underestimate of the significance of the relationship between job strain and CVD.

- Self-report bias is a danger in many job strain studies since data has been gathered through questionnaires completed by study participants. Self-reports may be inaccurate descriptions of job characteristics and health outcomes, or may be distorted by personality traits such as negative affectivity.

The biological mechanisms by which occupational stress acts to influence the development of CVD are not fully understood. Occupational stress may influence known risk factors for CVD, such as blood pressure, blood lipid levels, or smoking. Stress may precipitate heart attacks among vulnerable persons with underlying coronary artery disease through, for instance, increased sympathoadrenal activity. In response to stress, the sympathetic nervous system will act to accelerate the heart rate, constrict blood vessels and raise blood pressure. Adrenalin released into the blood stream from the adrenal gland in response to stress is a powerful heart stimulant. Dimsdale and Moss (1980, ref. no. 71) showed that adrenalin and noradrenalin levels increased in response to either psychological or physical stress. They found that noradrenalin levels were predominantly elevated in response to exercise, while adrenalin levels rose to a greater extent during stress-provoking public speaking. Frankenhaeuser has shown that in demanding, low-control jobs levels of both adrenalin and cortisol are elevated as effort with distress is experienced. On the other hand, under demanding conditions where the organism can exert control in the face of controllable and predictable stressors, adrenalin levels increase but cortisol decreases. Effort without distress is experience. Present models, however, are unlikely to capture the full complexity of the actual stress response. For example Rose in his longitudinal study of air traffic controllers (1987, ref. no. 401) found that men who showed a significant increase in cortisol as work increased were not more distressed, less competent or more dissatisfied. They suffered less frequent illness episodes that non-responders. They were judged by their peers to be more competent and described themselves as more satisfied with their jobs. These findings were opposite to expectations. That is, those with higher cortisol levels at work might be interpreted as being chronically stressed, which would lead to greater frequency of illnesses.

There is now general acceptance of the role of cholesterol and lipoprotein levels in human atherosclerosis (hardening of the arteries), and the benefits of lowering cholesterol by means of diet and drug therapy have been demonstrated. Cholesterol, lipids (free fatty acids) and cellular debris form plaques in the inner layers of arterial walls. The vessel walls become thick and hard and blood flow is reduced. Elevated concentrations of triglycerides and low-density lipoprotein (LDL) cholesterol especially in combination with low concentrations of high-density lipoprotein (HDL) cholesterol are associated with an increased risk of atherosclerosis, coronary heart disease and stroke. Triglycerides are compounds consisting of a fatty acid and glycerol. They are the principle lipids in the blood, where they circulate, bound to a protein, as high- and low- density lipoproteins. While several dietary and genetic factors contribute to atherogenic lipoprotein profiles, stress also has a role in producing unfavourable concentrations of lipoproteins which may predispose to cardiovascular disease. Blood lipid concentrations increase after brief exposure to acute stressors in uncontrolled naturally occurring settings and after stressful tasks and situations are presented in the laboratory. These tasks include mental arithmetic, the Stroop Colour-Work Interference test and speaking before a video camera. The effects of chronic stress on blood lipids have been documented most extensively in naturalistic studies with varying lengths or severity of the stressor. Results show that short term and moderate stressors do not appear to exert strong effects on blood lipids, and only relatively severe stressors are likely to lead to changes. For example, studies of job insecurity and occupational instability can demonstrate increased levels of total cholesterol which persist as long as the stress is present, often for one to two years.

One way in which stress may influence lipid concentrations is through stress-induced hormonal changes that affect lipid metabolism. Stress leads to increased concentrations of cortisol, catecholamines (adrenalin and noradrenalin) and fatty acids in the blood. Stress-induced increases in cortisol, catecholamines and fatty acids in turn have a number of effects on the metabolism of lipoproteins.

Individuals may attempt to cope with, or respond to, perceived stressors by altering their diet, smoking more or exercising less. These behavioural responses can, in turn, affect blood lipid concentrations. It is note-worthy that several such responses can occur simultaneously, further contributing to elevated lipid concentrations. Stress in various forms influences eating in humans. In a study of stress associated with work deadlines in office workers, subjects consumed more calories, fat and a greater proportion of calories from fat during periods of high rather than low workload. Given the role of dietary fat and obesity in determining blood lipid concentrations, this study points to a dietary influence mediating the relationship between stress and lipid levels (McCann, Warnick and Knopp, 1990, ref. no. 443). Cigarette smoking is associated with detrimental changes in almost all lipids and lipoproteins. Smoking often increases in response to stress, and smoking status and intensity is associated with certain personality characteristics, eg. hostility. This interrelation may also exert an influence on serum lipids, and it should be taken into account in studies of stress, personality and blood lipids (Conway *et al*, 1981, ref. no. 511).

5.8   Stress and the immune system

The role of stress in inducing immunological disturbances in humans has been the subject of keen interest over the past several years. To facilitate understanding of the evidence of how stress affects the immune system, it is useful to keep a basic model in mind. The model predicts that certain combinations of stress factors and stress buffers in the social environment will act through individual response and adaptation to produce biological changes in the immune system that can result in greater susceptibility to illness. For example, personal characteristics such as age and health and psychosocial and environmental factors such as social support and employment status interact with the individual's personality to predict that person's ability to cope with stress. Failure to cope adequately, as evidenced by symptoms such as insomnia, anxiety and/or depression, is thought to produce changes in neuroendocrine and autonomic pathways from the brain that alter immune function. Such impairment of the functioning of the immune system is thought to produce an increased susceptibility to diseases and changes in health outcomes. Increased incidence of influenza, pneumonia, tuberculosis, and streptococcal and herpes infections in stressed persons is thought to be associated with immunological under-activity, whereas stress-related increase in the rates of arthritis, other autoimmune disorders and allergies may reflect immune overactivity (Cohen and Williamson, 1991, ref. no. 403; Irwin, 1991, ref. no. 463).

A comprehensive description of the human immune system is well beyond the scope of this review. However, an understanding of basic immune function sufficient for comprehension of the research findings on interactions between stress and the immune system is not difficult to attain. The immune system is a surveillance mechanism whose general function is to identify and eliminate foreign, "non-self" materials that contact or enter the body. These foreign materials are called antigens and include bacteria, viruses, parasites and fungi. Components of the immune system are also capable of identifying and destroying cells that have undergone alterations associated with malignancy. The immune system is composed of specialised cells that originate in the bone marrow, mature and are stored in particular organs such as the thymus, spleen and lymph nodes and from there are released into the blood.

The most important cells in the immune system are the leukocytes, commonly called white blood cells. There are three main categories of leukocytes: granulocytic cells, monocytes/macrophages and lymphocytes. Granulocytic leukocytes include (a) neutrophils (also called polymorphonuclear leukocytes or PMNs) which are phagocytes that engulf and destroy bacteria in a nonspecific manner, (b) eosinophils, which engulf antigen-antibody complexes (described later), and (c) basophils, which release histamine to increase vascular permeability during inflammatory responses, thus facilitating the migration of other immune cells to the region. Monocytes/macrophages recognise certain carbohydrates on the surfaces of micro-organisms, which are then engulfed and destroyed. These cells also play other roles in the immune response, such as "presenting" antigens to lymphocytes. Monocyte is the name given to the cell in its less mature form, when it resides in the blood stream. When it enters tissue, the cell is referred to as a macrophage. Lymphocytes are cells designed to attack specific targets and are predominantly of two types: T and B cells. B lymphocytes comprise the humoral arm of the immune system and are responsible for the production and secretion of antibodies, highly specific molecules (immunoglobulins) that recognise and combine with their target antigens. When a B cell encounters its target antigen, it develops into an antibody-producing plasma cell and also proliferates so that the infection can be managed rapidly. This process is called clonal expansion or blastogenesis. Ultimately, the antigen-antibody complexes are destroyed by macrophages and other phagocytes. There are five classes of antibodies or immunoglobulins: IgG, IgA, IgM, IgD and

IgE. Immunoglobulins comprise the predominant response to bacterial infection and provide specific defence against some viruses. T cells comprise the cellular arm of the immune system. They make direct or close contact with the antigen, which may be a virally infected or cancerous cell. There are three general types of T cells: (a) cytotoxic T cells which are capable of destroying target cells, (b) helper T cells, which enhance the immune response, and (c) suppressor T cells which reduce it. Helper T cells are the primary target of the HIV virus and their destruction by it leads to the infection of AIDS sufferers with viruses, bacteria, fungi or parasites. Another type of lymphocyte-like cell, the natural killer (NK) cell, destroys virally infected cells and certain types of tumour cells.

Some immune cells secrete soluble factors called interleukins or lymphokines which provide communication between different cells within the immune system. This may involve amplification of the target cell's response, as in the case of T-cell-produced interleukin-2 and interferon, or direction of the target cell towards the inducing cell, a process called chemotaxis. Factors which influence the production of interleukins probably have an impact on the responsiveness of lymphocytes to antigens, and thus on the regulation of the immune system.

Hormonal changes in response to stress have been shown to result in changes in immune function. The release of catecholamines, for example, can result in redistribution of lymphocytes out of storage and into circulation while reducing their functional efficacy. On the other hand, cortisol and pharmacological corticosteroids seem to be primarily suppressive. Administration of corticosteroids results in reductions of lymphocyte numbers in the blood stream that are primarily T cell and monocyte specific. Numbers of neutrophils, on the other hand, increase with corticosteroid administration. In general cortisol seems to have greater suppressive effects on the cellular than the humoral arm of the immune response. Impaired IL-2 production by T cells has been noted following administration of corticosteroids. There is also evidence for suppressive effects on NK cell activity of cortisol and corticosteroids (O'Leary, 1990, ref. no. 460).

Experimental evidence also points to the importance of interactions between the nervous and immune systems. Examples of these interactions include neuroendocrinological regulation of some cells in the central nervous system, the ability of stimulated lymphocytes to synthesise neuro-endocrine hormones, and the presence of receptors for neurotransmitters on lymphocytes, monocytes, macrophages and granulocytes. The immune system also communicates with the central nervous system via cytokines, which, when released by leukocytes, influence activation of the hypothalamic–pituitary–adrenocortical axis of the endocrine system. Cytokines are thought to have behavioural, endocrinological and electrophysiological activity, as well as influence on sleep, temperature regulation, appetite and mood.

A model emerges from this research in which environmental factors such as stressful life events may result in endocrine system changes. The endocrine system changes may lead to immune system alterations which could then impact on the development of a physical disease.

A group of studies have demonstrated a link between occupational stress and changes in immune system function. A very recent study of Japanese taxi drivers by Nakano and colleagues (1998, ref. no. 476) showed that lymphocyte proliferative responses to mitogens and IL-2 production decreased during a severe economic depression in 1993, while IL-4 production was significantly elevated. A study of Norwegian female bank employees by Endresen and colleagues (1991, ref. no. 462) examined self-reported stress, emotional state, ego-strength and defensiveness in relation to measures of cellular and humoral immunity. Concentrations of Immunoglobulin M and complement component C3 were associated with strain concerning body posture at work. The number of T cells reflected both depression and workload. This group of studies do not, however, demonstrate that these immunological changes lead to health changes.

Other recent studies have implicated stress as a causal factor in a wide range of diseases including psoriasis (Ginsburg, 1995, ref. no. 464), cancer (Bryla, 1996, ref. no 472; Fife, Beasley and Fertig, 1996, ref. no. 471), inflammatory periodontal diseases (Da Silva, Newman and Oakley, 1995, ref. no. 468), upper respiratory infections (Cohen, 1995, ref. no. 465), infections diseases generally (Biondi and Zannino, 1997, ref. no. 474) and rheumatoid arthritis (Gio-Fitman, 1996, ref. no. 473). No study, however, has yet delineated a causal chain showing that a particular psychological state produces an immunological response that then results in an altered clinical outcome. What is missing in the literature is strong evidence that the associations between psychological factors and diseases that do exist are attributable to immune changes. Finally, it may be an oversimplification to suggest that stress-related decreases in any one immune measure may accurately reflect immunological competence and predict an increased susceptibility to illness. For example, the decrease in one immune parameter, the T-helper cell, may result in increased susceptibility to viral infection but decreased risk for autoimmune diseases. Thus, an association between susceptibility to illness and immune changes depends not only on the magnitude of the change but also on the specific parameter involved and its relationship to, and function within, the immune system.

5.9   Cancer

The concept that emotions play a part in cancer onset can be traced back to the 2nd century AD, when the Greek physician Galen noted that "melancholic" women developed breast cancer more frequently than those of a more "sanguine" nature. The potential causes of cancer currently recognised include external factors such as chemicals, radiation and viruses, and internal factors such as hormonal changes, immune system abnormalities and inherited mutations. It is hypothesised that psychosocial stress may adversely affect the functioning of the hormonal system. The hormonal system changes may then lead to immune system alterations. These changes may leave the organism vulnerable to oncogenic viruses, newly transformed cancer cells and other diseases subject to immunologic control (Fife, Beasley & Fertig 1996, ref. no. 471).

Three main hypotheses linking psychosocial factors to the development of cancer have been described. Firstly, cancer may be precipitated by significant life stress events, particularly those exceeding the individual's ability to cope. Secondly, improved psychological well-being is thought to lengthen survival, whereas impaired well-being may shorten survival. Finally, a cancer-prone personality has been proposed.

The contribution of stressful life events to cancer has been studied in both humans and animals. The most commonly used research approach has been the retrospective study. The strategy involves evaluation of stress histories of patients with cancer relative to people suffering from some other illness or unaffected individuals. Such studies have frequently, but not consistently, revealed that life stresses occurred more often among cancer patients than among cancer-free comparison groups. Indeed, the review conducted by Fox (1988, ref. no. 481) found seven studies showing a positive relationship between depression or stressful conditions and cancer, and seven studies showing no relationship at all. He concludes that if stressful events and/or other psychological factors do have an effect on cancer incidence, it is small. Even studies which do appear to show significant effects are inconclusive because of numerous flaws in their experimental designs. Retrospective studies are subject to recall bias, in that the subjects' memory may be defective, and recollection and interpretation of past events may be coloured by the subjects' current emotional states. Moreover in most studies life stress events are considered to have an equal impact on all individuals. Clearly, however, individuals do not all appraise life events in the same way. That which may be stressful to one individual may be a blessing to another, and, all things being equal, subjects may not be equally adept at coping. Clinical diagnosis of cancer may not be made until years after the appearance of the first malignant cells. Hence it cannot be demonstrated that the stressful life events antedate the onset of cancer (Anisman, Irwin and Sklar, 1989, ref. no. 483). Finally, studies typically do not consider factors which might interact with life events in provoking tumour development, e.g. age, sex, rural versus urban living, diet etc, or investigate the possibility that variations in tumour development may be associated with unhealthy behaviours promoted by stress factors, such as smoking, alcohol consumption or drug use.

Psychosocial interventions, offering a mixture of social support, health education, and training in coping skills, improve mood, adjustment to illness, fatigue, pain and possibly survival time in patients with cancer. Properly designed intervention studies provide a powerful tool for examining effects of psychosocial factors. By random assignment of patients who have the same kind and stage of cancer to control and intervention groups, researchers can assess psychological, immunological and disease changes. One of the best studies in the field, by Fawzy and colleagues, evaluated both the immediate and longer term effects of a six week structured group intervention that consisted of health education, stress management techniques, coping skills and supportive group psychotherapy. The patients had stage I or II malignant melanoma, and had not received any treatment after surgical excision of the cancer. At the end of the 6 weeks, the experimental subjects exhibited lower levels of distress and healthier coping styles than the control group; after 6 months the treatment group showed increases in natural killer (NK) cell cytotoxicity, and percentage of NK cells and large granular lymphocytes. After 6 years, lower rates of recurrence and mortality and greater activity of NK cells were found in the treatment group (Fawzy et al, 1993, ref. no. 486). Consistent with the results of this intervention study with melanoma patients, Spiegel and colleagues (1989, ref. no. 482) showed that a year of weekly supportive group therapy sessions with self-hypnosis for pain was associated with extended survival time in women with metastatic breast cancer. The 50 women in the treatment group survived an average of a year and a half longer than the 36 control patients.

A large body of literature has described the cancer patient's degree of emotional expressiveness and its purported effect on disease progression. Temoshok has hypothesised that the cancer-prone individual is co-operative and appeasing, unassertive, patient, unexpressive of negative emotions and compliant to external authorities (Temoschok, 1987, ref. no. 480). The Type C behaviour pattern contrasts with Type A, which has been much studied as a risk factor for cardiovascular disease. As we saw in Chapter 4, the Type A individual is impatient, competitive, hard-driving and hurried. The relationship between Type C and melanoma tumour thickness and invasion was investigated. Tumour thickness and measures of Type C personality correlated, especially in subjects under the age of 55 (Temoschok et al, 1985, ref. no. 479). Negative studies have also appeared such as that by Cassileth and colleagues (1985, ref. no. 478) which showed that none of the multiple psychosocial factors thought influence health (including hopelessness/helplessness) predicted cancer survival. Faragher and Cooper (1990, ref. no. 484) found that most of the personality aspects of women with breast cancer were Type B in nature, including being less competitive, less rushed and less eager to get things done than women without breast disease.

Depression has been identified as one of several emotional conditions that may influence immunologic and hormonal functioning. These effects appear to be similar to those associated with stress. Stress often precedes depression; therefore a considerable amount of effort as gone into elucidating the mechanisms relating depression to cancer development. On the basis of a critical review of the literature, Bieliauskas and Garron concluded that depression may be related to an increased risk of mortality from cancer (1982, ref. no. 477). A more recent meta-analysis by McGee and his colleagues inferred a small but statistically significant link between depression and the development of cancer (McGee, Williams and Elwood, 1994, ref. no. 488).

Studies examining depressive states and their association with cancer have been heavily criticised by Levenson and Bemis (1991, ref. no. 485) on methodological grounds. Most investigators have not differentiated among various depressive disorders or examined depressions from the point of view of past history, duration, chronicity or treatment pursued. Additionally, it is difficult to compare studies which use different instruments to measure the presence of depression. Another problem is that studies often do not adjust for the effects of other relevant psychosocial factors such as excessive drinking, poor diet or increased social isolation, which may independently influence the course of the disease. Bearing these methodological shortcomings in mind, it is hardly surprising that results are inconsistent.

5.10 Mental health

The link between stress factors and mental ill-health has been explored in a fleet of studies. Manifestations of psychological distress most commonly measured are anxiety and depression. Two kinds of anxiety have been distinguished in the literature: trait and state. The former is considered to be a personality trait of the individual which may be a handicap in coping with stress factors. In a study of Norwegian health care workers, Richardsen, Burke and Leiter (1992, ref. no. 496) found that trait anxiety contributed significantly to all aspects of burnout and was most strongly related to emotional exhaustion. They suggest that excessive work demands and the perception of limited resources to meet them effectively, which have been considered major contributors to emotional exhaustion, are exacerbated when the worker is already tense and anxious. In other words, trait anxiety may make people more prone to burnout. State anxiety and depressive symptoms are presumed to be caused or aroused by life events and to be situation-specific. The anxiety and depression mostly addressed in job stress research are presumed to be caused or precipitated by stress producing events or conditions in the workplace. Anxiety and/or depression at work have been associated with role stress (Jackson and Schuler, 1985, ref. no. 257), low levels of perceived control (Spector, 1986, ref. no. 276), on-going high job demands (Barnett and Brennan, 1995, ref. no. 499) occasional peaks in demand such as sitting examinations or meeting deadlines (Eden, 1982, ref. no. 396), and work-family conflict (Frone, Russell and Cooper, 1991, ref. no. 495). These studies have been largely cross-sectional in nature and have relied on a wide variety of self-report based assessment tools. Differences in results obtained can be partly explained by differences in emphasis in the measures used. More use of standardised measures would make it easier to synthesise results. To take a simple example quoted by Jackson and Schuler, the job related tension index developed by Kahn and his colleagues uses questions making direct reference to problems of role conflict and ambiguity eg. "being unclear on just what the responsibilities of your job are". On the other hand the anxiety-stress items developed by House and Rizzio have more face validity because they refer to psychological and psychosomatic symptoms often associated with the concept of tension eg. "I feel fidgety or nervous because of my job". Not surprisingly, when the Kahn questionnaire is used to measure tension, the associations with role conflict and ambiguity are much stronger than when the House and Rizzio questionnaire is used.

Theoretical models used in studies of anxiety and depression have included Karasek's job demands-decision latitude model (e.g. Fletcher and Jones, 1993, ref.

219

no. 83), Payne's demands-supports-constraints model (e.g. Payne and Fletcher, 1983, ref. no. 78) and various versions of Lazarus' transactional model (e.g. Cooper and Baglioni, 1988, ref no. 494). Results have been inconsistent and other factors clearly influence the relationship between job stressors and mental ill-health. One factor frequently hypothesised to impinge upon the relationship between occupational stress and mental well-being is social support. This has generally been treated as either having a direct effect on well-being or as buffering the stress-strain relationship. Direct effect means that workers with strong social support networks will be *de facto* happier and healther than those without, regardless of the presence of any overt stress factors. Buffering means that social support is hypothesised to interact with stress factors so that the adverse impact of the stess is more severe for persons with low levels of social support than for those with high levels of support.

There is a great deal of inconsistency in the research literature regarding the nature and definition of social support. Conceptual and empirical definitions have ranged from indices of various degrees of social integration, e.g. being married, through indices of various parameters of social networks, e.g. composition or types of people in them, to measures of the degree of intimacy of relationships the person has with particular individuals. Types of social support investigated include informational support, emotional support, in which supportive people show that they care for the stressed individual's welfare, instrumental support, in which supportive people try to help solve the problems caused by stress factors, and support that involves certain features of the frequency, style and contents of communications between the stressed person and supportive persons. Sources of social support are most often divided into supervisors, co-workers and people outside the organisation, such as family, friends and professionals (doctors, clergy, lawyers). It is assumed on both theoretical and empirical grounds that different sources and types of social support are likely to have different effects on the stress factor-psychological distress relationship (Beehr and McGrath, 1992, ref. no. 497).

The buffering hypothesis has probably been dominant in explaining the relation between work-related stress and social support. However, the results of research examining this buffering effect are far weaker than the popularity of the concept might suggest. For example, Ganster, Fusilier and Mayes found no evidence for a buffering effect of social support (1986, ref. no. 493) in their study of employees of a large contracting firm. They did however find a modest direct effect of social support in lowering experienced strain. On the other hand Iwata and Suzuki found that co-worker social support buffered the relationship between role overload and mental strain among Japanese bank workers. The buffering was only effective at low to medium levels of role overload among male clerks. It varied for female clerks and was not significant for chief clerks and above (Iwata and Suzuki, 1997, ref. no. 270). Similarly Payne and Fletcher, in a study of teachers, found very modest support for their model of stress as a function of the balance between job demands, supports and job constraints (1983, ref. no. 78). At the same time Fletcher and Jones (1993, ref. no. 83) found in their test of Karasek's model of job-strain that social support reduced psychological distress and increased job and life satisfaction.

It may be that there are higher order interactions involved in these mixed results regarding buffering effects. That is, expected effects might occur under some conditions but not others. Ganster and colleagues found no such effects in their 1986 study using employee sex, educational level and collar-colour as potential moderator variables. On the other hand, Daniels and Guppy (1994, ref. no. 498) found complex interactions between stress factors, locus of control, and social support or job autonomy in predicting psychological well-being. These interactions revealed that an internal locus of control, and social support/job autonomy synergistically reduce the effects of stressors on well-being. Complex effects were also reported by Schaubroeck and Fink (1998, ref. no. 296). Their findings showed that supervisor consideration improved job performance only when control was low. When control was high, consideration was negatively related to performance. This may be because persons with high job control who were also receiving high levels of managerial support were perceived as having too much responsibility and as being unable to perform their duties effectively. Alternatively, high support from the supervisor may have prevented employees from fully developing required job skills. On the other hand, high levels of worker control and social support appeared to aid in stress coping and to enhance well-being. Thus this study showed a conflict between the desirable outcomes of improving performance and improving mental health.

Moyle (1998, ref. no. 501) proposes an alternative approach to the role of social support in the stress process. She tested for mediating rather than moderating effects in a three wave longitudinal study of managers working for a food retail company. Results showed that job satisfaction could be predicted from a combination of high managerial support, high control and high role clarity. Good management communication skills (a facet of social support) led to high role clarity, which led in turn to high levels of job satisfaction. Supportive management was also associated with higher perceived job control, which also led to improved satisfaction.

5.11 Post-traumatic stress disorder

Post-traumatic stress disorder (PTSD) is characterised by three groups of symptoms. The first group relates to reliving aspects of the trauma, with nightmares or feelings that the traumatic event is happening again. The second group comprises symptoms related to avoiding anything likely to remind the individual of the trauma. For example, a person traumatised by a traffic accident might take to avoiding motorways. The third group includes symptoms indicative of heightened irritability, such as sleep disturbances, outbursts of anger or sudden shock reactions. PTSD can be triggered by an event which lies outside the normal pattern of human experience and which would clearly cause suffering in virtually everyone. It can thus be regarded as a normal human reaction to extremely unpleasant events (Gersons and Carlier, 1992, ref. no. 503). People in some occupations, such as the military in time of war, police, firefighters, rescue workers and health care providers, are routinely exposed to life threatening situations and violent or grotesque scenes and are most at risk of developing PTSD (Davis and Breslau, 1994, ref. no. 505). Carlier and her colleagues found that 7% of a sample of 262 traumatised police officers had PTSD, and 34% had post-traumatic stress symptoms or subthreshold PTSD. Apart from severity of the trauma, which predicted PTSD both 3 and 12 months after the event, symptoms at 3 months were more likely to occur in people who were introverted, were emotionally exhausted at the time of the trauma, had difficulty in expressing feelings, had been allowed insufficient time by the employer to come to terms with the trauma, were feeling insecure in their jobs and were dissatisfied with organisational support. Twelve months after the trauma, symptoms were further predicted by job dissatisfaction, social isolation, brooding over work, lack of hobbies and subsequent traumatic events (Carlier, Lamberts and Gersons, 1997, ref. no. 508). Marmar and colleagues (1996 ref. no. 507) studied the stress reactions of rescue workers to the collapse of the interstate 880 freeway following the Loma Prieta earthquake. They were able to compare different groups of emergency personnel including police, firefighters, paramedics and road construction personnel. Interestingly, police and firefighters had significantly lower distress levels than other groups.

It is clear, then, that not every traumatised individual will develop PTSD. The risks of so doing can be connected to the trauma itself, to pre-existing vulnerability factors, or to an interplay between the two. Predisposing vulnerability factors can include genetic susceptibility, early traumatic experiences, personality characteristics such as introversion, recent life stress, lack of support, perceived lack of control over the stressful event and recent heavy use of alcohol. The risk of developing PTSD can be seen both as a function of the trauma and as a function of the victim. Certain extreme events such as disaster rescue work that rise above a given severity threshold are likely to induce PTSD in most people regardless of predisposition. At the opposite end of the scale events that would be minimally stressful to most people such as corpse discoveries could prove traumatic in the presence of predisposing factors (McFarlane, 1989, ref. no. 502; Davidson and Fairbank, 1993, ref. no. 504).

Results of studies of the physiological mechanisms underlying PTSD suggest that the disorder occurs when the individual remains "mobilised" for fight or flight even when the external danger has passed away. Normal physiological reactions to external threat such as heightened perception, increased muscle tension and quickening heart beat can be experienced by the individual as a feeling of overwhelming fear, heightened alertness and tension. If the body does not return to normal once the danger has passed symptoms such as sleeping problems, irritability, concentration difficulties, extreme alertness and excessive shock reactions manifest themselves (Boudewyns, 1996, ref. no. 506).

5.12 Behavioural responses to stress factors

One possible mechanism linking stress factors to illness is that the experience of stress produces behaviours that are supportive in the short run but increase the risk of long term illness. Such behaviours include alcohol and drug consumption and cigarette smoking.

5.12.1 Smoking

People commonly turn to tobacco as a means of dealing with stressful situations. Perceptions of stress may result in mental strains such as depression, anxiety, tension and irritability. In turn these symptoms are associated with an increased desire to smoke (Perkins and Grobe, 1992, ref. no. 522) and with increased smoking intensity (i.e more cigarettes smoked per day) (Conway et al, 1981, ref. no. 511). Green and Johnson (1990, ref. no. 514) examined the relationship between job strain (high demands combined with low decision latitude), cigarette smoking and smoking cessation in male chemical plant employees. Results indicated that smokers who reported high job strain were more likely to smoke heavily, and those who reported low job strain were more likely to quit smoking.

Epidemiological studies have consistently linked cigarette smoking to coronary heart disease and angina pectoris. Nicotine causes an increase in heart rate and blood pressure, and carbon monoxide reduces the oxygen–carrying capacity of the blood, forcing the heart to work harder. In addition, smoking is associated with detrimental changes in blood lipids and makes it more likely that accumulations of cholesterol will occur in the blood vessels. Smoking is also linked to lung and bladder cancer, chronic bronchitis and emphysema. Sutherland and Cooper report that by 1990 approximately 30 major studies in 10 countries had produced irrefutable evidence of a link between smoking and lung cancer, and cigarette smoking has been identified as the major environmental cancer threat, perhaps followed by alcohol consumption (Sutherland and Cooper, 1990, ref. no. 56).

5.12.2 Alcohol/drug consumption

Alcohol and drug use in the workplace is considered one of the most critical problems facing business and industry today. The precise annual costs of alcohol and drug use to employers are probably impossible to determine, but the estimates can be staggering. Commonly accepted figures for the UK compiled by the charity Alcohol Concern and quoted in the Summer 1998 issue of their quarterly bulletin *Acquire* are:

- Up to 14 million working days are lost each year due to inappropriate drinking, about 3–5% of all absence.
- Sickness absence on this scale cost employers about £1,056 million in 1992.
- The cost of long-term sickness absence, unemployment and premature death due to alcohol is estimated at some £2,330 million.
- Hangovers alone cost industry between £53 million and £58 million.
- Alcohol is involved in 20% to 25% of all industrial accidents, rising to 60% of fatal accidents.

A number of researchers from a variety of disciplines have examined the relationship between working conditions and drug and alcohol abuse. Early studies on the basic relationship between working conditions and alcohol/drug use produced correlations, which although statistically significant in some cases, were quite weak. In most cases studies were cross-sectional and so unable to show causality and were based on self-reports of perceived job stress, job satisfaction and alienation. These studies also failed in most cases to take into account other factors which may impinge on the development of problem drinking. Sociodemographic characteristics, such as age, sex and education may influence both the likelihood of holding a stressful job and rates of alcohol/drug use and abuse, thereby creating a false relationship between work stress and alcohol outcomes. Similarly personality traits and social resources (e.g. self-esteem, social support) may influence the perception of work stressors on the one hand and psychological distress, patterns of alcohol/drug use and experience of drinking problems or drug addiction on the other.

Recent investigations have proposed or tested more complex models of the working conditions drug/alcohol relationship. Five different possible models for this relationship have been described: tension reduction, social learning theory, demands-control, lifestage transitions and demographic characteristics.

Tension reduction theory proposes that alcohol reduces tension and that people drink alcohol for its tension reducing properties. Tension here refers to various negative emotions such as fear, anxiety, or depression. Stressful conditions are hypothesised to increase negative emotions, which in turn increase alcohol use. This theory was tested by Cooper, Russell and Frone (1990, ref. no. 516) who examined work distress as a mediator between work stress factors and alcohol consumption in a random sample of 574 employed adults. Their results showed no significant relationship between work distress and alcohol consumption, leading them to conclude that the theory was not supported. However, further research is needed in the shape of a variety of studies using many different mediators (e.g. perceived efficacy) before any firm conclusions can be drawn about the plausibility of the model (Harris and Heft, 1992, ref. no. 519).

Social learning theory suggests that people are more likely to drink or take drugs in response to stress when they lack other, more appropriate coping responses and when they believe that alcohol enhances positive mood or reduces negative mood. In other words, people will engage in alcohol/drug use when they believe it will make them feel better and/or help them cope with stressful situations. This theory was also tested by Cooper and her colleagues (1990, ref. no. 516), who found only limited support for it.

Several studies have applied versions of Karasek's demands-control model to the drug-alcohol abuse/work stress relationship. In this context high demand implies high levels of physical exertion or exposure to psychological stressors. Control is expressed in relation to the degree to which a jobs tasks may be varied (skill discretion) as well as the ability to make autonomous decisions (decision authority). Crum and her colleagues tested this model (1995, ref. no. 525) using prospective data. They found that men in high strain jobs classified as having high psychological demands and low control were 27.5 times more likely to develop alcohol abuse/dependence than men in low strain jobs. Men employed in high strain jobs with high physical demands and low control were 3-4 times at higher risk for an alcohol disorder. No appreciable risk was found for women in any of the high strain job categories. However, the study did not examine personality and behavioural traits which might render individuals particularly vulnerable to alcohol/substance abuse and used mean scores of occupational strain imputed from work by Karasek and his colleagues instead of scores for each specific job. Richman and her colleagues, in a study of problem drinking among physicians, expanded the concept of lack of control to include experience of abuse or harassment in the workplace. Results showed that, while task-related stress factors such as overwork did not lead to problem drinking, most of the perceived abusive experiences did significantly predict deleterious drinking outcomes in men or women or both. Individuals with a fragile sense of self were most likely to experience psychological damage from abusive experiences and to use alcohol to mask the painful feelings arising from these experiences (Richman, Flaherty and Rospenda, 1996, ref. no. 527).

There has been increasing research interest in the effect of transitions from one life stage to another on a variety of behaviours including drug and alcohol use. A study by Johnson and White (1995, ref. no. 526) examined changes in alcohol and marijuana use and problems in relation to the transition to full time work, and the effects of work-related and generalised stress among a group of recent entrants to the labour force. Data indicated that when the impact of age, gender and marital status were excluded from the analysis, there were few significant effects of the transition to full-time work on alcohol and marijuana use and problems. Richman, in a longitudinal study of medical students, found that a sizeable proportion of pre-medical school problem drinkers "matured out" of their earlier patterns after entry into their roles as trainee doctors. Both male and female problem drinking declined during the preclinical years but tended to rise after the initiation of clinical training. The major predictors of alcohol abuse during clinical training involved pre-existing personality problems brought into the medical training context, lack of social support and stress factors related to patient care (Richman, 1992, ref. no. 523).

According to the demographic characteristics approach, alcohol/drug use is a function of the characteristics of the workforce rather than arising from adverse working conditions. The most thorough examination of this hypothesis was reported by Mensch and Kandel (1988, ref. no. 513) using a database containing over 5,000 working men and 4,000 working women. Very limited relationships between measures of work stress and job satisfaction and substance use were found. Conversely, various demographic characteristics such as education and race were more substantially related to alcohol and substance use. Similarly Steffy and Laker (1991, ref. no. 518) found that age, sex and race were more highly related to alcohol consumption than measures of job stress.

The weight of the evidence suggests that alcohol may be used to cope with job stressors only among a subset of vulnerable individuals. Three alternative models have been proposed to explain observed associations between occupations, alcohol consumption patterns and alcohol-related problems. The social control model suggests that under certain working conditions there is little to prevent drinking at work and under such circumstances, persons with a propensity to alcoholism are more likely to develop the condition. Drinking at work is less likely in occupations involving highly monitored performance with high levels of supervision where errors will be noticed immediately. Social availability theory identifies work group social norms about alcohol use as the determining factor in the inception of problem drinking. That is, in some occupations drinking with workmates is regarded as normal and to abstain means sticking out like a sore thumb and being regarded as odd. Here peer pressure may lead to problem drinking among the vulnerable. Occupations with such work group norms have been identified as restaurant workers, newspapermen and dealers in financial markets. Finally, a motivational model has been proposed in which separation from normal social and sexual relationship or noxious working conditions (cold, heat, dirt) causes people to drink (Mandell et al, 1992, ref. no. 520).

5.13 Costs and prevalence of work-related stress

In the United Kingdom, as in most countries, statistics are kept at national level on numbers of days lost from work due to certified incapacity for a variety of accidents and illnesses. There is no way of telling, other than by educated guesses, however, how much of this sickness absence is due to stress-related disorders. More adequate data on the relative architecture of stress-related illnesses can be found in general population surveys and in smaller scale studies of defined occupational populations, such as those carried out by Colligan and his colleagues on the occupational incidence of mental health disorders and Eaton and his colleagues on the prevalence of major depressive disorder (Colligan et al, 1977, ref. no. 491; Eaton, 1990, ref.

no. 530). Surveys have been carried out at national level by government, trades unions, employers groups and professional associations.

- The Health and Safety Executive commissioned a supplement to the 1990 Labour Force Survey (LFS) in which all adults from a representative sample of households in England and Wales were asked about workplace accidents occurring in the previous 12 months and work-related illnesses they had suffered in the previous year. Follow-up questions established the nature of the illness and the job that was thought to have given rise to it, whether the work caused the condition or was thought to have simply made it worse and the number of days sick-leave due to the complaint (Health and Safety Commission, 1992, ref. no. 531). Based on these figures Davies and Teasdale estimate 182,700 cases of work-related stress/depression. Interestingly, 57% of these cases thought their condition was caused by work. Self-reported stress and depression taken together were second in the league table after musculoskeletal disorders as causes of work-related illness (Davies and Teasdale, 1994, ref. no. 534).

- The Confederation of British Industry (CBI) has conducted a series of surveys on absence from work since 1987. In 1996 work-related stress was seen as a medium to strong factor in absence from work for 22% of manual workers and 35% of non-manual workers. This is down from 1995, when the figures were 37% and 55% respectively (CBI 1995 and 1997, ref. nos. 535 & 541).

- The TUC's 1996 survey of Safety Reps identified work-related stress as the top workplace safety concern. More than two-thirds of respondents (68%) identified stress as the main hazard in their workplace (TUC, 1996, ref. no. 540). Even in the manufacturing and construction sector, where workers are faced with a wide range of chemical, physical and environmental hazards, 44% and 45% of reps respectively still identified significant stress problems in their workplaces.

- The Institute of Management has conducted a series of surveys of management morale. Results of a survey published in 1995 showed that 63% of respondents felt their work to be a source of stress. The greatest levels of stress were felt by women and those in the 35-44 age group, around 70% of whom felt under pressure at work (Benbow, 1995, ref. no. 536).

The European Foundation for the Improvement of Living and Working Conditions has developed models for the measurement of work-related stress at both the organisational and the national level. At the organisational level costs lie in the areas of:

- Employee health and related costs (direct costs of sickness absence, administrative costs involved in processing employee claims and benefits, costs of accident insurance premiums).

- Human resource development costs (recruitment, education and training).

- Productivity loss (low morale, reduced performance, high staff turnover).

The costs of work-related stress do not stop at the company level but extend to national governments. For example, stress may cause an illness which results in the employee needing treatment by the NHS and having to take early retirement and claim Incapacity Benefit. Levi and Lunde-Jensen (1996 ref. no. 538) have developed a model for measuring the costs of stress at national level. Their costs-of-illness model adds the direct costs of health care to the loss of potential output caused by sickness absence, early retirement and premature death.

5.14 Legal consequences of work-related stress

5.14.1 Stress-related ill-health

There are no legislative provisions in the UK which deal specifically with the control of stress at work or with the mental and psychological well-being of employees and workers. However, employers have a duty under the Health and Safety at Work Act 1974 to ensure, as far as is reasonably practical, that their workplaces are safe and healthy. Under the Management of Health and Safety at Work Regulations 1992 employers are obliged to assess the nature and scale of risks to health in their workplace and base their control measures on it. Ill-health arising from work-related stress has to be treated in the same way as ill-health due to other, physical, causes present in the workplace. Employers therefore have a legal duty to take reasonable care that health is not placed at risk through excessive and sustained levels of stress arising from the way that work is organised, the way people deal with each other at work or the day-to-day demands placed on their workforce. Employers are not, however, under a legal duty to prevent ill-health due to stress arising from outside circumstances such as personal or domestic problems, but where such stress is exacerbated by work it cannot be ignored.

In order to succeed in a claim for failure to provide a safe system of work, an employee must first show that the employer was, or should have been, aware of the risk. When the employee is known to have suffered a mental illness, the employer must be aware of the risk. However, when the employee is of normal health and the workload is not unusual, there is no apparent risk and no duty to take preventive action. The employee will also have to show that their ill-health was caused by the employers failure to amend or ameliorate the working conditions. When an employee is known to be particularly at risk, the employer must not ignore signs of stress or complaints by the employee. An employer must take the steps that any reasonable employer in its position would take to protect the employee. The employer's liability depends on its knowledge of the risk.

5.14.2 Bullying

There is no legislation in the UK which deals specifically with workplace bullying. Bullied employees are in practice most likely to resign and complain that they have been unfairly constructively dismissed. An employee must prove that the employer is in breach of its implied contractual duty to maintain trust and confidence, to give reasonable support or to provide a safe workplace. When an employee is bullied or harassed by his employer, this is likely to amount to a breach of the implied contractual duty to maintain trust and confidence. A breach of this term may also arise where the employer fails to protect the employee against bullying or harassment by colleagues, customers or members of the public. Alternatively, the employee may seek to establish that the employer, in failing to prevent the bullying, is in breach of its implied duty to give reasonable support or to provide a safe workplace.

5.14.3 Harassment

Two of the most common forms of workplace bullying are sexual and racial harassment. Since harassment is simply a convenient term for a particular form of sex or race discrimination, there is no specific legal definition of it as such. In order to succeed in a claim for sex or race discrimination, the victim of harassment must satisfy the definition of direct discrimination contained in the Sex Discrimination Act 1975 and Race Relations Act 1976. Thus an employee will have to show:

• That he/she has been treated less favourably than an actual or hypothetical comparator in the same or similar relevant circumstances.

- That the treatment was on the grounds of sex or race.

- That the treatment resulted in dismissal, denial of opportunities within or for employment, or any other detriment.

It should be noted that the employment provisions of the Disability Discrimination Act 1995 use the same formula as the sex and race discrimination legislation. Thus the Act may afford protection to employees who are harassed or bullied at work due to their disability.

5.14.4 Legal actions

The decision in the landmark case of *Walker v Northumberland County Council* embraced psychiatric damage within the employers' legal duty of care to their workforce. Mr John Walker worked for Northumberland County Council from 1970 to December 1987 as an area social services officer responsible for four teams of field social workers. In November 1986 Mr Walker suffered a nervous breakdown due to overwork. He returned to work on March 4th 1987, having negotiated an agreement that assistance should be provided to him on his return. The promised assistance was withdrawn early in April and the workload continued to increase. In September 1987 Mr Walker suffered a second nervous breakdown and was forced to retire from his post due to ill-health. The judge in the case found the council liable for Mr Walker's second nervous breakdown but not his first.

Following the decision in the John Walker case, the floodgates have opened and the number of claims arising out of workplace stress has increased exponentially. Latest figures from the TUC (1998, ref. no. 551) show that there are a total of 459 legal actions against employers brought as a result of stress suffered by workers currently in progress. A rise in the cases of stress among members was reported by 22% of trade unions. However, the majority of stress actions are still settled out of court. In one case the widow of a Unison member who was driven to suicide by stress at work received a £25,000 out of court settlement from North East Essex Mental Health NHS Trust. The man had been subjected to a "vindictive, oppressive, ruthless and macho style of management" according to Unison. His managers had been aware that he was suicidal, but had done nothing about it.

A 1995 survey of law firms handling personal injury cases reported by Earnshaw and Cooper (1996, ref. no. 548) found that 20% of respondents indicated that they were involved in a workplace stress claim. The most prevalent trigger for the stress injury was alleged bullying in some shape or form, and the most common injury was nervous breakdown followed by depression.

5.15 Bibliography

5.15.1 Stress and health

(396)
CRITICAL job events, acute stress and strain: a multiple interrupted time series
D Eden
Organizational behavior and human performance, vol.30, 1982, p.312-329.

The effects of acute objective stress on subjective stress and on psychological and physiological strain were assessed among 39 first-year student nurses. Strain was measured five times, twice in anticipation of critical job events interspersed with three low-stress occasions. The critical job events were providing the first comprehensive patient care and the final exam in nursing. Anxiety, systolic blood pressure and pulse rate showed a consistent pattern of significant changes as predicted. Qualitative overload and serum uric acid changed significantly as predicted three out of four times.

DSC Shelfmark: 6290.750000

See also: Acute and chronic job stress, strain and vacation relief by D Eden. (Organizational behavior and human decision processes, vol.45, 1990, p.175-193. DSC Shelfmark: 6290.749000)

(397)
STRESS and the development of somatic disorders
L S Zegans
In Handbook of stress: theoretical and clinical aspects edited by L Goldberger and S Breznitz. New York: Free Press, 1982. p.134-152.

Argues that somatic diseases develop through an exposure to stressors which is severe, frequent, or of long duration, combined with an interaction between stress responses and other physiological systems, particularly control systems. The potentially pathogenic effects of the stress response express themselves by challenging the various body systems which integrate and defend physiological function, and which underpin its link with behaviour. These systems include the hypothalamic-pituitary-adrenal-cortical axis, the autonomic nervous system-adrenal-medullary axis, the immune system, the reticular activating system and the cognitive affective centres of the brain.

DSC Shelfmark: 83/05846

(398)
HEALTH psychology
D S Krantz, N E Grunberg and A Baum
Annual review of psychology, vol.36, 1985, p.349-383.

Describes mechanisms linking behaviour to physical disease, covering stress and its effects on health, psychoneuroimmunology, behavioural factors in cardiovascular disease, tobacco use, eating disorders, and health promotion.

DSC Shelfmark: 1528.400000

(399)
STRESS and disease in the workplace: a methodological commentary on the accumulated evidence
S V Kasl
In Health and industry: a behavioral medicine perspective edited by M F Cataldo and T J Coates. New York: Wiley, 1986. p.52-77.

Argues that the objective of research in this field is to identify causal linkages between exposure to objective environmental conditions at work and health related outcomes. Presents a strong critique of subjective measures of exposure which are seen as precipitating numerous problems, especially confounding and triviality.

DSC Shelfmark: 86/10188

(400)
WORK and non-work correlates of illness and behaviour in male and female Swedish white collar workers
R A Karasek, B Gardell and J Lindell
Journal of occupational behaviour, vol.8, 1987, p.187-207.

Analyses surveys of 5000 male and 3700 female workers who were members of a Swedish labour federation. Assesses four classes of outcome variables: (1) psychological health (depression, exhaustion, job dissatisfaction), (2) physical health, (3) health-related behaviours (pill consumption, smoking, absenteeism), and (4) social participation (sports, politics, entertainment). For both males and females, decision latitude was significantly associated with psychological and physical symptoms, although less strongly with the latter. No tests were made of an interaction between demands and decision latitude.

DSC Shelfmark: 5026.085000

(401)
NEUROENDOCRINE effects of work stress
R M Rose
In Work stress: health care systems in the workplace edited by J C Quick and others. New York: Praeger, 1987. p.130-147.

Summarises results of the Air Traffic Controller Health Change Study, a five-year project to study a group of about 400 air traffic controllers. Findings support the interpretation that the hypothalamic-pituitary-adrenal-cortical system does adapt to stressful stimuli, and that, therefore, cortisol mostly increased only slightly with increasing workload. Men who showed a significant increase in cortisol as work increased were judged to be more competent, described themselves as more satisfied with their jobs and did not show more health change but, on the contrary, less frequent illness episodes.

DSC Shelfmark: 87/29739

(402)
STRESS: neurobiology and neuroendocrinology
M R Brown, G F Koob and C Rivier
New York: Dekker, 1991. 703p.

Covers the role and integration of regulatory processes in human physiology, the role of the regulatory processes in the development of stress-induced diseases, and a description of stress management.

DSC Shelfmark: 91/04595

(403)
STRESS and infectious disease in humans
S Cohen and G M Williamson
Psychological bulletin, vol.109, no.1, Jan–May 1991, p.5–24.

Reviews research on the role of stress in infectious disease as measured either by illness behaviours (symptoms and use of health services) or by verified pathology. Substantial evidence was found for an association between stress and increased illness behaviour and less convincing but provocative evidence was found for a similar association between stress and infectious pathology. Introverts, isolates and persons lacking social skills may also be at increased risk for both illness behaviours and pathology.

DSC Shelfmark: 6946.300000

(404)
WORK stress and employee health
D C Ganster and J Schaubroeck
Journal of management, vol.17, 1991, p.235–271.

Review and critique of studies which examined the effects of work characteristics on employee health. Concludes that the evidence as a whole is highly suggestive that work experiences play a significant role in mental and physical health. There is good evidence that certain job characteristics produce elevated neuroendocrine and cardiovascular responses, and there are plausible models for theorising that over time such elevations might lead to disease. Argues that studies relying on self-reports, whether longitudinal or cross-sectional, are unlikely to add significantly to the evidence, and makes recommendations as to how organisational researchers might in future contribute to this knowledge.

DSC Shelfmark: 5011.100000

(405)

MENTAL load and work stress as two types of energy mobilization

A W K Gaillard and C J E Wientjes

Work and stress, vol.8, 1994, p.141–152.

The differing characteristics of two mental states, arbitrarily labelled 'mental load' and 'stress' are explored. The concept of mental load stems from cognitive-energetical theories based on human information-processing theories. Energy mobilisation under mental load is tuned by the demands of the task and aimed at improving performance by focusing attention. It is for a limited period and is a reponse to a situation seen as a challenge not a threat. Under stress, energy mobilisation is not instrumental to the execution of the task, persists outside of the task situation and inhibits recovery, and is a response to a situation perceived as a threat. Study goes on to explore the role of stress in triggering disease.

DSC Shelfmark: 9348.102000

(406)

PSYCHOSOCIAL work characteristics and social support as predictors of SF-36 health functioning: The Whitehall II study

S A Stansfeld *et al*

Psychosomatic medicine, vol.60, 1998, p.247–255.

Study sought to determine whether psychosocial work characteristics and social support at baseline predict physical functioning, mental health and social functioning longitudinally at follow-up in the Whitehall II Study of British civil servants. Results showed that negative aspects of work (high demands and effort-reward imbalance) and negative aspects of close relationships predicted poor physical, psychological and social functioning after controlling for age, employment grade, baseline ill-health and negative affectivity.

DSC Shelfmark: 6946.555000

(407)

TEAM cultures, stress and health

I Smit and M Schabracq

Stress medicine, vol.14, 1998, p.13–19.

Article describes a method for in-depth analysis of team cultures. Culture may be defined as the way in which a group of people solve problems. Four cultural dimensions are analysed: solution of external problems, attainment of goals of team members, integration within the team, and maintenance of cultural patterns. Cultural maps so obtained can be used to identify areas where existing culture can be enriched to improve the coping capability of the team.

DCS Shelfmark: 8474.129500

5.15.2 Gastrointestinal disorders

(408)
OCCUPATIONAL stress and health among factory workers
J S House *et al*
Journal of health and social behavior, vol.20, 1979, p.139-160.

Results of a large-scale study of male manufacturing plant workers showed a link between work stress and ulcers after controlling for seven possible confounding variables. Supervisor support had significant effects on health outcome measures. Low levels of reported support from the boss were related to the occurrence of ulcers, angina pectoris, itch and rash.

DSC Shelfmark: 4996.730000

(409)
LIFE event stress and chronic difficulties in duodenal ulcer: a case control study
I Gilligan *et al*
Journal of psychosomatic research, vol.31, 1987, p.117-123.

Investigated 66 consecutive out-patients with duodenal ulcer and compared them with a matched healthy control group. Applied the Bedford College Life Events and Difficulties Schedule covering a 12-month period. Results showed that, in all instances except one, duodenal ulcer patients experienced more chronic difficulties than matched pair controls.

DSC Shelfmark: 5043.480000

(410)
ROLE of stress in the development of disorders of gastrointestinal motility
T F Burks
In Stress: neurobiology and neuroendocrinology edited by M R Brown, G F Koob and C Rivier. New York: Dekker, 1991, p.566-583.

Stress-induced effects on motility apparently result from brain and spinal cord selection of specific motility programmes directed by the enteric nervous system. Stressors may influence the central nervous system to select stereotype motility programmes. Experimental stress in humans can affect gastric emptying, small intestinal motility and colonic motility. Evidence has been put forward that some of the components of the gastrointestinal response to stress may be mediated by extra-pituitary actions of corticotrophin releasing factor (CRF).

DSC Shelfmark: 91/04595

(411)

ORGANIC and psychosocial risk factors for duodenal ulcer

J Lewin and S Lewis

Journal of psychosomatic research, vol.39, 1995, p.531-548.

Evidence for the contribution of psychosocial factors to the onset of duodenal ulcer is reviewed in the context of evidence of organic, genetic and environmental factors, with special reference to the role of *H pylori*. Although psychosocial factors may be of significance, their contribution to etiology is likely to be modest.

DSC Shelfmark: 5043.480000

(412)

DUODENAL ulcer: the helicobacterization of a psychosomatic disease

R N Melmed and Y Gelpin

Israel journal of medical sciences, vol.32, 1996, p.211-216.

The discovery of *Helicobacter pylori* has revolutionised thinking about the causes of duodenal ulcer, where it is now thought to play a central role in the vast majority of cases. However, given the widespread occurrence of infection with *H pylori* in first and third world populations, only a very few numbers of subjects actually develop duodenal ulcers. The epidemiological, clinical and genetic evidence suggests that host factors, especially the effects of psychological stress, may be decisive in determining who develops duodenal ulcer.

DSC Shelfmark: 4583.812000

(413)

THE RELATIONSHIP between daily stress and symptoms of irritable bowel: a time series approach

C P Dancey, M Taghavi and R J Fox

Journal of psychosomatic research, vol.44, 1998, p.537-545.

Study used a within-person, lagged time-series approach to investigate the links between daily stress and symptoms in 31 IBS sufferers. Results showed that for 43% of the participants symptoms could be significantly predicted by hassles in the previous 4 days, and that for 37% of them hassles could be predicted by symptoms in the previous 4 days. In the latter case, an attack of IBS heightened perceptions of stress.

DSC Shelfmark: 5043.480000

5.15.3 Diabetes

(414)

THE RELATIONSHIP between psychological stress and insulin-dependent blood diabetic control: preliminary investigations
D J Cox *et al*
Health psychology, vol.3, 1984, p.63–75.

Reported a significant correlation between blood glucose and daily hassles in a sample of adult Type 1 patients. Neither the presence of social support nor compliance with health care recommendations were correlated with blood glucose levels. Patients reported that different types of hassles had different effects on their blood glucose level. Stressors producing happiness frequently sent blood glucose down, while stressors producing feelings of worry, sadness or frustration drove it upwards.

DSC Shelfmark: 4275.105200

(415)

PERCEIVED stress and diabetes control in adolescents
S L Hanson and J W Pichert
Health psychology, vol.5, 1986, p.439–452.

Found that as the number of reported hassles increased so also did blood glucose even after the effects of diet, exercise, etc. had been controlled for. The camp setting of the study allowed the monitoring of food intake, exercise, and timing of insulin injections to be reasonably accurate.

DSC Shelfmark: 4275.105200

(416)

PSYCHOLOGY and diabetes: psychosocial factors in management and control
R W Shillitoe
London: Chapman and Hall, 1988. 288p.

Contains chapter examining the relationships between personality, the emotions and the disease. Considers possibilities that diabetes can be triggered by emotional problems or predisposing personality traits, and that emotional and personality factors can influence metabolic control both directly and indirectly.

DSC Shelfmark: 88/26487

(417)

GLYCAEMIC reactivity to stress: a biologic marker for development to Type 2 diabetes (Abstract)

R S Surwit *et al*

Diabetes, vol.39, suppl.1, 1990, p.8A.

A ten-minute mental arithmetic test induced an increase in blood glucose levels in Pima Indians who have a strong genetic predisposition to NIDDM but not in a control group of white subjects. Both groups showed similar cardiovascular and neuroendocrine responses to the stress.

DSC Shelfmark: 3579.600100

(418)

DOES psychological stress cause diabetes?

J K Wales

Diabetic medicine, vol.12, 1995, p.109-112.

Many patients believe their diabetes has been caused by stress or an adverse life event. While there is strong evidence that psychological stress is related to a deterioration in blood sugar control in established diabetes, there is much less evidence that it can cause diabetes in humans *de novo*.

DSC Shelfmark: 3579.606000

5.15.4 Musculoskeletal disorders

(419)

OCCUPATIONAL causes of low-back pain

K Walsh *et al*

Scandinavian journal of work, environment and health, vol.15, 1989, p.54-59.

Obtained life-time histories of low-back pain from a retrospective postal survey of 545 randomly selected adults and related incidence of low-back pain to occupational activities prior to onset of symptoms. For men the strongest associations were with heavy lifting and prolonged car driving. There was also an association with heavy lifting among the women. However, in this sample, less than 20% of cases could be attributed to such activities.

DSC Shelfmark: 8087.568000

(420)

A PROSPECTIVE study of work perceptions and psychosocial factors affecting the report of back injury

S J Bigos *et al*

Spine, vol.16, 1991, p.1-6.

A longitudinal prospective study was conducted on 3020 aircraft employees to identify risk factors for reporting back-pain at work. During slightly more than 4 years of follow-up, 279 subjects reported back problems. Other than a history of back trouble, the factors found to be most predictive in a multivariate model were work perceptions and certain psychological responses identified on the Minnesota Multiphasic Personality Inventory. Subjects who stated that they 'hardly ever' enjoyed their job were 2.5 times more likely to report back injury than subjects who 'almost always' enjoyed their jobs. The quintile of subjects scoring highest on Scale 3 (Hysteria) of the MMPI were 2.0 times more likely to report a back injury than subjects with the lowest scores.

DSC Shelfmark: 8413.903000

(421)

PSYCHOSOCIAL job factors and symptoms from the locomotive system: a multicausal analysis

T Theorell *et al*

Scandinavian journal of rehabilitation medicine, vol.23, 1991, p.165-173.

The effects of physical and psychosocial work environment factors on emotions, psychosomatic and endocrine (cortisol and testosterone) states, back pain, symptoms of degenerative joint disease and absenteeism for sickness were studied in 147 men and 60 women in six occupations. Measurements were carried out twice to four times over a year. It was found that psychological work demands were associated with physiological indicators of strain (plasma cortisol and self-reported muscle tension), and that self-reported muscle tension was associated with several emotional reactions as well as with symptoms from the back, neck and shoulders. Little possibility for decision making was associated with a high rate of sickness absence. A high plasma testosterone level in men was associated with self-reported muscle tension.

DSC Shelfmark: 8087.530000

(422)

DEPRESSIVE and distress symptoms as predictors of low back pain, neck-shoulder pain and other musculoskeletal morbidity: a 10-year follow-up of metal industry employees

P Leino and G Magni

Pain, vol.53, 1993, p.89-94.

607 employees in 3 metal industry plants were studied for depression and somatic responses to stress, self-reported musculoskeletal problems, and clinical findings in the musculoskeletal

system made by a physiotherapist. Measurements were made 3 times at 5-year intervals. Predictive effects of depressive and somatic stress symptoms on the five-year development of musculoskeletal symptoms in both women and men and on the development of clinically identifiable findings in men were found. None of the musculoskeletal morbidity indices significantly predicted the development of depressive symptoms in either sex.

DSC Shelfmark: 6333.795000

(423)
MUSCLE pain and coping with working life in Norway: a review
H Ursin *et al*
Work and stress, vol.7, 1993, p.248-258.

Argues that there is clear statistical evidence of a link between psychological factors and muscle pain. The authors' interpretation of this is that a sense of helplessness and hopelessness leads to a psychological state which leads to a physiological state (muscle tension) which predicts muscle pain. A review of intervention studies suggests that combined interventions (physical exercise plus stress management training) had better effects than exercise alone.

DSC Shelfmark: 9348.102000

(424)
PSYCHOSOCIAL factors at work and musculoskeletal disease
P M Bongers *et al*
Scandinavian journal of work, environment and health, vol.19, 1993, p.297-312.

Qualitative review of 44 cross-sectional and 15 longitudinal studies. It is concluded that monotonous work, high perceived workload, and time pressure are related to musculoskeletal symptoms. The data also suggest that low control on the job and lack of collegial support are also positively associated with musculoskeletal disease. Perceived stress may be an intermediary in the process.

DSC Shelfmark: 8087.568000

(425)
JOB task and psychosocial risk factors for work-related musculoskeletal disorders among newspaper employees
B Bernard *et al*
Scandinavian journal of work, environment and health, vol.20, 1994, p.417-426.

Results suggest a high prevalence of musculoskeletal disorders of the upper extremities among newspaper employees and they provide additional evidence that increased workload, time pressure and greater hours of computer use are related to the occurrence of work-related musculoskeletal disorders among these workers, particularly for disorders in the hand or wrist area.

DSC Shelfmark: 8087.568000

(426)
PSYCHOSOCIAL stressors at work and musculoskeletal problems
I L D Houtman et al
Scandinavian journal of work, environment and health, vol.20, 1994, p.139-145.

Secondary analyses were performed on data from the Dutch National Work and Living Conditions Survey, 1977, 1983 and 1986. Factor analysis identified work pace, intellectual discretion and physical stressors as risk dimensions in the survey. Psychosocial stressors were found to be associated not only with psychosomatic complaints and health indicators but also with musculoskeletal problems. The relationship between intellectual discretion and musculoskeletal problems can be partly attributed to physical load. Even after adjustment for physical stressors and personality variables, the relationship between the psychosocial stressors and musculoskeletal problems remained significant.

DSC Shelfmark: 8087.568000

(427)
MUSCULOSKELETAL disorders among operators of visual display terminals
C N Ong et al
Scandinavian journal of work, environment and health, vol.21, 1995, p.60-64.

Debate about the relationship of musculoskeletal disorders and VDT usage usually centres around occupational factors (e.g. constrained posture, poor ergonomic design of the workplace), psychosocial factors (e.g. age, previous musculoskeletal injuries, emotional stress, family burden, environmental factors) and work-related psychological factors (e.g. high job demands, mundane, boring and repetitive job activity, little control, lack of social support). Improving workstation design, changing occupational legislation and improving occupational health services have been suggested as means to decrease the incidence of musculoskeletal disorders among VDT workers.

DSC Shelfmark: 8087.568000

(428)
PSYCHOSOCIAL factors at work in relation to back and limb disorders
P I Leino and V Hänninen
Scandinavian journal of work, environment and health, vol.21, 1995, p.134-142.

A sample of 902 blue-and-white collar employees in the metal industry was studied. Measurements were made twice at 10-year intervals by questionnaire and clinical examination. Work-related psychosocial factors were associated with, and predicted, changes in the occurrence of musculoskeletal disorders when age, gender, social class and physical workload were controlled for.

DSC Shelfmark: 8087.568000

(429)

SOCIAL support, job strain and musculoskeletal pain among female health care personnel

G K Ahlberg-Hultén, T Theorell and K Sigala

Scandinavian journal of work, environment and health, vol.21, 1995, p.435–439.

Ninety registered nurses and nurse's aids working in different hospitals in or just outside Stockholm and working in different kinds of care completed self-report questionnaires. Results showed that symptoms from the back were significantly related to job strain – the higher the strain the more symptoms in the low back. Symptoms from the neck and shoulders were more associated with social support at work – the lower the support score, the more severe the symptoms.

DSC Shelfmark: 8087.568000

(430)

UPPER extremity disorders: a literature review to determine work-relatedness

M J Vender, M L Kasdan, K L Trappa

Journal of hand surgery, vol.20, 1995, p.534–541.

The objective of this review was to establish whether the medical literature supported a causal relationship between upper extremity disorders and work activities. None of the reviewed studies did in fact establish such a causal relationship. Further research is needed using studies that incorporate reliable epidemiologic and accepted diagnostic criteria.

DSC Shelfmark: 4996.620000 (American vol.)

(431)

PSYCHOSOCIAL and physical risk factors for musculoskeletal disorders of the neck, shoulders and lower back in salespeople

T Skov, V Borg and E Ørhede

Occupational and environmental medicine, vol.53, 1996, p.351–356.

Data were collected from a sample of 1306 salespeople who completed a questionnaire on job characteristics, personality characteristics, social network, smoking, drinking and symptoms of the neck, shoulders and low back. High job demands were related to neck and shoulder symptoms, and tendency to become overworked and lack of social support from colleagues were related to back pain. Lack of variation in the job, low control over time and high competition were related to neck symptoms, but there was an interaction so that low control over time and high competition both had to be present to increase the risk.

DSC Shelfmark: 6227.833000

(432)

IS ergonomic intervention alone sufficient to limit musculoskeletal problems in nurses?

A K Burton *et al*

Occupational medicine, vol.47, 1997, p.25–32.

Report of a retrospective survey of 1216 nurses in hospitals in Belgium and the Netherlands. Prevalence rates for musculoskeletal problems and low back trouble were significantly lower in the Dutch hospitals, but a significantly higher proportion of Dutch nurses had 'heavy' workloads. Overall, symptoms and work loss in the previous 12 months were not related to workload; nor was there a perception that work was causative. The Dutch nurses differed strikingly from the Belgian nurses in that they were less depressed, and significantly more positive about pain, work and activity.

DSC Shelfmark: 6229.610000

(433)

MUSCULOSKELETAL symptoms and headaches in VDU users: a psychophysiological study

C Wiholm and B B Arnetz

Work and stress, vol.11, 1997, p.239–250.

Data were collected by self-report questionnaire from 116 employees of a high-tech telecommunications company. Blood samples were also analysed for testosterone, prolactin and cortisol. Dissatisfaction with line management, work/family conflict, younger age and lower levels of testosterone predicted symptoms of the back and neck. For symptoms of the lower arm, years of computer work, underutilisation of skills, younger age and poor balance of job autonomy were predictive. It is concluded that musculoskeletal symptoms in high-tech environments might be mediated via neuroendocrine mechanisms.

DSC Shelfmark: 9348.102000

(434)

PSYCHOSOCIAL stressors at work, psychological stress and musculoskeletal symptoms in care for the elderly

M Elovainio and T Sinervo

Work and stress, vol.11, 1997, p.351–361.

Study investigated how psychosocial stressors and physical load are related to psychological stress symptoms among staff in Finnish care homes and home help services. Results supported the mediating effect of psychological stress between psychosocial stress factors (troublesome patients and time pressure) and musculoskeletal symptoms. Findings concerning the mediating effect of physical load between psychosocial stress factors and musculoskeletal symptoms were not so substantiating.

DSC Shelfmark: 9348.102000

(435)

UPPER limb disorders and work: the importance of physical and psychosocial factors

P Buckle

Journal of psychosomatic research, vol.43, 1997, p.17-25.

Epidemiological literature provides substantive evidence of a relationship between exposure to factors in the work system and development of disorders of the soft tissues of the neck, shoulder and upper limb. The strongest relationships have been found for physical factors, but psychosocial factors such as work involving time pressures or low job control, also show significant associations. The complex interactions between variables make it difficult to estimate how much each factor contributes to the overall problem.

DSC Shelfmark: 5043.480000

(436)

OCCUPATIONAL factors affecting sick leave attributed to low back pain

G J Wickstrom and J Pentti

Scandinavian journal of work, environment and health, vol.24, 1998, p.145-152.

A sample of 117 white- and 189 blue-collar workers from two metal industry companies completed a questionnaire on recurrent low back pain and exposure to potential risk factors at work on two occasions, with a 24 month interval. Sick leave was monitored for the period between the questionnaires. Sick leave attributed to back problems was predicted by biomechanical loads at work and by a lack of recognition and respect among blue-collar workers. Self-reports of recurrent low back pain were preceded by reports of harmful biomechanical loads at work among blue- and white-collar workers, by stress among white-collar workers and by exposure to drafts among blue-collar workers.

DCS Shelfmark: 8087.568000

5.15.5 Cardiovascular disorders

(437)

CHANGES in the serum cholesterol and blood clotting time in men subjected to cyclic variation of occupational stress

M Friedman, R H Rosenman and V Carroll

Circulation, vol.17, 1958, p.852-861.

Serum cholesterol was obtained biweekly and blood coagulation time at monthly intervals from 40 volunteer accountants during the first 5 months of 1957 in order to study the effects of stress arising from deadlines in the tax calendar on these 2 factors. Results indicate that severe occupational stress or other forms of unusual emotional tension are associated both with a sudden and often profound rise in serum cholesterol and a marked acceleration of blood coagulation time.

DSC Shelfmark: 3265.200000

(438)

JOB decision latitude, job demands and cardiovascular disease: a predictive study of Swedish men

R A Karasek *et al*

American journal of public health, vol.71, 1981, p.694-705.

Performed prospective analyses on data from the Swedish national Level of Living Surveys for 1968 and 1974. In addition to the demands and decision latitude variables previously studied, the impact of 'personal schedule freedom at work' was examined. Skill level and job demands were each predictive of coronary heart disease indicators after controlling for age, education, smoking and obesity. The personal schedule freedom variable was not predictive. The interaction between job demands and decision latitude as specified in the original model was not tested.

DSC Shelfmark: 0835.900000

(439)

JOB characteristics of occupations and myocardial infarction risk: effect of possible confounding factors

L Alfredsson and T Theorell

Social science and medicine, vol.17, 1983, p.1497-1503.

Some previously found associations between occupational characteristics and myocardial infarction risk were scrutinised regarding counfounding effects. Possible confounding factors were smoking, low level of education, high proportion of immigrants and heavy lifting. Standardised occupational characteristics were utilised in a case-control study of 1216 men aged 40-64 years living in the Stockholm area. Results showed that occupations characterised by high demand and low possibilities of control or growth were significantly associated with an elevated MI risk regardless of the confounding factors.

DSC Shelfmark: 8318.157000

(440)

JOB strain and ischaemic heart disease: an epidemiologic study of metal workers

M N Haan

Annals of clinical research, vol.20, 1988, p.143-145.

Report of research conducted using data collected between 1973 and 1983 on 902 employees of a metal fabrication company in Finland. Baseline data were collected in 1973 with follow-up in 1978 and 1983. On all three occasions, a survey questionnaire was administered and a 25-minute medical examination was conducted. Results suggest an association between job strain and ischaemic heart disease not accounted for by differences in age, sex, serum cholesterol, systolic blood pressure, relative weight, smoking or alcohol consumption. Persons exposed to high job strain who smoke are at significantly greater risk of IHD than non-smokers exposed to low job strain.

DSC Shelfmark: 1040.250000

(441)

COMBINED effects of job strain and social isolation on cardiovascular disease morbidity and mortality in a random sample of the Swedish male working population

J V Johnson, E M Hall and T Theorell

Scandinavian journal of work, environment and health, vol.15, 1989, p.271-279.

Examined the prevalence of CVD morbidity and cardiovascular-specific mortality in a nine-year longitudinal study of 7219 Swedish employed men. A multiplicative measure was constructed to model the combined effects of job demands, work-related social support and work control. Results supported the hypothesis that workers exposed to adverse psychosocial conditions of high strain and social isolation would have an elevated risk of CVD morbidity and mortality.

DSC Shelfmark: 8087.568000

(442)

THE RELATION of psychosocial dimensions of work with coronary heart disease risk factors: a meta-analysis of five United States data bases

C Pieper, A Z Lacroix, and R A Karasek

American journal of epidemiology, vol.129, 1989, p.483-494.

Results shown utilise a new imputation strategy to test the relation of job variables with 4 cardiovascular risk factors (cholesterol, smoking, diastolic and systolic blood pressure) in five major US databases. When age, race, education, body mass index, and Type A behaviour were controlled for, there was evidence that the main effects of job decision latitude were related to at least two risk factors: smoking and systolic pressure. There was no support for the original hypothesis that the interaction of demands with decision latitude related to the risk factors.

DSC Shelfmark: 0824.600000

(443)

CHANGES in plasma lipids and dietary intake accompanying shifts in perceived workload and stress

B S McCann, G R Warnick and R H Knopp

Psychosomatic medicine, vol.52, 1990, p.97-108.

Measures of plasma lipids, dietary intake and perceived stress and workload were obtained from individuals experiencing periodic increases in work demands in their workplace. Increases in total plasma cholesterol were significantly positively correlated with increases in perceived stress and perceived workload. Relative to a low workload period, significant increases in the intake of foods known to raise plasma cholesterol levels were observed during periods of high workload.

DSC Shelfmark: 6946.555000

(444)

FAMILY history of hypertension: an individual trait interacting with spontaneously occuring job stressors
T Theorell
Scandinavian journal of work, environment and health, vol.16, suppl.1, 1990, p.74–79.

Objective of the study was to test the hypothesis that men with a family history of hypertension differ from other men with regard to both blood pressure and endocrine reactions to occupational strain. Results showed that systolic blood pressure at work increased successively with increasing job strain, mainly, as expected, in the 31% of the sample with a family history of hypertension. These also showed low cortisol levels during peak strain, and a lack of prolactin response and a strong decrease in testosterone levels during job strain.

DSC Shelfmark: 8087.568000

(445)

THE RELATIONSHIP between 'job strain', workplace diastolic blood pressure and left ventricular mass index
P L Schnall *et al*
Journal of the American Medical Association, vol.263, 1990, p.1929–1935.

Conducted a case-control study at seven urban worksites of 215 employed men aged 30-60 years without evidence of coronary heart disease. After a comprehensive blood pressure screening of male employees at the worksite, 87 cases of hypertension and a random sample of 128 controls were studied. Job strain was significantly related to hypertension with an estimated odds ratio of 3.1, after adjusting for age, race, body-mass index, Type A behaviour, alcohol intake, smoking, worksite, 24-hour urine sodium excretion, education and physical demand level of the job. Controlling for these variables in subjects aged 30 to 40 years with job strain, the echocardiographically determined left ventricular mass index was on average 10.8 glm2 greater than in subjects without job strain.

DSC Shelfmark: 4689.000000

(446)

THREAT of unemployment and cardiovascular risk factors: longitudinal study of quality of sleep and serum cholesterol concentrations in men threatened with redundancy
I Mattiasson *et al*
British medical journal, vol.301, 1990, p.461–466.

Longitudinal study of a cohort of middle aged shipyard workers followed up for a mean of 6.2 years and a group of controls observed for the same period. The first investigation took place during a period of relative economic stability for the shipyard, and the second during the phase of its closure. Indications were found of a relation between imminent risk of job loss and increases in serum cholesterol concentrations. The increases were more pronounced in

248

men with sleep disturbance and in immigrants and almost non-existent among men offered early retirement on full pay.

DSC Shelfmark: 2330.000000

(447)
THE EFFECTS of the strain of returning to work on the risk of cardiac death after a first myocardial infarction before the age of 45
T Theorell *et al*
International journal of cardiology, vol.30, Jan 1991, p.61-67.

Seventy-nine men who had suffered a heart attack before the age of 45 while they were vocationally active in the greater Stockholm area were followed for five years. Forty-nine survived without cardiac complications and 13 died of ischaemic heart disease during the period of follow up. Results showed that subjects who reported having a psychologically demanding and intellectually boring job before the onset of myocardial infarction, and who then returned to it after the infarction, were more likely than other subjects to die because of a re-infarction during the five year follow-up.

DSC Shelfmark: 4542.158000

(448)
JOB strain and ambulatory blood pressure profiles
T Theorell *et al*
Scandinavian journal of work, environment and health, vol.17, 1991, p.380-385.

Ambulatory 24-h recordings of blood pressure were made for 161 men with borderline hypertension. From the occupational classification system, scores for psychological demands, control, support, physical demands and occupational hazards were obtained. An association was found between job strain measured by means of this occupational inference system and diastolic blood pressure during work hours and sleep. The association was strengthened when subjects with occupations classified as physically demanding were excluded from the analysis.

DSC Shelfmark: 8087.568000

(449)
JOB strain and prevalence of hypertension in a biracial population of urban bus drivers
C L Albright *et al*
American journal of public health, vol.82, 1992, p.984-989.

1,396 bus drivers underwent a physical examination measuring height, weight and blood pressure and gave their medical histories. Subjects completed a questionnaire assessing their work schedules, personal habits, job demands and decision latitude. After 12 confounding variables were controlled for, the association between occupational stress and hypertension became non-significant.

DSC Shelfmark: 0835.900000

(450)

LIPIDS in psychological research: the last decade

R Niaura, C M Stoney and P N Herbert

Biological psychology, vol.34, 1992, p.1-43.

Mild forms of chronic or episodic stress are apparently not associated with alterations in lipids and lipoproteins, but severe forms of real or perceived stress do appear to alter lipid levels. Acute laboratory stress is frequently associated with short term alterations in lipids and lipoproteins, but the significance of this is unclear. Several individual characteristics such as Type A behaviour and other personality variables appear to be associated with an atherogenic lipid profile. The physiological and behavioural mechanisms through which stress influences lipid concentrations and metabolism are not fully understood.

DSC Shelfmark: 2077.560000

(451)

RELATION between job strain, alcohol and ambulatory blood pressure

P L Schnall *et al*

Hypertension, vol.19, 1992, p.488-494.

A total of 264 men at eight worksites wore an ambulatory blood pressure (AmBP) monitor for 24 hours on a working day. Job strain was associated with an increase in both systolic and diastolic ambulatory blood pressure after adjusting for age, race, body mass index, Type A behaviour, alcohol behaviour, smoking, worksite, 24-hour urine sodium excretion, education and physical demand level of the job. Alcohol use and job strain interacted so that workers in high strain jobs who drank regularly had significantly higher AmBP at work. Job strain also had significant effects on AmBP at home and during sleep.

DSC Shelfmark: 4352.629000

(452)

THE RELATIONSHIP between job strain and blood pressure at work, at home and during sleep

L F von Egeren

Psychosomatic medicine, vol.54, 1992, p.337-343.

Eleven normotensive workers in 'high strain' jobs were compared with 26 normotensive workers in 'low strain' jobs on ambulatory blood pressure at home, at work and during sleep. High strain workers' systolic BP was higher at work and at home in the evening after adjusting for pre-work casual BP, body mass index, gender, Type A behaviour, and coffee consumption. Under certain conditions, systolic BP during sleep and diastolic BP at work were higher as well.

DSC Shelfmark: 6946.555000

(453)
STRESS and lipoprotein metabolism: modulators and mechanisms
D N Brindley *et al*
Metabolism, vol.42, no.9, Suppl.1, Sept. 1993, p.3-15.

Data from human and animal studies generally support a relationship between stress and blood lipid concentrations. Human studies include investigations of acute and chronic stress, and of individual differences in how stress is handled. Direct evidence in support of exact mechanisms to account for this relationship is lacking. Nevertheless, it appears that a causal link between stress and lipid concentrations may be supported by at least three mechanisms. These include effects of stress on hormonal responses that can affect lipoprotein concentrations and turnover, on haemoconcentration, and on behaviour.

DSC Shelfmark: 5683.300000

(454)
ASSOCIATION between ambulatory blood pressure and alternative formulations of job strain
P A Landsbergis *et al*
Scandinavian journal of work, environment and health, vol.20, 1994, p.349-363.

Examined whether 4 formulations of a job strain construct were associated with ambulatory blood pressure and the risk of hypertension in a study of 262 male employees in 8 worksites. Subjects completed a casual blood pressure screening, medical exams and questionnaires, and wore an ambulatory BP monitor for 24 hours during a normal workday. All formulations of high job demands and low decision latitude were significantly associated with elevated ambulatory systolic BP.

DSC Shelfmark: 8087.568000

(455)
JOB strain and cardiovascular disease
P L Schnall, P A Landsbergis and D Baker
Annual review of public health, vol.15, 1994, p.381-411.

Comprehensive review of the efficacy of Karasek's job demands-control model in linking job strain to risk factors for cardiovascular disease. Investigates whether the observed effect of job strain could be due to confounding by other CVD risk factors or some forms of bias, or the biological mechanisms underlying the association. Explores whether the effect is direct or mediated by known cardiovascular risk factors and the nature of the interaction between the constructs job demands and job decision latitude in the job strain model.

DSC Shelfmark: 1528.450000

(456)

CONTRIBUTION of job strain, job status and marital status to laboratory and ambulatory blood pressure in patients with mild hypertension

J A Blumenthal, E T Thyrum and W C Siegel

Journal of psychosomatic research, vol.39, 1995, p.133-144.

The effects of job strain, occupational status and marital status were evaluated in 99 men and women with mild hypertension. Blood pressure was measured during daily life at home and at work over 15 hours of ambulatory blood pressure monitoring. On a separate day blood pressure was measured in the laboratory during mental stress testing. High strain women, but not men, displayed higher systolic blood pressure levels during ambulatory monitoring than their low strain counterparts. Married persons and individuals with high job status had elevated blood pressures during mental stress testing.

DSC Shelfmark: 5043.480000

(457)

PSYCHOSOCIAL work characteristics and cardiovascular disease risk factors in young adults: the CARDIA study

K J Greenlund *et al*

Social science and medicine, vol.41, 1995, p.717-723.

Examined the associations of high demands, low decision latitude and job strain with cardiovascular disease risk factors (high blood pressure, alcohol/cigarette use or high cholesterol). The Job Content Questionnaire was administered to assess the relationship of job demands, decision latitude and job strain with CVD risk factors. Resting blood pressure was measured and alcohol intake derived from interviewer-administered questions. Analysis revealed an inverse association with risk factors in high job demands, low decision latitude and job strain. Few associations supported the hypothesis that high job demands, low decision latitude or job strain are associated with increased levels of CVD risk factors.

DSC Shelfmark: 8318.157000

(458)

EFFECTS of work overload and burnout on cholesterol and triglycerides levels: the moderating effects of emotional reactivity among male and female employees

A Shirom *et al*

Journal of occupational health psychology, vol.2, 1997, p.275-288.

The effects of objective and subjective overload, and of physical and emotional burnout on cholesterol and triglycerides levels were studied in a quasi prospective design. Results suggest that stress may impact serum lipids by means of burnout and that burnout is directly implicated in elevations of cholesterol, and, for female employees, also of triglycerides.

DSC Shelfmark: 5026.095000

(459)
CARDIOVASCULAR and immune responses to acute psychological stress in young and old women: a meta-analysis
R J Benschop *et al*
Psychosomatic medicine, vol.60, 1998, p.290-296.

Analyses of data from 8 independent studies reveal a medium to large significant correlation between natural killer (NK) cell number changes and heart rate responses to acute stress, and small to medium correlations between NK cell number changes and blood pressure responses. NK cell changes and heart rate responses induced by acute stress in women appear to be regulated, to some extent, by the same mechanism. Neither type of stressor nor age seem to be very important when considering correlations between NK cell and cardiovascular changes.

DSC Shelfmark: 6946.515000

5.15.6 Stress and the immune system

(460)
STRESS, emotion and human immune function
A O'Leary
Psychological bulletin, vol.108, 1990, p.363-382.

Provides a review of empirical evidence linking emotional processes to immune function in humans. Chronic stress has been associated with suppression of immune function. Effects of stress accompanying social disruption and depression have been consistently adverse. Certain personality styles may enhance or degrade the immune response. Relationships between psychosocial factors and immunity have been identified for several diseases, including cancer, AIDS and autoimmune diseases.

DSC Shelfmark: 6946.300000

(461)
EFFECTS of experimental psychological stress on T-lymphocytes and NK cells in man: an exploratory study
J F Brosschot *et al*
Journal of psychophysiology, vol.5, 1991, p.59-67.

Eleven experimental subjects were exposed to a mild and potentially uncontrollable interpersonal stress situation. Before, directly after, and half an hour after the stress situation, blood was drawn, in which percentages of total T-cells, T-helper/inducer cells, T-suppressor/cytotoxic cells and NK cells were determined. Results showed that a brief period of experimentally induced stress influenced the distribution of T-lymphocytes and NK cells in peripheral blood. Percentages of T-helper/inducer cells were significantly decreased during the stress period and returned to baseline levels afterwards. In contrast, NK cells increased during the stress period and returned to baseline afterwards.

DSC Shelfmark: 5043.465000

(462)

STRESS at work, and psychological and immunological parameters in a group of Norwegian female bank employees
I M Endresen *et al*
Work and stress, vol.5, 1991, p.217-227.

Self-reported stress, emotional state, ego-strength and defensiveness were examined in relation to measures of cellular immunity (T-cell response to Con A and number of T4 and T8 cells) and humoral immunity (concentrations of immunoglobulins and complement components in plasma) in a group of 96 Norwegian female bank employees. The analyses showed that workload, the stress factor with the highest group mean, was associated with the number of T-cells while strain due to body posture at work was related to concentrations of IgM and C3. Depression was significantly correlated with IgM concentration and T-cell number and anxiety with C3 concentration.

DSC Shelfmark: 9348.102000

(463)

STRESS-INDUCED immune dysfunction in humans
M Irwin
In Stress: neurobiology and neuroendocrinology edited by M R Brown, G F Koob, and C Rivier. New York: Dekker, 1991, p.589-611.

Evidence for diminished cell-mediated immune function during life threatening events and clinical depression is reviewed. A model is presented to organise clinical research relevant to the association between stress and immune dysfunction. To characterise the mechanisms by which the brain influences immune cells, an interdisciplinary approach involving the efforts of researchers with expertise in the neuroendocrine and autonomic physiology of the stress response is needed.

DSC Shelfmark: 91/04595

(464)

PSYCHOLOGICAL and psychophysiological aspects of psoriasis
I H Ginsburg
Dermatologic clinics, vol.13, 1995, p.793-804.

Psychoneuroimmunologic pathways between stressful life experience and onset and exacerbation of psoriasis are beginning to be explored, and are a likely focus for future interdisciplinary research. It seems likely that having psoriasis acts as a stressful life event in itself.

DSC Shelfmark: 3555.138000

(465)

PSYCHOLOGICAL stress and susceptibility to upper respiratory infections

S Cohen

American journal of respiratory critical care medicine, vol.152, 1995, p.553-558.

Although there is substantial evidence for the association between psychological stress and both cellular and humoral immune response, these data do not necessarily suggest increased susceptibility to infectious agents among stressed persons. Epidemiologic and viral challenge studies suggest that psychological stress is a risk factor for upper respiratory infections, with strongest evidence supplied by recent well-controlled prospective viral challenge trials. However, there is still little direct evidence for the nature of the neuroendocrine, immune or behavioural pathways through which stress might alter susceptibility.

DSC Shelfmark: 0836.590000

(466)

PSYCHONEUROIMMUNOLOGY: interactions between the nervous system and the immune system

R Ader, N Cohen, and D Felten

The Lancet, vol.345, 1995, p.99-103.

The innervation of the lymphoid organs and the availability of neurotransmitters for interactions with cells in the immune system have changed our understanding of the environment in which immune responses occur. The interaction between pituitary, endocrine and lymphocyte derived hormones which define the neuroendocrine environment in which immune responses take place adds another level of complexity to the analysis of cellular interactions that drive immune responses. Collectively, these observations provide the basis for behaviourally induced alterations in immune function and immunologically based changes in behaviour. They may provide the means by which psychosocial factors and emotional states influence development and progression of infections, autoimmune and neoplastic disease.

DSC Shelfmark: 5146.000000

(467)

PSYCHONEUROIMMUNOLOGY and health consequences: data and shared mechanisms

J K Kiecolt-Glaser and R Glaser

Psychosomatic medicine, vol.57, 1995, p.269-274.

Data reviewed suggest that immune modulation by psychosocial stressors and/or interventions may influence health status. The impact of chronic stressors and psychosocial factors on sympathetic nervous system and endocrine function influences the immune system, thereby providing shared mechanisms that may impact on disease susceptibility and progression.

DSC Shelfmark: 6946.555000

(468)

PSYCHOSOCIAL factors in inflammatory periodontal diseases: a review

A M Da Silva, H N Newman and D A Oakley

Journal of clinical periodontology, vol.22, 1995, p.516–526.

It is not clear that the scientific evidence is sufficient to substantiate the hypothesis that psychosocial factors are of etiological importance in periodontitis. The proposed mechanisms which may mediate the relationship between psychosocial conditions and inflammatory periodontal diseases remain to be tested. However, psychoneuroimmunologic studies make lowered host resistance especially interesting as a possible mechanism.

DSC Shelfmark: 4958.672000

(469)

CATECHOLAMINE induced leukocytosis: early observations, current research, and future directions

R J Benschop, M Rodriguez-Feuerhahn and M Schedlowski

Brain, behaviour and immunity, vol.10, 1996, p.77–91.

Acute psychological stress in man affects lymphocyte circulation. It has been suggested that catecholamines are responsible for these changes. Review summarises findings regarding catecholamine-induced lympho- and leukocytosis. Particular attention is given to the mechanisms of this phenomenon and the potential site of newly appearing leukocytes. Results from acute psychological stress or physical exercise models corroborate the results obtained with catecholamine administration. Together, the data demonstrate that components of the innate immune system participate in the classical fight/flight response.

DSC Shelfmark: 2268.101000

(470)

HEALTH psychology: psychological factors and physical disease from the perspective of human psychoneuroimmunology

S Cohen and T B Herbert

Annual review of psychology, vol.47, 1996, p.113–142.

Psychoneuroimmunology provides psychologically and biologically plausible explanations of how psychological factors might influence immunity and immune system-mediated disease. There is substantial evidence that factors such as stress, negative affect, clinical depression, social support and repression/denial can influence both cellular and humoral indicators of immune status and function. Existing data also offer convincing evidence of links between stress and negative affect and the onset and progression of infectious diseases such as colds, flu and herpes. Evidence for the effects of stress, depression and repression/denial on the onset and progress of AIDS and cancer is less convincing, probably due to methodological difficulties in studying these complex diseases.

DSC Shelfmark: 1528.400000

(471)
PSYCHONEUROIMMUNOLOGY and cancer: historical perspectives and current research
A Fife, P J Beasley and D L Fertig
Advances in neuroimmunology, vol.6, 1996, p.179-190.

The belief that emotions play a part in the onset and progression of cancer has been emphasized throughout the history of medicine. A substantial literature has emerged supporting the theory that depression and stress can result in altered endocrine and immune system functioning. Methodological problems are a major obstacle in clarifying the true impact of psychological factors on cancer; how a particular individual copes with a particular stress factor is likely to be an important variable.

DSC Shelfmark: 0709.479000

(472)
THE RELATIONSHIP between stress and the development of breast cancer: a literature review
C M Bryla
Oncology nursing forum, vol.23, 1996, p.441-448.

Studies show that a relationship exists between stress and the development of breast cancer. Most of the literature describes this relationship according to the patient's personality traits, their response to stress, or the occurrence of stressful life events. The immune system may mediate the physiologic influence of stress on breast cancer. Although the difficulty of measuring stress makes it difficult to demonstrate a tangible relationship between stress and breast cancer, studies reveal that stress is associated with breast cancer in various ways. Dealing positively with stress may improve the patient's quality of life.

DSC Shelfmark: 6256.980000

(473)
THE ROLE of psychological stress in rheumatoid arthritis
J Gio-Fitman
Medsurg. nursing, vol.5, 1996, p.422-426.

Psychological stress affects the immune system and is linked to disease onset and exacerbation in the rheumatoid arthritic patient. Stress may precede the onset of disease or flare-ups.

DSC Shelfmarks: 5535.589000

(474)

PSYCHOLOGICAL stress, neuroimmunomodulation and susceptibility to infectious diseases in animals and man: a review

M Biondi and L G Zannino

Psychotherapy and psychosomatics, vol.66, 1997, p.3-26.

Reviews research on the role of psychological stress, personality, social support and other psychosocial factors in bacterial, viral and parasitic infections. Psychological stress is considered as a potential cofactor in the pathogenesis of infectious diseases. It seems able to alter susceptibility to infectious agents, influencing the onset, course and outcome of certain infectious pathologies. Many experiments have identified in neuroimmunomodulation the principal mediator of the alterations associated with conditions of stress.

DSC Shelfmark: 6946.559000

(475)

SEARCHING for the biological pathways between stress and health

S Kelly, C Hertzman and M Daniels

Annual review of public health, vol.18, 1997, p.437-462.

Review found virtually no research that measured chronic stress, physiological responses to it and health status outcomes related to these responses over the long term. Population-based, person-specific health surveys, with concomitant biological measures, should provide important information about the processes whereby socioeconomic and psychosocial factors embed themselves in human health. Questionnaire responses allow for assessment of the perceived psychosocial environment, but biological measurements will measure the status of the psychoneuroimmunologic/psychoneuroendocrinologic pathways and may allow us to identify people who have successfully coped with their stress because of experience, expectations, stoicism, etc. Properly designed longitudinal studies would help determine whether PNI/PNE pathways function differently in people who have more income, better jobs, more social support, etc. than in those who are less advantaged.

DSC Shelfmark: 1528.450000

(476)

IMMUNE function and lifestyle of taxi drivers in Japan

Y Nakano *et al*

Industrial health, vol.36, 1998, p.32-39.

Examined randomly selected male taxi drivers aged 40-59 years who were members of a labour union in Kansai in 1992 and 1993. At the end of 1993 business was adversely affected by an economic depression. Results showed that mitogen response and interleukin-2 production decreased in 1993, while interleukin-4 production was significantly elevated. Immune system changes in drivers prohibited from working overtime were more pronounced than those of drivers allowed to do so.

DSC Shelfmark: 4454.700000

5.15.7 Cancer

(477)
PSYCHOLOGICAL depression and cancer
L A Bieliauskas and D C Garron
General hospital psychiatry, vol.4, 1982, p.187-195.

Studies are reviewed which relate to five areas of research concerning depression and cancer: significant loss experience, emotional inhibition, hopelessness, psychiatric assessment of depression and test measurement of depression. There is no evidence that cancer patients have an increased experience of emotional loss prior to their disease, while there is some support for increased emotional inhibition and hopelessness in patients who already have cancer. There is no solid evidence that cancer patients have increased depression in the psychiatric sense compared to other patients, relatives or normal control groups. Psychometric assessment of depression also does not indicate increased prevalence of pathologic depression in cancer patients, though there is some suggestion that mild elevations in depressive symptomology may be prospectively linked to cancer incidence.

DSC Shelfmark: 4104.344000

(478)
PSYCHOSOCIAL correlates of survival in advanced malignant disease
B R Cassileth *et al*
The New England journal of medicine, vol.312, 1985, p.1551-1555.

Study assesses the ability of psychosocial factors (social ties, job satisfaction, use of psychotropic drugs, life satisfaction, subjective view of adult health, hopelessness/helplessness and perception of the adjustment required to cope with the diagnosis) to predict survival and the time to relapse after a diagnosis of cancer. Results showed that none of these factors were useful clinical predictors of length of survival in newly diagnosed patients with advanced metastatic disease. Secondly, they did not predict the time to recurrence of disease in patients with high risk primary melanoma or Stage II breast cancer.

DSC Shelfmark: 6084.000000

(479)
THE RELATIONSHIP of psychosocial factors to prognostic indicators in cutaneous malignant melanoma
L Temoshok *et al*
Journal of psychosomatic research, vol.29, 1985, p.139-153.

Several personality characteristics conceived as part of a theoretical Type C constellation were found to be significantly positively correlated with tumour thickness, which is the best prognostic indicator for malignant melanoma.

DSC Shelfmark: 5043.480000

(480)

PERSONALITY, coping style, emotion and cancer: towards an integrative model

L Temoshok

Cancer surveys, vol.6, 1987, p.545–567.

Research evidence suggests a constellation of factors that appears to predispose some individuals to develop cancer more readily or to progress more quickly through its stages. These factors include (a) certain personality traits and coping styles discussed under the heading of 'Type C', (b) difficulty in expressing emotions, (c) an attitude or tendency towards helplesssness/hopelessness. To explain discrepant results across studies, a process model of coping style and psychological-physiological homoeostasis is proposed. This model may be used to explain why some studies have found that Type C is associated with cancer outcome measures, while others have found that helplessness/hopelessness or emotional expression is related to outcome. It is expected that these differences are attributable to the point in the cancer and coping process at which psychological assessment was conducted.

DSC Shelfmark: 3046.610000

(481)

EPIDEMIOLOGIC aspects of stress, ageing, cancer and the immune system

B H Fox

Annals of the New York Academy of Science, vol.521, 1988, p.16–28.

Concludes that biological phenomena suggest that stress can increase cancer susceptibility with age, but that it must ride on top of biological causal agents for cancer whose effects are much greater. The probability is that stress affects survival, or progress of cancer, more than it does initiation.

DSC Shelfmark: 1031.000000

(482)

EFFECT of psychosocial treatment on survival of patients with metastatic breast cancer

D Spiegel *et al*

The Lancet, no. 8668, 1989, p.888–891.

Patients with metastatic breast cancer randomised to weekly group therapy for a year lived significantly longer than did controls, by an average of nearly 18 months. This difference was statistically and clinically significant.

DSC Shelfmark: 5146.000000

(483)
THE INFLUENCE of stressors on the progression of neoplastic change
H Anisman, J Irwin and L S Sklar
Cancer growth and progress, vol.2, 1989, p.7-18.

There appears to be a substantial literature suggesting that stressful events may influence the course of tumour development. Factors such as the organism's ability to cope with the stressor, the chronicity of the stressor, and the social back drop upon which the stressor is applied may also contribute to neoplastic change. The mechanisms of stressor-provoked alterations in tumour growth remain to be determined.

DSC Shelfmark: Not found.

(484)
TYPE A, stress prone behaviour and breast cancer
E B Faragher and C L Cooper
Psychological medicine, vol.20, 1990, p.663-670.

Quasi-prospective study of 2163 women attending breast-screening clinics (and controls) indicated a link between personality factors and breast disease. Relative to normal control women studied, the women with malignancies tended to be more 'laid-back', deliberate and patient. They were less competitive, ambitious and hard driving. They had a slow and casual approach to activities, but with a keen desire to achieve personal satisfaction from tasks irrespective of the effect on others. Finally, they exhibited an increased level of introversion and decreased level of social contacts.

DSC Shelfmark: 6946.450000

(485)
THE ROLE of psychological factors in cancer onset and progression
J L Levenson and C Bemis
Psychosomatics, vol.32, 1991, p.124-132.

Article critically reviews the literature on cancer and its potential connections to depression, personality traits, and stressful life events. Much of the existing research is flawed by poor study design and analysis that have limited the reliability and validity of negative and positive studies. While some psychological factors have been associated with cancer onset and progression, no direct links have been established.

DSC Shelfmark: 6946.557000

(486)

MALIGNANT melanoma: effects of an early structured psychiatric intervention, coping, and affective state on recurrence and survival 6 years later

F I Fawzy *et al*

Archives of general psychiatry, vol.50, 1993, p.681–689.

Evaluated recurrence and survival for 68 patients with malignant melanoma who had participated in a 6-week structured psychiatric group intervention 5 to 6 years earlier, shortly after their diagnosis and initial surgical treatment. For control patients, there was a trend for recurrence (13 out of 34) and a statistically significant greater rate of death (10 out of 34) than for experimental patients (7 out of 34 and 3 out of 34, respectively).

DSC Shelfmark: 1634.350000

(487)

PSYCHOSOCIAL factors in the development and progression of breast cancer

L Hilakivi-Clarke *et al*

Breast cancer research and treatment, vol.29, 1993, p.141–160.

The relevant evidence linking psychosocial factors to breast cancer is suggestive but not conclusive. Authors propose that the crucial factor affecting mammary tumour growth is not the presence of a stressor itself, but an individual's ability to cope with the stressor. The number of stressful events an individual has been exposed to, their significance to the individual, personality characteristics and social support all affect the ability to cope with stress. Existing data also suggest that survival is shortened by exposure to severe stressors which impair psychological well-being and lengthened by improving the patient's well-being through social support and psychological therapies.

DSC Shelfmark: 2277.494000

(488)

DEPRESSION and development of cancer: a meta-analysis

R McGee, S Williams and M Elwood

Social science and medicine, vol.38, 1994, p.187–192.

Review of evidence supporting the view that depression is a causal factor in the development of cancer based upon prospective longitudinal studies measuring depression at time 1 and subsequent incidence of cancer over the intervening period to time 2. A meta-analysis of available studies indicates a small, but marginally statistically significant association between depression and the later development of cancer.

DSC Shelfmark: 8318.157000

(489)
CRITICAL review of psychosocial interventions in cancer care
F I Fawzy and N W Fawzy
Archives of general psychiatry, vol.52, 1995, p.100-113.

This article reviews the four interventions most commonly used in the treatment of cancer patients (1) education about the disease and its treatment, (2) behavioural training, including relaxation techniques, hypnosis, deep breathing, meditation, biofeedback and guided imagery, (3) individual psychotherapy and (4) group interventions.

DSC Shelfmark: 1634.350000

(490)
GROUP therapy in the cancer setting
F I Fawzy and N W Fawzy
Journal of psychosomatic research, vol.45, 1998, p.191-200.

Review of the literature on psychosocial interventions with cancer patients shows that structured interventions consisting of health education, stress management/behavioural training and group support seem to offer significant benefits for patients in the early stages of treatment. For patients with advanced metastatic disease, on-going support programmes dealing with pain management, daily coping and issues related to death are helpful.

DSC Shelfmark: 5043.480000

5.15.7 Mental health

(491)
OCCUPATIONAL incidence rates of mental health disorders
M J Colligan *et al*
Journal of human stress, vol.3, 1977, p.34-39.

Examined the admission records of community mental health centres in Tennessee to determine incidence rate of diagnosed mental health disorders for 130 major occupations. Results indicated a disproportionate incidence of mental health anomalies among the hospital/health care professions.

DSC Shelfmark: 5003.440000

(492)

OCCUPATIONAL stress and health among men and women in the Tecumseh Community Health Study

J S House *et al*

Journal of health and social behavior, vol.27, 1986, p.62-77.

Reports on the relationship in the Tecumseh Community Health Study of a variety of measures of occupational characteristics and stressors collected 1967-69 to biomedical and questionnaire assessments of health behaviour and morbidity taken at the same time and to mortality over the succeeding nine to twelve year period. Results indicate that job pressures and tensions may constitute a consequential risk factor for poor health behaviour, morbidity and even mortality. Firmer validation of this result requires longitudinal or prospective studies in which job pressures and tensions and other occupational stressors are ascertained at multiple time points.

DSC Shelfmark: 4996.730000

(493)

ROLE of social support in the experience of stress at work

D C Ganster, M R Fusilier and B T Mayes

Journal of applied psychology, vol.71, 1986, p.102-110.

Study was designed to examine the role of social support in the experience of work stress with a sample large enough to provide statistically powerful tests of models of social support that specify two-way and three-way interactions. No support for higher order interactive models was found. No evidence emerged of any buffering or moderating effect of social support. Results, however, did show that social support had a modest direct effect of lowering experienced strain.

DSC Shelfmark: 4947.000000

(494)

A STRUCTURAL model approach toward the development of a theory of the link between stress and mental health

C L Cooper and A J Baglioni

British journal of medical psychology, vol.61, 1988, p.87-102.

Explores, through structural equation modelling, three different models of the stress process (interactional, dispositional and indigenous). The indigenous model was found to be the most predictive of mental ill-health. In this model personality and coping strategies precede and determine the perception of job stressors, which ultimately affect the mental well-being of the individual.

DSC Shelfmark: 2311.850000

(495)

RELATIONSHIP of work and family stressors to psychological distress: the independent moderating influence of social support, mastery, active coping and self-focused attention

M R Fronc, M Russell and M L Cooper

Journal of social behavior and personality, vol.6, 1991, p.227-250.

Data were obtained via questionnaire from a set of 596 employed individuals drawn from a random community sample. Results showed that job stressors, family stressors and work-family conflict each made an independent contribution to the prediction of psychological distress (depression and somatic symptoms), even after controlling for sociodemographic characteristics and the four psychological resources/vulnerabilities. The only consistent moderator of the relationships between stressors and psychological distress was self-focused attention. High levels of self-focused attention exacerbated the stressor-distress relationships.

DSC Shelfmark: 5064.751500

(496)

OCCUPATIONAL demands, psychological burnout and anxiety among hospital personnel in Norway

A M Richardsen, R J Burke, and M P Leiter

Anxiety, stress and coping, vol.5, 1992, p.55-68.

Reports results of a study conducted among health care workers at a regional university hospital in Norway. Data were collected by self-report questionnaire. Results showed that trait anxiety contributed significantly to all three aspects of burnout and was most strongly related to emotional exhaustion. Trait anxiety combined with workload and interpersonal conflicts to produce a considerable amount of the variance in burnout, especially emotional exhaustion (45%) and depersonalisation (22%). Trait anxiety may function as a relatively stable individual difference in burnout-proneness.

DSC Shelfmark: 1566.612000

(497)

SOCIAL support, occupational stress, and anxiety

T A Beehr and J E McGrath

Anxiety, stress and coping, vol.5, 1992, p.7-19.

Social support is hypothesised to reduce anxiety in one of three ways: by directly reducing the anxiety, by interacting with the stress factors to reduce the strength of their effects on anxiety and by weakening the strength of the stress factors themselves. Future research on the relationships between anxiety, social support and job stress needs to design investigations that allow causality to be determined, test hypotheses derived from theory and examine potential cross-cultural differences in the nature of, and reactions to, social support.

DSC Shelfmark: 1566.612000

(498)

OCCUPATIONAL stress, social support, job control and psychological well-being

K Daniels and A Guppy

Human relations, vol.47, 1994, p.1523-1543.

Study aimed to empirically synthesise models of social support, worker control and locus of control and to show how they relate to well-being in the workplace. In order to synthesise these areas of research a one-month follow-up study of 244 accountants was conducted. Results showed a complex interaction whereby internal locus of control, social support and job autonomy together buffered the effects of stress factors on well-being.

DSC Shelfmark: 4336.400000

(499)

THE RELATIONSHIP between job experiences and psychological distress: a structural equation approach

R C Barnett and R T Brennan

Journal of organizational behavior, vol.16, 1995, p.259-276.

Using structural equations, estimated the relationship between 7 potential job stressors (skill discretion, decision authority, schedule control, job demands, pay adequacy, job security and relations with supervisor) and psychological distress in a random sample of 504 employed men and women in dual-earner couples. Results showed that skill discretion and job demands were related to psychological distress, but that the other five conditions were not. The additive effects of feeling concerned about having to do dull monotonous work and having to work under pressure of time and conflicting demands were associated with mental strain.

DSC Shelfmark: 5027.066000

(500)

WORK and psychiatric disorder in the Whitehall II study

S A Stansfeld *et al*

Journal of psychosomatic research, vol.43, 1997, p.73-81.

Effects of changing work practices on mental health were studied in a cohort of 6895 male and 3413 female, London-based civil servants aged 35-55 years at baseline in 1985. Results show that high job demands are a risk factor for future psychiatric disorder. Social support at work has a consistently protective effect both on mental health and on taking short spells of psychiatric sickness absence. Decision authority and skill discretion do not predict better mental health, but are protective against taking short spells of psychiatric sickness absence.

DSC Shelfmark: 5043.480000

(501)
LONGITUDINAL influences of managerial support on employee well-being
P Moyle
Work and stress, vol.12, 1998, p.29–49

A three wave longitudinal survey of 148 managers working for a food retailer assessed both job characteristics and well-being during a period of organizational restructuring. Results showed that job satisfaction could be predicted from a combination of high managerial support, high control, and low ambiguity. These factors have in common the theme of clarification and information flow as necessary for high job satisfaction. Mental health was consistently predicted by low work demands and in addition was associated with high managerial support.

DSC Shelfmark: 9348.102000

5.15.8 Post-traumatic stress disorder

(502)
THE AETIOLOGY of post-traumatic morbidity: predisposing, precipitating and perpetuating factors
A C McFarlane
British journal of psychiatry, vol.154, 1989, p.221-228.

A group of 469 firefighters were studied 4, 11 and 29 months after having an extreme exposure to a bushfire disaster. The study found neither the severity of exposure nor the losses sustained to be the major determinant of post-traumatic morbidity in firefighters. While these factors appeared to play a significant role in the immediate post-traumatic morbidity experienced, no detectable contribution was present at 29 months. At all three stages of the study pre-morbid vulnerability (neuroticism and past history of psychiatric disorder) accounted for a greater percentage of the variance than the impact of the disaster.

DSC Shelfmark: 2320.800000

(503)
POST-traumatic stress disorder: the history of a recent concept
B P R Gersons and I V E Carlier
British journal of psychiatry, vol.161, 1992, p.742-748.

Review describes the history of PTSD in relation to military psychiatry, physiology and crisis theory. PTSD may be explained as an initially adequate reaction to danger that becomes pathological if it does not disappear when the danger has gone.

DSC Shelfmark: 2320.800000

(504)
THE EPIDEMIOLOGY of post-traumatic stress disorder
J R T Davidson and J A Fairbank
In post-traumatic stress disorders: DSM-IV and beyond edited by J R T Davidson
and E B Foa. Washington, DC: American Psychiatric Press, 1993, p.147-169.

Several studies are reviewed, grouped into high risk groups (combat veterans, victims of
disaster) and non-high risk general population samples. Prevalence rates, duration of
symptoms, co-morbidity patterns, pretrauma and trauma risk factors, interaction of pre-
existing risk factors with trauma and PTSD symptomology are evaluated.

DSC Shelfmark: 93/09505.

(505)
POST-traumatic stress disorder in victims of civilian trauma and criminal violence
G C Davis and N Breslau
Psychiatric clinics of North America, vol.17, 1994, p.289-299.

Review of the post-traumatic stress disorder (PTSD) literature that explores the consequences
of civilian stressors such as rape, assault, road traffic accidents, work-related stressors such as
those experienced by police or firefighters, and sudden and catastrophic medical events such
as severe burns and heart attacks.

DSC Shelfmark: 6946.212500

(506)
POST-TRAUMATIC stress disorder: conceptualization and treatment
P A Boudewyns
Progress in behavior modification, vol.30, 1996, p.165-189.

Theoretical and conceptual formulations regarding both the etiology and treatment of PTSD
are in the early stages of development. Researchers need to explore issues such as predisposing
factors, how the nature and intensity of the stressor relates to the severity of the disorder and
how biological, psychological, social and cultural variables interact to result in PTSD. Studies
indicate that the most effective treatment for PTSD is some form of exposure therapy.

DSC Shelfmark: 6865.957000

(507)
STRESS responses of emergency services personnel to the Loma Prieta earthquake interstate 880 freeway collapse and control traumatic incidents
C R Marmar *et al*
Journal of traumatic stress, vol.9, 1996, p.63-85.

Report focuses on responses of emergency services personnel at the time of critical incident exposure and the dimensions and severity of stress-specific, general and somatic symptom responses as well as occupational and social functioning at the time of assessment. Findings showed that a large scale disaster rescue and recovery operation such as the one that occurred at the I-880 freeway collapse, compared to critical incidents occurring in the routine line of work, is associated with greater immediate but not longer term distress. Compared with lower distress responders, those with greater distress reported greater exposure, greater peritraumatic emotional distress, greater peritraumatic dissociation, greater perceived threat and less preparation for the critical incident.

DSC Shelfmark: 5070.520000

(508)
RISK factors for post-traumatic stress symptomology in police officers: a prospective analysis
I V E Carlier, R D Lamberts and B P R Gersons
Journal of nervous and mental disease, vol.185, 1997, p.498-506.

Study examined internal and external risk factors for post-traumatic stress symptoms in 262 traumatised police officers. Trauma severity was the only predictor of post-traumatic stress symptoms both 3 and 12 months post-trauma. At 3 months post-trauma, symptomatology was further predicted by introversion, difficulty in expressing feelings, emotional exhaustion at the time of the trauma, insufficient time allowed by employers to come to terms with the trauma, dissatisfaction with organisational support and job insecurity. At 12 months post-trauma, symptoms were further predicted by lack of hobbies, acute hyperarousal, subsequent traumatic events, job dissatisfaction, brooding over work and lack of social support in private life.

DSC Shelfmark: 5021.400000

(509)
DISASTER-related post-traumatic stress in police officers: a field study of the impact of debriefing
I V E Carlier *et al*
Stress medicine, vol.14, 1998, p.143-148.

Eight and 18 months after they had assisted at a civilian plane crash, symptoms were assessed in 46 debriefed and 59 non-debriefed police officers, using structured clinical interviews. Eight months after the disaster, debriefed and non-debriefed officers did not differ significantly in PTSD symptoms. Eighteen months after the disaster, however, debriefed officers showed significantly more disaster-related hyperarousal symptoms.

DSC Shelfmark: 8474.129500

5.15.9 Alcohol, drug and tobacco use

(510)
RELATIONSHIPS of cessation of smoking with job stress, personality and social support

R D Caplan, S Cobb and J R P French.
Journal of applied psychology, vol.60, 1975, p.211-219.

The hypotheses that quitting smoking is greatest under low occupational stress, and that quitters are Type B rather than Type A employees were tested through self-report data gathered from a sample of 200 male administrators, engineers and scientists. Results showed that quitters had the lowest levels of quantitative work load, responsibility and social support and scored low on Type A personality characteristics. Social support and job stress interacted so that decreases in stress were associated with increases in the quit rate only for persons with low social support.

DSC Shelfmark: 4947.000000

(511)
OCCUPATIONAL stress and variation in cigarette, coffee and alcohol consumption

T L Conway *et al*
Journal of health and social behavior, vol.22, 1981, p.155-165.

A sample of 34 US Navy petty officers recently assigned to the Naval Training Center, San Diego, to become company commanders were followed through their first two recruit training cycles. Data were collected on 14 study days spread over an eight month period. Results showed an increase in smoking and coffee drinking but a decrease in alcohol consumption under high perceived stress. These general effects of stress appeared to depend largely on the behaviour of only a few of the participants, as the association between subjective stress indicators and substance consumption within individuals was not consistent across all of them. Findings suggest that there can be important individual differences in the tendency to increase or decrease habitual substance consumption in response to varying levels of stress.

DSC Shelfmark: 4996.730000

(512)
JOB stress, cigarette smoking and cessation: the conditioning effects of peer support

M Westman, D Eden and A Shirom
Social science and medicine, vol.20, 1985, p.637-644.

Relationships between self-report measures of job stress, smoking intensity (SI) and cessation were studied among 560 healthy smoking males and 310 quitters, all members of 22 kibbutzim. Hours of work, work addiction, lack of influence, intrinsic impoverishment and lack of support were positively associated with SI. Conflict, responsibility, hours of work, low status, lack of influence and harsh working conditions were negatively associated with cessation. Persons reporting low social support smoked significantly more than those who reported high support. For respondents reporting low support, more stress factors were correlated with a decreased likelihood of quitting than among those reporting high support. Concludes with the hypothesis that social support may be detrimental to the smoker, if the 'supportive others' themselves smoke.

DSC Shelfmark: 8318.157000

(513)
DO job conditions influence use of drugs?
B S Mensch and D B Kandel
Journal of health and social behavior, vol.29, 1988, p.169–184.

Results for a national sample of young adults suggest little concentration of drug users or on-the-job drug use in specific occupations or industries. Multivariate analyses show that marijuana use and cigarette smoking are predicted among both men and women by individual attributes indexing lack of conformity or attachment to social institutions, such as having dropped out of school, having participated in delinquent activities, or not being married.

DSC Shelfmark: 4996.730000

(514)
THE EFFECTS of psychosocial work organization on patterns of cigarette smoking among male chemical plant employees
K L Green and J V Johnson
American journal of public health, vol.80, 1990, p.1368-1371.

Tested the hypothesis that job strain was positively associated with smoking prevalence and intensity in a sample of 389 males employed in a chemical plant using a self-administered questionnaire. Smokers in high strain jobs smoked more heavily than those in lower-strain positions and were more likely to increase the amount they smoked.

DSC Shelfmark: 0835.900000

(515)
JOBS, occupations and patterns of alcohol consumption: a review of literature
J K Martin
In Alcohol problem intervention in the workplace edited by P M Roman. New York: Quorum Books, 1990. p.45-65.

Reviews early literature on the relationship between work and problem drinking. Apart from some epidemiological studies which attempted to link prevalence of alcohol abuse to a particular occupation, research used either on alienation or job stress theory. Alienation theory postulates that as jobs have become bureaucratised, routinised, depersonalised and repetitive, workers have become alienated and have experienced feelings of powerlessness and non-involvement. This leads to a decline in physical and mental health, family stability and community participation, and an increase in drug and alcohol addiction. The job stress perspective holds that certain features of modern work are potentially and frequently stressful. For certain individuals these stresses translate into strain outcomes, including alcohol abuse. Overall, empirical studies testing both of these theories find modest, if not always consistent, support for them.

DSC Shelfmark: 90/21869

(516)
WORK stress and alcohol effects: a test of stress-induced drinking
M L Cooper, M Russell, and M R Frone
Journal of health and social behavior, vol.31, 1990, p.260–276.

Drawing on both tension reduction and social learning theories, the authors hypothesise that work stressors lead to distress which in turn leads to problem drinking among vulnerable individuals. Model was tested on a random sample of 574 employed adults using a combination of path analytic and hierarchical moderated regression techniques. Results revealed no support for a simple tension reduction model of work stress induced drinking and only limited support for a social learning model.

DSC Shelfmark: 4996.730000

(517)
SMOKING and sedentary behaviour as related to work organization
G Johansson, J V Johnson and E M Hall
Social science and medicine, vol.32, 1991, p.837–846.

In investigating whether the psychosocial structure of work might affect smoking and sedentary behaviour, a subsample of a representative sample of the Swedish population aged 16-65 years was selected for study. Self-reports on job characteristics and health behaviours were obtained in telephone interviews. For both sexes, physical load, hazardous exposure, shift work and piece work were associated with smoking behaviour. Among women, psychological demands and monotonous work were also significantly related to smoking. Of the four work resource factors, only one, the opportunity for social interaction, was significantly associated with smoking, and that only among women. The opportunity for social interaction slightly increased the risk of smoking among women. Sedentary behaviour was positively associated with hazardous exposure and monotonous work among both men and women. Among men, job resources like personal freedom, learning opportunities, job control and social interaction decreased the risk of sedentary behaviour. Among women, this was true of learning opportunities and job control.

DSC Shelfmark: 8318.157000

(518)
WORKPLACE and personal stresses antecedent to employee's alcohol use
B D Steffy and D R Laker
Journal of social behavior and personality, vol.6, 1991, p.115-126.

Study evaluates impact of work role stressors (role overload, role ambiguity and boredom), job insecurity and recent life stressors on level of drinking and use of alcohol to relax. A large heterogenous sample of more than 8,600 health care workers was surveyed. Findings suggest that stressful life events and job insecurity predict greater alcohol intake and use of alcohol to relax. Workplace stressors generally failed to explain drinking behaviour.

DSC Shelfmark: 5064.751500

(519)
ALCOHOL and drug use in the workplace: issues, controversies and directions for future research
M M Harris and L L Heft
Journal of management, vol.18, 1992, p.239-266.

Review of extant research on drug and alcohol use in the workplace covering the relationship between working conditions and substance use, drug testing, Employee Assistance Programmes and legal issues.

DSC Shelfmark: 5011.100000

(520)
ALCOHOLISM and occupations: a review and analysis of 104 occupations
W Mandell *et al*
Alcoholism: clinical and experimental research, vol.16, 1992, p.734-746.

Establishes an association between occupations and diagnoses of Alcohol Dependence Disorder and Alcohol Abuse Disorder using data from a large population-based household interview study. Associations between some occupations and alcohol-related disorders are due to demographic characteristics of those employed in them. Employment in some occupations may be protective for Alcohol Dependence. Analyses of data from individuals currently employed or not employed in their occupation reveals a reduction of risk for those who leave some occupations and increased risk for those who leave others.

DSC Shelfmark: 0786.789300

(521)
DRINKING to cope and self-medication: characteristics of jobs in relation to workers' drinking behaviour
J M Martin, Y C Blum and P M Roman
Journal of organizational behavior, vol.13, 1992, p.55-71.

Working within the context of a generalisation model of worker behaviour, the authors have attempted to determine whether characteristics of jobs are meaningfully related to worker's patterns of alcohol consumption. Analyses of data drawn from the 1973 Quality of Employment Survey (QES) indicate that job characteristics operate on alcohol consumption by conditioning a set of justifications supportive of the use of alcohol to avoid or escape unpleasant emotional states. Work characterised by high levels of pressure, and/or low levels of extrinsic reward is significantly and independently related to escapist drinking.

DSC Shelfmark: 5027.066000

(522)
INCREASED desire to smoke during acute stress
K A Perkins and J E Grobe
British journal of addiction, vol.87, 1992, p.1037–1040.

In this study, 16 male and 16 female smokers either smoked or sham-smoked with an unlit cigarette after brief abstinence during two sessions, one involving a stressful and one involving a non-stress task. Desire to smoke was greater during the stressful vs non-stress task for sham-smokers, and, to a lesser extent for smoking smokers. There were no differences between males and females.

DSC Shelfmark: 2303.880000

(523)
OCCUPATIONAL stress, psychological vulnerability and alcohol-related problems over time in future physicians
J A Richman
Alcoholism: clinical and experimental research, vol.16, 1992, p.166–171.

Study addressed the course and psychosocial contributors to alcohol abuse in a cohort of future physicians undergoing the initial 2 years of medical training. Results showed that the initial transition to medical training was accompanied by varied changes in alcohol abuse patterns. While a sizeable proportion of medical students 'matured out' of their previous alcohol abuse patterns, a smaller segment of students manifested the onset of alcohol abuse or a continuation of abuse patterns during the first training year. A trend to increasing alcohol abuse after the initiation of clinical training in the third year was demonstrated. Alcohol abuse at this time was predicted by initial personality deficits and subsequent medical training-related experiences involving limited social support and patient-care related stressors.

DSC Shelfmark: 0786.789300

(524)
CIGARETTE smoking under stress: the role of coping expectancies among smokers in a clinic based smoking cessation program
W G Shadel and R J Mermelstein
Health psychology, vol.12, 1993, p.443–450.

Study examined two expectancies to explain smoking under stress: smokers' expectations about their ability to remain abstinent under stress and their expectations about the stress-ameliorating benefits of smoking under stress. Retrospective data revealed that the interaction of smokers' expectations about their ability to remain abstinent under stress and their expectations about the coping benefits of smoking was strongly related to their smoking urges and smoking under stress. In the prospective design, the interaction of end-of-treatment coping expectations predicted smoking status three months after treatment.

DSC Shelfmark: 4275.105200

(525)
OCCUPATIONAL stress and the risk of alcohol abuse and dependence
R M Crum *et al*
Alcoholism: clinical and experimental research, vol.19, 1995, p.647-655.

Using prospective data, study examined the relationship of occupational stress to the development of alcohol disorders, hypothesising that individuals who reported working in jobs characterised by high strain would be at greater risk of alcohol abuse and dependence than those in low-strain employment. Relative to low-strain employment, men were found to be 27.5 times more likely to develop alcohol abuse or dependence if they had been employed in a high-strain job classified as having high psychological demands and low control and 3.4 times at higher risk for an alcohol disorder if they were employed in high-strain jobs with high physical demands and low control. No significant risk was found for women in any of the high-strain job categories.

DSC Shelfmark: 0786.789300

(526)
THE RELATIONSHIP between work-specific and generalized stress and alcohol and marijuana use among recent entrants to the labour force
V Johnson and H R White
Journal of drug issues, vol.25, 1995, p.237-251.

Longitudinal study examining changes in alcohol and marijuana use, problems in relation to the transition into full-time work and the effects of work-related and generalised stress among a group of recent entrants to the labour force. Subjects were originally interviewed at the age of 18 and followed up twice at three year intervals. When age, gender and marital status were controlled, there were few significant effects of the transition to full time work on use measures. Data provided evidence of a stronger role for generalised stress over work-specific stress in predicting changes in drug use in young adulthood.

DSC Shelfmark: 4970.570000

(527)

PERCEIVED workplace harrassment experiences and problem drinking among physicians: broadening the stress/alienation paradigm

J A Richman, J A Flaherty and K M Rospenda
Addiction, vol.91, 1996, p.391–403.

Hypothesised that personal vulnerabilities would interact with perceived abusive experiences in the prediction of deleterious coping styles such as alcohol use and abuse. Tested this hypothesis on a sample of 184 students who were surveyed yearly through medical school and in their internship year. Results showed that task-related stressors such as overwork and lack of control did not significantly relate to deleterious drinking outcomes. In contrast, most of the perceived abusive experiences did significantly predict one or more drinking outcomes in men or women or both. Drinking outcomes were most strongly predicted by perceived abusive experiences in interaction with personality deficit (narcissism).

DSC Shelfmark: 0678.548000

(528)

EMPLOYEE stress levels and the intention to participate in a worksite smoking cessation program

W F Chan and C A Heaney
Journal of behavioral medicine, vol.20, 1997, p.351–364.

Study examines the nature and extent of the relationship between stress levels and intentions to participate in a worksite smoking cessation programme among current male smokers employed in a vehicle factory. Results show that high stress levels, stemming from exposure to work and non-work stress factors, are associated with modest increases in the likelihood of intending to participate in a worksite smoking cessation programme.

DSC Shelfmark: 4951.262000

(529)

WORK stress and problem alcohol behavior: a test of the spillover model

L Grunberg, S Moore and E S Greenberg
Journal of organizational behavior, vol.19, 1998, p.487–502.

Authors propose that job dissatisfaction may increase drinking among those who believe that alcohol consumption is an effective means to reduce stress. On the other hand, those who are dissatisfied with their jobs but do not believe that alcohol is an effective coping strategy will drink less. These hypotheses were tested in a sample of 972 production workers in the Northwest USA. Results showed moderate support for the existence of both responses.

DSC Shelfmark: 5027.066000

5.15.10 Organisational costs of stress

(530)
OCCUPATIONS and the prevalence of major depressive disorder.
W W Eaton *et al*
Journal of occupational medicine, vol. 32, 1990, p.1079–1087.

Analysis reveals considerable range in the prevalence of major depressive disorder in 104 occupations. Three occupations yielded prevalances significantly above the norm for employed persons generally. The three are lawyers with an odds ratio of 3-16; other teachers and counsellors with an odds ratio of 3-8; and secretaries with an odds ratio of 1-9.

DSC Shelfmark: 5026.100000

(531)
HEALTH and Safety Commission. Annual report 1991/92
London: HMSO, 1992. 145p.

Reports results of the health and safety supplement to the 1990 Labour Force Survey.

DSC Shelfmark: Not found.

(532)
MANAGERS under stress: a survey of management morale in the nineties.
Personal Performance Consultants UK Ltd
London: Institute of Management, 1993. 31p.

Overall, 71% of respondents reported work as a source of stress and over half reported it as a source of worry. Some 54% reported taking work home once or twice a week; 53% worked at weekends once or twice a month. Main sources of stress reported were incompetence of supervisors, poor internal communications, time pressures and deadlines. Just over 70% of respondents believed their overall health was affected by stress and anxiety. Symptoms reported included disturbed sleep, undue exhaustion, irritability, headaches and gastrointestinal disturbances.

DSC Shelfmark: q95/13176

(533)
STRESS at work: do managers really count the costs?
M McHugh
Employee relations, vol. 15, 1993, p.18–32.

Reports results of an investigation of attitudes of managers to work-related stress in the Northern Ireland clothing industry. Results suggest that while many admit that stress is a problem for employees and their organisations, few have implemented preventive and curative measures

DSC Shelfmark: 3737 040000

(534)
THE COSTS to the British economy of work accidents and work-related ill-health.
N V Davies and P Teasdale
Sudbury: HSE Books, 1994. 73p.

Study draws upon a special health and safety supplement to the 1990 Labour Force Survey (LFS) and a series of special in-depth company studies of accidental loss carried out by HSE's Accident Prevention Advisory Unit. Based upon these, the authors provide the most comprehensive estimates of the costs of accidents and ill-health at work ever undertaken.

DSC Shelfmark: GPC/03761

(535)
MANAGING absence: 1995 CBI/Centre-file survey results.
London: Confederation of British Industry, [1995].

Data were collected from almost 400 organisations with a combined workforce of three-quarters of a million in April 1995. Respondents identified work-related stress and mental illness as a medium to high factor in sickness absence in 37% of manual and 55% of non-manual workers.

DSC Shelfmark: q97/08967

(536)
SURVIVAL of the fittest: a survey of managers' experiences of, and attitudes to, work in the post recession economy.
N Benbow
London: Institute of Management,1995. 70p.

63% of respondents reported work as a source of stress and 47% reported it as a source of worry. The most stressed individuals are in the 35-44 age group, and those with young children. 55% of respondents claim always to work excess hours, and over a quarter state they often do. Only 2% say they never work over their contracted hours.

DSC Shelfmark: Not found

(537)
ARE managers under stress? a survey of management morale.
K Charlesworth

London: Institute of Management, 1996. 31p.

More than 80% of managers reported increased workloads, of which 47% felt their workloads had increased greatly. Unpaid overtime hours are widespread, with nearly 60% always working in excess of their contracted hours. Symptoms of stress such as tiredness, irritability and disturbed sleep were experienced by 80% of respondents. Only 11% believed their health was not affected by stress. The major cause of stress in the workplace are unreasonable deadlines and office politics, while 30% of women had suffered stress due to bullying.

DSC Shelfmark: 96/33109

(538)
A MODEL for assessing the costs of stressors at national level: socio-economic costs of work stress in two EU member states.
L Levi and P Lunde-Jensen
Dublin: European Foundation for the Improvement of Living and Working Conditions, 1996. 82p.

Reports results of project to develop a practical model for assessing the costs associated with work-related stress. Proposes a cost-of-illness model which uses available market prices in the health care sector and a loss of potential output principle for time lost due to sickness absence, early retirement, and deaths.

DSC Shelfmark: OP-EC/4167

(539)
STRESS prevention in the workplace: assessing the costs and benefits to organisations.
C L Cooper, P Liukkonen and S Cartwright
Dublin: European Foundation for the Improvement of Living and Working Conditions, 1996. 107p.

Report details three European case studies which illustrate how organisations have identified the costs of stress, the kinds of interventions they have introduced, and the way they have demonstrated the cost benefits associated with the interventions.

DSC Shelfmark: OP-EC/4004

(540)
STRESSED to breaking point: how managers are pushing people to the brink: 1996 TUC survey of safety reps: initial findings
London: TUC, 1996. 4p.

68% of Safety Reps identified stress as one of the top 5 health and safety concerns of their work colleagues. Overall 89% of Reps in the voluntary sector cited stress as a major issue, followed by 80% in education and 78% in the finance sector. Main causes of stress are new management techniques, long hours, redundancies, harassment, shiftwork and bullying. [Unfortunately the full report of this survey was never produced].

DSC Shelfmark: Not found.

(541)
MANAGING absence: in sickness and in health
London: Confederation of British Industry, 1997. 18p.

Reports results of a 1996 survey of 691 organisations with a combined work-force of over 1.5 million employees. Work-related stress was seen as a medium to strong factor in sickness absence for 35% of non-manual workers and 22% of manual workers.

DSC Shelfmark: q 97/16549

(542)
THE QUALITY of working life: 1997 survey of managers' changing experiences
L. Worrall and C L Cooper
London: Institute of Management. 1997. 114p.

Results showed that the restructuring and organisational change which had taken place in the previous year had significantly decreased employee loyalty, morale, and sense of job security. The majority of managers were working in excess of their contract hours and almost 40% were working over 50 hours per week. Roughly one in six had taken time off with stress related illness during the year. Major differences in the perceived quality of working life came to light, with top management clearly having higher net job satisfaction scores across the board.

DSC Shelfmark: 98/03797

(543)
SECOND European Survey on Working Conditions
P Paoli
Dublin: European Foundation for the Improvement of Living and Working Conditions, 1997. 384p.

Reports that 57% of workers think that their work negatively affects their health. The most important problems indicated were backache (30%), stress (28%) overall fatigue (20%), muscular pains (17%) and headaches (13%).

DSC Shelfmark: 3830.237V

(544)

MISSING out: 1998 absence and labour turnover survey

London: Confederation of British Industry, 1998. 24p.

For manual workers, high workload pressure was ranked low at 9th out of 14 as a cause of absence. However, it was ranked higher (5th) for non-manual workers. Pressure from managers was ranked 12th for manual employees and 11th for non-manual. No significant relationship was found between length of hours worked by employees and levels of absence.

DSC Shelfmark: 0551.465200

5.15.11 Stress and the law

(545)

CRONER'S health and safety at work

S Tullett (editor)

New Malden: Croner, 1979 – Loose-leaf in binder; kept up to date by monthly amendment sheets.

DSC Shelfmark: 3487.825000

(546)

BULLYING and harassment at work

London: Incomes Data Services, 1996. 50p.

(IDS employment law supplement; 76)

In the UK there is as yet no legislation which deals specifically with bullying and harassment at work. The victims of bullying and harassment are therefore forced to rely on existing legal remedies, which, because they are not specifically designed to deal with the problem, are often less than satisfactory. The supplement deals with the circumstances under which bullied employees may bring unfair constructive dismissal claims and actions for damages against their employers, and examines potential criminal liability of workplace bullies. The circumstances in which sexual or racial harassment amount to direct discrimination under the Sex Discrimination Act 1973 and the Race Relations Act 1976 are also covered.

DSC Shelfmark: 4362.5961/00

(547)

SEXUAL harassment at work

Health and safety monitor. Special report no. 32, Apr. 1996. 2p.

The accepted remedy in the UK is for victims of sexual harassment to make sex discrimination claims to industrial tribunals. Intentional harassment is now also a criminal offence under the Criminal Justice and Public Order Act 1994. Employers have a duty of care under the Health and Safety at Work Act 1974 to provide and maintain a safe working environment. Fulfilling this duty should include the conduct of a risk assessment to mental health and the development of policies to prevent the occurrence of sexual harassment which may lead to negative psychological health effects.

DSC Shelfmark: 4274.86500

(548)
STRESS and employer liability
J Earnshaw and C L Cooper
London: Institute of Personnel and Development, 1996. 156p.

Outlines major sources of stress and explains the law of negligence and liability for foreseeable stress-based injuries caused by the working environment. Covers employers' responsibilities under the Health and Safety at Work Act and subsequent regulations, employment protection legislation and claims for unfair or constructive dismissal and discrimination, harassment, and compensation for injury to feelings.

DSC Shelfmark: 96/22593

(549)
HEALTH and safety at work brief. 1998 ed.
G Myles
Sidcup: Locksley, 1998. 2 vols.

DSC Shelfmark: Not found.

(550)
LAW of health and safety at work. 7th ed.
N M Selwyn
Kingston-upon-Thames: Croner, 1998. 416p.

DSC Shelfmark: Not found.

(551)
TRADE union trends: focus on union legal services.
J Gallagher
London: TUC, 1998. 16p.

DSC Shelfmark: Not found.

6 Stress management: Theory Into Practice

6.1 Introduction

As concern about the impact of stress on the individual and the organisation has grown, so has the literature on stress management. A plethora of self-help books on how to manage stress are now available, (e.g. Watts and Cooper, 1998, ref. no. 584) alongside a growing academic literature on stress management interventions in organisations. In the last few years there has also been an explosion of health promotion or 'wellness' programmes in US and UK industry. Activities such as exercise, stress management, training, smoking cessation and counselling are being encouraged by the mass media and are taking place in the workplace as well as at home.

The motivation for employers to initiate stress management programmes arises from five sources (Briner, 1997, ref. no. 667):

- The need to reduce the costs to the organisation of stress related illness, absenteeism and staff turnover.

- A humanitarian desire to improve working conditions.

- The legal requirement under the *Health and Safety at Work Regulations* for employers to list and assess all workplace hazards, including hazards to mental health such as psychological stress, and to provide a safe working environment.

- A wish to be seen as a caring organisation which looks after its employees in order to raise morale or improve the company image.

- A tendency to follow current fashion, when everyone else is introducing stress management interventions under the influence of a vociferous stress management industry.

As shown in our review of the literature in previous chapters, much of the research on stress has collected data on a self-report basis, focusing on individual outcomes resulting from stress. Similarly, the focus of research on stress management has been on how the individual can cope better with stress. The result is that there is now extensive advice available on individual stress management techniques at both the popular and the academic level. Stress supplies us with a way of attributing cause to a wide range of negative emotions and health outcomes. At the same time, many sources of advice on stress management promote the idea of individual empowerment, and suggest that people can take control of, and resolve, stressful situations.

6.2   Classification of intervention strategies

By the late 1980s, reviews of the literature identified a broad range of interventions which were being used to manage stress in a work context. These included interventions which were not only aimed at changing the individual, but also at changing the individual's relationship with the organisation, or the organisation itself. DeFrank and Cooper (1987, ref. no. 553) postulated three levels of stress management interventions and outcomes, focusing on the individual, the individual/organisation interface and the organisation. Interventions which empower the individual to cope more effectively with a stressful environment include relaxation techniques, cognitive coping strategies, biofeedback and meditation. These techniques have become the staple fare of traditional stress management programmes and are designed to alleviate some of the negative health consequences of stress, such as psychosomatic complaints, sleep disturbance, depression, anxiety, muscle tension and blood pressure. The next level emphasises the interface between the individual and the organisation. Stress factors here include role problems, poor person–environment fit, and issues of control and autonomy. Negative outcomes at this level affect both the individual in the shape of burnout and/or job dissatisfaction and the organisation in the shape of absenteeism, high staff turnover, low productivity and poor performance. The third level of intervention focuses on the areas in which organisational environment, structure and policies produce stress for employees. Problems at the organisational level can include physical characteristics of the workplace such as exposure to excessive heat or noise, shiftworking, or inadequate training. Negative outcomes here are at the organisational level and include high staff turnover, absenteeism, and poor productivity. Bearing these categories in mind helps in understanding what organisations are trying to achieve in introducing stress management interventions, and in understanding the research on stress management.

Cox, Leather and Cox (1990, ref. no. 557) identify three broad aims for stress management interventions:

- Prevention, through control of hazards by design and worker training to reduce the likelihood of workers experiencing stress.

- Timely reaction, to improve the ability of managers to recognise and deal with problems as they arise.

- Rehabilitation, often involving offering enhanced support such as counselling to help distressed workers cope and recover.

This model, phrased in terms of the organisation, can be contrasted with that outlined by Quick and his colleagues (1992, ref. no. 562) and phrased in terms of the individual. They classify interventions in terms of three levels, primary, secondary and tertiary:

- Primary prevention aims to improve occupational mental health by reducing the risk factor or changing the nature of the stressor through, for example, redesign of the physical work environment to eliminate hazards, or, through developing clear job descriptions to reduce role ambiguity.

- Secondary prevention aims at the recognition of early warning signs of distress and the alteration of ways in which individuals respond to risks and stressors, through traditional stress management techniques such as muscle relaxation, meditation, biofeedback and assorted cognitive strategies.

- Tertiary prevention is to do with healing those who have been traumatised or distressed at work, and usually manifests itself in the form of the provision of counselling or an employee assistance programme.

6.3   Intervention evaluation

Before introducing a stress management intervention, organisations will need to determine the effectiveness of such programmes. Despite a burgeoning literature on the subject, the relative effectiveness of stress management programmes and interventions has been difficult to determine, largely because of methodological deficiencies in much of the relevant research and lack of adequate evaluations. Murphy, Hurrell and Quick (1992, ref. no. 564), for example, consider that evaluations should include cost benefit analyses and assessments of employee satisfaction, job stressors, performance, absenteeism and health status. However, they rarely do so. In addition, stress management interventions are diverse, and, as a result, research findings can be difficult to compare. Some persistent evaluation problems which repeatedly emerge from the literature are:

- Lack of longitudinal study designs. A stress management intervention may produce a reduction in levels of distress at the conclusion of the programme, but a longitudinal design would be needed to establish whether or not the improvement was sustained. Unfortunately longitudinal studies are expensive to carry out and consequently rare.

- Lack of control groups. One of the common criticisms of research evaluating the effectiveness of programmes aimed at enhancing well-being is that many factors other than the treatment programme itself can influence results. In order for an evaluation to be strong methodologically, the research needs to demonstrate not only that benefits exist, but that these benefits can be attributed to the provision of the programme. This is extremely difficult without comparative data from individuals who have not used the programme.

- Selection effects. Since participation in most secondary and tertiary stress management interventions is voluntary, selection effects may operate and the characteristics of participants and non-participants may be quite different. Selection effects have been discussed in detail in the context of employee fitness programmes (Jex, 1991, ref. no. 559).

- Non-specific effects. Many studies claim to show improvements resulting from interventions which may arise from completely different sources such as treatment expectations or even the benefits of just sitting quietly. Sallis and colleagues (1987, ref. no. 613) allocated 76 participants to one of three intervention groups: multi-component stress management training, relaxation training and an education support group. Results showed that participants in all three groups made similar gains, which suggests that any benefits were due to non-specific factors such as group support and encouragement rather than any of the 'active' components of stress management training or relaxation.

- Lack of hard data. Many studies rely of self-reports by participants, rather than using hard data such as records of sickness absence or staff turnover.

In the following sections we shall look at the content, strengths, weaknesses and available evaluation of tertiary, secondary and primary interventions.

6.4   Employee assistance programmes

In essence an employee assistance programme (EAP) is a systematic, on–going and organised service, funded by the employer and providing counselling, advice and help to employees and their families with problems arising from both work–related and external sources. EAPs are comprehensively described in a recent book by Berridge, Cooper and Highley-Marchington (1997, ref. no. 600).

Employee assistance programmes originated in the United States where they were originally developed to deal with problems of alcohol abuse. Early programmes were established following the foundation of Alcoholics Anonymous (AA) in 1935 and were usually led by lay people, often reformed alcoholics. From the 1960s occupational alcohol programmes became increasingly professionalised and were run by social workers. They expanded into drug abuse from the 1970s. The second origin of employee counselling schemes was in the Hawthorne studies of Mayo in the Chicago plant belonging to Western Electric in the 1930s. A programme of advice and counselling grew out of these. It was staffed by lay counsellors drawn from supervision and management and was clearly aimed not only at promoting the social and psychological adjustment of the employee at work, but also at integrating individual behaviour and corporate goals. Current US corporate EAPs have increasingly adopted a 'broad-brush' approach and cover a wide range of social issues arising outside as well as inside the workplace.

In Britain, the first EAPs appeared on an in-house basis around 1980, notably in the electronics, chemical and oil industries in UK subsidiaries of US companies. They were at first closely linked to the practice of the US parent companies, but soon demonstrated differences of approach in adaptation to local conditions. In Britain, EAPs tend to have two main objectives:

* To help employees distracted by a range of personal concerns, including emotional, stress, relationship, family, alcohol, drug, financial, legal and other problems to cope with such concerns and to learn to manage the stresses produced (EAPA, 1995, ref. no. 598).

* To assist the organisation in the identification and amelioration of productivity problems in workers whose performance is adversely affected by such concerns (EAPA, 1995, ref. no. 598).

From the start, British programmes have provided counselling for a wide range of concerns to both employees and family members. Employees may either contact the service themselves, or, if appropriate, be referred by management. The service may either be provided in-house through staff employed by Occupational Health or Human Resources Management departments, or delivered by an external contractor. In Britain the customary delivery method is by external contractors who use a network of counsellors to provide services for a variety of large and smaller employers. Most counselling within employee assistance is short term therapy, aimed at helping the client at a time of change, choice or crisis. People are viewed as basically healthy, not pathological, and it is assumed that they have the ability to use their own internal coping skills to solve their problems. Counselling is viewed as an opportunity to learn problem solving skills and to create new life choices. Workplace counselling does not aim at the kind of personal restructuring effected by a psychoanalyst. If deep-seated psychological problems are detected the norm in the British context would be referral for specialist treatment in the NHS.

The upshot of all this is that EAPs can vary widely. Provision can be in-house or by an external contractor, and services can be delivered by telephone, or face to face, or both. The service can be narrowly focused on a limited range of problems such as alcohol or substance abuse or 'broad-brush' covering a very wide range of problems from divorce to AIDS. It can be available to employees only or can be extended to cover their families. Clients may be self-referred or referred by management. The precise configuration of an EAP will depend very much on local conditions and the policies and objectives of individual organisations.

Provision and management of EAPs is not as simple as it might appear as there is a delicate balance between assisting individuals and promoting the interests of the organisation. The problem, according to Berridge and Cooper (1993, ref. no. 594) lies in attempting to ally a mental-health driven therapy to a performance- and profit-dominated system of production of goods and services. 'An implicit unstated process of mutual exploitation may well have been created around EAPs, whereby counsellors pursue their professional goals, and enterprises seek to attain their economic goals in uneasy alliance'. In the Human Resource Management context, EAPs may be seen as assisting the personnel specialist in moving problems forward. EAPs are a humane and efficient alternative to exclusively disciplinary methods of dealing with problem employees. For the disciplinarian, the EAP is the ultimate deterrent, requiring conformity with the programme to avoid dismissal. In the wider organisational context, EAPs can be viewed simply as another method of job performance control designed with special reference to problem employees. The degree of benefit gained by the organisation will correlate with the extent to which the EAP is integrated into the control structure (Berridge and Cooper, 1993, ref. no. 594).

6.4.1   Evaluation of EAPs

With the growing acceptance of EAPs in UK organisations, there has been an increasing demand for information on their effectiveness. In Britain evaluations have been almost exclusively qualitative in nature, other than basic statistical reports on usage rates. In the US, however, there has been a move away from such anecdotal evidence of effectiveness towards insistence on hard data such as cost–benefit analysis (Highley and Cooper, 1994, ref. no. 596). Results of evaluations carried out, with varying degrees of scientific rigour, in the US have been almost uniformly positive. One of the most ambitious cost–benefit analyses undertaken in the US looked at the Department of Health and Human Services Employee Counselling Service. The design was rigorous, relying on the collection of individual level data, and so results were credible. Employees who had not used the EAP acted as the control group. Cost–benefit analyses showed an estimated cost per client of $991; the estimated benefit in six months was $1274 per employee (Maiden, 1988, ref. no. 587). Nadolski and Sandonato (1987, ref. no. 586) examined the work performance of employees referred for counselling over a period of six months at the Detroit Edison Company. Outcome measures used were lost time, health insurance claims, discipline warnings and accidents, and a longitudinal design was used. Results showed instances of lost time reduced by 18%, and the number of lost days reduced by 29%. Health insurance claims were reduced by 26% and written warnings diminished by 13%. There was also a 40% decrease in suspensions and a 41% fall in the number of accidents. No control group, unfortunately, was used in this study.

The first nationwide independent evaluation of UK EAPs was carried out by Highley and Cooper for the Health and Safety Executive in 1995. Data were collected via self-report questionnaires completed by both clients and providers. Outcome measures were provided by scrutiny of employers' records, especially sickness absence data. Matched control groups were established, and a longitudinal design employed. Results showed that the mental and physical health of client groups improved significantly after counselling, while no improvement was detected for the control groups. Absence levels of clients and controls were identical before counselling, but while clients had less absence after counselling, the controls showed no reduction (Berridge, Cooper and Highley-Marchington, 1997, ref. no. 600). An earlier evaluation of the impact of stress counselling at the Post Office showed significant reductions in frequency of absence, duration of absence, and numbers of disciplinary proceedings (Allinson, Cooper and Reynolds, 1989, ref. no. 588; Cooper and Sadri, 1991, ref. no. 590).

The relative lack of evaluations of counselling services has attracted considerable comment in the literature and has been attributed to a variety of causes (Highley and Cooper, 1993, ref. no. 593):

- Difficulty of accessing organisational level data such as absence records. Many UK organisations do not monitor absenteeism, so records may not exist. Where records do exist, employers may be unwilling to allow access for ethical reasons.

- Reluctance of both providers and participant organisations to take part in research. Evaluation studies are expensive and time-consuming, requiring effort which busy professionals may be unwilling to provide. Some providers are unwilling to be evaluated in case their service is shown to be ineffective; some organisations have implemented an EAP as a public relations exercise and may not be interested in its effectiveness.

- Evaluation may undermine trust in the confidentiality of the service, and give rise to a fear that individual clients may be identified. The perception of a service being truely confidential is vital to a successful EAP. The reputation of a service could be destroyed if employees perceive the evaluation negatively.

- In order to demonstrate that use of the service and not some other factor has improved well-being, a comparison group of people who have not used the programme is required. Selecting this group again raises major issues of confidentiality. It can also be argued that selecting individuals who have not used the service can tell us very little about the effectiveness of the treatment since these people are psychologically healthy to begin with and improvement over time is unlikely.

- Finally, most EAPs attempt to assist clients in a variety of ways, with a mixture of 'hard' and 'soft' benefits, ranging from improving self-esteem to reducing absenteeism. Their simultaneous provision to the same employees makes the identification of clear outcome measures difficult if not impossible.

6.4.2   Conclusions

There is a well-established evidence base for the provision of workplace counselling services. These appear to be acceptable to managers and staff, demand little in the way of organisational change, can easily be costed and are reasonably easy to evaluate. On the other hand, counselling services are only useful to those who choose to use them, and users may not be those in greatest need. They do nothing to address the problem of noxious work environments, and may fall into the trap of victim blaming.

6.5   Stress management training

At the individual level, the employee can attempt to manage his or her personal perception of stress by reappraising situations more realistically, reducing Type A behaviour, etc. He or she can improve their management of their work environment by developing and using time management, assertiveness and communication skills, and of their lifestyle by appropriate use of leisure time, eating a balanced diet, etc. Individuals can also attempt to alter ways in which they respond to stress through use of relaxation techniques, such as progressive muscle relaxation or biofeedback, through physical outlets such as aerobic exercise, jogging or walking, or through emotional outlets such as talking or writing about their problems (Palmer, 1996, ref. no. 632).

In recent years, it has become popular to offer training in stress management techniques of these kinds in a work setting. Individual level stress management training seeks to educate staff about stress and its attendant health effects, and to teach coping and stress reduction skills. Interventions have more often than not been offered in a preventive context to participants not suffering from any evident stress-related problems. Training usually consists of some form of relaxation exercise in combination with cognitive techniques borrowed from the fields of counselling and psychotherapy. Elements of management skills, such as time management, and of interpersonal skills, such as delegation and assertiveness, may be included.

6.5.1   Relaxation training

The objective of relaxation training is to reduce the individual's arousal level both psychologically and physiologically. Psychologically, successful relaxation results in enhanced feelings of well-being, peacefulness and control, and a reduction in tension and anxiety. Physiologically, decreases in blood pressure, respiration and heart rate should take place. There are a number of different relaxation techniques, including muscle relaxation, biofeedback, and various forms of meditation (Matteson and Ivancevich, 1987, ref. no. 611).

6.5.1.1   Progressive Muscle Relaxation

Progressive muscle relaxation involves focusing attention on muscle activity, learning to identify even small amounts of tension in a muscle group, and practicing releasing tension from the muscles. Muscle relaxation is usually accomplished by a series of alternating tensing and relaxation exercises and involves creating tension in a muscle group (e.g. by clenching one's fist), studying the feelings of tension, and then allowing the muscles to relax.

6.5.1.2   Meditation

The most widely practiced form of meditation is Transcendental Meditation (TM), which involves sitting upright in a comfortable position, in a quiet place, with eyes closed and mentally repeating a secret mantra while maintaining a passive mental attitude. Meditation methods taught in stress management training are often secular versions of transcendental meditation. For example, the Respiratory One Method developed by Herbert Benson requires a person to sit comfortably in a quiet place for 20 minutes twice a day and repeat the word 'one' or some other neutral word with each exhalation while maintaining a passive mental attitude.

6.5.1.3   Biofeedback Training

In biofeedback training, a person is provided with information or feedback about the status of a physiologic function and over time learns to control the activity of that function. For example, the electrical activity produced when muscles contract or tense can be recorded and transformed into a tone, whose pitch rises and falls when muscle activity increases and decreases. Using the feedback tone as an indicator of muscle tension level, a person can learn how to reduce activity and achieve a state of relaxation. Potentially, biofeedback techniques can be used to bring a wide range of physiological functions under control, including heart rate, blood pressure, stomach acidity and body temperature.

6.5.2   Cognitive Behavioural Skills Training

Cognitive-behavioural techniques refer to a range of skills designed to help participants to appraise situations more realistically so as to reduce the threat that they present, and to develop behavioural skills to manage stress factors successfully. Cognitive reappraisal or restructuring focuses on removing distorted views of a situation that can arise from over-generalisation, personalisation and exaggeration of its impact. It is an important part of such approaches as stress inoculation training, rational–emotive therapy and cognitive behaviour modification. All these approaches aim to help individuals to gain a higher degree of control over their reactions to stress factors by modifying unhelpful patterns of thinking. Stress inoculation, the most widely used of these approaches in practical stress management training, has three stages. The first phase is educational and aims to help the individual to understand the nature of stress and stress effects. The second phase consists of skill acquisition and rehearsal, and has the objective of teaching individuals a range of coping skills to reduce anxiety and enhance their capability to respond effectively in stressful situations. The final phase, application and follow through, involves the application of coping skills through role play or guided imagery in conditions that increasingly approximate real life (Meichenbaum, 1993, ref. no. 609).

6.5.3   Programme effectiveness

An examination of the research literature on individual stress management programmes shows that they differ widely in intervention technique used and outcomes measured. This makes it very difficult to evaluate their general effectiveness. However, Murphy has recently attempted a review of their health effects, and his conclusions are summarised here (1996, ref. no. 636). He grouped health outcomes of the 69 studies included in his review into four categories: physiological/biochemical, psychological/cognitive, somatic and job/organisational.

Physiologic/biochemical. The most common outcome variable measured was blood pressure. A close examination of the literature revealed that studies reporting the largest decreases in blood pressure after training also reported large and significant reductions in control and comparison groups. Murphy therefore concludes that stress interventions have a minimal unique effect on worker blood pressure.

Psychological cognitive. Examination of 16 studies using the State-Trait Anxiety Inventory as an outcome measure revealed that the average pre-training anxiety level score was 41.17, the average post-training level score was 35.91 and the net reduction in anxiety levels was about 5.00. Results support the conclusion that stress management training has a positive and specific effect on anxiety. Murphy's conclusions are supported by a meta-analysis of the effect of stress inoculation training on anxiety by Saunders and colleagues (1996, ref. no. 633). Their analysis of 37 studies showed stress inoculation training to be an effective approach for reducing performance anxiety, reducing state anxiety and enhancing performance under stress.

Somatic (physical health) complaints. Comparison of results was found to be difficult due to the general lack of uniformity in the measures used, and methodological validity was questionable as many studies did not use a control group. Murphy therefore considers the effects of stress management training on health complaints to be equivocal.

Job/organisational. Self-reported job satisfaction was the organisational outcome variable most commonly measured. Studies which reported increases in satisfaction after training were not randomised controlled experiments, and half did not use a control group. Murphy therefore concludes that stress management training has little effect on job satisfaction.

Murphy's analysis confirms the conclusions reached by Reynolds, Taylor and Shapiro (1993, ref. no. 623) that stress management interventions generally produce modest reductions in psychological symptoms which are maintained for up to six months after the training programme. Physiological indices of arousal and job-related attitudes and perceptions are less amenable to change. Thus, at the end of a well designed study, Ganster and his colleagues (1982, ref. no. 605) found only modest effects of training on employee strain as shown by measures of epinephrine execretion, depression and irritation. Reynolds and Briner (1994, ref. no. 568) suggest that the modest impact of SMT may be due to:

- The limited extent to which stress management training programmes are designed to meet the individual needs of participants. SMT is typically offered in as a standardised package, which may or may not meet the needs of the particular individuals in the group (Kolbell, 1995, ref. no. 631).

- Problems experienced by groups of participants may not be amenable to individually orientated interventions, and may be caused by organisational features such as insufficient resources or high workloads (Reynolds, Taylor and Shapiro, 1993, ref. no. 623).

- SMT participants are mostly recruited on a voluntary basis from the working population and have normal levels of psychological well-being. The extent to which clinically significant change, which will be of lasting benefit to the participants, can be expected in the context of SMT is very limited.

• Design shortcomings which make it very difficult to assess the effectiveness of SMT as a prevention strategy. The effectiveness of SMT could be best evaluated using large samples and assessing incidence of disorder in the long term. SMT outcome studies generally report follow-ups of between three and six months with sample sizes of less than 80 participants. This is not long enough to judge the effectiveness of SMT in preventing the outbreak of stress-related disorders.

6.5.4 Methodological problems

In order to develop more effective interventions, outcome research needs to concentrate on elucidating how the various techniques used in stress management programmes actually work to bring about beneficial change. The basic hypothesis underlying stress management programme design is that specific interventions produce observed effects. However, some research suggests that different components lead to the same outcomes. For example, Sallis and his colleagues (1987, ref. no. 613) compared the results of three different interventions: relaxation training, a multicomponent stress management programme, and an educational/social support group. Results showed that no intervention was more effective than the others in changing any of the psychological, work-related or physiological outcomes measured. There were significant reductions in anxiety, depression and hostility, but no group improved significantly on job satisfaction, work stress, resting blood pressure or blood pressure reactivity to mental arithmetic or cold pressor stressors. Non-specific effects are also evident in a study by Kagan, Kagan and Watson (1995, ref. no. 630) of workers in an emergency medical service and a municipal fire department. The research compared all possible combinations of three different intervention strategies: muscle relaxation, interpersonal skills training and cognitive-behavioural training. Measures tapping job-related stress and psychological well-being were administered before and after one week training programmes, with follow up nine to sixteen months later. Results showed that, although overall improvement was found on the majority of measures, and was maintained at follow-up, the benefits of one type of programme over another were found only in a minority of measures. Thus, equivalence of outcome was predominant. Equivalence of outcome between interventions of different technical content can be explained in a number of ways. It is possible that non-specific factors such as warmth and support may be responsible for any change.

Alternatively, apparent outcome equivalence may be caused by weaknesses in the study design and methodology. Methods used may not be sensitive enough to detect subtle differences in outcome (Bunce, 1997, ref. no. 637). Thirdly, each intervention method may have different but equally effective change mechanisms, leading to the same outcomes by different routes (Reynolds, Taylor and Shapiro, 1993, ref. nos. 623 & 624).

Studies by Reynolds and colleagues have used session impact methodology to identify active elements of stress management training. Session impact methodology was developed as a way of inferring change mechanisms in psychotherapy. Clients complete questionnaires immediately after therapy sessions and these immediate evaluations are assumed to reflect session contents and processes. Session impact research indicates that psychotherapy clients and SMT participants do experience different therapies and different components of SMT in different and predictable ways. A study of health service workers by Reynolds Taylor and Shapiro (1993, ref. no. 623), evaluated the outcomes of a stress management training programme in which the standard components of training were delivered in discrete and pre-ordered sessions. Results showed that participants who reported more positive mood after sessions also reported less psychological distress after training. Specific session impacts were also associated with specific outcomes. Impacts such as gaining insight into one's own or others' feelings and behaviour, and improved capacity to clearly define problems were related to improvements in non-job satisfaction levels one month after training, although only the impact 'personal insight' remained significant at three month follow-up. Emotional impacts such as feelings of support and relief due to attendance at the group also led to improved levels of life satisfaction one month after training, although the improvement was not sustained. There was also some evidence that whether the subjects found group particpation to be a good or bad experience overall was related to post-intervention psychological distress. Those participants whose ratings became more positive and enthusiastic over the course of the six sessions reported less distress after training.

Similarly, a study by Bunce and West (1996, ref. no. 635) compared a multicomponent SMT programme to one promoting innovation in the workplace as a stress coping strategy. Results showed that how the participants viewed and experienced the intervention influenced outcomes. Measures of perceptions of session depth, smoothness and insight were administered to assess this. At first sight, the training in innovation was more successful in reducing stress than the SMT programme. However, differences in outcome became non-significant when measures of perception of session comfort and safety were taken into account.

Several studies have used designs incorporating placebo conditions which primarily control for expectancy effects. That is, distress may be reduced because people have been told that they will be receiving treatment and expect it to work, not because of the technical content of the training. Placebo groups may, for example, be educated about the causes and effects of stress, or receive training in personal development skills, but still benefit just as much as groups which have received formal stress management training. Although giving an indication that factors other than the technical content of the intervention influence outcomes, this method does not pinpoint specific change agents. The weight of the evidence from studies incorporating education or other placebo groups suggests that non-specific factors do affect outcomes. For example, Drazen and colleagues (1982, ref. no. 606) found no differences in diastolic or systolic blood pressure between education and treatment groups. Similarly, Sallis and his colleagues (1987, ref. no. 613) were only able to distinguish between groups receiving different forms of training on diastolic blood pressure, and found little variation on a range of other outcomes.

Strategies to improve research methodologies to the point that they become sensitive enough to detect subtle differences between interventions are discussed by Bunce (1997, ref. no. 637). Design failings which need to be addressed include small sample sizes, overly restricted ranges of outcomes measured and uncontrolled participant heterogeneity. The greater the initial variation in level and type of strain within the sample, the more unlikely it is that all individuals in the sample require intervention, and the more uncertain it is whether a particular intervention is appropriate to every individual's own needs. Finally, researchers do not distinguish between contrasting treatments with sufficient rigour. In consequence it is not possible to tell which component is responsible for change when it occurs.

A methodological problem with many studies is that the follow-up period is short (generally three months) and little is known about the longer term benefits of stress management. In order to address this problem the study by Bunce and West (1996, ref. no. 635) extended follow-up to one year. Results suggested that short term gains in psychological well-being were not maintained at follow-up one year after the intervention, but that increases in levels of innovative coping, although not apparent three months after the intervention, were significant after one year. A complex pattern of outcomes over time was also found in a worksite coping skills intervention for employed mothers in secretarial positions. It was expected that changes in selected stress factors, social support and coping, at work and in the family, would be accompanied by reductions in psychological distress and substance use over time. Outcomes were measured immediately after the training and at six month follow-up. Not all of the original hypotheses were supported and a complex pattern of results across the two time periods emerged. Programme participants reported lower levels of role stress than controls immediately after training, but this effect was not maintained at six month follow-up. In contrast, the positive effects of the intervention on work/family conflict and stress factors in the work environment did not emerge until follow-up. Intervention participants reported lower levels of psychological symptoms than controls, and this effect strengthened over time. On the other hand, while tobacco and alcohol use levels were reduced in the short term, the changes were not maintained at six month follow-up (Kline and Snow, 1994, ref. no. 625). More longitudinal studies are needed to investigate the long term results of SMT.

Thirty of the 64 studies reviewed by Murphy (1996, ref. no. 636) used a combination of stress management techniques and these studies appear to produce most consistent significant effects on health across a range of outcome measures. The most common combination of techniques is relaxation plus cognitive-behavioural skills training. For example, in the study by Kagan, Kagan and Watson (1995, ref. no. 630) the combination of interpersonal skills training and cognitive behavioural therapy was associated with less emotional exhaustion immediately after the intervention than cognitive-behavioural training alone. Personal accomplishment significantly improved for a combination of relaxation training and interpersonal skills training over all other possible combinations and relaxation training alone. Similarly, there was also evidence that combinations of cognitive-behavioural skills and interpersonal skills training and of relaxation and interpersonal skills training were more effective for highly depressed individuals than relaxation or interpersonal skills training alone. Interestingly, the effects of combining treatments appears to have been multiplicative rather than additive in that some combinations proved more potent while other combinations weakened one another. For instance, combining interpersonal skills training with cognitive behavioural training was preferable to relaxation with cognitive behavioural training for strain reduction. Thomason and Pond (1995, ref. no. 629) investigated whether training in self-management consisting of self-monitoring, specifying goals, evaluating monitored behaviour against goals, and self-reinforcement would augment the effects of traditional SMT. Participants were volunteers from the custody staff of a large US prison and were randomly assigned to four groups: a group receiving training on both stress management and self-management skills, a group receiving training on stress management only, a placebo group receiving training on personal development skills and a no-treatment control group. Results showed that the additional training on self-management skills appeared to augment the SMT. Specifically, the group that received both programmes exhibited significant differences across time on blood pressure, health symptoms and state anxiety. No significant differences were found between groups in levels of job satisfaction after the intervention.

6.5.5   Conclusions

Ganster and his colleagues (1982, ref. no. 605) conclude that while stress management training may be of value in helping workers to cope with unavoidable pressures, it deals with only part of the problem and needs to act as a supplement to organisational change programmes that tackle the root causes of stress in noxious work environments. Individual level interventions need to include an assessment of stress factors in the work environment in order to understand the stress–health dynamics and to target the intervention properly. Research demonstrating the importance of process variables (i.e. how the intervention is done) in determining its effectiveness points to the importance of employee involvement in programme design. Finally, stress management studies would benefit from being done within the context of a well-defined theoretical model that would guide the choice of stress factors to measure, the targeting of intervention strategies, implementation decisions and evaluation of effectiveness.

6.6   Crisis intervention

Traumatic events in the workplace can arise from many sources. Some jobs, such as law enforcement, emergency response, and retail banking carry higher than normal risks of exposure to crime or injury. However, sudden death, violence or the threat of violence can strike any workforce and can have a profound effect on individual and group functioning. Other threats or traumas can also disrupt the functioning of a workforce. For example, the discovery that the head of a residential children's home was a paedophile so traumatised the staff that they lost their capacity to look after the children effectively (Webb and McCaffrey, 1998, ref. no. 646). While many organisations have developed disaster control plans for responding to crisis situations, which may include plans for evacuations, policies for public relations, and procedures to protect the organisation from legal action, etc., few have developed comprehensive plans to deal with the acute and long term effects of traumatic events on the health and morale of employees.

6.6.1   Intervention models

People exposed to traumatic events in the workplace may exhibit a range of reactions including emotional numbing, withdrawal, irritability, fearfulness, depression, sleep disturbances, substance abuse, and prolonged medical problems. Braverman (1992, ref. no. 639) regards the mobilisation of social support at work as vital to the restoration of general morale and the protection of the health of individual workers. A primary goal of post-trauma crisis management is to ensure that these resources are mobilised. He proposes a crisis response plan which provides structures within which communication and group support can take place. The proposed model crisis intervention consists of:

- Crisis readiness – a set of procedures needs to have been prepared in advance, including communication plans, security procedures, handling shutdowns, etc. (Kutner, 1996, ref. no. 644).

- Formation of a crisis response team, including high level management whose visibility will be reassuring to staff.

- Meetings with affected groups which combine an informational, educational and emotion-sharing approach. Accurate and authoritative information is essential to avoid speculation and the spread of wild rumours. People in crisis can cope better if they are clear about where they stand. Managers should provide facts, address rumours, answer questions and explain company policy. In the educational section of the meeting a qualified expert should explain the normal range of post-traumatic stress reactions to warn people of what they may experience in coming days and weeks. Finally, employees and management need to be offered a process and forum through which they can share reactions to the event. It is through this process that group support is activated.

- Crisis counselling for individual employees, especially primary victims and witnesses.

- Follow-up, including evaluation of the success of the intervention and planning for the future.

An integrated system for the management of traumatic stress in the workplace implemented by Leeds Permanent Building Society is described by Richards (1994, ref. no. 641). It is designed to deal with trauma following robberies and involves:

- Pre-raid training, including security procedures and training in psychological coping techniques.

- Provision of an emergency pack to be opened immediately after a raid.

- Immediate local management visit to provide support.

- Peer counsellors made available to advise staff concerned about how they are feeling after the robbery.

- Critical incident stress debriefing by professional counsellors.

- Psychological health screening, continued for up to two years after the robbery.

- Cognitive behavioural therapy and/or medical treatment offered to staff experiencing continuing problems.

Stress debriefing has been widely promoted as a means of preventing or reducing psychological distress experienced following a severe trauma. The Assaulted Staff Action Plan (ASAP) described by Flannery and his colleagues (1995, ref. no. 642) is an intervention for mental health care providers assaulted by patients in a US state mental hospital. It operates on a voluntary basis to avoid passive resistance by staff victims and offers peer help, with services provided by colleagues who themselves understand the risks. Within twenty minutes of an assault an ASAP team member debriefs the victim at the site and provides other services such as referral to the Staff Victims Support Group as required. Results of the ASAP intervention have been encouraging in that, with the exception of severely injured victims, most staff remained at the worksite or were able to return within 24-48 hours. Few needed to be referred to the Staff Victims Support Group, and 90% of victims regained caring attachments to others, a sense of control over their lives, and of meaningful purpose in life itself.

6.6.2   Critical incident stress debriefing

Critical incident stress debriefing (CISD) appears to be the most widely used group intervention technique for the prevention of work-related traumatic stress disorder amongst high-risk emergency reponse personnel. It was developed by J T Mitchell as a result of his field experience with firefighting and emergency medical service workers. It may be defined as group meetings or discussions designed to mitigate the psychological impact of a traumatic event, prevent the development of post-traumatic stress disorder and serve as an early identification mechanism for individuals requiring professional counselling. Participants are given the opportunity to discuss their thoughts about, and emotions following, a traumatic event, are taught about normal reactions to trauma and stress management techniques, and get the opportunity to see they are not alone in their responses (Everly and Mitchell, 1995, ref. no. 643). However, despite the growing popularity of psychological debriefing, there are few evaluations of its effectiveness and results of studies are inconsistent. In a recent study of the effects of stress debriefing on rate of recovery of 195 helpers after an earthquake in Newcastle, Australia, Kenardy and his colleagues found no evidence of improved rate of recovery among those helpers who were debriefed, even when level of exposure and degree of helping-related stress experienced were taken into account (Kenardy *et al*, 1996, ref. no. 645). On the other hand, Robinson and Mitchell (1993, ref. no. 640) found in a descriptive study of 172 emergency service, hospital and welfare personnel, who took part in 31 debriefings, that most participants who experienced stress at the time of the incident attributed a reduction in symptoms, at least in part, to the debriefing. More rigorous investigation of the effectiveness of stress debriefing and its role in post-trauma recovery is urgently required.

6.7   Stressor reduction interventions

Models of occupational stress identify a range of job characteristics that can be associated with poor levels of mental and physical health. Stress factors which fall into this category typically include role ambiguity, role conflict, job insecurity, low involvement in decision-making, and work overload among others. In spite of these factors being endemic in many organisations, relatively little attention has been focused on organisational change as a way of improving health. Initiatives aimed at reducing work environment stress factors can be costly and difficult to implement. Stressor reduction requires an identification of the stress agents followed by planned changes in organisational structure and function, which are potentially expensive and disruptive to work processes. It is therefore more palatable for organisations to concentrate on cheaper individual-centred approaches, such as stress management training, to help employees cope more effectively, than to tackle the root of the problems in the work environment.

This tendency is reinforced by the transactional model of stress causation. According to this model, the individual appraises real-world events as stressful or non-stressful. For example, a Type A individual who complains of overload may perceive his or her workload as excessive when it is objectively no greater than that of the Type B at the next desk who is coping nicely. Thus people can be regarded as responsible for 'causing' their own stress (Karasek, 1994, ref. no. 664). The remedy for the stress in this model is to treat the victim by improving his or her coping skills rather than by reducing the objective workload.

However, opinion in the research community supports organisational level interventions as the preferred approach to dealing with employee stress because they concentrate on eliminating the source of the problem rather than simply treating the symptoms (Burke, 1993, ref. no. 662).

Newman and Beehr in their seminal work (1979, ref. no. 552) identify a range of organisation level interventions:

- Changing organisational characteristics, such as reward systems, staff selection systems, or training and development systems.

- Changing role characteristics through role redefinition, reduction in role underload or overload, reduction in role conflict and increasing participation in decision-making.

- Changing task characteristics through job redesign to take account of workers' abilities, use of workers' preferences in selection and placement, provision of training programmes and treatment of workers as individuals.

Evidence for the impact of interventions in these areas remains very limited. Robust research evidence on their effectiveness is scarce and results are mixed. However, the past 15 years have seen the design and implementation of a number of methodologically rigorous organisational level interventions to reduce work stress, of which we will now consider some illustrative examples.

6.7.1   Autonomous work groups

Wall and Clegg (1981, ref. no. 647) undertook a work redesign project involving blue collar workers in a particular department of a confectionery company which was characterised by low morale and poor motivation. The study involved three phases: problem assessment, implementation of redesign intervention and follow-up six and eighteen months after the intervention. The initial investigation revealed problems of lack of group autonomy and group work identity (a sense of being responsible for a meaningful task), and of poor quality of feedback from management. Employees exhibited low levels of work motivation and job satisfaction, combined with considerable emotional distress. The intervention involved increasing control by implementing autonomous work groups. Each team was given control over setting the pace of production, the distribution of tasks among team members, the organisation of breaks and changeover between different lines, and the allocation of overtime. The role of the supervisor was changed to that of providing support with daily operations. Results showed significant increases on measures of group autonomy and group work identity six months after the intervention. These improvements were maintained but not increased eighteen months after the intervention. Emotional distress was significantly reduced, and job satisfaction increased at both follow-up periods, with the greatest change occurring eighteen months after the intervention.

A later field experiment with autonomous work groups by Wall and his colleagues produced somewhat different results. The study was set in a confectionery company where senior management had decided to implement autonomous work groups at a new factory. Team members were collectively responsible for allocating jobs among themselves, reaching production targets, meeting quality and hygiene standards, solving local production problems, organising breaks, ordering and collecting raw materials, delivering finished goods to stores, and training new recruits. Groups reported to a support manager whose role was to provide guidance for the development of social and technical skills within the work groups. The design consisted of two experimental groups of day and night shift workers at the new factory and two non-equivalent control groups at existing factories where work was conventionally organised. It was hypothesised that implementation of autonomous work groups would enhance work motivation, job satisfaction and group performance, reduce labour turnover, improve mental health and increase organisational commitment. The study involved three waves of measurement of the experimental groups, with measures after 6, 18 and 30 months of production, and two waves of measurement for the control groups at times corresponding to the first two collections of data for the groups at the new factory. Results showed that implementation of the new work design substantially enhanced job satisfaction, but did not demonstrably affect job motivation, organisational commitment, mental health, work performance and labour turnover (Wall *et al*, 1986, ref. no. 652).

Cordery, Mueller and Smith (1991, ref. no. 654) conducted a longitudinal study of autonomous work groups at a new and an established minerals processing plant in Australia. Employees at the established site operating under traditional work design acted as controls. The study tested hypotheses that employees in autonomous work groups would report higher levels of job satisfaction, organisational commitment and trust in management and show lower levels of absenteeism and turnover than counterparts in traditionally designed jobs. Results showed that employees in the autonomous work groups did indeed report more favourable work attitudes than those in traditionally designed jobs. However, levels of turnover and absenteeism were higher among the autonomous groups.

6.7.2   Participatory action research projects

In the studies considered above, outside experts were pivotal in assessing need, designing the intervention and evaluating outcomes. An alternative approach, participatory action research (PAR), places the employees themselves centre stage and both involves them actively in, and gives them control over, programme planning, implementation and evaluation under the guidance of the research team. The approach is described in detail in a case study of a stressor reduction intervention in a car components manufacturing plant in Michigan (Schurman and Israel, 1995, ref. no. 666). The project began in 1985 and ended in 1992. It was put into operation by creating a representative group of employees to work in collaboration with the research team in designing, implementing and evaluating stress reduction initiatives. The researchers contributed their theoretical knowledge to help the employees to gain understanding and insights which they could then use to change the organisation. Employees were enabled to develop the skills to engage in a cyclical process of diagnosing and analysing problems, and then planning, implementing and evaluating interventions aimed at solving the problems they had identified.

The results of this intervention are described in detail by Heaney and her colleagues (1993, ref. no. 659). Overall objectives of the intervention included changing the work environment to eliminate stress factors, strengthening factors that mitigate the effects of stress on health such as social support and perceived control, and promoting employee mental and physical health. During the course of the study the original manufacturing facility was reorganised into two separate factories. One was managed in a traditional hierarchical fashion, with little trust between management and employees. The second had a moderately co-operative labour-management relations system which incorporated elements of joint problem solving. The impact of the PAR stress project differed markedly in the two plants. Involvement in the project enhanced co-worker support and decreased depressive symptoms only in the plant with adversarial industrial relations. As expected, involvement in the project was more strongly associated with increased perceptions of management's openness to suggestions in the plant with cooperative industrial relations. Employees involved in the project in both plants perceived themselves as participating more often in decision-making. Whatever the effects of the project on those involved, results indicated that, in general, the social environment at work and employee well-being did not improve in the course of the study.

Landsbergis and Vivona-Vaughan (1995, ref. no. 665) describe a PAR project at a large public health agency where physicians conducting medical examinations of employees had reported that many symptoms appeared to be stress-related. Two pairs of 'matched ' departments were selected to participate in the project. Within each pair, one department was randomly assigned to intervention status, while the other became a waiting list control group. Within each intervention department, representatives were elected to serve on employee problem-solving committees. Committee members identified and prioritised aspects of work organisation causing stress. Subsequently the committees developed proposals and action plans to reduce stress factors, provided feedback to other employees, and assisted management in implementing change. The impact of the intervention was assessed using data collected through a self-report survey completed in all four departments before the problem-solving committees were elected and one year later after the committees had concluded their formal meetings. Results suggested that the intervention in Intervention Department 1 had a negligible or adverse impact while intervention in Department 2 had a mixed impact. Scores for Intervention Department 1 suggested a reduction in group goal clarity, skill utilisation, decision latitude, and organisational involvement, and an increase in job demands and job dissatisfaction relative to Control Department 1. In Intervention Department 2, results showed an improvement in all aspects of job satisfaction, except influence satisfaction, compared to Control Department 2. In Intervention Department 2 also reported an increase in open group process and group goal clarity. In defence of their project the authors point out that the intervention was of relatively short duration, and several years work may be required to implement substantive change. Lack of resources prevented the collection of objective measures of health status or of organisational outcomes such as absenteeism or staff turnover. There was also some evidence of lack of commitment by the organisation to true worker participation, except as a limited experiment. Finally, a major internal restructuring of the agency took place during the project as the result of a crisis. This may have adversely affected its impact.

A final illustrative example of the PAR approach is an intervention by Cahill (1993, ref. no. 657) in the State of New Jersey child protection agency where an unsuitable computerised record keeping system combined with heavy case loads were causing strain. In this case the union used the results of a survey of burnout in the agency conducted by Cahill as evidence in a legislative hearing concerning the agency's performance and staff morale. As a result of the hearing a joint labour-management stress committee was formed to work on the problems of the agency. Strategies were designed to both improve the coping skills of the workers and to reduce the sources of stress in the work environment. A new microcomputer based information system was developed with employee participation. It offered multiple software applications including a timekeeping system, operational plan programme, caseload trend analysis, mailing lists, inventory tracking system, providers resource directory, critical indicators programme, and clients programme. Implementation of the new systems improved task variety and raised the skills levels of the clerical staff. New ergonomically correct computer equipment was purchased and a computer health and safety training programme was designed. The impact of the intervention was evaluated using self-report data from two surveys conducted before and after the intervention. Results showed that the intervention had a positive impact on decision latitude, skills levels, attitudes towards technology and job satisfaction. However, measures of strain did not show any change over time, which was positive in that the intervention did not increase stress.

6.7.3   The integrated model

Criticisms and shortcomings of both organisational level and individual level interventions have led researchers to develop integrated models of stress management which allow practitioners to use comprehensive approaches that address individual, psychosocial, environmental and organisational factors together. In this context, 'psychosocial factors' mean the availability of coping resources such as social support or perceived control, and 'environmental factors' refer to the physical environment. The integrated model of Israel and her colleagues (Baker, Israel and Schurman, 1996, ref. no. 572; Israel et al, 1996, ref. no. 575) incorporates a number of objective stress factors, and individuals' perception of these conditions as stressful. It suggests that stress factors may be a wide variety of demands and exposures including job, interpersonal, organisational, environmental and physical demands. These stress factors may have direct effects physical and mental health, or they may act through the perception of events as stressful to produce short term physiological, psychological or behavioural changes. These short term responses may be healthy or unhealthy and may include individual lifestyle behaviours such as smoking or exercise. These behaviours may exist prior to, and be exacerbated or enhanced, by, the stress factor, or the response may be initiated by the stressor. For example, individuals may drink or smoke more in response to increased task demands. The integrated model also suggests that psychosocial factors, such as social support and control, may have direct effects on both short term responses and enduring health outcomes or may affect the relationship of the stress factors to these outcomes. The model suggests that health is the result of interrelationships among a number of factors. It is therefore important for practitioners designing an intervention aimed at one area of the model, for example short term responses such as individual behaviour, to understand the effects of other factors in the model on the targeted area and on health outcomes. A practitioner developing an intervention to enhance, for example, problem-solving coping skills, needs to take into account the effect that organisational constraints and decision-making authority will have on the desired behaviour changes. It is no use teaching workers to identify and solve problems if they have no authority to make necessary changes. The Integrated Model, as a guide for developing interventions, allows practitioners to target any of the factors in the model, from eliminating stressors to enhancing modifiers like social support. It suggests that the effectiveness of programmes focused on either individual behaviour change or stressor elimination can be enhanced by strengthening psychosocial resources such as social support or control, and that practitioners should consider using comprehensive approaches that address individual, psychosocial, environmental and organisational factors.

Arguing from a transactional perspective, Dewe (1994, ref. no. 567) suggests that attempts to reduce stress by altering working conditions fail because change for some may simply add to their strain. Helping those who are at risk by offering a standard stress management training package is also liable to fail because the intervention again treats people as if they were all alike. To reconcile environmental and individual focused strategies, Dewe proposes looking at the individual in relationship with the work environment. 'This approach requires a greater matching of the individual and the environment, recognises that each is bound to the other through the adaptational encounter, and forces a more comprehensive strategy to evolve'.

6.7.4   Frameworks for intervention

Various frameworks for planning and implementing stress management interventions have been proposed by researchers. We will review three contrasting approaches here.

6.7.4.1   *The Participatory Action Research (PAR) framework*

PAR can be defined as 'a methodology in which researchers and members of a social system collaborate in a process of data-guided problem solving for the dual purposes of (a) improving a system's ability to provide members with desired outcomes and (b) contributing to general scientific knowledge'. PAR methodology involves assembling a representative group of stakeholders and helping them to design a knowledge acquisition and change strategy. The approach is essentially cyclical and iterative and involves the team in:

* Identifying aspects of the system they wish to change.
* Analysing root causes of the problems.
* Developing and implementing action plans.
* Creating a plan to evaluate the effects of their interventions.
* Specifying lessons learned from the evaluations.
* Creating and implementing revised action plans.

From a practical point of view, PAR initiatives tend to be costly and time-consuming to implement and difficult to evaluate because of problems in establishing control groups.

6.7.4.2   *Total stress management*

The concept Total Stress Management (TSM) was developed by McHugh and Brennan (1993, ref. no. 661) and can be viewed as a derivative of Total Quality Management. TSM may be viewed as both a pervasive organisational philosophy and as a practical approach to stress management which aims to establish optimum levels of stress for effective functioning in all areas of the organisation and in all individual employees. The four stage model involves:

* Stage 1: Stress audit to identify problems.
* Stage 2: Training of all organisation members in stress recognition and helping them to appreciate the value of a holistic approach to stress management.
* Stage 3: Development of organisation-wide skills in the prevention,

identification and management of stress at both the organisational and individual level. All organisation members will be helped to acquire skills which enable them to recognise stress in themselves and others and introduced to techniques which permit them to search actively for sources of stress and to present creative solutions.

- Stage 4: Evaluation through the collection of data on current organisational stress levels plus the cost of implementing TSM and comparing results with the initial stress audit.

Organisations approaching stress in this way would be unusual in their sensitivity to the welfare of employees and in their acceptance that individual and organisational health are interdependent.

6.7.4.3   Problem solving cycle

Rick and colleagues have identified five key areas of good practice in the research literature which they have consolidated into a problem solving cycle (Rick *et al*, 1997, ref. no. 579):

- Assessment and diagnosis of specific problems in the workplace based on solid evidence gleaned both from self-report surveys and hard data such as sick absence levels and staff turnover, (Briner, 1997, ref. no. 667).

- Solution generation based clearly defined objectives and investigation of options for intervention available.

- Implementation, if possible in a way that allows for controlled comparisons over a clearly defined timescale.

- Evaluation of the consequences of the intervention against objectives and expected positive and negative outcomes.

- Ongoing monitoring of the intervention, and feedback into the assessment process.

This proposed framework for intervention has the advantage of being flexible and can be adapted to many different organisational settings. It can be applied at both the individual and organisational level, regardless of whether the interventions are primary, secondary or tertiary.

6.7.5   Effectiveness of organisational level interventions

Employee well-being is determined by a wide range of related factors, some of which, like control and social support, are relevant features of work and employment, and some of which, like early experience and temperament, are matters on which work cannot have any impact. Organisational level interventions can have no effect on the latter. Weak results may also arise from the fact that researchers may have wrongly diagnosed the problem and have chosen an inappropriate target for their intervention. The interventions we have reviewed have largely concentrated on increasing employees' control over their work environment, with mixed results. However, many work characteristics other than control have been identified as causing stress, including job insecurity, role conflict and ambiguity, high workloads, poor social support and shiftworking. Some of these factors are probably impossible to change. There is resistance to legislation limiting working hours, and shift patterns are often inflexible because of service demands. Technological change and economic globalisation will continue to lead to job insecurity (Reynolds, 1997, ref. no. 668).

Causal associations between job conditions and well-being have to be shared or common among employees for organisational level interventions to be effective. For example, increased levels of job control may not be seen as a bonus by all employees. If 50% of the workforce want more responsibility and control and the other 50% do not, then increasing levels of autonomy by job redesign may benefit only half the workforce and perhaps be detrimental to the rest. Because our understanding of organisations and how they work is still rudimentary, changes introduced may have quite unforeseen effects (Briner, 1997, ref. no. 667).

It is difficult to evaluate the effectiveness of primary prevention interventions. In an organisational context it is impractical to randomly assign employees within the same workplace to intervention and control groups. It is difficult to distinguish the effects of the intervention from effects of other changes occuring within the organisation such as restructuring. Studies reported to date tend to have focused on small groups of employees within well defined occupational sectors. Prevention activities need to be evaluated in terms of long term health outcomes in a relatively large population. Long term evaluations, however, are complicated by mobility in the workforce and incomplete response rates at different times.

6.7.6 Conclusion

There is a need for a clearer understanding of the dynamics of organisational change and of the causal relationships between stress factors and illness to provide a sound conceptual basis for the design of primary prevention interventions. Prevention is in principle better than cure and this may encourage researchers to develop their understanding of, and methods for, organisational change.

6.8 Bibliography

6.8.1 Stress management overviews

(552)
PERSONAL and organizational strategies for handling job stress: a review of research and opinion
J E Newman and T A Beehr
Personnel psychology, vol. 32, 1979, p.1-43.

Reviews literature pertaining to personal and organisational strategies for handling job stress. Personal strategies are categorised as those aimed at changing (1) the person's psychological condition, (2) the person's physical condition, (3) the person's behaviour, and (4) the person's work environment. Organisational strategies are divided into those aimed at changing (1) organisational characteristics or conditions, (2) role characteristics or conditions, and (3) task/job characteristics or conditions. Concludes by emphasising the need for more evaluative research in the area, and by calling for more involvement by organisational psychologists.

DSC Shelfmark: 6428.095000

(553)
WORKSITE stress management interventions: their effectiveness and conceptualisation
R S DeFrank and C L Cooper
Journal of managerial psychology, vol.2, 1987, p.4-10.

Presents a model classifying stress management interventions as focusing either on the individual, the individual/organisational interface or the organisation. Individual level interventions include relaxation techniques, cognitive coping strategies, biofeedback and meditation. Interventions at the individual/organisational interface target known stressors such as role issues, relationships at work and person-environment fit. Organisation level interventions focus on selection and placement, training, health concerns and resources and job rotation.

DSC Shelfmark: 5011.530000

(554)

WORKPLACE interventions for stress reduction and prevention

L R Murphy

In Causes, coping and consequences of stress at work edited by C L Cooper and R Payne. Chichester: Wiley, 1988. p.301–339.

Reviews workplace interventions designed to reduce or prevent employee distress. Three classes of intervention are discussed: employee assistance programmes, stress management training and stressor reduction strategies. For each intervention an historical context is offered first, followed by a description of the intervention and review of empirical research.

DSC Shelfmark: 88/19899

(555)

STRESS management in work settings

L R Murphy and T F Schoenborn (editors)

New York: Praeger, 1989. 174p.

Summarises scientific evidence and reviews conceptual and practical issues relating to worksite stress management. Highlights the limitations of individual level interventions and argues that stress management needs to be seen as a complement to job redesign and organisational change interventions. Emphasises the importance of clear definition of the purpose and goals of any programme, of gaining organisational support, and of integrating the programme with existing occupational safety and health efforts.

DSC Shelfmark: 89/24186

(556)

BROADENING the scope of worksite stress programs: a guiding framework

C A Heaney and M van Ryn

American journal of health promotion, vol. 4, 1990, p.413–420.

Worksite stress programmes can be developed to reduce stressors, to modify employee perceptions of conditions in their environment, to reduce individual reactivity to a stressor, or to enhance the social environment as a buffer against stress. Article describes a decision tree designed to aid in the process of choosing the target of intervention. In order to make best use of the decision tree, information about the prevalence of particular stressors, the distribution of perceived stresses across the workforce and the health status of employees should be gathered through a needs assessment.

DSC Shelfmark: 0824.760000

(557)

STRESS, health, and organisations

T Cox, P Leather and S Cox

Occupational health review, vol. 23, 1990, p.13–18.

Argues that the organisation offers a number of different environments to employees, including a task environment, a problem-solving environment, and personal development and professional development environments. Measures based on the quality of these environments offer powerful predictors of organisationally relevant outcomes such as staff turnover and absence. Stress identified in an organisation can be controlled in three ways:

(1)   by the organisation putting its house in order.

(2)   by the organisation taking steps to help its employees.

(3)   by employees helping themselves.

DSC Shelfmark: 6228.990000

(558)

WORKSITE stress management interventions

J M Ivancevich *et al*

American psychologist, vol. 45, 1990, p.252–261.

Offers a theoretical framework for stress and stress management interventions. Interventions can (a) aim to reduce the number or intensity of stress factors present, (b) help employees to modify their appraisal of a potentially stressful situation, or (c) help employees to cope more effectively with the outcomes of stress. Intervention programmes can target the individual, the organisation, or the interface between the individual and the organisation. Outcomes can be similarly categorised.

DSC Shelfmark: 0853.400000

(559)

THE PSYCHOLOGICAL benefits of exercise in work settings: a review, critique and dispositional model

S M Jex

Work and stress, vol. 5, 1991, p.133–147.

Review suggests that evidence for the psychological benefits of exercise is largely inconclusive due to methodological flaws. The most pervasive flaw is that potential differences between exercisers and non-exercisers are not controlled. It is argued, on both theoretical and empirical grounds, that people who are high in dispositional optimism and self-motivation, low in negative affectivity and high in internal locus of control are most likely to adhere to an exercise programme and least likely to suffer from job stress. This may account for the apparent relationship between exercise and enhanced coping with stress.

DSC Shelfmark: 9348.102000

(560)

STRESS reduction in transition: conceptual problems in the design, implementation and evaluation of worksite stress management interventions

S Reynolds and D A Shapiro

Human relations, vol. 44, 1991, p.717-733.

Interventions to reduce occupational stress have focused primarily on strategies which target individual employees despite recommendations that researchers address organisational issues in occupational stress. Paper describes how the medical model has constrained the development and evaluation of stress management interventions. Proposes the adoption of the organisation development approach as a more fruitful basis for building new strategies for reducing work-related stress.

DSC Shelfmark: 4336.400000

(561)

STRESS and well-being at work: assessments and interventions for occupational mental health

J C Quick, L R Murphy, and J J Hurrell (editors)

Washington, DC: American Psychological Association, 1992. 372p.

Collection of papers covering causes of workplace stress, strain outcomes for both the individual and the organisation, and interventions aimed at ameliorating the situation for both parties.

DSC Shelfmark: 93/12260

(562)

THE VALUE of work, the risk of distress, and the power of prevention

J C Quick *et al*

In Stress and well-being at work edited by J C Quick, L R Murphy and J J Hurrell. Washington, DC: American Psychological Association, 1992. p.3-13.

Presents an overview of the value of work in the life experience, identifies the risks of distress within the framework of public health notions of disease, and argues the case for implementation of preventive measures. Proposes a three-tiered approach to prevention. Primary prevention aims to reduce the risk factor or change the nature of the stressor, secondary prevention aims to alter individual stress response, and tertiary prevention aims to heal those who have been distressed at work.

DSC Shelfmark: 93/12260

(563)

WORK and well-being : an agenda for the 1990s

G P Keita and S L Sauter (editors)

Washington, DC: American Psychological Association, 1992. 250p.

Part of the proceedings of a conference held in Washington DC in 1990 at which participants finalised an action plan to protect the psychological health of workers based on formulations contained in the NIOSH-proposed National Strategy for Prevention of Work-Related Psychological Disorders. Three panels were organised to develop more specific action plans in job design, education/mental health service delivery, and surveillance.

DSC Shelfmark: q93/11604

See also: Prevention of work-related psychological disorders: a national strategy proposed by the National Institute for Occupational Safety and Health (NIOSH) by S L Sauter, L R Murphy and J J Hurrell (American psychologist, vol.45, 1990, p.1146-1158 *DSC Shelfmark: 0853.400000*).

(564)

WORK and well-being: where do we go from here?

L R Murphy, J J Hurrell and J C Quick

In Stress and well-being at work edited by J C Quick, L R Murphy and J J Hurrell. Washington, D C: American Psychological Association, 1992. p. 331-347.

Argue that if occupational stress research and occupational mental health are to be advanced, improved surveillance systems at national level are needed, and at least five methodological problems in the field must be addressed. Major methodological needs are: (1) more longitudinal designs; (2) more standardised measurement instruments; (3) extensive use of collateral measures for assessing working conditions and strain outcomes, including assessments by co-workers and mangers, objective measurements obtained by job analysis, psychophysiological measures, performance and attendance data and information from medical and personnel records; (4) representative sampling procedures and replications to ensure generalisability of results; (5) use of advanced statistical methods such as structural equations analysis to improve understanding of causal relationships.

DSC Shelfmark: 93/12260

(565)

PROMOTING mental health policies in the workplace

R Jenkins and D Warman (editors)

London: HMSO, 1993. 115p.

A mixture of theoretical articles and case studies, covering, from a UK perspective, a definition of the problem of mental ill-health at work and solutions at the organisational and individual levels.

DSC Shelfmark: OP-93/H

(566)
CREATING healthy work organizations
C L Cooper and S Williams (editors)
Chichester: Wiley, 1994. 250p.

Presents a series of case studies of health promotion and stress management interventions in a range of organisations.

DSC Shelfmark: 94/16144

(567)
EAPs and stress management: from theory to practice to comprehensiveness
P Dewe
Personnel review, vol. 23, no.7, 1994, p.21-32

Attempts to search for reasons why stress interventions have failed to realise their potential. Recommends integrating the transactional model of stress into the design of intervention programmes that are truly comprehensive, thus translating theory into practice. The transactional strategy sees the individual in a relationship with the work environment. It requires a greater matching of the individual and the environment, recognises that each is bound to the other via the adaptational encounter, and forces a more comprehensive strategy to evolve.

DSC Shelfmark: 6428.098000

(568)
STRESS management at work: with whom, for whom and to what ends?
S Reynolds and R B Briner
British journal of guidance and counselling, vol. 22, 1994, p.75-89.

Argue that the whole area of occupational stress management research requires fundamental reconsideration. Stress management interventions are based on inadequate and over-simplistic theories which obscure the conflicting interests of employees, employers and researchers, and ignore empirical evidence that suggests that individual well-being, attitudes to work and work behaviours are minimally linked.

DSC Shelfmark: 2308.700000

(569)
STRESS-management interventions in the workplace: stress counselling and stress audits.
C L Cooper and S Cartwright
British journal of guidance and counselling, vol. 22, 1994, p.65-73.

Argues that both stress management training and counselling and substantive organisational change to eliminate sources of stress are important in meeting the needs of individuals and organisations.

DSC Shelfmark: 2308.700000

(570)
JOB stress interventions
L R Murphy *et al* (editors)
Washington, D.C.: American Psychological Association, 1995. 439p.

Collection of research studies of individual and organisational level stress management interventions.

DSC Shelfmark: q96/00105

(571)
OCCUPATIONAL stress management: current status and future directions
L R Murphy
Trends in organizational behaviour, vol. 2, 1995, p.1-14.

Proposes four directions for future work in stress management research: (1) design of comprehensive stress management interventions, (2) development and use of conceptual models of stress interventions, (3) improvements in the assessment of job and organisational stressors, and (4) increasing worker involvement in stress-management interventions.

DSC Shelfmark: 9049.668800

(572)
THE INTEGRATED MODEL: implications for work site health promotion and occupational health and safety practice
E Baker, B A Israel and S Schurman
Health education quarterly, vol.23, 1996, p.175-190.

Atricle describes a model of occupational stress that incorporates a broad definition of stress and includes, but is not limited to, the domains traditionally covered by both health promotion and health and safety practitioners. Practice examples from both fields are used to illustrate interventions that focus on different areas of the model (individual behaviour, psychosocial, organisational and contextual factors).

DSC Shelfmark: 4275.011400

(573)
MENTAL health and stress in the workplace: a guide for employers
C L Cooper and S Cartwright
London: HMSO, 1996. 25p.

Provides some factual information about mental health and well-being at work, and guidelines for employers wishing to create and maintain a healthy and productive workforce. It also offers general information on publications and other available sources of help and assistance.

DSC Shelfmark: OP-96/H

(574)
OCCUPATIONAL stress intervention
J J Hurrell and L R Murphy
American journal of industrial medicine, vol. 29, 1996, p.338–341.

Defines primary, secondary and tertiary occupational stress interventions. Primary prevention interventions involve job redesign and organisational change. Secondary interventions involve efforts to help employees either modify or control their appraisal of stressful situations, while tertiary interventions aim to help people to cope more effectively. Examples of secondary interventions are relaxation techniques, meditation and biofeedback. Tertiary interventions usually manifest themselves as employee assistance programmes.

DSC Shelfmark: 0826.750000

(575)
OCCUPATIONAL stress, safety and health: conceptual framework and principles for effective prevention interventions
B A Israel *et al*
Journal of occupational health psychology, vol.1, 1996, p.261–286.

Presents a comprehensive model of occupational stress, safety and health. Examines implications of the model for developing prevention interventions. Recommends that interventions should be context-specific, comprehensive and evaluated on multiple outcomes. Participants should be actively involved and the intervention should be led by interdisciplinary teams of researchers and practitioners. Concludes with four case studies addressing exposure to environmental, ergonomic and psychosocial stressors, and a combination of physical-environmental and psychosocial stressors.

DSC Shelfmark: 5026.095000

(576)
WHY aren't managers concerned about occupational stress?
K Daniels
Work and stress, vol.10, 1996, p.352-356.

Paper attempts to draw attention to the cognitive and cultural characteristics of risk perception in order to explain managers' apparent lack of interest in the effects of occupational stress and stress management. It is concluded that occupational stress is a risk with a low 'signal potential': that is, characteristics of the risk lead to little general concern. Managers may also consider stress management to be inappropriate since individuals, not organisations, should be responsible for coping with stress. Risk communication is discussed as a means through which the risks of stress may be more fully communicated to managers.

DSC Shelfmark: 9348.102000

(577)
AN INTERVENTION strategy for workplace stress
C L Cooper and S Cartwright
Journal of psychosomatic research, vol. 43, 1997, p.7-16.

Recommends a comprehensive three-pronged approach to tackling workplace stress consisting of primary, secondary and tertiary initiatives. Primary is concerned with stressor reduction, secondary with individual level stress management and tertiary with remedial support. Secondary and tertiary levels of intervention are likely to be insufficient in maintaining employee health without the complementary approach of stressor reduction initiatives.

DSC Shelfmark: 5043.480000

(578)
PREVENTIVE stress management in organizations
J C Quick *et al*
Washington, D.C: American Psychological Association, 1997. 368p.

Examines the sources of stress, the stress response and its modifiers, and the individual and organisational consequences of stress. Then sets forth a basis for organisational stress diagnosis and elaborates the principles of preventive stress management. Finally explores organisational and individual stress reduction and management strategies.

DSC Shelfmark: 98/06758

(579)
STRESS: big issue, but what are the problems?
J Rick *et al*
Brighton: Institute for Employment Studies, University of Sussex, 1997. 97p.
(IES report; 331)

Report draws together evidence from the literature and from a number of case studies to examine the good practice principles underlying the effective management of work-based stress. It moves away from traditional concepts of stress management to propose a pragmatic problem-solving framework. This facilitates a systemic analysis and a better understanding of workplace issues.

DSC Shelfmark: 7520.30000

(580)
CASES in stress prevention: the sources of a participative and stepwise approach
M A J Kompier *et al*
Stress medicine, vol. 14, 1998, p.155–168.

Recommends a five stage approach to stress management interventions involving: (1) a stepwise and systematic approach, (2) an adequate diagnosis or risk analysis, (3) a combination of individual level and organisation level interventions, (4) a participative approach involving both employees and middle management, and (5) top management support.

DSC Shelfmark: 8474.129500

6.8.2   Self-help books

(581)
NO hassle! : taking the stress out of work
S Cartwright and C L Cooper
London: Century Business, 1994. 207p.

Presents a range of coping strategies for managing stressful situations at work including dealing with difficult people, coping with organisational culture, handling unexpected events such as sexual harassment, redundancy or unethical behaviour, and achieving a healthy life/work balance.

DSC Shelfmark: Not found

(582)
MANAGING workplace stress
S Cartwright and C L Cooper
Thousand Oaks, Calif : Sage, 1997, 185p.

Self-help book gives practical advice on how to cope with a range of work-related stress factors such as organisational change, sexual harassment, unethical behaviour and difficult colleagues. Suggests strategies for dealing with everyday stressful events such as travel, heavy work load and meetings, and explores issues related to home/work conflict.

DSC Shelfmark: 97/08410

(583)
STRESS work book: how individuals, teams and organisations can balance pressure and performance. 2nd ed.
E Warren and C Toll
London: Brealey, 1997. 190p.

Authors place stress management within the mainstream of management skills, and draw upon current best practice to provide a straightforward guide to the topic.

DSC Shelfmark: Not found.

(584)
STOP the world: finding a way through the pressures of life
M Watts and C L Cooper
London: Hodder and Stoughton, 1998. 229p.

Part one introduces the stress equation (life stress + work stress + individual vulnerability = stress symptoms/outcomes) and focuses on identifying stress and on knowing yourself. Part 2 considers the mistakes people make and where power and responsibility really lie. Part 3 covers the range of coping strategies an individual needs to deal with stress.

DSC Shelfmark: Not found.

(585)
THE STRESS workbook
J Gutmann
London: Sheldon, 1998. 115p.

A self-help book written in an easy to ready style with lots of exercises. Covers causes of stress, self-evaluation (strengths, weaknesses and personal goals), energy wasting through emotions such as worry and guilt, coping skills and self-care.

DSC Shelfmark: Not found.

6.8.3   Employee assistance programmes

(586)
EVALUATION of an employee assistance program
J A Nadolski and C E Sandonato
Journal of occupational medicine, vol. 29, 1987, p.32-37.

Examined the work performance of employees of Detroit Edison referred to the EAP Jan-Dec 1982. Five measures were chosen to assess overall work performance of the subjects: (a) lost time, (b) health insurance claims, (c) disciplinary action, (d) accidents, and (e) work productivity. Data were collected at their initial appointment with the EAP and for the 6 months following treatment. Results showed that employees who received help from the EAP subsequently improved their work performance.

DSC Shelfmark: 5026.100000

(587)
EMPLOYEE assistance program evaluation in a Federal government agency
R P Maiden
Employee assistance quarterly, vol.3, 1988, p.191-203

Discusses the cost-benefit and cost-effectiveness evaluation conducted by the US Department of Health and Human Services Employee Counselling Services programme. Describes the development of the evaluation plan, data collection processes and strategies for maintaining client confidentiality while analysing personnel data. Results showed that ultimately the HHS should realise a $7.01 return per dollar invested in the programme.

DSC Shelfmark: 3737.032400

(588)
STRESS counselling in the workplace: the Post Office experience
T Allinson, C L Cooper and P Reynolds
The Psychologist, vol. 2, 1989, p. 384-388.

In-house counselling service was independently evaluated using a time series analysis of absenteeism, sickness and disciplinary records prior to and following counselling. Found 53% reduction in the frequency of absence events, and a 74% reduction in the duration of absence for the six months pre- and post- counselling. The number of recorded disciplinary proceedings fell by 50%.

DSC Shelfmark: 6946. 534680

(589)
EVALUATING the benefits of employee assistance programmes
V Orlans
Employee counselling to-day, vol.3, no.4, 1991, p.27-31.

Proposes a form of evaluation of employee assistance programmes (EAPs) which includes qualitative as well as quantitative factors, and which seeks to highlight contradictions and difficulties as potential sources of learning rather than reporting only statistically significant outcomes. Evaluation should also address itself to the relationship between a particular programme and the rest of the organisation in which it is located. Feedback mechanisms should be built into programmes to facilitate learning and insights.

DSC Shelfmark: 3737.037330

(590)

IMPACT of stress counselling at work

C L Cooper and G Sadri

Journal of social behavior and personality, vol. 6, 1991, p.111-423.

Study systematically assessed the impact of stress counselling in the UK Post Office among postal employees from shop floor level to senior management. Results showed a significant improvement pre- to post- counselling in unauthorised absence events and days lost among participants. Self-reported levels of anxiety, somatic anxiety and depression were reduced, and self-esteem increased significantly. However, there was no significant improvement in job satisfaction and organisational commitment.

DSC Shelfmark: 5064.751500

(591)

OCCUPATIONAL stress, clinical treatment and changes in job perceptions

J Firth-Cozens and G E Hardy

Journal of occupational and organizational psychology, vol.65, 1992, p.81-88.

Longitudinal study looked at individual change over a 16-week period in response to psychotherapy. Results suggest that as symptom levels are reduced, perceptions of jobs become more positive.

DSC Shelfmark: 5026.082000

(592)

EMPLOYEE Counselling Service: evaluating a service

P McAllister and P Bryan

Employee counselling today, vol. 5, no.2, 1993, p.4-8.

The Employee Counselling Service is a registered charity offering a free service. The primary aim of the ECS is to help individuals who are in danger of losing their jobs as a result of personal difficulties affecting work performance. Results of an evaluation carried out through questionnaires completed by employers and employees showed that 64.4% of clients referred for alcohol-related problems were still in the same employment one year after counselling ceased.

DSC Shelfmark: 3737.037330

(593)

EVALUATING employee assistance/counselling programmes: practical problems.

J C Highley and C L Cooper

Employee counselling today, vol.5, no.5, 1993, p.13-18.

Major problem with carrying out counselling evaluation research in organisations are questionnaire administration, selecting a comparison group, confidentiality, extracting hard data from company records and gaining access to providers and organisations.

DSC Shelfmark: 3737.037330

(594)
STRESS and coping in US organizations: the role of the Employee Assistance Programme
J Berridge and C L Cooper
Work and stress, vol. 7, 1993, p.89–102.

Reviews and evaluates scope and coverage of Employee Assistance Programmes (EAPs), theoretical models of the configuration of EAPs , selection criteria for the EAP, and methods of introduction. Analyses the roles of participants within the EAP process, and the ethical and professional conflicts which an EAP may introduce into organisational functioning.

DSC Shelfmark: 9348.102000

(595)
EFFECTIVE employee assistance programs: a guide for EAP counsellors and managers
G Cunningham
Thousand Oaks, Calif.: Sage, 1994. 249p.

Surveys US philosophies and practices of EAPs, which are designed to provide a balance of benefits for both employing organisations and individual workers. Sees a fully professionalised service as the future model, replacing the lay origins of EAPs in the employee alcoholism movement. Proposes that EAP professionals must keep the personnel function at arms length to maintain their integrity, and envisages the evolution of EAPs into wider intervention programmes in organisational analysis and development, and in management consultancy.

DSC Shelfmark: 8069.271100

(596)
EVALUATING EAPs
J C Highley and C L Cooper
Personnel review, vol. 23, no.7, 1994, p.46–59.

EAP evaluation should include process evaluation (service audit and quality assurance) and outcome evaluation (effectiveness of the service). Major problems in conducting an evaluation are questionnaire administration, selection of a control group, confidentiality, extracting hard data from company records and gaining access to providers and organisations.

DSC Shelfmark: 6428.098000

(597)

PSYCHIATRIC morbidity in policemen and the effect of brief psychotherapeutic intervention: a pilot study
R S Doctor, D Curtis and G Isaacs
Stress medicine, vol. 10, 1994, p.151-157.

Levels of psychiatric morbidity and perceived sources of stress among police officers were investigated using the General Health Questionnaire (GHQ) and a stress situation questionnaire in a sample of 171 officers. Half of the 61 responders were invited to attend group counselling sessions weekly for 12 weeks. Of these 22 attended at least one session. Outcome measures were studied with a second GHQ completed at the end of the treatment and the amounts of sick leave taken before, during and after the treatment period. There were no significant changes in GHQ score within or between groups, nor were there significant differences in amounts of sick leave taken.

DSC Shelfmark: 8474.129500

(598)

UK standards of practice and professional guidelines for employee assistance programmes
Employee Assistance Professionals Association, Britannic Chapter
London, 1995. 47p.

Covers programme design, implementation, management, direct service links with the organisation and external resources, and evaluation.

DSC Shelfmark: Not found

(599)

REDUCING absenteeism by stress management: evaluation of a stress counselling service
S Michie
Work and stress, vol. 10, 1996, p.367-372.

A stress counselling service for hospital staff is described and evaluated. A total of 163 staff were seen over a two year period. Subjects were asked to complete a questionnaire immediately before and after counselling, and at six month follow-up. Results showed that staff reported less distress and had lower absenteeism due to sickness following short term stress counselling compared to before. Due to lack of a control group, the results suggest, but do not prove, the beneficial effects of stress management.

DSC Shelfmark: 9348.102000

(600)

EMPLOYEE assistance programmes and workplace counselling
J Berridge, C L Cooper and C Highley-Marchington

Chichester: Wiley, 1997. 249p.

The employee assistance programme (EAP) is a development of employee counselling which grew up in the U.S. in the 1960s, and in Britain in the 1980s. It involves the employer who funds the counselling, and management if appropriate, and is concerned that the outcomes of counselling can be related to the employee's job context as well as to his or her personal life. Within the EAP, solutions are sought simultaneously to individual and corporate problems in a professional and purposive, yet cost driven, manner.

DSC Shelfmark: 97/17352

(601)
UK guidelines for audit and evaluation for employee assistance programmes
UK Employee Assistance Professionals Association
London, 1998. 15p.

DSC Shelfmark: Not found.

6.8.4   Individual level training

(602)
THE RELAXATION response
H Benson
London: Collins, 1976. 158p.

DSC Shelfmark: Not found

(603)
DAILY relaxation response breaks in a working population. II. Effects on blood pressure
R K Peters, H Benson, and J M Benson
American journal of public health, vol. 67, 1977, p.954-959.

Volunteers were recruited at the corporate offices of a manufacturing concern, and, after a baseline measurement period, were randomly assigned to three groups. Group A was taught a relaxation technique, Group B was taught to sit quietly, and Group C was taught nothing. Groups A and B were asked to take two 15-minute relaxation breaks daily. Mean decreases in blood pressure in the group practising the relaxation technique were 6.7 mm Hg for systolic blood pressure SBP and 5.2mm Hg for diastolic blood pressure DBP. For both SBP and DBP mean changes in group A were significantly greater than those in Group B and in Group C.

DSC Shelfmark: 0835.900000

(604)

CONTROLLED trial of biofeedback-aided behavioural methods in reducing mild hypertension

C Patel, M G Marmot and D J Terry

British medical journal, vol. 282, 1981, p. 2005-2008.

A total of 204 employees in a large industry with two or more coronary risk factors, (serum cholesterol greater than 6.3 mmol/1, blood pressure greater than 140/90 mm Hg and current cigarette consumption greater than 10 cigarettes per day) were randomly allocated to a biofeedback group receiving training in relaxation and management of stress or a control group. Both groups received simple health education literature. The treatment group received training in breathing exercises, deep muscle relaxation, and meditation. The relaxation was enhanced by means of a multicircuit galvanic skin resistance feedback machine developed for group use. After 8 weeks of training, and again 8 months later, the biofeedback group showed a significantly greater fall in systolic and diastolic blood pressure than the control group.

DSC Shelfmark: 2330.000000

(605)

MANAGING organizational stress: a field experiment

D C Ganster *et al*

Journal of applied psychology, vol.67, 1982, p.533-542.

A stress management training programme was evaluated in a field experiment with 79 public agency employees who were randomly assigned to treatment and control groups. The programme consisted of 16 hours of group exposure to stress inoculation training over 8 weeks. Participants were also taught progressive relaxation techniques to supplement the process. Epinephrine and norepinephrine excretion at work, anxiety, depression, irritation and somatic complaints were all measured at pre-test, post-test and 4 month follow-up. Subjects exhibited significantly lower epinephrine and depression levels than the controls at post-test and 4 months follow-up. However, results were not reproduced in a subsequent intervention on the original control group.

DSC Shelfmark: 4947.000000

(606)

WORKSITE-based behavioral treatment of mild hypertension

M Drazen *et al*

Journal of occupational medicine, vol.24, 1982, p.511-514.

The relative effectiveness of two behaviourally oriented, non-pharmacological treatments, rational-emotive therapy/assertiveness training and anxiety management training, were compared in reducing blood pressure of white-collar employees with mild hypertension. A third treatment comparison group, hypertension education counselling, was used to control for non-specific effects. Significant reductions in diastolic pressures from pre-treatment to post-treatment were found in the two behavioural treatment groups, but significant pre-post reductions in systolic pressure were found only in the rational–emotive therapy/assertiveness training condition. These reductions were generally maintained at two–month follow–up.

DSC Shelfmark: 5026.100000

(607)
OCCUPATIONAL stress management: a review and appraisal
L R Murphy
Journal of occupational psychology, vol. 57, 1984, p.1–15.

Reviews the literature on occupational stress management, comparing studies along the dimensions of type of work group, programme orientation and format, stress management methods, non–specific effects, and long term maintenance of skills and benefits.

DSC Shelfmark: 5026.120000

(608)
STRESS management at the worksite for hypertension: compliance, cost–benefit, health care and hypertension–related variables
E A Charlesworth, B J Williams and P E Baer
Psychosomatic medicine, vol.46, 1984, p.387–397.

A group of 22 hypertensive employees showed significant reductions in both systolic and diastolic blood pressure at the end of a 10-week stress management training programme. A control group showed no significant reduction in either systolic or diastolic blood pressure over a comparable time period. When the control group was given stress management training, the resulting systolic and diastolic blood pressure reductions were significant. When blood pressure was recorded 3 years later, there were significant reductions in both systolic and diastolic blood pressure. The frequency of relaxation practice and the amount of blood pressure reduction achieved during relaxation practice were significantly correlated with blood pressure reduction after the training programme.

DSC Shelfmark: 6946.555000

(609)
STRESS inoculation training
D Meichenbaum
New York: Pergamon, 1985. 114p.

Introduces stress inoculation training (SIT) as consisting of (1) conceptualisation phase in which clients are taught the transactional nature of stress, and how to analyse their own responses, (2) skills acquisition in which clients are taught coping and problem solving skills, and (3) application and follow through, in which clients practice their newly acquired skills through role play, etc.

DSC Shelfmark: 85/23724

See also: Stress inoculation training: a 20-year update by D Meichenbaum. In Principles and practice of stress management edited by P M Lehrer and R L Woolfolk. 2nd ed. New York: Guilford Press, 1993. p.373-406. *DSC Shelfmark: q93/09892*

(610)
EFFECTS of exercise, relaxation, and management skills training on physiological stress indicators: a field experiment.
N S Bruning and D R Frew
Journal of applied psychology, vol. 72, 1987, p.515-521.

Sixty-two volunteer subjects were randomly assigned to one of four groups as follows: (1) management skills, (2) meditation, (3) exercise, and (4) control group. Results showed that each of the intervention strategies improved two of the four physiological indicators, pulse rate and systolic blood pressure. Combination strategy analyses indicated that all dual combination strategies produced significant decreases in pulse rate, with no combination being superior to the others. No reliable results were found for combination strategies when examined for order effects.

DSC Shelfmark: 4947.000000

(611)
INDIVIDUAL stress management interventions: evaluation of techniques
M T Matteson and M Ivancevich
Journal of managerial psychology, vol.2, 1987, p.24-30.

Reviews what is known about the effectiveness of individual or personal stress management techniques by examining four different categories: (1) relaxation training, (2) biofeedback (3) cognitive techniques, and (4) exercise. Points to the need for use of multiple measures, adequate control groups, longitudinal research and representative samples to improve evaluation research on stress management techniques.

DSC Shelfmark: 5011.530000

(612)
RELAXATION training for essential hypertension at the worksite: 1. The untreated mild hypertensive
M A Chesney *et al*
Psychosomatic medicine. vol.49, 1987, p.250-263.

An industry-based randomised study compared the effects of behavioural treatment and blood pressure monitoring on blood pressure change in 158 untreated persons with mild hypertension. Participants were randomly assigned to BT or BPM groups and stratified by entry diastolic blood pressure, age and sex. BT participants received relaxation training with or without the addition of cognitive restructuring, biofeedback and health behaviour change components. At 18 weeks into the study, when BT groups had completed training, both the BT and BPM groups showed significant reductions in systolic and diastolic blood pressure. These reductions were maintained throughout the 36 week follow-up period.

DSC Shelfmark: 6946.555000

(613)
WORKSITE stress management: a comparison of programs
J F Sallis *et al*
Psychology and health, vol 1, 1987, p.237-255.

Randomised controlled group outcome study compared three intervention conditions: relaxation training, multicomponent stress management and an education/support comparison group. Assessments were conducted at baseline, post-intervention and at three month follow-up. For this non-clinical population, results were constant with an interpretation that non-specific intervention factors produced significant improvements in psychological functioning (reductions in depression, anxiety and hostility), but there were no improvements in job satisfaction, work stress, blood pressure or blood pressure reactivity to stress. No intervention was more effective than the others in changing any of the psychological, work-related or physiological variables measured.

DSC Shelfmark: 6946.535325

(614)
EMPLOYEE behaviors before and after stress management
L R Murphy and S Sorenson
Journal of organizational behavior, vol.9, 1988, p.173-182.

Organisational records on employee absenteeism, performance ratings, equipment accidents and work injuries were obtained for highway maintenance workers who received biofeedback or muscle relaxation training. Similar data were gathered for a comparison group of 80 employees who did not volunteer for training. Employee records were analysed for the two years before training. (time 1), the year after training (time 2), and the six months after that (time 3). Results indicated that workers who received muscle relaxation (but not biodfeedback) had significantly lower absenteeism and higher attendance ratings for the year immediately following training relative to non-volunteers. These differences were not evident beyond the first post-training year. No group differences were found on performance ratings, equipment accidents or work injuries.

DSC Shelfmark: 5027.066000

(615)
DESIGNING worksite stress-management programs
P J Rosch and K K Pelletier
In Stress management in work settings edited by L R Murphy and T F Schoenborn. New York: Praeger, 1989, p.65-85.

Reviews and evaluates formal stress management training programmes which consist of a mixture of physiologic techniques (muscular relaxation, meditation and biofeedback), cognitive training and physical fitness.

DSC Shelfmark: 89/24186

(616)
REDUCING teacher stress
M R Bertoch *et al*
Journal of experimental education, vol. 57, 1989, p.117-128.

Thirty participants scoring high on occupational stress were randomly assigned to treatment and control groups. The intervention consisted of 12 2-hour treatment sessions covering relaxation and breathing, meditation, nutrition and exercise advice, general information about stress, and discussions of assertiveness, coping with disappointment, and social support. Subjects were assessed on environmental, personality and emotional variables using self-report and expert judge measures at both pre- and post-treatment. Significant differences on the post-test means, favouring the treatment group, were found for 23 of the 39 variables measured on the self-report instruments.

DSC Shelfmark: 4981.500000

(617)
STRESS reduction at the worksite: an evaluation of two methods
R B Goodspeed and A G DeLucia
American journal of health promotion, vol. 4, 1990, p.333-337.

The Time-Life Stress Management Program and a Myers-Briggs Personality Type approach were used in a study of the relative effectiveness of contrasting interventions. Some 35 employees participated in the Myers-Briggs programme and 113 in the Time-Life programme. Baseline strain scores were obtained using a standardised strain survey instrument. Follow-up strain scores were obtained six to eight months after baseline for 62% of individuals. Both groups showed significant reductions in follow-up strain scores when compared to baseline.

DSC Shelfmark: 0824.760000

(618)
EFFECTIVENESS and cost efficiency of interventions in health promotion
R H Pruitt
Journal of advanced nursing, vol.17, 1992, p.926-932.

Study evaluated the stress management component of an overall employee fitness programme using psychological, physiological and economic parameters. The stress management course consisted of strategies involving stress awareness and principles of time management, environmental modification, and assertiveness, as well as multiple methods of relaxation. A sample of 31 subjects participated in the experimental group and 33 in a no treatment control group. The treatment group showed significant differences in stress-related physical symptoms. There was no statistically significant difference between groups for state anxiety and blood pressure. This was due to improvements in control group members who were also participating in the wider fitness programme. Those who practised relaxation on a regular basis had significantly lower systolic blood pressure.

DSC Shelfmark: 4918.947000

(619)
IMPROVED health and coping by physical exercise or cognitive behavioral stress management training in a work environment
H Grønningsæter *et al*
Psychology and health, vol. 7, 1992, p.147-163.

The effects of two types of stress management training on physically inactive employees in an insurance company were studied. Subjects were randomly allocated to: (a) aerobic exercise, (b) stress management training, or (c) a no-treatment control group. Participants were tested after 10 weeks of training and at 6 month follow up. Aerobic exercise resulted in improved aerobic capacity, perceived general health and muscle pain but significantly reduced job satisfaction. The SMT group reported increased coping abilities both in work and leisure time and showed improved knowledge about stress, but fewer health effects. No non-specific treatment effects were observed across groups.

DSC Shelfmark: 6946.535325

(620)
BEHAVIOURAL and cognitive psychotherapies: past history, current applications and future registration issues
A Hackmann
Behavioural and cognitive psychotherapy, vol. 21, 1993, Supplement. 75p.

Report covers the nature, origins and guiding principles of the behavioural and cognitive psychotherapies, the main treatment techniques used and their current applications together with an evaluation of their efficacy in a variety of settings.

DSC Shelfmark: 1877.293500

(621)
EFFECTS of the transcendental meditation program on stress reduction, health and employee development: a prospective study in two occupational settings
C N Alexander *et al*
Anxiety, stress and coping, vol. 6, 1993, p.245-262.

Three-month prospective study evaluated the effects of transcendental meditation (TM) on stress reduction, health, and employee development in a large manufacturing plant and a small distribution sales company in the car industry. Subjects were 27 volunteer employees in the treatment group and 23 controls at Site 1 and 18 treatment subjects and 18 controls at site 2. Regular meditators improved significantly more than controls on multiple measures of stress and employee development including reduced physiological arousal (measured by skin conductance levels) during and outside TM practice, decreased trait anxiety, job tension, insomnia and fatigue, cigarette and alcohol use, improved general health and enhanced employee effectiveness, job satisfaction and relationships with colleagues.

DSC Shelfmark: 1566.612000

(622)
PRINCIPLES and practice of stress management. 2nd ed.
P M Lehrer and R L Woolfolk (editors)
New York: Guilford Press, 1993. 621p.

Describes a range of stress management techniques including progressive relaxation, meditation, biofeedback and cognitive therapies.

DSC Shelfmark: q93/09892

(623)
SESSION impact and outcome in stress management training
S Reynolds, E Taylor and D Shapiro
Journal of community and applied social psychology, vol.3, 1993, p.325–337.

Sixty-two female health service workers participated in six standardised sessions of stress management training, each of which contained specific techniques. After training, participants reported statistically significant reductions in psychological distress, which were maintained at three-month follow-up. There were no significant changes in job or non-job satisfaction. Specific task impacts, such as insight and problem definition, and non-specific impacts, such as support, relief and involvement, were significantly related to non-job satisfaction one month after training. In addition, the slope of ratings of support and relief was negatively correlated with psychological symptoms at one month and three months after training.

DSC Shelfmark: 4961.693000

(624)
SESSION impact in stress management training
S Reynolds, E Taylor and D A Shapiro
Journal of occupational and organizational psychology, vol.66, 1993, p.99–113.

To test the proposition that specific skills-related interventions produce differential effects, a multi-component stress management training programme was designed in which six sessions presented specific topics and related techniques in a pre-determined order. Participants rated each session in terms of depth, smoothness, post-session mood and 12 specific impacts, including task and interpersonal positive impacts and problematic, negative impacts. Impact ratings were of three types: those which did not differ between sessions; those which appeared to reflect non-specific and group processes and showed a significant linear trend over time; and those which reflected specific session content where no linear trend was detected but one or more sessions differed significantly from others.

DSC Shelfmark: 5026.082000

(625)
EFFECTS of a worksite coping skills intervention on the stress, social support and health outcomes of working mothers
M L Kline and D L Snow
Journal of primary prevention, vol.15, 1994, p.105–121.

Paper reports the results of a study which evaluated the immediate and longer term effectiveness of a 15-session worksite coping skills intervention for working mothers. A sample of 142 mothers employed in secretarial positions was assessed at pre-test, immediately following the intervention and at 6-month follow-up using self-report measures. At post-test participants reported lower levels of role stress, higher levels of perceived social support at work, reduced alcohol and tobacco use, less use of avoidance coping and lowered psychological symptomology. At 6 month follow-up, they reported lower work-family and work environment stress, less avoidance coping, lower psychological symptomology and higher social support from work sources.

DSC Shelfmark: 5042.370000

(626)
RELAXATION with guided imagery: effects on employees' psychological distress and health seeking behaviors
S W Vines
AAOHN journal, vol.42, 1994, p.206–213.

Study examined the effects of relaxation with guided imagery (RGI) on decreasing psychological distress and improving health seeking behaviours with a working population. Psychological distress was measured using SCL-90-R and health seeking behaviours by the Personal Lifestyle Activities Questionnaire. The practice of RGI did not significantly reduce employees' psychological distress or improve their health seeking behaviours. Anecdotal data suggest that RGI may be useful for some individuals.

DSC Shelfmark: 0537.501300

335

(627)

STRESS inoculation for reduction of burnout: a Conservation of Resources approach

J R Freedy and S E Hobfoll

Anxiety, stress and coping, vol. 6, 1994, p.311-325.

Evaluated the efficacy of two programmes designed to reduce stress among nurses by increasing their coping resources. A dual resource intervention targeted the enhancement of both social support and mastery resources. A single resource intervention targeted the enhancement of only mastery resources. Both interventions were contrasted with a no intervention control group. Participants in the dual resource intervention experienced significant increases in social support and mastery compared to the control group. The social support enhancement persisted through a five week follow-up. Participants in the dual resource intervention with low initial levels of social support or mastery experienced significant reductions in psychological distress. Participants in the single resource intervention experienced a slight increase in mastery compared to the control group.

DSC Shelfmark: 1566.612000

(628)

COURSES on work stress: a growing market , but what about their quality?

I L D Houtman and M A J Kompier

In Job stress interventions edited by L R Murphy and others. Washington, DC: American Psychological Association, 1995, p.337-349.

Describes a study carried out to inventory, characterise and assess the quality of courses on work stress offered on the 'open market' in the Netherlands. Results showed that most training institutions did not specify course objectives, target groups or course content. Evaluation of the courses was often unstructured and oral, an evaluation report was often not written and the evaluation was not always available to the organisation purchasing the course. Emphasis was on changing the individual, yet how a link was made between course content and stress problems of participants was unclear.

DSC Shelfmark: q96/00105

(629)

EFFECTS of instruction on stress management skills and self-management skills among blue-collar employees

J A Thomason and S B Pond

In Job stress interventions edited by L R Murphy and others. Washington, DC: American Psychological Association, 1995, p.7-20.

Study was designed to assess the effects of instruction on stress management skills among blue collar workers, and to assess whether instruction in self-management would enhance the effects of stress management training. Participants were prison officers at a large prison in the US. They were randomly assigned to a group receiving training in both self-management and stress management skills, a group receiving training in stress management skills only, a placebo group receiving personal development training and a no intervention control group. Physiological, psychological and health symptoms were measured at pre-test, post-test, 3 month follow-up and 6 month follow-up. Results showed that self-management training augmented instructional programmes and that the effects of stress management instruction were modest for blue collar workers.

DSC Shelfmark: q96/00105

(630)
STRESS reduction in the workplace: the effectiveness of psychoeducational programs
N I Kagan, H Kagan and M G Watson
Journal of counseling psychology, vol 42, 1995, p.71-78.

Study focused on determining if stress levels could be reduced by psychoeducational training programmes, if reduced stress levels were sustained over time, and if any programme was more effective than any other over short or long term. Studied the effects of three individual programmes and all four possible combinations of these programmes. The individual techniques were: progressive muscle relaxation, assertiveness training, crisis intervention, suicide prevention and hostage negotiations, and interpersonal process recall. Outcomes were measured using standardised psychological self-report instruments and job performance measures. Results supported the value of psychoeducational training programmes in preventing mental ill-health in the workplace.

DSC Shelfmark: 4965.450000

(631)
WHEN relaxation is not enough
R M Kolbell
In Job stress interventions edited by L R Murphy and others. Washington, DC: American Psychological Association, 1995. p.31-43.

Study investigated whether meditation as a stress management intervention could significantly affect health and cognitive function in an at risk population of employees of a children's services division. Results showed that a brief training in meditation was no different from social support or no intervention controls on measures of health and cognitive functioning among social service workers.

DSC Shelfmark: q 96/00105

(632)
DEVELOPING stress management programmes
S Palmer

In Handbook of counselling psychology edited by R Woolfe and W Dryden. London: Sage, 1996. p. 528-552.

After an overview of stress theory and models, discusses development of stress management programmes for the individual, the family and the organisation. In the organisational context, summarises common stress factors and briefly reviews research on the effectiveness of stress management interventions in the workplace.

DSC Shelfmark: 96/19083

(633)
THE EFFECT of stress inoculation training on anxiety and performance
T Saunders *et al*

Journal of occupational health psychology, vol. 1, 1996, p.170-186.

Results of a meta-analysis provide strong support for the effectiveness of stress inoculation training as a stress management intervention. It was shown to be effective in reducing performance anxiety and state anxiety and enhancing performance under stress. The examination of moderators such as the experience of the trainer, the type of setting in which the training was implemented, and the type of trainee population, revealed no significant limitations on the application of stress inoculation training.

DSC Shelfmark: 5026.095000

(634)
THE EFFECTIVENESS of massage therapy intervention in reducing anxiety in the workplace
K R Shulman and G E Jones

Journal of applied behavioral science, vol. 32, 1996, p.160-173.

A sample of 18 volunteers from an organisation undergoing downsizing participated in a chair massage therapy programme for 6 weeks. A control group of 15 subjects participated in break therapy. For 15 minutes weekly, subjects either received a massage or were allowed a break, depending on their assignment to either the treatment or control condition. The State-Trait Anxiety Inventory was administered before the intervention, during the intervention and after the intervention was completed. Significant reductions in state anxiety were found for the treatment group. Trait anxiety significantly decreased as well, although there were no significant differences between treatment and control groups.

DSC Shelfmark: 4940.500000

(635)
STRESS management and innovation interventions at work
D Bunce and M A West
Human relations, vol.49, 1996, p. 209-232.

Reports a study among health care workers where a traditional stress management programme was compared with an intervention promoting innovation at work as a form of stress management and a control group. The traditional programme, emphasising cognitive behavioural and arousal reduction techniques, was associated with improvements in general psychological strain and job satisfaction. The intervention promoting innovative response to stressors, eg changing work methods, was associated with improvements in job-related stress and innovation. Follow-up data, one year after the intervention, suggested short term gains in psychological well-being were not maintained. However, increases in levels of innovation, although not apparent 3 months after the intervention, were significant after one year.

DSC Shelfmark: 4336.400000

(636)
STRESS management in work settings: a critical review of the health effects
L R Murphy
American journal of health promotion, vol. 11, 1996, p.112-135.

Article reviews the health effects of stress management interventions implemented in work settings. These are defined as techniques and programmes designed to help employees modify their appraisal of stressful situations or deal more effectively with the symptoms of stress. Concludes that the large number of different techniques coupled with the wide range of health outcome measures used make it difficult to draw firm conclusions about the effectiveness of each technique. The most positive results across the various health outcomes were obtained with a combination of two or more techniques. None of the interventions was consistently effective in ameliorating organisation relevant outcomes such as absenteeism or job satisfaction.

DSC Shelfmark: 0824.760000

(637)
WHAT factors are associated with the outcome of individual-focused worksite stress management interventions?
D Bunce
Journal of occupational and organizational psychology, vol. 70, 1997, p.1-17.

The empirical evidence suggests that across a range of self-report measures, outcome equivalence is a common feature of contrasts between multicomponent cognitive-behavioural arousal reduction and personal skills training approaches. Design and methodological shortcomings may limit the identification of between-treatment differences, or non-specific elements common to all types of SMI may be responsible. Evidence from several studies reviewed suggests that both non-specific factors and factors related to technical content of interventions are associated with outcomes. It is argued that a new generation of research is required that makes clear distinctions between interventions of differing technical content, includes session process measures to help elucidate the degree to which outcome variables are associated with specific and non-specific factors, focuses on the moderators of change, enabling greater understanding of the circumstances in which a particular intervention is appropriate, and examines the mediators of change, to increase understanding of the psychological mechanisms underlying outcomes.

DSC Shelfmark: 5026.082000

(638)
HOLISTIC stress management at Corning, Incorporated
J Monroy *et al*
In The new organizational reality: downsizing, restructuring and revitalization edited by M K Gowing, J D Kraft and J C Quick. Washington, DC: American Psychological Association, 1998. p.239-255.

Describes two-pronged stress management strategy implemented by Corning, Inc, which consisted essentially of organisational and individual assessment and skills development. The individual stress management programme lasted 12 weeks and taught muscle relaxation, biofeedback, meditation and cognitive restructuring. Self-report evaluations were conducted at weeks 1, 8, and 12. Results showed significant positive changes on measures of stress symptoms (eg restlessness, depression, sleep disturbance and anxiety), stress management skills (e.g. ability to relax) and life areas such as exercise and nutrition habits after the 8th week of training. After 12 weeks training, additional reductions were found in the frequency of some stress symptoms (depression, anxiety and restlessness) and in problems in other life areas (overeating, talking with spouse). No further improvements in stress management skills were seen.

DSC Shelfmark: 98/18938

6.8.4   Crisis intervention

(639)
POST-TRAUMA crisis intervention in the workplace
M Braverman
In Stress and well-being at work: assessments and interventions for occupational mental health edited by J C Quick, L R Murphy and J J Hurrell. Washington, DC: American Psychological Association, 1992. p.299-316.

Describes a model crisis intervention that focuses on the emotional well-being of managers and employees in the aftermath of a traumatic event. The intervention is composed of 5 key elements: (1) crisis readiness, (2) consultation with management, (3) meetings with affected groups, (4) assessment and counselling of individuals at risk, and (5) follow-up and recommendations.

DSC Shelfmark: 93/12260

(640)
EVALUATION of psychological debriefings
R C Robinson and J T Mitchell
Journal of traumatic stress, vol. 6, 1993, p.367–382.

Paper describes the impact of critical incident stress debriefings on 172 welfare, hospital and emergency service personnel in Australia. Participants completed questionnaires two weeks following the debriefing. Psychological debriefing was reported to reduce strain symptoms in almost all personnel who reported a stress response.

DSC Shelfmark: 5070.520000

(641)
TRAUMATIC stress at work: a public health model
D Richards
British journal of guidance and counselling, vol. 22, 1994, p.51–64.

An organisational response is described which tries to use primary, secondary and tertiary prevention strategies to reduce the impact of traumatic incidents in the workplace. Inter-departmental working, use of management and peer support, pre-incident training, cognitive-behavioural therapy and post-incident psychological health monitoring are all used to tailor support to individual needs.

DSC Shelfmark: 2308.700000

(642)
THE ASSAULTED staff Action Program: an approach to coping with the aftermath of violence in the workplace.
R B Flannery *et al*
In Job stress interventions edited by L R Murphy and others. Washington, DC: American Psychological Association, 1995. p.199–212.

The Assaulted Staff Action Program (ASAP) is a treatment intervention for mental health care providers assaulted by patients in a US State mental hospital. Within 20 minutes of an assault, an ASAP team member debriefs the victim at the site and provides any further ASAP services needed, such as referral to the staff victim support group, or arrangement of family meetings. The system is voluntary and is a peer help model so that services are supplied by colleagues who understand the risks.

DSC Shelfmark: q96/00105

(643)

PREVENTION of work-related post-traumatic stress: the critical incident stress debriefing process

G S Everly and J T Mitchell

In job stress interventions edited by L R Murply and others. Washington, DC: American Psychological Association, 1995. p.173-183.

Describes the development of critical incident stress debriefing (CISD), its basic components and its 12 year operational history as a preventive intervention for PTSD among high risk occupational groups. CISD may be defined as group meetings or discussions about a traumatic event or a series of traumatic events. CISD is designed to mitigate the psychological impact of a traumatic event, prevent the subsequent development of PTSD, and serve as a mechanism for identifying individuals who will require professional mental health follow-up after a traumatic event.

DSC Shelfmark: q96/00105

(644)

COPING with crisis

M Kutner

Occupational health and safety, vol. 66, no. 2, 1996, p.22-24.

Recommends the development in advance of a crisis response plan which can be used as a guide to addressing key issues such as communicating with employees, addressing operational issues and security concerns, and working with police and emergency services.

DSC Shelfmark: 6228.858000

(645)

STRESS debriefing and patterns of recovery following a natural disaster

J A Kenardy *et al*

Journal of traumatic stress, vol. 9, 1996, p.37-49.

Paper reports the effects of stress debriefing on the rate of recovery of 195 helpers (emergency service personnel and disaster workers) following an earthquake at Newcastle, Australia (62 debriefed helpers and 133 who were not debriefed). Post-trauma stress reactions and general psychological morbidity were assessed on four occasions over the first two years after the earthquake. Results provided no evidence of a more rapid rate of recovery for those who were debriefed compared to those who were not debriefed.

DSC Shelfmark: 5070.520000

(646)
EMOTIONAL repair for organisations: intervening in the aftermath of trauma

L Webb and T McCaffrey

In Stress in social work edited by R Davies. London: Jessica Kingsley, 1998. p.165–182.

Describes psychotherapeutic intervention by external consultants in a residential children's home where staff had been traumatised by the revelation that the Team Manager was paedophile. Group sessions enabled team members to talk about and share reactions to the traumatic event, with the aim of repairing their capacity to function effectively.

DSC Shelfmark: 98/03522

6.8.5   Organisation level interventions

(647)
A LONGITUDINAL field study of group work redesign

T D Wall and C W Clegg

Journal of occupational behaviour, vol.2, 1981, p.31–49.

Describes an action research project on group work redesign which involved blue collar employees in a confectionery company. The findings, based on evaluations after 6 and 18 months, show that group work redesign, which substantially enhances group task indentity and group autonomy, leads to improvements in internal work motivation, general job satisfaction, mental health, performance and staff turnover.

DSC Shelfmark: 5026.085000

(648)
THE DESIGN of flexible work schedules and employee responses: relationships and process

J L Pierce and J W Newstrom

Journal of occupational behaviour, vol. 4, 1983, p.247-262.

Study examines the relationship between six dimensions of flexible work schedules and employee job satisfaction, organisational commitment, psychological stress symptoms, performance and absenteeism. Results suggest that perceived time autonomy mediates the relationship between flexible work schedules and employee attitudes. Employees who experienced increased time autonomy were increasingly job satisfied, organisationally committed and experienced fewer symptoms of psychological stress. However, there appears to be a significant main effect of schedule flexibility on absenteeism and performance.

DSC Shelfmark: 5026.085000

(649)

DEVELOPING a corporate policy for managing stress

C R Stoner and F L Fry

Personnel, May/June 1983, p.66–76.

Proposes a three stage process for corporate stress management interventions. The first stage is to identify problem areas where signals such as deteriorating performance, increased absenteeism and turnover, and a rise in employee dissatisfaction reveal organisational strain. The second stage involves an analysis to pinpoint the sources of stress and determine the scope of the undesirable outcomes. The third stage involves the formulation of a corrective policy at either individual or organisational level.

DSC Shelfmark: 6428.033000

(650)

PARTICIPATION in decision–making as a strategy for reducing job-related strain

S E Jackson

Journal of applied psychology, vol. 68, 1983, p.3–19.

To establish causal effects of participation in decision-making, a longitudinal field experiment was conducted. Workers who had been given more frequent opportunities to participate in decision-making were compared to workers who had fewer such opportunities. The effects of participation on personal and job related communications, perceived influence, role conflict and ambiguity, social support, psychological health, job satisfaction, absenteeism and turnover intention were examined after 3 months and after 6 months. After 6 months, participation was shown to have reduced role conflict and ambiguity and increased perceived influence. Role conflict and ambiguity were, in turn, related to increased emotional strain and lowered job satisfaction. Perceived influence was related to increased job satisfaction and increased intention to quit.

DSC Shelfmark: 4947.000000

(651)

ORGANIZATIONAL level stress management interventions: a review and recommendations

J M Ivancevich and M T Matteson

Journal of organizational behavior and management, vol. 8, 1986, p.229–248.

Organisational level stress management intervention programmes which incorporate well-designed evaluations have rarely been attempted. After presenting a stress management framework, the authors propose that investigations of stress management interventions at organisational level should begin with needs diagnosis, use a longitudinal design, incorporate outcome and consequence measures and include a control group where possible.

DSC Shelfmark: 5027.068000

(652)
OUTCOMES of autonomous work groups: a long-term field experiment
T D Wall *et al*
Academy of Management journal, vol.29, 1986, p.280-304.

A quasi-experimental design was used to study the long-term effects of implementation of autonomous workgroups in a manufacturing environment. Results showed that, although implementation of this work design substantially enhanced intrinsic job satisfaction, it did not demonstrably affect job motivation, organisational commitment, mental health, work performance and voluntary labour turnover. At organisational level, implementation increased productivity through the elimination of supervisory positions; a side effect was increased dismissals.

DSC Shelfmark: 0570.587000

(653)
REDUCING the cost of stress: an organisational model
T Arroba and K James
Personnel review, vol. 19, no.1, 1990, p.21-27.

Model presents organisational stress management as a four-stage process consisting of (1) raising awareness of stress within the organisation, (2) training individuals in stress management, (3) providing organisational support, and (4) audit of stress factors in the work environment, and action to remove them.

DSC Shelfmark: 6428.098000

(654)
ATTITUDINAL and behavioral effects of autonomous group working: a longitudinal field study
J L Cordery, W S Mueller, and L M Smith
Academy of Management journal, vol.34, 1991, p.464-476.

Reports a longitudinal study of autonomous work groups at a new and an established minerals processing plant. Results support the hypothesis that employees in autonomous work groups would report more favourable work attitudes than those operating under traditional work structures. Absenteeism and staff turnover, however, were higher among autonomous work groups. This may be due to the unusual demands of plant start up.

DSC Shelfmark: 0570.587000

(655)
AN ACTION research approach to workplace health: integrating methods
M K Hugentobler, B A Israel and S J Schurman
Health education quarterly, vol. 19, 1992, p.55-76.

Article describes the implementation of a longitudinal multi-methodological research and intervention project aimed both at examining the relationship between occupational stress and psychosocial moderating factors (eg social support, participation, and influence over decision-making) and health outcomes, and reducing stress and improving employee health. Combining qualitative and quantitative research techniques, such as semi-structured individual and focus group interviews, field notes and survey data, increases confidence in research findings and strengthens the process and outcomes of needs assessments, programme planning, implementation and intervention.

DSC Shelfmark: 4275.011400

(656)
PREVENTING stress at work
Conditions of work digest, vol. 11, no.2, 1992. 275p.

Contains an annotated bibliography on stress and its prevention, and 19 international case studies on stress prevention through work reorganisation.

DSC Shelfmark: 3405.870000

(657)
COMPUTERS in child welfare: planning for a more serviceable work environment
J Cahill and L H Feldman
Child welfare, vol.72, 1993, p.3-12.

Describes a programme to reduce stress and improve the work environment by introducing a microcomputer-based information system. The principal goals of the project were to increase local control of, and access to, information and reduce the amount of redundancy in processing case records. Other goals included increasing skill levels of the clerical staff, streamlining the information flow between the local and central offices and improving health and safety factors by installing ergonomically correct equipment.

DSC Shelfmark: 3172.950000

See also: Computers and stress reduction in social service workers in New Jersey by J Cahill (Conditions of work digest, vol.11, no.2., 1992, p.197-203. *DSC Shelfmark: 3405.870000*)

(658)
A FIELD experiment testing supervisory role clarification
J Schaubroeck *et al*
Personnel psychology, vol.46, 1993, p.1-25.

An intervention designed to clarify individual roles was tested experimentally on the business service division of a major university. Results showed that the intervention appeared to reduce role ambiguity and supervisor dissatisfaction, but had no effect on other aspects of subjective strain, physical symptoms or time lost through illness. Role conflict was reduced throughout the organisation during the experiment.

DSC Shelfmark: 6428.095000

(659)

INDUSTRIAL relations, worksite stress reduction, and employee well-being: a participatory action research investigation
C A Heaney *et al*
Journal of organizational behavior, vol. 14, 1993, p.495-510.

Describes and evaluates a participatory action research (PAR) stress reduction project in two different labour-management relations contexts. In one organisation, industrial relations incorporated elements of joint problem-solving. The other organisation had a traditional approach where labour-management relations were formally adversarial. Management in the adversarial organisation showed little interest in implementing project recommendations, whereas management in the co-operative organisation took them on board. The potential for long term benefits from the PAR project is much greater in the latter than the former.

DSC Shelfmark: 5027.066000

(660)

JOB stress and heart disease: evidence and strategies for prevention
P A Landsbergis *et al*
New solutions, vol.3, no.4, Summer 1993, p.42-58.

Reviews the evidence linking 'job strain' as defined by Karasek to heart disease. Evaluates preventive strategies based on Expert-Dominated Action Research, Participatory Action Research, and collective bargaining approaches.

DSC Shelfmark: 6088.645000

(661)

MANAGING work stress: a key issue for all organization members
M McHugh and S Brennan
Employee counselling today, vol.5, no.1, 1993, p.16-21.

Introduces the concept of Total Stress Management (TSM), which may be viewed as a pervasive organisational philosophy and a practical approach to stress management. The TSM model is implemented in four stages: (1) stress audit; (2) raising awareness company-wide of stress; (3) development of organisation-wide skills in the prevention, identification and management of stress; (4) evaluation of results.

DSC Shelfmark: 3737.037330

(662)

ORGANIZATIONAL level interventions to reduce occupational stressors

R J Burke

Work and stress, vol. 7, 1993, p.77-85.

Paper reviews 10 organisational level interventions to reduce stress at work which have been examined in field studies. These interventions were generally found to have positive effects and, given the limited success of individual-level interventions in reducing levels of occupational stress, should be encouraged.

DSC Shelfmark: 9348.102000

(663)

HEALTHY mind; healthy organization: a proactive approach to occupational stress

C L Cooper and S Cartwright

Human relations, vol. 47, 1994, p.455-471.

Growing health and safety legislation, escalating insurance costs and fear of litigation will force organisations to take a move responsible attitude towards stress reduction. On the basis of a review of the empirical literature, it is argued that organisations need to focus more on identifying and reducing or eliminating environmental sources of stress, which may include role problems, interpersonal relationships at work, job insecurity, organisational structure and climate and home/work interface.

DSC Shelfmark: 4336.400000

(664)

STRESS at work: an integrative approach

R A Karasek

New solutions, vol. 4, no.4, Summer 1994, p.28-35.

Proposes reduction of work-related stress through a participative multi-level job redesign process. Workers gain new awareness in areas such as stress-task organisation and work system issues through stress education. They then evolve for themselves new vocabularies of explanations to build action plans. Finally they develop ever expanding work system-based understanding of solution possibilities and limits.

DSC Shelfmark: 6088.645000

(665)

EVALUATION of an occupational stress intervention in a public agency

P A Landsbergis and E Vivona-Vaughan

Journal of organizational behavior, vol. 16, 1995, p.29-48

Study evaluates the impact of an intervention based on organisational development, action research and Karasek's job strain model. Employee committees conducted problem diagnosis, action planning and action taking in two departments in a public agency. Waiting list control departments and pre-, post-, and follow-up assessment were utilised. Results indicated a mixed impact in one department of the agency, and a negligible or negative impact in the other.

DSC Shelfmark: 5027.066000

(666)
REDESIGNING work systems to reduce stress: a participatory action research approach to creating change
S J Schurman and B A Israel

In Job stress interventions edited by L R Murphy and others. Washington DC: American Psychological Association, 1995, p.235-263.

Introduces Participatory Action Research (PAR) as a methodology in which researchers and members of a social system collaborate in a process of data-guided problem solving for the purposes of improving the system's ability to provide members with desired outcomes and of contributing to scientific knowledge. Describes use of the PAR methodology to design, implement and evaluate an intervention aimed at reducing sources of stress in an automobile factory.

DSC Shelfmark: q96/00105

See also: A participatory action research approach to reducing occupational stress in the United States by B A Israel and others (Conditions of work digest, vol. 11, no.2, 1992, p.152-163. *DSC Shelfmark: 3405.870000*).

(667)
IMPROVING stress assessment: toward an evidence-based approach to organizational stress interventions
R B Briner

Journal of psychosomatic research, vol.43, 1997, p.61-71.

Study aims to describe features of an evidence-based approach to organisational stress interventions in which evidence gathered from valid assessments is used as the basis for choosing and implementing an intervention. Valid stress assessment requires a relatively sophisticated and comprehensive approach to measurement, designs that permit causal relationships between phenomena of interest to be established, a healthy scepticism towards claims made by organisations about stress, and a willingness to allow other types of problems and solutions to emerge.

DSC Shelfmark: 5043.480000

(668)

PSYCHOLOGICAL well–being at work: is prevention better than cure?

S Reynolds

Journal of psychosomatic research, vol. 43, 1997, p.93–102.

Article compares impacts of an individual level intervention (counselling) and an organisational level intervention (increasing employees' participation and control). Results suggest that the organisational intervention had no impact at all on employees' psychological well-being, physical well-being or absence from work. Individual counselling was effective in improving the psychological well-being of employees who used the service.

DSC Shelfmark: 5043.480000

(669)

THE IMPACT of a stress management programme on staff well-being and performance at work

J Rose, F Jones and B Fletcher

Work and stress, vol. 12, 1998, p.112-124.

Study evaluated the effects of treatment packages designed for staff working within group homes for people with learning disabilities. The packages were designed by first identifying important perceived demands and supports/constraints. Interventions were aimed at reducing demands/constraints and increasing supports and thus reducing anxiety and depression. The intervention group reported lower levels of anxiety and increased perceived support compared to the control group. There were also changes in some observational measures, particularly increased assistance given to clients.

DSC Shelfmark: 9348.102000

7 New Labour, the EU and the world of work

7.1 The Third Way

In Chapter 1 the impact of Thatcherism and the New Right on the worlds of work and welfare were examined in some detail. In this final chapter the likely implications of Tony Blair's version of social democracy, currently called the 'Third Way', are briefly considered. For Tony Blair, the First Way is Individualism or Thatcherism whose weakness lies in its neglect of social solidarity and national cohesion. The Second Way is old-fashioned socialism with its commitment to nationalisation, redistribution of wealth and comprehensive welfare provision. The Third Way remains committed to ideals of social solidarity, social inclusion and opportunities for poor people to better themselves, but is pragmatic about how to achieve these goals. In the new mixed economy which it advocates, there will be a synergy between the public and private sectors, utilising the dynamism of the markets but with the public interest in mind. The government's role is to ensure that business is confident, successful and profitable by fostering innovation, promoting competitive markets and investing in education and training to equip citizens with the skills that employers need. Citizens in the new dispensation have a responsibility to work if they are able and to equip themselves through lifelong learning with skills that will attract a range of employers. They have a social obligation to bring up children to be competent and responsible citizens and to co-operate with those who share this task, such as teachers. Third Way government is strongly committed to public spending restraint. Inflation must be kept under control and government must only borrow money for capital investment, not for current operating costs. Any surplus in the public funds should go towards paying off the national debt, rather than towards bailing out the cash-strapped public services. This means that Third Way government will be inherently limited, and will look for partnerships with the private sector and with voluntary organisations to deliver public services. Welfare provision will be far from universal, and as far as they can, citizens will be encouraged to provide for themselves. In the following sections we will look at the outworking of some of these ideas in the policies of the new Labour government.

7.2 UK economic prospects

There is nothing more calculated to raise levels of work-related stress than a recession in the UK economy. This would bring in its wake job losses and job insecurity. For survivors of the layoffs, it would mean increased pressures to perform, heavier workloads, and long hours. Over the Summer of 1998 there was a sharp decrease in confidence in the economic situation in the UK. This was evidenced by:

- A series of high profile job losses such as those incurred by the closure of the Fujitsu plant in County Durham with the loss of 570 jobs and the 1500 redundancies announced by Rover in late July.

- Lowering of interest rates in October and November by the Bank of England Monetary Policy Committee. The cut in November 1998 especially gave rise to suspicions in the City of something very nasty in the way of an economic downturn lurking in the proverbial woodshed.

- A series of surveys reporting reduced business and consumer confidence. For example, September results of the highly respected CBJ Industrial Trends Survey showed reduced business confidence and weakened demand for manufactured goods, with output set to fall. The CBI survey has in the past been successful and accurate in giving early warning of recession.

- Downwards revisions in economic forecasts. For example, in his pre-budget statement on November 3rd 1998, the Chancellor of the Exchequer forecasted that the GDP (Gross Domestic Product) would grow by $1-1\frac{1}{2}$ per cent in 1999. In his March 1998 budget the equivalent figure was $1\frac{3}{4}-2\frac{1}{4}$ per cent.

Pressure on the UK economy arose from a number of internal and external sources:

- The collapse of export markets due to economic turmoil in Russia and the Far East.

- A substantial decline in share prices. After falling by 25% from a peak in late July to a low of 4649 in early October, the FT-SE 100 had made up over a third of the losses by 23rd October. This may represent either a genuine recovery or an upward blip in a continuing downward correction.

- The fear that losses made by banks and other financial institutions in the Far East and Russia may lead to a credit squeeze at home.

Against these dangers there were a number of grounds for optimism:

- The last recession in the early 1990s coincided with increasing personal and company debt, and depressed housing and labour markets. This time the UK economy has been experiencing falling unemployment and relatively low levels of debt.

- Policymakers both in the UK and abroad are aware of the dangers faced by the global economy. The Bank of England Monetary Policy Committee responded to evidence of an economic downturn by cutting interest rates by 0.25% in October 1998 and by a further 0.50% in November. With underlying inflation now at 2.5% there seems to be ample scope for further large cuts in rates. This is in marked contrast to the recession of the early 1990s when interest rates could not be cut because of the need to maintain the value of the pound in the European Union Exchange Rate Mechanism (ERM).

- Finally, the new public spending plans announced in the Comprehensive Spending Review in July 1998 will also support the economy. Funded by a continuing squeeze on public sector pay and sales of national assets, there is likely to be a sharp rise in the share of current government spending devoted to goods and services.

The combination of relatively low levels of debt and easing of monetary and fiscal policy reduced the risks of the UK economy sliding into recession. In the event, despite the continuing strength of the pound, the UK economy did not slide into recession and a golden future of steady growth combined with low inflation is now being forecast (*Daily Telegraph*, May 13th 1999, p.35). At the time of writing the spectre of pressure on the workforce due to the threat of job losses and financial insecurity has receeded.

7.3 New Labour and welfare

The Conservative governments 1979 to 1997 argued that reform of welfare provision was essential and had the clear intention of 'rolling back the state' and keeping the lid on public spending. How far they succeeded in these policy aims is explored in detail in Chapter 1. To recap, when it came to power in 1997 New Labour inherited a welfare state where:

- A quarter of the national income was spent on welfare. This was almost the same as when the Conservatives came to power in 1979. Rising demand due to high levels of unemployment, demographic change, such as increasing longevity, and social change, such as the increase in one-parent families, meant that in spite of a series of measures to keep its growth in check, the Conservatives had not actually succeeded in reducing the overall scale of the welfare state. However, constrained budgets meant that the welfare jam was being spread more thinly over a greater number of claimants.

- The role of the private sector in welfare had increased. However, this increased role was more important in service provision than in terms of finance. For example, residential care for the elderly has been increasingly provided by the private sector, though it is still funded from the public purse.

- Means testing had become much more important under the Conservatives as far as housing and cash benefits were concerned. This led in particular to the polarisation of social housing, which increasingly housed only the poorest. Wherever possible, people were encouraged to buy their own homes. The very poor tended to become concentrated on sink estates racked by decaying housing, unemployment, street crime and drugs (Social Exclusion Unit, 1998, ref. no. 683).

- Social inequality had increased during the 1980s. Earnings inequality grew due to technological change which led to the disappearance of large numbers of low skill manual jobs, to the declining influence of trade unions, and to the loss of minimum wage protection through the Wages Councils. Rising unemployment led to larger numbers subsisting on benefits, with a particularly rapid growth in the proportion of families with no-one in work. Over the period 1979 to 1995, the incomes of the poorest 10-20% of the population were little or no higher in real terms, despite overall income growth of 40% (Hills, 1998, ref. no. 693).

How then have New Labour handled this inheritance? In their 1997 Manifesto Labour pledged to 'help build strong families and strong communities, and lay the foundations of a modern welfare state'. At the same time they committed themselves to shedding their old 'tax and spend' image. They promised economic stability, a tough inflation target, no increase in income tax rates and no increase in public spending for two years. Specific promises on welfare reform were modest. They included a welfare to work programme for the young unemployed (financed by a windfall tax on the privatised utilities), the introduction of stakeholder pensions, a reduction of class sizes for 5–7 year olds (financed by the withdrawal of the Assisted Places Schemes whereby the state paid for some children to go to private schools) and a pledge to reduce NHS waiting lists (financed from cost savings accruing from the abandonment of the internal market). In office, the government have concentrated on increasing welfare spending by reallocation of existing resources through the Comprehensive Spending Review (1998, ref. no. 688). Increased spending on health care and education will be funded by reductions in the defence, agriculture and legal aid budgets, a continuing squeeze on public sector pay, and the sale of national assets, i.e. further privatisations. Revenue will also be raised by increases in taxes on petrol and tobacco, and on the investment income of pension funds. Over the three years 1998/1999 to 2001/02 for which new spending plans have been, made health spending is planned to increase by 4.7% per year in real terms, and education spending by 5.1%. Allowing for the freeze of the first two years, the average growth rate for the Parliament as a whole falls to 3.7% for health and 2.9% for education. These rates are faster than projected national income growth and the increase in government spending as a whole.

The second major theme of the Labour government's welfare policies has been its promotion of work and the work ethic. The first principle quoted in the Government's green paper on welfare, *New Ambitions for Our Country*, is that 'The new welfare state should help and encourage people of working age to work where they are capable of doing so'. (1998, ref. no. 689). The flagship programme, the New Deals for the unemployed, aims to move people from social security benefits into work. The New Deal for the young unemployed offers participants four options: work with an employer, who will receive a job subsidy of up to £60.00 per week, full-time education or training, work with a voluntary sector organisation, or work on an Environmental Taskforce. An additional grant of £750 is available to employers who provide training towards a recognised qualification. There is no fifth option of continued life on benefits. For long term unemployed adults, the New Deal offers a job subsidy of £75.00 per week for employers for six months and changes to benefit rates to improve access to full-time education and training. Further measures to encourage unemployed people, including lone parents and the disabled, to work were unveiled by Alistair Darling, the Social Security Secretary, in October 1998. Under the proposed system claimants would have to provide basic information about themselves and their claim when they first made contact. In return they would receive a 'balanced package' of financial support and advice on work. They would be required to attend an interview with a personal adviser to receive employment advice, or lose benefit.

The new Working Families Tax Credit (WFTC) introduced in the March 1998 budget is intended to increase the differentials between incomes in and out of work. By linking support directly to the pay packet it will demonstrate the rewards of work and remove the stigma associated with claiming benefit. WFTC is intended to boost the incomes of households moving off benefits and into paid work. Working families earning up to a net £90.00 per week remain eligible for the maximum amount of WFTC. This means that every family with a full-time worker will be guaranteed an income of at least £180.00 per week. For many families, the cost of childcare is an obstacle to work. In order to encourage mothers to go out to work, the WFTC will include a Childcare Tax Credit for low-income working families. This credit will be worth up to 70% of eligible childcare costs, subject to a maximum payment of £70.00 per week for a family with one child and £105.00 per week for a family with two or more children. The government appears to believe that being paid to look after other people's children is to be positively encouraged, while staying at home to look after one's own is not.

The priority given by the Labour Government to education flows from its perception that growing earnings inequality and the trapping of workers in low-paid and insecure jobs are rooted in a workforce that lacks the skills required by the contemporary global economy. The Welfare Reform green paper points out that the average gross weekly earnings of an individual with no qualifications is £240.00 compared with £470.00 for a graduate. Similarly 40% of those unemployed for more than two years have no qualifications compared with 19% of those unemployed for less than a year. Education and skills help individuals survive and prosper in a labour market in which employment security depends not on attachment to a single employer but on having skills that will attract a range of employers. The Government set out a comprehensive programme of measures to improve schools in England in the white paper 'Excellence in Schools' (1997, ref. no. 680). Proposed strategies to improve educational standards include:

*   Expanding pre-school education.

*   Reducing class sizes in infant schools.

*   Introducing education action zones. These will be run by forums including representatives of local authorities, business, teachers and parents. All zones will receive £750,000 from government and £250,000 from business for three years and must set targets to demonstrate improvements made.

- Establishing after school clubs to enhance children's opportunities to learn.

- Promoting setting in comprehensive schools so that children of similar levels of ability are taught together.

The most heavily criticised aspect of the government's education reform programme is its proposals for school management. There will be a massive centralisation of powers away from schools and into the hands of Local Education Authorities (LEAs) and the Secretary of State for Education and Employment. LEAs will control staffing, implementation of class sizes and early education. They will be able to instruct schools how to raise standards through Education Development Plans. Articles of government, valued by many schools as a definition of their ethos, will be replaced by standardised 'instruments of government' drawn up by the DfEE. Other standardisation measures include the abolition of grant maintained schools, definition of rules of admission for all schools by the DfEE, and the requirement for church schools to get LEA approval for their religious admissions policy every year. Critics argue that such centralising and standardising measures will reduce standards rather than raise them (Williams, 1998, ref. no. 687).

The government has also demonstrated its commitment to widening access to higher education by implementing, with modifications, the recommendations of the Dearing Committee (1997, ref. no. 681). The key changes involve the introduction from October 1998 of a standard annual fee for previously free university education (although this is waived on a means-tested basis for students from poor families) and the replacement of the previous mixture of loans and means-tested grants for living costs with a system of loans repaid as a percentage of future income. How exactly this transfer of the costs of higher education from the taxpayer to the recipient will widen access remains to be seen.

With the relentless advance of technology, knowledge and skills become obsolete much faster. By the end of a four year engineering degree, half of the knowledge gained in the first year will be out of date. Business places a high value on knowledge creation, and on innovation in working methods and product development. All this means that people will have to return to formal education more often during their lifetime. Offering opportunities for training and personal development will become a means whereby organisations both attract high quality staff and ensure their own survival (Bentley, 1998, ref. no. 686). Recognising that learning must now be lifelong to enable people to prosper in a rapidly changing work environment, the government is committed to developing an infrastructure to support continuing education. Initiatives include a University for Industry and Individual Learning Accounts, which will allow adults to invest public, private and personal finances in their own learning choices (1998, ref. no. 685). The University for Industry will connect those who want to learn with ways of doing so. Individuals and companies will be able to contact the University for information and advice about options. The University will then provide a course that meets the enquirer's needs. Training may be full-time or part-time and may be delivered through study at home, at work or at a local learning centre. The University could deliver a learning package by email, contract with a college for an evening course or broadcast a TV programme. Individual Learning Accounts will be offered to anyone at work wishing to learn. Everyone would have to invest a minimum amount of their own money in their account. The government would contribute a maximum of £150 per account and employers could also offer support in cash or in kind. The account would then be used, at the learner's discretion, to meet the costs of study.

How, then, does New Labour's approach to welfare impinge on work-related stress? Four main points emerge:

• New Labour does not want to offer an easy safety net, and will encourage citizens to take responsibility for themselves and their families. This will mean people in employment having to take out private insurance to provide, for example, for their own retirement and their children's education and to protect against risks such as accidents or illness.

• The government's recognition of the need to create an infrastructure to support lifelong learning should help people to cope with a world where the old-fashioned job for life has been replaced by a variety of flexible working practices such as short term contracts, part-time work and teleworking.

• The government's commitment to raising standards in schools and in adult education and training should prevent workers becoming trapped in low-paid, low-skill jobs.

• The government's policy of encouraging mothers to work through help with costs of childcare may exacerbate stress arising from work/family conflict.

7.4 Private finance initiatives and privatisation of services

7.4.1 Private finance initiatives

In opposition, the Labour Party was highly critical of the Private Finance Initiative (PFI), anathematising it as the back door to privatisation. In power, Labour has embraced it with evangelical fervour. In the 1997 general election campaign, the Labour Party committed itself to sticking to the Conservative government's public spending allocations for 1997-98 and 1998-99, in which were embedded assumptions about PFI-financed investment and privatisation proceeds. Labour were further pledged to no increase in income tax rates for five years, to take no risks with inflation, and to keep public borrowing at a stable and prudent level (Labour Party. Manifesto, 1997, ref. no. 670). Hemmed in by these constraints and commitments, Labour has turned to the PFI as a way of delivering new hospitals and schools which would not otherwise be built.

Intriguing questions arise, however, as to the effect of this reliance on private funding on the provision of services to the vulnerable, and on the working conditions of employees in the new facilities. Private investment is efficient when it maximises the returns on capital. Public investment is efficient when achieves public policy goals like meeting the population's health care needs. Gaffney and Pollock (1997, ref. no. 698) have investigated what these differing aspirations mean in practice when private finance funds hospital redevelopment. In a detailed study of the 14 PFI schemes approved in June 1997, the authors conclude that reliance on private investment inflates costs as bidders propose lavish large-scale schemes to maximise their rate of return. This cost escalation puts new demands on the NHS which then has to search for economies and/or sell assets to pay off the private partners. Economies include bed reductions, staff reductions and hospital closures. If economies and asset sales are inadequate to pay for the new facilities, new subsidies have to be sought. In some cases investigated by Gaffney and Pollock, privately financed projects had to be subsidised out of the equipment and maintenance budgets of other hospitals within the group through the translation of block grant capital into revenue payments. In other cases, health authorities had to transfer money from other projects or sectors such as community services. Finally, in order to bail out cash-strapped health authorities and trusts, the NHS Executive has introduced a direct annual subsidy for the first thirty years of any private finance contract. Gaffney and Pollock cite the example of a hospital in Swindon where costs rose by a staggering 219%. Hospital closures helped meet the cost by releasing land for sale. Bed reductions allowed economies to be made in the new buildings. So a private finance initiative can become a costly burden and the means of implementing a savage squeeze on services, increasing levels of stress, insecurity and general unhappiness in society.

7.4.2   Privatisation of services

The next logical step after the private funding of buildings is the privatisation of care provision. This has already happened in the long term care sector. Private-sector provision of long-term care increased when the Conservative government amended the Social Security Act to allow residents entering private sector homes to claim board and lodging allowance to pay for their care. Residents under local authority or NHS care could not claim this allowance. As a result, local authorities encouraged residents to opt for private care and closed their own homes. Then the NHS and Community Care Act 1990 devolved responsibility for funding care to local authorities and 'turned off' the social security funding. At the same time the NHS was reduced to a residual role in long term care, catering for only the most sick and dependent patients. Local authorities retained discretionary powers to charge for community-based services. As cash-strapped local authorities tightened eligibility criteria, individuals were forced to either go without or pay for their own care. Because of the expense of nursing-home care, up to 40,000 individuals a year may now sell their homes to pay for it. With NHS support and central funding withdrawn, local authorities are left struggling to provide care for increasingly dependent groups out of local taxation and charges. In response to these changes, the number of residential care home places has declined in spite of the growth of the aged population. What has become of their former clients is not known, but an increasing number of individuals probably pay for their own care, rely on families and friends, or do without (Harrington and Pollock, 1998, ref. no. 700).

Service privatisation has also been held to adversely affect the working conditions of employees. Privatised services may turn out cheaper only because they employ fewer staff, pay lower wages, and offer less generous pensions and other benefits. Walsh and Davis (1993, ref. no. 694), in a major report on the impact of competition in local government services, found the most common changes to be reductions in staffing (in 56% of cases) and rearrangement of working hours (in 51% of cases). Competition had also led to the greater casualisation of work. Existing staff found both their hours and the number of weeks worked per year reduced. Temporary staff were often hired to cope with peaks in demand. Similarly, the Centre for Public Service estimated that competitive tendering in local authorities had led to 15,000 workers having their hours cut to take them below the then National Insurance threshold of £56.00 per week (1995, ref. no. 696).

7.5   Minimum wage

According to the Low Pay Unit, (1998, ref. no. 704) half the British workforce are low paid by European standards. The Council of Europe's decency threshold is set at 68% of national average earnings. Based on the New Earning's Survey, the level for 1997 was £6.60 per hour. A total of 10.47 million UK workers earned below this level in 1997, a slight increase on 1996 and nearly three million more than in 1979. Another commonly accepted threshold of poverty pay is half median male earnings. In 1997 this would have been £4.61 per hour. Analysis of the same data set showed that 4.76 million adult employees were earning less than this.

The Labour Party in its 1997 manifesto committed itself to a sensibly set national minimum wage. This would remove the worst excesses of low pay while cutting the massive £4 billion bill by which the taxpayer subsidies low paying employers through in-work benefits (Labour Party, 1997 ref. no. 670). In government Labour duly appointed the Low Pay Commission which reported in June 1998 recommending a minimum wage of £3.60 per hour for adults and a development rate of £3.20 per hour for 18-20 year olds, to be introduced in April 1999. They proposed that the development rate should also be paid to workers over 21 on accredited training courses for a maximum of 6 months when they began work with a new employer (Low Pay Commission, 1998, ref. no. 709). The Treasury then diluted these recommendations and fixed rates of £3.60 per hour for adults aged 22 and above and £3.00 per hour for 18 to 21 year olds to be implemented in mid-1999.

Pressure groups such as the Low pay Unit (LPU) expressed deep disappointment and argued that the impact of a wage of £3.60 per hour for adults would be minimal in most sectors of industry. It would tackle only the worst cases of exploitation in exceptionally low paying sectors such as security, cleaning, catering, agriculture and social care. Firms such as McDonalds where over two-thirds of the staff are aged 20 or under would be barely affected (Sachdev and Wilkinson, 1998, ref. no. 705). There was felt to be a risk that a low minimum wage could actually entrench low pay. It might, for example, legitimate low pay in public services, undermining higher rates set for those who are directly employed but who have to compete for contacts with private sector firms. The LPU (1998, ref. no. 708) also criticised the Commission proposals on the grounds that they:

- Have not set an uprating mechanism.

- Ignore the plight of single people and childless couples who do not qualify for in-work benefits.

- Will promote the casualisation of work. Those on short term contracts may end up being paid the lower development rate of £3.00 per hour as they move from job to job and employers avoid paying the minimum wage.

- Perpetuate the flawed reasoning that people in low-paid occupations are low skilled. It can be argued that low pay is the result of low value set on the skills and experience of disadvantaged workers. For example, child carers are expected to be highly skilled, yet over 60% of female, full-time carers earn less than £4.00 an hour.

The main argument against the use of a minimum wage as an instrument for combating social exclusion and poverty is that it destroys jobs. The basis for this view is the competitive model of the labour market which predicts that employment will fall at the introduction of a minimum wage. In this model, wages are determined by the market and firms paying below the market rate would instantly lose all their workers. Recent theories of the labour market have challenged the competitive model and proposed that where there is uncertainty about what jobs are available and what wages are on offer, firms paying below the market rate may not lose all their workers immediately. This labour market is said to be characterised by 'monopsony'. In this situation, a judiciously set minimum wage will not cause job losses. Employers will be forced to pay more for their labour but will still make a profit. However, if the minimum wage is set too high, firms will be unable to afford to pay as many workers and employment will fall. Evidence on the impact of the minimum wage on employment is, as ever, contradictory. Card and Krueger (1995, ref. no. 702), in a study of employment and wages in fast food establishments in New Jersey, found that employment actually rose when the State's minimum wage was increased from $4.25 per hour to $5.05 per hour in 1992. However, a reanalysis of Card and Krueger's data by Williams and Mills (1998, ref. no. 707), in the light of recent developments in time series methods, showed that a hike in the minimum wage had a negative effect for both men and women.

Following a 10% increase in the minimum wage, both male and female employment dropped by 2-4% over a two year period. Research work in the UK has looked at the impact of Wages Councils on employment. These used to set pay rates in various low paying industries until their abolition in 1993. Dickens and Manning (1995, ref. no. 701) have shown that while real wages have fallen in industries previously covered, there has been no sudden increase in numbers of workers employed. Finally, a cross-country statistical comparison of the impact of minimum wages on employment levels by the OECD (1998, ref. no. 706) suggests that a rise in the minimum wage has a negative effect on teenage employment but no impact at all on the employment outcomes of prime-age adults. Overall, the weight of the available evidence suggests that a sensibly set minimum wage will not cause serious job losses.

Opponents of the minimum wage also suggest that it is an ineffective tool for tackling poverty because the truly needy live in households where no-one is working and the low-paid often do not live in poor households (OECD, 1998, ref. no. 706). While it is undeniable that the minimum wage will not help the unemployed and pensioners for whom work is not an option, the premise that most of the low-paid are teenagers or working women living with another earner is challenged by Dickens (1998, ref. no. 710). He uses data from the 1992 British Household Panel Survey to show that 50% of those paid below £3.50 per hour at that date belonged to the bottom 30% of households. These figures support the argument that a wisely set minimum wage has a role in reducing inequalities of household income and helping reduce the financial stresses on the working poor.

7.6 The European dimension

7.6.1 Impact of EMU

Levels of work-related stress can be linked to the general economic situation. In times of recession, pressure on employees increases through threat of job loss and the effects of downsizing and restructuring on the working environment. The feelgood factor disappears, and all sorts of anxieties surface. What impact is advent of economic and monetary union (EMU) in January 1999 likely to have on the UK? In his statement to the House of Commons on 27th October 1997, the Chancellor of the Exchequer committed the new Labour government in principle to joining the single currency when economic conditions are right. The Prime Minister reaffirmed this position when he told the House of Commons on 15th

December 1997, 'We should judge whether we enter monetary union according to our national interest, and that is defined by the economic tests we have set'. However, by November 1998 the Blair government had started to shift its ground on the Euro. The question for ministers became less whether or not Britain should adopt the Euro than when and how entry should be effected. The Chancellor of the Exchequer announced to the Confederation of British Industry Conference on November 2nd plans to publish a 'national changeover strategy' in January 1999 setting out the practical steps Britain will have to take to join the single currency. The government's present strategy is to commit the UK to full preparations for joining that will allow a decision to be made, subject to a referendum, early in the next Parliament. What, then, are the pros and cons of EMU for Britain? These questions have been hotly debated in the literature, and only a brief summary of the arguments for and against joining, based on very selective reading, is attempted here.

Lower transaction costs. For companies operating across national boundaries in Europe, the euro eliminates the costs of converting money from one currency to another within the EMU zone. These costs would be quite small for big companies which enjoy the benefits of scale, but may be more significant for small and medium-sized companies which lack expertise in proper foreign exchange management. At the macroeconomic level, estimates of the possible savings vary, but the usual range is around 0.2-0.5% of GDP. At this level, the costs of converting to the euro would be likely to be higher than the savings.

Elimination of exchange rate volatility. The single currency eliminates the possibility of exchange rate variation within the EMU zone which should make life easier for businessmen wishing to trade. On the other hand, countries using the euro lose the ultimate economic weapon of devaluation of their currency to escape, in the short term at least, economic and financial pressures. Devaluation has been used in the past to boost a flagging economy and reduce unemployment by making exports cheaper. However, it may be a curse if the freedom to devalue the currency is used as a substitute for tackling structural problems. Monetary freedom has not significantly benefited the UK over the past 30 years. In 1966 Sterling traded against the German mark at about DM11; by 1996 this had slipped to around DM 2.3, an average depreciation of nearly 5% per year over 30 years. The principal result of this has been that the UK has experienced nearly 5% more inflation than Germany. The UK economy has also exhibited greater instability over the same period than any of its major competitors. From 1970-93 the UK's GDP increased by 1.9% per year compared with 2.3% in West Germany. GDP actually fell in 6 years out of the 23, compared with a decline in only 3 years out of 23 in West Germany. However, although variation in exchange rates for macroecomonic adjustment can be helpful, their erratic movement due to arbitrary speculation is disruptive. Elimination of the kind of volatility must be counted as an advantage of EMU.

EMU will clearly achieve the objective of eliminating exchange rate uncertainty within the euro zone. However, it cannot eliminate exchange rate volatility between the euro and other world currencies such as the dollar and the yen. Members of the euro zone have significant trade with countries outside the zone, both in Europe and elsewhere. They are therefore still faced with the familiar problems of a strong euro making their exports less competitive and a weak euro pushing up the cost of imports.

Lowering of interest rates and control of inflation. In the EMU zone interest rates are under the control of an independent European Central Bank (ECB), which is in theory immune from political interference and sets rates on purely economic grounds. It should be free from the temptation experienced by politicians to lower interest rates in advance of an election to stimulate the economy, thus triggering an inflationary boom. It is argued that full EMU should lead to permanently lowered interest rates because:

- It will no longer be necessary for countries other than Germany to raise their interest rates above the German level to stop their currencies falling against the Deutschmark.

- The Maastricht rules on keeping budget deficits down will mean that interest rates do not have to be kept high to finance excessive government spending.

Permanently lowered interest rates and inflation should stimulate long term investment and growth. However it remains to be seen how immune the ECB will prove to lobbying by governments of participating countries. A report in the *Financial Times* of Oct. 27th 1998 showed the ECB already embroiled in a policy conflict with left-leaning European governments over whether to cut interest rates.

Control of Government Borrowing. Central bankers argue that the main obstacle to lowered interest rates at the time of writing is politicians. High levels of government borrowing in several EU member states is keeping interest rates higher than they would be in the absence of a structural deficit. According to the Maastricht Treaty, powers over taxation and public spending remain at national level, although governments are expected to conduct their fiscal policy after EMU so as not to breach the economic convergence criteria which enabled the single currency to be launched. The Council of Ministers (Ecofin) oversees the conduct of fiscal policy and is able to fine governments which breach the fiscal criteria. Under the terms of the Maastricht convergence criteria, government deficit to GDP ratios must be less than 3%. Under the terms of the Stability and Growth part agreed at the Dublin Summit in December 1996, governments breaching the 3% ceiling would be fined 0.2% of GDP, with a further 0.1% fine for each further 1% breach of the ceiling up to a maximum of 0.5% of GDP. This half-way house on control of fiscal policy has prompted many questions. Will the fines be an insufficient deterrent to irresponsible government borrowing? Or will the constraints imposed prove unduly severe, worsening the problems of unemployment and slow growth? In a recession, a larger budget deficit helps to mitigate the economic downturn. In order to avoid breaching the 3% ceiling, governments may have to raise taxes or cut spending to balance their books as the economy moves into recession, thus exacerbating the downward spiral.

Managing the economic cycle. Eddie George, the governor of the Bank of England, blundered into a political storm in October 1998 when he said in an interview with a journalist that job losses in the North East of England were an acceptable price to pay to beat inflation. The point that Mr George was making was that interest rates have to be set for the country as a whole to counter inflation. They cannot be set to deal with the problems of a particular distressed region. The same reasoning, writ large, applies to the European Central Bank setting interest rates for the whole Euro zone. Inside EMU, monetary policy cannot respond to the particular and distinct circumstances of a particular national economy; instead it must be set to reflect average circumstances across the participating countries. This would not matter if economic cycles in different EMU countries coincided and if the effects of a given monetary policy were the same in all the EMU countries. Unfortunately neither condition applies. Economic cycles across European economies have a common element due to aggregate shocks affecting all in the same way, and a national element due to asymmetric or asynchronous shocks which affect only a particular country or region. An example of an aggregate shock is the turmoil in South East Asia in the summer of 1998 leading to a general fall in demand. An example of an asymmetric shock is an increase in the price of oil. In this case the UK, as an oil exporter, gains; other European countries, as oil importers, lose. The problem of the 'one-size-fits-all' monetary policy is also a function of the differences in the relative importance of services and industry in the various countries of the EU. Some countries, like Italy and Germany, have large and important manufacturing sectors, while others, such as the Netherlands, are heavily service oriented. Manufacturing will always be more affected by external shocks such as the economic turmoil in Asia than services, where demand tends to be internally determined. So measures appropriate for manufacturing may not be right for the services, and vice versa.

If countries experience asynchronous shocks that lead to an economic downturn relative to other participants in EMU, their economies will be forced to adjust somehow. Within EMU, it is not possible for countries to stimulate their economies through devaluation, so adjustment will be forced through other channels, primarily falling wages and labour mobility. In Europe, mass migrations of the unemployed from countries in recession to those experiencing labour shortages are not feasible due to language and cultural barriers and national loyalties. Therefore economies are most likely to adjust through falling wages.

Increased competition. Economic and monetary union will eventually create an integrated market across Europe. Customers will be able to purchase across national boundaries unimpeded by the complexities of different currencies and the risk of exchange rate variation. Companies across Europe will be competing head on without the currency barrier. The opportunities this presents for capital flight from high wage to low wage regions, and from countries with highly regulated employment practices to those favouring labour market flexibility, are obvious. The more competitive market created by EMU will offer the efficient company opportunities of operating across a much larger customer base, whether as a large or niche player. However, inefficient companies will find themselves under pressure from more intense competition. The resulting rationalisation and restructuring of European industries will certainly result, in the short term, in further waves of job insecurity.

Loss of influence. By choosing not to join the single currency in the first wave, the UK may seen by other members as opting-out of the mainstream of the EU. This may well diminish the UK's influence over key issues, both now and in the future, and could mean that the UK's national interests will be given little weight when important decisions are made.

The decision on when to join EMU is one of the most important facing the British government at this time. Our current position of voluntarily staying out of the single currency in the short term has many advantages but some costs. Euro-enthusiasts argue that European Monetary Union will usher in a golden age of economic stability and growth; Euro-sceptics compare joining EMU to jumping over a precipice with one's hands tied behind one's back. Who is right only time will tell.

7.6.2　Impact of European Social Policy

The Labour government made a formal commitment in June 1997 to adhere to the provisions of the Social Policy Agreement made between 11 Member States of the European Union at Maastricht in December 1991. This Agreement is commonly referred to as the 'Social Chapter' because the European Commission had originally hoped to replace the existing Social Chapter of the Treaty of Rome with a new version. The UK's opposition in 1991 prevented this and the original Social Chapter remains within the body of the Treaty of Rome. The Social Policy Agreement is contained within the Social Protocol to the Treaty of Maastricht, also known as the Treaty on European Union. In the Protocol itself all 12 Member States agreed that the UK would be excluded from the Agreement. This opt-out was relinquished by New Labour in June 1997 but the UK will not be formally covered until the Treaty of Amsterdam, which will incorporate the Social Policy Agreement and Protocol, comes into force following ratification by all member states.

The Social Policy Agreement does not, of itself, require the introduction of new policies. It merely changes the procedure by which new policies can be introduced in future. In effect, it brings more 'social' topics within the scope of qualified majority voting in the Council of Ministers, the body which adopts legislation. Thus, for example, proposals on the information and consultation of workers require unanimous support under the Treaty of Rome's Social Chapter but only qualified majority support under the Treaty of Maastricht's Social Policy Agreement. The Agreement also enhances the role of organised management and labour in implementing EU legislation. At management and labour's joint request, a Member State may allow a Directive to be implemented by collective agreement on condition that this leaves the State in a position to guarantee the results required by the Directive. Furthermore, the Agreement introduces a new procedure under which the Commission must consult management and labour, the social partners, at Community level before submitting proposals for legislation in the social policy field.

So far three pieces of legislation which may impact on stress at work have been adopted under these procedures:

- **The Parental Leave Directive**. This gives all employees the right to a minimum of three months parental leave when they have a baby or adopt a child and entitles them to take time off for urgent family reasons such as looking after a sick child. The government is committed to implementing this Directive by December 1999. The legislation aims to make it easier for parents to balance work and family life and so should help to reduce stress arising from work/family conflict.

- **The Part-time Work Directive**. This aims to remove discrimination against part-time employees, promote the development of part-time working on a voluntary basis and encourage more flexible working arrangements. It should mean better quality part-time jobs and more choice, and aims to help parents to combine work with family life. The Government promises to implement this Directive by April 2000.

- **The European Works Councils Directive**. This requires companies within its scope to establish a European Works Council (EWC) or equivalent procedure for informing and consulting employees. It covers companies with at least 1,000 employees located within the EU and the other three European Economic Area states and at least one establishment employing a minimum of 150 workers each in two of these Member States. The Government's proposals for implementing this Directive were expected in the Autumn of 1998 and the regulations should come into force in December 1999. Meanwhile, the European Commission has announced its intention to publish a draft Directive which would require all firms with 20 or more employees to set up consultative bodies. The UK government has signalled opposition to this (*Independent*, 14/9/98). The role of Works Councils in the reduction of stress would lie in the improvement of communications, with better information exchange and provision. In very large multinational corporations the remoteness of the EWC and the infrequency of meetings may preclude it from having much impact in practice.

The Social Chapter is sometimes confused with the Social Charter. This is the popular name for The Community Charter of the Fundamental Social Rights of Workers which was signed in December 1989 by all Heads of Governments of Member States except Mrs Thatcher. The Charter has no legal force and was intended to act as a stimulus to further EC legislation and activity in the social field. At the end of 1989 the Commission published an Action Programme for the implementation of the Charter. It contained 43 new initiatives, 17 of which were for legally binding Directives to be brought forward in 1990, 1991 and 1992. Among these was the controversial Directive on Working Time. This was brought into force in the UK through the *Working Time Regulations 1998*. Among other things the Regulations impose:

- A limit of 48 hours on the working week.

- A limit of 8 hours on night work.

- An entitlement to three weeks' paid annual leave rising to four from November 1999 after 13 weeks' continuous service.

- Rest breaks of 20 minutes for adults working more than 6 hours in the day.

- A limit of 13 hours on the working day.

However, there are many derogations and exemptions from these rules. For example, the transport sector, the armed forces, police, doctors in training and those working at sea are completely excluded from the Regulations and other groups are excluded from some of the provisions or allowed to observe them flexibly. Any worker can opt out of the Regulations by agreement with their employer. These opt outs can be negotiated with a trade union, with elected employee representatives where there is no trade union, or with individual workers. The Regulations are so hedged about with exemptions, derogations and opt outs that their utility in combating the long hours culture must be questioned.

Future directions in EU social policy are outlined in the Commission's 1998-2000 Social Action Programme. Recognising that the world of work is undergoing rapid change due to new technology, evolving markets and the growth of the service sector, the Commission states that, in adapting to this new environment, the right balance needs to be struck between flexibility and security. Greater flexibility is required by employers, while employees need security in terms of their employability and job prospects. The Commission argues that better organisation of work can give workers increased security through greater involvement in work planning, a greater choice of working arrangements, increased job satisfaction and the possibility of developing skills. This also provides employers with increased flexibility in the form of a more skilled, motivated and versatile labour force which is better able to cope with change. The Commission commits itself to promoting a new framework for the modernisation of work organisation and a better balance between work and family life. To this end, it will:

- Present a Communication on work organisation and adaptability.

- Present proposals on the protection of workers currently excluded from the Working Time Directive based on the 1997 White Paper.

- Launch an initiative designed to encourage greater financial participation in companies by employees.

Finally, the current prevalence of social-democratic national governments in the EU may lead to a shift to the left in social policy. The PES ECOFIN Group brings together Socialist and Social-Democratic Ministers of Finance and party spokespersons on finance from member parties of the Party of European Socialists. A recent paper published by the Group urges the adoption of full employment policies, an active welfare state, and extension of co-operation and integration within the EU, including tax harmonisation (PES-ECOFIN Group, 1998, ref. no. 719). The task is to find a way of marrying an open, competitive and successful economy with a just, decent and humane society.

7.7   Bibliography

7.7.1   The Third Way

(670)
NEW Labour because Britain deserves better
Labour Party
London: 1997. 40p.
Labour Party manifesto for the 1997 general election.

DSC Shelfmark: Not found

(671)
NEW Labour in power: precedents and prospects
B Brivati and T Bale (editors)
London: Routledge, 1997. 212p.

Combines historical, political and practical approaches to the questions raised by Labour's election victory. Addressing core themes such as Europe, the economy, welfare, education and the constitution, it provides an assessment of the new era.

DSC Shelfmark: Not found

(672)
THE THIRD way: new politics for the new century
T Blair
London: Fabian Society, 1998. 20p.
(Fabian pamphlet; 588)

Sets out his vision of the Third Way as a modernised social democracy, committed to social justice and other goals of the centre-left, but flexible, innovative and forward looking in the means to achieve them. Makes the case for a dynamic economy based on individual empowerment and opportunity, a strong civil society enshrining rights and responsibilities, a modern government based on partnership, innovation and decentralisation and a foreign policy furthering international co-operation.

DSC Shelfmark: 3863.107000

(673)
THE THIRD way: renewal of social democracy
A Giddens
Cambridge: Polity Press, 1998. 160p.

Explores the idea of the social investment state in the positive welfare society. Expenditure on positive welfare would be generated and distributed by the state working in partnership with other agencies including business. In the positive welfare society, the contract between government and the individual would shift as autonomy, self-development and the expansion of individual responsibility became the prime focus.

DSC Shelfmark: 98/28856

(674)
TOMORROW'S politics: the Third Way and beyond
I Hargreaves and I Christie (editors)
London: Demos, 1998. 148p.

Collection of essays exploring the so-called 'Third Way', a new approach to political economy that will help meet the challenges of the next century. It seeks to reconcile capitalism and social justice, modernise welfare systems, public services and labour markets, deepen democracy and make a transition to environmentally sustainable development.

DSC Shelfmark: 99/14423

7.7.2   UK economic propsects

(675)
MONTHLY trends enquiry Sept 1998
[London]: Confederation of British Industry, 1998. 43p.

Findings show that demand for manufactured goods has weakened with output set to fall.

DSC Shelfmark: 5959.558000

(676)
OECD economic outlook, no.63, 1998

Analyses prospective economic developments in the OECD area over the two years to 2000 and makes reommendations on economic policies needed to ensure sustainable growth in OECD Member states. Detailed country notes provide an assessment of the economic situation and assessment for each member country, including the UK.

DSC Shelfmark: 6235.251000

(677)
STEERING a stable course for lasting prosperity: pre-budget report November 1998
Treasury
London: TSO, 1998. 134p. (Cm 4076)

Forecasts that the UK economy will grow by 1-1.5% in 1999 0.75% less than forecast in the March budget. This slowdown can be accounted for by the effect of the deterioration in the world economy. Slower growth in 1999 is forecast to be followed by GDP growth of 2.25 to 2.75% in 2000. The slowdown in growth in 1998, should, in turn dampen domestic inflationary pressures. With import price inflation likely to start picking up through 1999, Retail Prices Index inflation is forecast to return to its target level of 2.50% by the end of 1999, after temporarily dipping below it earlier in the year.

DSC Shelfmark: OP-CM/4076

(678)
THE UK economy
R Kneller, R Riley and G Young
National Institute economic review, no.166, 1998, p.8-27.

Forecasts that the economy will grow at 1.1% in 1999, but manufacturing output will decline by 0.5% and there is a one in three chance of outright recession. Cuts in interest rates to 5.75% by the end of 1999 together with higher government spending should sustain continuing growth.

DSC Shelfmark: 6025.580000

(679)
UNITED Kingdom
Paris: OECD, 1998. 186p.
(OECD economic surveys; 1997-98)

Gives an overview of the New Labour government's monetary and fiscal policies, and analyses its attempts to integrate work and welfare, and to reform corporate governance.

DSC Shelfmark: 3656.650000

7.7.3   Welfare reform

(680)
EXCELLENCE in schools
London: TSO, 1997. 84p. (Cm 3681)

Sets out policy principles guiding educational reform: (1) education will be at the heart of government, (2) policies will be designed to benefit the many, not the few, (3) intervention in schools will be in inverse proportion to success, (4) there will be zero tolerance of under-performance, and (5) government will work in partnership with parents, teachers and governors, local authorities, churches and business to raise standards.

DSC Shelfmark: OP-CM/3681

(681)
HIGHER education in the learning society
R Dearing (Chairman)
[S l]: National Committee of Inquiry into Higher Education, 1997-98. 14 Reports and 5 Appendices.

Report recommending, among other things, that the costs of higher education should be shared among those who benefit from it. So, for example, students should contribute to their tuition fees.

DSC Shelfmark: GPE 1729 (summary report)

(682)
REFORMING welfare
F Field
London: Social Market Foundation, 1997. 129p.

Collection of speeches and essays presenting Frank Field's ideas on welfare reform.

DSC Shelfmark: 8310.951000

(683)
BRINGING Britain together: a national strategy for neighbourhood renewal
Social Exclusion Unit
London: TSO, 1998. 84p. (Cm 4045)

Sets out a national strategy for tackling poor neighbourhoods. New funding programmes, including the New Deal for Communities, will support their regeneration. This will provide funds to develop and implement local, community-based plans covering everything from jobs and crime to health and housing. It will give local leaders power and resources to turn their community around.

DSC Shelfmark: OP-CM/4045

(684)
THE FUTURE of welfare
London: Social Market Foundation, 1998. 141p.
(SMF paper; No. 35)

Debates how far Britain is willing and able to follow America down the path to radical welfare reform.

DSC Shelfmark: 8310.951000

(685)
THE LEARNING age: a renaissance for a new Britain
London: TSO, 1998. 82p. (Cm 3790)

Green paper encourages adults to enter and re-enter learning at every point in their lives to update and extend their skills. Two new initiatives are proposed to support lifelong learning: individual learning accounts which will enable people to take responsibility for their own learning with support from employers and government, and a University for Industry which will offer access to a learning network.

DSC Shelfmark: OP-CM/3790

(686)
LEARNING beyond the classroom
T Bentley
In Tomorrow's politics: the Third Way and beyond edited by I Hargreaves and I Christie. London: Demos, 1998, p.80-95.

Argues the case for continuous, lifelong learning delivered through systems which are demand led and individualised. They will employ information and communications technologies, weak control structures and network forms of organisation.

DSC Shelfmark: 99/14423

(687)

LEVELLING down: the School Standards and Framework Bill

S Williams

London: Centre for Policy Studies, 1998. 39p.

The Government's education reforms represent a massive centralisation of powers away from schools and into the hands of Local Education Authorities and the Secretary of State for Education and Employment. Centralising measures in the Bill include giving LEAs power to employ all school staff and to intstruct schools how to raise standards through Education Development Plans. Articles of government, valued by many schools as a definition of their ethos, will be abolished and replaced by standardised 'instruments of government' drawn up by the DfEE. Standardisation measures include the abolition of grant maintained schools, definition of rules of admission for all schools by the DfEE, and the requirement for church schools to get LEA approval for their religious admissions policy every year.

DSC Shelfmark: 98/15728

(688)

MODERN public services for Britain: investing in reform: comprehensive spending review: new public spending plans 1999-2002

London: TSO, 1998. 117p. (Cm 4011)

On the welfare front promises more than £20bn to modernise the NHS over the next three years, build hospitals and cut waiting lists; £19bn extra for education and doubling of investment in schools to cut class sizes; £4.4bn to regenerate cities, improve council houses and extend the 'new deal' to the most deprived estates; a new minimum guaranteed pension for the poorest pensioners, plus abolition of eye test charges and more help with fuel bills; a new means tested educational maintenance allowance for teenagers who stay on at school to replace child benefit for over-16s. Spending is to be financed by reductions in the Defence, Legal Aid and Agriculture budgets, a continuing squeeze on public sector pay and the sale of national assets. Department's spending will be subject to continuous scrutiny and audit. Each department will be expected to achieve quantifiable targets and to produce an annual output and performance analysis. The public will also be given more information about public sector performance through League Tables.

DSC Shelfmark: OP-CM/4011

(689)

NEW ambitions for our country: a new contract for welfare

London: TSO, 1998. 96p. (Cm 3805)

Proposes a welfare system that is proactive, preventing poverty by ensuring that people have the right education, training and support. People of working age will be encouraged to work where they are capable of doing so. The public and private sectors should work in partnership to ensure that, wherever possible, people are insured against foreseeable risks and make provision for their retirement. The system should support families and the disabled, and tackle social exclusion.

DSC Shelfmark: OP-CM/3805

(690)
THE NEW deal handbook
C Donnelly, M Nimmo and P Convery
London: Unemployment Unit and Youthaid, 1998.

Covers key elements of the New Deal for the Young Unemployed: eligibility and recruitment, the 'Gateway' (supporting young people to become 'option ready'), referral to the New Deal options, the four options themselves (work with an environmental taskforce, work with a voluntary organisation, a job with an employer or full-time education), leaving the New Deal, and the follow-through strategy. Also explores the relationship between the New Deal and the benefits regulations, particularly in terms of sanctions.

DSC Shelfmark: Not found

(691)
PUBLIC attitudes on the future of welfare: research findings
Fabian Society
London: 1998. 11p.

Paper summarises research findings on public attitudes towards the National Insurance (NI) system. Research indicates that the public is losing confidence in it. This leaves it in danger of being undermined by default. A substantial private insurance system would exclude the poor and raise costs. The government needs to rebuild public confidence by clarifying what people are paying into and the benefits they can expect to receive in return.

DSC Shelfmark: Not found

(692)
TECS: meeting the challenge of the millennium: consultation paper
Department for Education and Employment
Sudbury: DfEE Publications, 1998.

Assures the Training and Enterprise Councils (TECs) of a key role in raising standards of education and training, making lifelong learning a reality, helping people move from welfare into sustainable employment, tackling deprivation and social exclusion and supporting community regeneration. TECs will be required to work in partnership with the new Regional Development Agencies in developing regional economic strategies and National Training Organisations in designing national skills strategies. Also considers the TEC funding and audit system in depth to allow the strength and weaknesses of current arrangements to be set out and practical possiblities for change to be considered.

DSC Shelfmark: GPE 4110

(693)

THATCHERISM, New Labour and the Welfare State

J Hills

London: Centre for Analysis of Social Exclusion, London School of Economics, 1998. 37p.

(CASE paper; 13)

Examines the extent to which the policies towards the Welfare State pursued by the Labour Government represent a break with those of its Conservative predecessor and with earlier policies put forward by Labour in opposition. Identifies four linking themes: the importance to Labour of shedding its 'tax and spend' image leading to tight budgetary constraints; the promotion of paid work; the new dominance of the Treasury in making welfare policy; and the drive to reduce inequality and relative poverty.

DSC Shelfmark: 3058.251430

7.7.4 Privatisation

(694)

COMPETITION and service: the impact of the Local Government Act 1988

K Walsh and H Davis

London: HMSO, 1993. 167p.

The major impact of competitive tendering was found to have been on the staff. Manual staff, in particular, had borne the brunt of changes in working methods, pay and conditions. The large majority of authorities had made significant changes to staff pay, conditions or numbers in introducing competition, and many had continued to make changes after winning tenders. Management had become both more powerful and formal.

DSC Shelfmark: OP/93-ENV

(695)

COMPULSORY competitive tendering for local government services: the experiences of local authorities in the North of England 1988-1992

K Shaw, J Fenwick and A Foreman

Public administration, vol.72, 1994, p.201-217.

Article examines the different reactions to the development of a more commercial approach to the management of local authority services among officers, councillors and trade union representatives.

DSC Shelfmark: 6962.400000

(696)
THE GENDER impact of CCT in local government: calculation of the costs and savings of CCT
Centre for Public Services
Sheffield, 1995. 26p.

Argues that competitive tendering was not saving public money which could be invested in other services or used to reduce government expenditure. Whilst public sector employment was reduced by contracting out and private sector employment increased, the latter was in effect being subsidised by the public purse.

DSC Shelfmark: q96/01244

(697)
ACCOUNTING for the private finance initiative
D Heald and N Geaughan
Public money and management, July/Sept 1997, p.11-16.

Considers the ideological and spending context out of which the PFI emerged and discusses how accounting and public expenditure scoring issues have been addressed.

DSC Shelfmark: 6967.781000

(698)
CAN the NHS afford the private finance initiative?
D Gaffney and A M Pollock
London: Health Policy and Economics Research Unit, British Medical Association, 1997. 25p.

Argues that reliance on private investment inflates the scale of capital schemes to levels which far exceed more prudent public proposals as bidders try to improve their rate of return. This cost escalation puts new demands on public revenue which in turn leads to the search for new economies and subsidies. The economies inspire bed reductions and unpiloted innovations in health care provision, while the subsidies entail transfers from sectors such as equipment and maintenance budgets.

DSC Shelfmark: Not found

(699)
PRIVATELY financed capital in public services
D Heald
The Manchester School of Economic and Social Studies, vol.65, 1997, p.568-598.

Recent changes in UK policy, notably the retirement of the 1981 Ryrie rules, predict a substantial increase in the use of private finance for public sector projects.

DSC Shelfmark: 5359.645000

(700)

DECENTRALISATION and privatisation of long-term care in UK and USA

C Harrington and A M Pollock

The Lancet, vol.351, 1998, p.1805-1808.

Transfer of funding responsibilities for long term care from central to local government and privatisation of services are causing the USA and UK systems of financing and delivery to converge. Access to care is increasingly on the basis of ability to pay. Sold under the rubric of increasing user choice, these shifts are largely directed towards decreasing central government costs. There is, however, no evidence that devolution of funding responsibility and privatisation have actually lessened the costs to taxpayers.

DSC Shelfmark: 5146.000000

7.7.5   Minimum wage

(701)

AFTER wages councils

R Dickens and A Manning

New economy, vol.2, 1995, p.223-227.

Demonstrates that the abolition of the wages councils in 1993 led to downward pressure on wages in the sectors they had covered but no increase in employment.

DSC Shelfmark: 6083.670500

(702)

MYTH and measurement: the new economics of the minimum wage

D Card and A B Krueger

Princeton, N J: Princeton University Press, 1995. 422p.

An empirical study of employment in the fast food industry after the 1992 increase in the New Jersey minimum wage showed that employment was not adversely affected. Relative to restaurants in Pennsylvania, where the minimum wage remained unchanged, results show that employment in New Jersey expanded with the increase. Moreover, a cross-state analysis found that 1990 and 1991 increases in the Federal minimum wage did not adversely affect teenage employment.

DSC Shelfmark: 95/13473

(703)

WAGE mobility in Great Britain

R Dickens

Employment audit, issue 3, 1997, p.20-28.

It is generally agreed that wage inequality has risen over the last 20 years. More contentious is the issue of the degree to which individuals progress out of low pay. The evidence points to a significant degree of wage immobility and individuals being caught in a cycle of low pay and unemployment. Wage mobility appears to have decreased since the 1970s and people find themselves trapped in low-paid, dead end work.

DSC Shelfmark: 3737.213700

(704)
LESS than common decency
Anon
New review of the Low Pay Unit, no. 49, 1998, p.15–17.

Presents data suggesting that half the British workforce are low paid by European standards.

DSC Shelfmark: 6087.760895

(705)
LOW pay, the working of the labour market and the role of a minimum wage
S Sachdev and F Wilkinson
London: Institute of Employment Rights, 1998. 74p.

Presents the case that low pay is primarily the result of the low value placed on the skills and experience of disadvantaged workers rather than their personal shortcomings. Low pay remains overwhelmingly a problem of women's pay, often exacerbated by race discrimination. Argues that labour market changes over the last 20 years have allowed the economically powerful to secure the lion's share of the productivity gains at the expense of the low-paid, who have largely carried the cost of change. Over a quarter of the population have not gained from economic growth and in sectors like contract cleaning or fast food any wage floor has collapsed.

DSC Shelfmark: 98/31701

(706)
MAKING the most of the minimum: statutory minimum wages, employment and poverty
In Employment outlook June 1998. Paris, OECD, 1998, p.31–77.

Report states that minimum wages are not the solution for family poverty and may lead to job losses, especially for young people. The higher the minimum wage the more it hits youth employment. A 10% rise in the minimum rate is associated with a fall of 1.5 to 3 per cent in teenage employment. Minimum wages tend to help families with above average incomes because many low-paid workers live in such households, while failing to help households with no workers at all. The OECD estimates that 40% of people on low incomes live in households where nobody has paid work.

DSC Shelfmark: 6235.251500

(707)

MINIMUM wage effects by gender

N Williams and J A Mills

Journal of labor research, vol.19, 1998, p.397–414.

Reanalysis of data in the light of recent developments in time-series methods shows that the minimum wage has a negative impact on both men and women. Results show that following a 10% hike in the minimum wage, both male and female employment drops by between 2 and 4% over a two-year period.

DSC Shelfmark: 5009.960000

(708)

MINIMUM wage goes down in history

Anon

New review of the Low Pay Unit, no.52, 1998, p.6–8.

Summary and critique of 'The national minimum wage: first report of the Low Pay Commission.'

DSC Shelfmark: 6087.760895

(709)

THE NATIONAL minimum wage: first report of the Low Pay Commission

Low Pay Commission

London: TSO, 1998. 285p. (Cm 3976)

Describes the work of the Low Pay Commission in establishing the pattern of low pay, defining earnings which may count towards the minimum wage, choosing the rate for the minimum wage, assessing its impact and considering how it should be implemented and enforced. Recommends an initial rate of £3.60 per hour to be introduced in April 1999, rising to £3.70 in June 2000. The initial development rate for young people should be £3.20 per hour in April 1999 rising to £3.30 per hour in June 2000.

DSC Shelfmark: OP-CM/3976

(710)

WHY we need a national minimum wage

R Dickens

Chartered Banker, vol.4, no.3, 1998, p.51–54.

Argues that although the minimum wage is not the perfect policy tool for tackling poverty, it will go some way to alleviating the plight of the working poor. Set at a sensible level, it should not increase unemployment.

DSC Shelfmark: 3129.983000

7.7.6   Economic and monetary union

(711)
IN with the Euro, out with the pound: the single currency for Britain
C Johnson
London: Penguin, 1996. 256p.

Argues that in return for short-run transition costs, the single currency will lead to a more stable economic environment, with lower inflation and interest rates combined with increased investment and economic growth. Businesses will be able to trade in the euro zone without losing on exchange rate conversions and fluctuations. The Euro will mean lower prices, more jobs and higher living standards. In spite of some pooling of economic sovereignty, Britain will remain politically independent.

DSC Shelfmark: 97/05627

(712)
THE OSTRICH and the EMU: policy choices facing the UK: report of an Independent Panel ....
R Pennant-Rea (Chair)
London: Centre for Economic Policy Research, 1997. 51p.

Considers the economic policy implications for the UK of four different strategies on membership of EMU: joining in the first wave, joining later, waiting to see how EMU works out and deciding, in principle, not to join.

DSC Shelfmark: 97/14281

(713)
THE PROS and cons of EMU
D Currie
London: Economist Intelligence Unit, 1997. 102p.
(EIU research report; no.519)

Argues that EMU will be a partial success, though not necessarily for all its members. Going forward to EMU does not condemn Europe to failure nor guarantee its success. The pros and cons are finely balanced, and success or failure will depend on the wisdom of the choices governments make in implementing the single currency.

DSC Shelfmark: 3668.239000

(714)
UK membership of the single currency: an assessment of the five economic tests
Treasury
London: 1997. 40p.

Argues that we need to demonstrate sustainable and durable convergence before we can be sure that British membership of EMU would be good for growth and jobs. Joining before such convergence is secured would risk harming both.

DSC Shelfmark: Not found

(715)
EMU: the debate gathers pace
Anon
European industrial relations review, no. 296, 1998, p.13-16.

Summarises the debate over the potential effects of EMU on pay and collective bargaining in Europe.

DSC Shelfmark: 3829.720500

(716)
EUROPE beyond the millennium: making sense of tomorrow
Andersen Consulting
London, 1998. 56p.

Presents three different possible outcomes of the implementation of the single currency. In the 'Competitive Europe' scenario capitalism is dominant in an enlarged EU with a single market and single currency. Competition is encouraged and the labour market is lightly regulated. The gap between rich and poor is widening. The 'Conscience Europe' scenario envisages an enlarged and integrated EU with interventionist social and economic institutions ensuring high minimum social standards, more regulation and less innovation. In the 'Patchwork Europe' scenario, the euro has collapsed and different national currencies have reappeared. In a highly fragmented EU, regions pursue their own very different agendas based on differing socio-economic models.

DSC Shelfmark: Not found

(717)
EUROPEAN monetary integration: 1958-2002
E Apel
London: Routledge, 1998. 222p

Book describes the monetary integration of Europe from 1958 to 2002. The Community progression from the co-ordination of economic and monetary policies between Member

States to the convergence of these policies is described and analysed. Provides an overview of the historical background and economic framework of European monetary integration.

DSC Shelfmark: 98/05028

(718)
EUROPEAN monetary integration. 2nd. ed.
D Gros and N Thygesen
Harlow: Longman, 1998. 574p.

Provides the reader with a complete analysis of European monetary integration, its history, including the achievements of the European Monetary System, its current economics, and the outlook for EMU.

DSC Shelfmark: Not found

(719)
THE NEW European way: economic reform in the framework of EMU
PES–ECOFIN Group: 1998. 7p.
URL: http://www.pes.org/english/content4-4b.htm

Sets out a policy agenda which aims to restore growth and employment in Europe, develop the contract for social justice and promote a market economy which is socially and environmentally responsible.

DSC Shelfmark: Not applicable

(720)
THE RISK of deflation in the future EMU: lessons of the 1990s
P de Grauwe
London: Centre for Economic Policy Research, 1998. 22p.
(Discussion paper; no.1834)

Argues that in the first half of the 1990s, inspired by the Treaty of Maastricht, European countries followed a policy of monetary and fiscal contraction. This policy mix contributed to the severity of the 1992-93 recession and was partly responsible for the surge in unemployment during 1992-93. If the EMU participants continue to apply this policy mix for too long, there are grounds to fear that the Euro zone will be an area of deflation.

DSC Shelfmark: 3597.951200

7.7.7   European Union Social Policy

(721)
EUROPEAN social policy: a way forward for the Union: a white paper
Commission of the European Communities
Luxembourg: Office for Official Publications of the European Communities, 1994.
(COM (94) 333).

DSC Shelfmark: 3337.665000

(722)
SOCIAL Europe: the economic implications of current European social policy
C Hanson
London: Institute of Directors, 1996. 40p.

Argues that the inflexibilities, burdens and costs imposed by European social policy on employers are a major cause of structural unemployment in the EU.

DSC Shelfmark: Not found

(723)
PARTNERSHIP for a new organisation of work: green paper
Commission of the European Communities
Brussels, 1997. 16p. (COM (97) 128).

Presents the issues raised by the policy challenge of how to reconcile the security that workers need with the flexibility that firms need to prosper in an increasingly competitive world economy. Looks at the scope for improving employment and competitiveness through a better organisation of work based on high-skill, high trust and high quality.

DSC Shelfmark: 3337.665000

(724)
THE SOCIAL chapter
J Lourie
London: House of Commons Library, 1997. 61p.
(Research paper; 97/102)

Looks at the effect of EU employment legislation on UK law in the areas of working time, maternity leave, young workers, European Works Councils, parental leave, part-time and temporary workers, posted workers, transfer of undertakings, consultation with workers, sexual harrassment and discrimination, and equal treatment in occupational social security.

DSC Shelfmark: 7752.135000

(725)
BEYOND the market: the EU and national social policy
D Hine and H Kassim (editors)
London: Routledge, 1998. 231p.

Examines the impact of the European Union on the formation and content of national social policy in France, Germany, Italy and the UK.

DSC Shelfmark: 98/16874

(726)
EU social policy in the 1990s: towards a corporatist policy community
G Falkner
London: Routledge, 1998. 254p.

Explores the background and development of social policy content and process in the European Union since the policy innovations of the 1991 Maastricht Treaty came into force. Case studies of European Works Councils, parental leave, and atypical work are included to highlight the day to day processes at work in social policy formation and the major interest groups and EU institutions involved.

DSC Shelfmark: Not found

(727)
FAIRNESS at work
London: TSO, 1998. 47p. (Cm 3968)

States the Labour government's commitment to family-friendly policies to ensure that parents are better able to balance work and family life. Includes pledges to implement the Working Time Directive, Young Workers Directive and Parental Leave Directive.

DSC Shelfmark: OP-CM/3968

(728)
SOCIAL Action Programme 1998–2000
Commission of the European Communities
Brussels: 1998. 18p. (COM (98) 259).

Commission aims to direct social policy to meet the challenges of high unemployment, the changing world of work, poverty and social exclusion.

DSC Shelfmark: 3337.665000

(729)
SOCIAL policy state of play
Anon
European industrial relations review, no. 294, 1998, p.13–19.

Reports progress on important 'live' items of EU draft social policy legislation which are still in the pipeline. Notes the extension of two Directives progressed under the Social Policy Agreement route to the UK: the Directive on part-time work and the Directive on the burden of proof in sex discrimination cases.

DSC Shelfmark: 3829.720500

(730)
WORKING time regulations: SI 1998 No.1833
J Lourie
London: House of Commons Library, 1998. 27p.
(Research paper; 98/82).

Summarises the main provisions of the EC Working Time Directive and the UK Working Time Regulations, their potential costs and benefits and some of the criticisms which have been made of their provisions.

DSC Shelfmark: 7752.135000

8 Conclusions

1 Stress, or pressure, is an inescapable part of life. In moderation it can be challenging and stimulating and enhances performance. Pressure only becomes harmful when demands exceed the individual's ability to cope.

2 Much of the research on the link between stress at work and serious illness is methodologically flawed. Most studies use cross sectional designs in which measurements are taken at a single point in time. In this kind of research it is impossible to prove the direction of causality. A family row, for example, may cause one to perceive work as stressful, but equally the experience of stress in the workplace could make one irritable and result in rows at home. Data is normally collected by self-report survey. People's answers to the questions may be inaccurate for a variety of reasons ranging from lapses of memory to the fact they were in a bad mood when they completed the questionnaire. Other examples of dubious methodology are pointed out from time to time in the text.

3 Methodological improvements required include more use of longitudinal designs where measurements are taken at at least two different points in time and more use of objective measures such physiological tests or levels of absenteeism to corroborate the self-report data.

4 Due to the methodological problems noted, results of research studies are often inconsistent and difficult to interpret.

5 For all of the above reasons, the evidence for a link between stress and impaired mental and physical health must be considered suggestive rather than conclusive. There is a very strong suspicion that stress is guilty as charged, but proof positive is lacking.

6 There has been an explosion of interest in stress over the past 20 years which has given rise to a large and vociferous stress management industry offering a variety of interventions. The effectiveness of these interventions is debatable.

7 Employee assistance programmes and counselling services are well accepted by employees. They can be implemented with minimal disruption to the

organisation and are relatively easy to evaluate. Evaluations of their effectiveness to date have been positive.

8   Individual level stress management training programmes are the most popular form of intervention. They generally consist of a mixture of relaxation techniques and enhancement of coping skills through training in assertiveness, time management, etc. Their effectiveness is difficult to establish because (a) research has not demonstrated the relative efficacy of the different components of the training, (b) there is a suspicion that beneficial effects may attenuate over time and (c) many studies lack a valid comparison group who have not received training to show differences in outcomes.

9   Organisation level interventions which aim to reduce sources of stress in the work environment are few in number as they are expensive and difficult to implement. Although in principle prevention should be better than cure, in practice the results of these interventions have been mixed. Most have concentrated on increasing control. However, while some individuals thrive on increased responsibility and autonomy, others may find too much freedom threatening. Lack of control may be a stress factor for some individuals but not others. Increasing control may reduce stress for the one group but increase it for the other. A much greater understanding of how people function within organisations is needed to ensure that we can design organisational level changes which do not have unforeseen adverse effects.

10   An integrated approach to stress management which combines individual and organisational level approaches is recommended. Organisational redesign should eliminate unnecessary sources of stress while stress management training should help people cope with stress factors which cannot be avoided.

11   Stress management interventions should begin with a diagnosis of the problem, should have clear objectives, and should undergo continuous monitoring and feedback.

INDEXES

General index

A

Abridged Hardiness Scale 164
Absenteeism 136, 138, 146, 161, 182, 186, 233, 240, 283, 286, 305, 323, 326, 331, 339, 343–5
Accidents, workplace 125, 228, 278
  Accident Prevention Advisory Unit 278
Acquisitions 13, 153
Active jobs, definition of 35
Adrenal gland 203, 210
Adrenal medullary axis 34, 52–54, 202–3, 232
Adrenal system, in stress responses 34, 53, 202–3
Adrenalin 203, 210–11
  excretion rate of, 54
Affectivity, negative 143, 151, 161–5, 167–70, 178, 182, 188–92, 201, 235
  definition of 167–8
  links to ill health 168–70, 188
  role in stress/strain relations 168–9, 188–91
  see also Neuroticism
Affectivity, positive 190–1
Aggression 172, 185, 194
AIDS 253, 256, 288
Alarm stage, of stress 34, 52
Alcohol abuse 136, 141, 224–7, 270–6, 287
  Alcohol Abuse Disorder 273
  Alcoholics Anonymous 287
  links with violence 127

Alcohol consumption 224–7, 246, 270–6, 308, 334–5
  economic consequences of 224
  occupational analysis 271–4
  psychosocial contributors 274
  relationship to working conditions 224–5
Alertness, in shiftworkers 108–9
Alienation 126, 276
  alienation theory 272
Anger
  relationship to coronary heart disease 194
  relationship to Type A Behaviour Pattern 172
Antigens 213
Anxiety 32, 37, 136, 139, 147, 165, 177, 183, 186, 197, 200, 212, 219–20 , 223, 232, 265, 284, 295, 331, 338, 340, 350
  association with burnout 115, 219
  association with control 92
  association with immune function 254
  association with ulcers 205
  effect of stress management programmes 293–4
  in assault victims 126
  in shiftworkers 108, 110
  personality effects of 160
  state anxiety 219
  State-Trait Anxiety Inventory 293, 338

trait anxiety 219, 265, 333-4
  see also Affectivity, negative
Arteriosclerosis 211
Arthritis, rheumatoid 257
Asia, industry in 7
Assault 85, 126, 301, 341
  Assaulted Staff Action Plan 301
  Assaulted Staff Action Program 341
Assembly line work, stress in 93
Asset testing, of long term care 17
Assisted Places Schemes 355
Australia, burnout studies in 181
  working conditions in 99
Autoimmune diseases 253
  association with stress 213
Automation 10-11, 24-5
Autonomic nervous system 202-3,
  232

B

Back pain 206-7, 239-45
  association with depression 240
  occupational causes 239
  psychosocial factors in 240
Bacteria 213, 234, 258
Bank of England 366
  Monetary Policy Committee of
    352-3
Basophils 213
Bedford College Life Events and
  Difficulties Schedule 236
Biofeedback, training in 284, 292,
  312, 319, 328, 330-2, 334, 340
Biorhythms, disruption in shiftwork
  75-7, 104-6, 204
Blair, Tony 351, 363-4
Blood clotting, stress effects on 245
Blood pressure 210, 232, 246-51, 295,
  327, 329-31, 333

association with hardiness 163
effects of hostility 198
effect of stress management
  programmes 293
  see also Hypertension
Blood sugar 203
  effects of stress on 206
Blue collar workers 303-4, 336-7
  cardiovascular disease in 209-10
  gastrointestinal disorders in 204
  musculoskeletal disorders in 242,
    245
  stress in 35
Boredom 147, 242
  health consequences of 93
  models of 143
Bortner Scale, measure of Type A
  personality 172-3, 194, 196-7
Breast cancer 216, 257, 259, 262
Bullies, classification of 83
Bullying 82-5, 121-6
  categories 124
  health effects of 83
  institutional 121
  legislation on 230, 281-2
  surveys 123
Burnout 45, 50, 64, 78-82, 111-21, 138,
  140-1, 165, 181-2, 265, 284, 336
  association with role stress 89
  Cherniss model of 79, 112, 116
  effect on cholesterol levels 252
  Maslach Burnout Inventory 81-2,
    112, 118
  Maslach model of 79, 112, 118
  models of 79-81, 112-4, 116-20
  personality correlates of 81, 181
  recovery from 115, 121
  relationship to inequity 117
  relationship to locus of control 185

relationship to organisational commitment 112
Business process re-engineering 12-13, 25-8, 125

C

Cancer 216-8, 257, 259-63
  association with depression 218, 259
  association with psychosocial factors 34
  association with stress 216, 257, 261-2
  influence of emotional state 217-8, 259-62
  intervention studies in 217
  psychoneuroimmunology of 257
  psychosocial correlates of survival 259
  psychosocial treatment of 217, 260, 263
  relationship to coping style 260
  role of psychosocial factors 216, 261-2
  see also Breast cancer, Melanoma
Carbohydrates, metabolism of 203
Cardiovascular disease 119, 209-12, 245-53
  association with boredom 93
  association with job strain 91-2, 209-10, 245-53
  association with shift work 76, 104-5
  in Karoshi victims 99
  in unemployed 98
  in women 98
  links with job control 145-6
  prediction by demands–control model 91-2
  see also Coronary heart disease

Care provision, privatisation of 360
Carpal tunnel syndrome 98
Catecholamines 256
  association with job demands 93
  effect on lymphocyte trafficking 214
  excretion of 54
  in responses to stress 53, 212
  see also Adrenalin
Cholesterol, levels of 202, 211-2, 246-8
  effects of burnout 252
  in arteriosclerosis 211
  stress effects 245
Church, as stabilising institution 125
Circadian rhythms, effects of shiftwork on 75-7, 104-9
COBRA project, of European Commission 27
Cognitive Behavioural Skills Training 292-3, 298, 312, 328-40
Cognitive Hardiness Scale 164
Cognitive tasks, in shiftwork 103
Colon, stress effects on function 205, 236
Computers, use in child welfare 307, 346
Confederation of British Industry 228, 252, 364
Conference Board, business research organisation 97
Conservative government 1979-97 3-4, 6, 30-1, 353, 360, 378
  monetary policy of 19
  reduction of pensions by 17
  welfare retrenchment by 16, 30-1, 354
see also Thatcher, Margaret

Control
 association with cardiovascular
  disease 209-10, 245-53
 association with drug/alcohol abuse
  225-6, 275-6
 association with organisation level
  stress management 303-7, 311,
  343-50
 association with shiftwork tolerance
  75, 77
 association with Type A behaviour
  175, 197-8
 demands–control model 35-6, 55-9
 in workplace 90-3, 143-51
Control coping 43, 64
Coping 41-6, 49, 51, 53, 61-71, 120,
 146, 150
 definition of 41, 61, 69
 in working mothers 131
 measurement of 44-6, 70
 resources, 42-3
 Ways of Coping Checklist (Lazarus)
  44-5
Coping inventories 45-6
Coping measures 44-6, 65
 evaluation framework of 44
Coping strategies 41, 45, 61-9, 119,
 197, 284
 association with personality 43-4
 categories of 43
 of shiftworkers 106, 108
Coping style 42, 67, 117, 150
 association with stress responses
  203
 in predisposition to cancer 260
 in shiftworkers 77-8
Coping taxonomy 44-5
Coronary artery disease 210

Coronary heart disease 209-12, 245-
 53
 association with smoking 224
 association with Type A behaviour
  170-2, 192-6
 prediction by demands–control
  model 36-7
 see also Cardiovascular disease
Corporations
 hierarchical organisation of 1, 27
 social responsibility of 22
 transnational 7-8
Corticosteroids, immunosuppressive
 effects 214
Corticotrophin releasing factor 236
 in gastrointestinal stress responses
  205
Cortisol 203, 210-12, 234, 240, 244,
 248
 as measure of strain 165, 179
 immunosuppressive effects 214
 in repetitive work 93
 levels associated with chronic stress
  211-12
Council of Europe 361
Counselling services, workplace
 287-91, 322-7
Criminal Justice and Public Order Act
 1974 281-2
Crisis intervention 299-302, 340-3
 models of 300-1, 317
Crisis response plans 342
Critical Incident Analysis 46, 67, 69
Critical Incident Stress Debriefing
 301-2, 342
Customer focused operating units 11
Cytokines 214-5

D

Dearing Committee 357
Decision latitude 35, 209
Demands–Abilities fit 37-9, 60
Demands–control model (Karasek)
    35-6, 55-9, 90-3, 143-51, 347, 349
    criticisms of 36
    in mental health studies 57, 219-20
    in prediction of cardiovascular
        disease 209-10, 245-53
    in prediction of coronary heart
        disease 36
    in prediction of drug/alcohol abuse
        225-6, 275-6
Demands–supports–constraints model
    (Payne), in mental health studies
    220
Demos, independent think tank 73
Depersonalisation 79, 81-2, 112-21,
    265
Depression 32, 37, 136-9, 141, 146-7,
    177, 184, 191-2, 194, 197, 200, 212,
    215, 219-21, 223, 227-8, 233, 240,
    256, 265, 284, 295, 300, 331, 350
    association with back pain 240-1
    association with bullying 121
    association with cancer 218, 259,
        261-2
    association with control 92
    association with coronary heart
        disease 194
    association with ulcers 205
    in assault victims 126
    in shiftworkers 108
    occupational analysis 277
    personality effects 161
Deregulation 23
    effect on economy 20

Derivatives 23
Devolved decision-making authority
    12
Diabetes 205-6, 238-9
    association with stress 206
    psychology of 238
Diet
    association with cardiovascular
        disease 212
    association with workload 247
    of shiftworkers 76
Dispositional Resilience Survey 164
Downsizing 13, 29-30, 125, 153, 363
Drug abuse 127, 217, 224-7, 259,
    270-6, 300
Dutch National Work and Living
    Conditions Survey 242

E

Eating disorders 233
Economic cycles, in world economy
    21, 366-7
Economic policy, changes in 18-20
Education, higher 374
Educational reform 374-5
Elderly, long term care for 16-17
Electronic Performance Monitoring,
    stress responses to 93-4, 147-9
Emotions
    association with malignant disease
        216, 255, 257
    links with immune function 253,
        255
Emotional expressiveness, effects on
    cancer progression 217-8, 259-60
Emotional state, in predisposition to
    cancer 217-8, 259-60
Employee Assistance Programs 125,
    287-91, 322-27, 389-90

Employees
    effects of restructuring on 28
    psychological contract of 158
Employment policies, post-war 2
Employment Policy Institute 6
Endocrine system
    role in cancer development 216,
        257
    role in cardiovascular disease
        210-2, 251
    role in disease development 202-3
    role in immune system 214-5,
        255-8
    role in stress response 34, 52-54
Enteric Nervous system 205, 236
Environmental Fit theory (French,
    Caplan, van Harrison) 37-9, 59-60
Eosinophils 213
Escapism, as coping strategy 45
Essex University, Centre for Micro-
    Social Change 94
European Central Bank 365
European Commission 368-71
    COBRA project 27
    Social Action Programme 370
European Economic Area 369
European Enterprise Centre, working
    hours survey 73
European Foundation for the
    Improvement of Living and
    Working Conditions 228
European Survey on Working
    Conditions 84
European Union 4, 363-71, 383-88
    Community Charter of the
        Fundamental Social Rights of
        Workers 369-70
    Council of Ministers (Ecofin) 366

economic and monetary union
    363-8, 383-5
European Works Councils Directive
    369
Exchange Rate Mechanism 353
Parental Leave Directive 369, 387
Part-time Work Directive 369
Social Action Programme 370-1
social policy of 368-70, 386-88
Social Policy Agreement 368
Working Time Directive 370,
    387-8
European Works Councils Directive
    369
Exercise, effects on stress 330, 333
    health effects of 179
    psychological benefits of 314
Exhaustion 233
    exhaustion stage of stress 34, 52
Exhaustion, emotional 79, 81-2,
    117-20, 138, 185, 265, 269
    role in post-traumatic stress
        disorder, 222

F

Family, as stabilising institution 125
Family Credit 6
Family support 134
Family–work conflict 85-87, 129-135
Fatherhood
    father-child interaction 133
    work-family stress 134
Fatigue 334
    association with shiftwork 109-10
    association with working hours 74,
        107
Feel-good factor 97, 157
Fight-or-Flight response 202, 256

Finance, effects of new technology 25
   globalisation of 22
Finland
   ischaemic heart disease in 246
   shiftwork in 106
   work-family conflict in 134
   workplace violence in 85
Flexible working practices 29
Flexitime 28, 144
Flight attendants, shiftwork effects in
   107
Framingham Heart Study 170, 192
Framingham Scale, measure of Type A
   personality 172-3, 196-7
France
   social policy in 387
   unemployment in 4
   working hours in 102
Freelance workers 15

G

Gastric emptying, stress effects on
   205, 236
Gastritis, association with boredom
   93
Gastrointestinal disorders 204-5,
   236-9
   association with shiftwork 76
Gastrointestinal function, effect of
   shiftwork 105, 108
Gastrointestinal motility
   disorders of 205
   stress effects on 236
George, Eddie, governor of Bank of
   England 366
Germany
   economy of 3, 364-5
   manufacturing sector in 366
   productivity in 26

shiftwork in 104
   social policy in 38
   unemployment in 4
   working hours in 102, 110
Globalisation, economic 6-9, 21-3, 311
   environmental consequences of 21
Glucocorticoids 203
Glycaemic reactivity 239
Glycogen 203
Governments, national
   borrowing of 8
   effects of new technology 25
   relationship to multinational
      corporations 9
   see also Conservative Government,
      Labour Government
Granulocytes 213-4
Grocery checkers, carpal tunnel
   syndrome in 98
Group therapy, as cancer intervention
   263
Growth, personal 35

H

Haarland and Wolff, Belfast shipyard,
   labour practices in 15
Harassment 122, 124, 276
   legislation on 230, 281
   racial 281
   sexual 281, 321
Hardiness 163-4, 177, 179-83
   association with cardiovascular
      disease 181
   commitment component of 180
   resistance to stress 179, 182
Health and Safety at Work Act 1974
   229, 282
Health and Safety Executive, UK 50,
   84, 228

Health authorities, withdrawal of long term care 17
Heart rate, stress effects on 181
Hedge funds 23
Helicobacter pylori
  role in aetiology of ulcers 204, 237
Herpes infections, association with immune system impairment 212
Homicide, workplace 124
Hormones 214, 255-8
  levels in stress response 34-35, 52-54
  role in disease development 202-3
  role in immune system 214, 255-8
Hostility 171, 192-3, 197-8, 212, 295, 331
  relationship to disease 172, 194
Households, surveys of 155
Human Immunodeficiency Virus 214
  see also AIDS
Hyperactivity 121
Hypertension 248-9, 251
  behavioural methods of reduction 329-30
  relation to occupational strain 248
Hypothalamic–pituitary–adrenal–cortical axis 215, 232, 234

I

IBM, 12
  Credit Corporation of 12
Immune system
  cellular components of 213
  effects of stress 212-5, 253-8
  function of 213-4, 258
  humoral components 214
  impairment by psychosocial factors 34, 54
  interaction with nervous system 255
  links with emotional state 253
  suppression of 202
Immunoglobulins 213-4
  association with depression 254
  association with strain 215
  Immunoglobin A 213
  Immunoglobin D 213
  Immunoglobin E 213
  Immunoglobin G 213
  Immunoglobin M 213
Industry, inefficiency of 29
Inequity, relation to burnout 117
Infections 212, 256, 258
  association with stress 215, 234, 255
Inflation 373
  control of 3-4
Influenza, association with immune system impairment 212
Information technology 10-11, 13, 24-5
  displacement of labour 24
  in business process re-engineering 12
Injuries, in shiftwork 109
Innovation, effect on competitiveness 27
Insomnia 212, 334
Institute of Management 228
Intellectual property, effect on competitiveness 27
Interest rates, in control of inflation 19
Interferon 214
Interleukins 214
  interleukin-2 214, 258
  interleukin-4, 258
  stress effects 215

Internal markets, in public sector 2
Interpersonal relationships, association
    with stress 78-82
Intimidation 126
Introversion 23, 269
    association with cancer 261
Ireland, labour market in 20
Irritable bowel syndrome 237
Isolation, social, association with
    cardiovascular disease 247
Israel
    coronary heart disease in 136
    role conflict studies in 142
Italy
    manufacturing sector in 366
    social policy in 387
    unemployment in 4
    working hours in 102

J
Japan
    cardiovascular disease in 99
    economy of 3
    productivity in 26
    role stress surveys in 142
    working hours in 100, 107
Japanese industry, just-in-time
    manufacturing methods in 26
Jenkins Activity Scale, measure of Type
    A personality 171-3, 193-4, 196-8
Job characteristics 147
    relationship to job satisfaction 143
Job conditions 311
    influence on drug usage 271
Job control 35-6, 55-9, 90-3, 143-51
    see also Control
Job creation 27
Job decision latitude, association with
    cardiovascular disease 246

Job demands 35-6, 55-60, 150-1, 177,
    186
    association with cardiovascular
        disease 246
    job demands–control model
        (Karasek) 35-7, 55-9, 90-3,
        143-51
Job–demands–decision latitude model
    (Karasek) 35-7, 55-9, 90-3, 143-51,
    347, 349
Job descriptions 1-2
Job exit, association with burnout
    119
Job insecurity 5-6, 21, 94-7, 125, 127,
    152-9, 269, 273, 302
    buffering effects 158-9
    effects on health 156
    measures of 153
    models of 152
    psychological impact of 95
    surveys of 159
Job losses 13, 352
Job pacing 93-4, 144, 147-9
Job satisfaction 58, 115, 130, 136-40,
    143-4, 151, 156, 161, 165, 169,
    177-8, 182-3, 186-7, 191-2, 196,
    221, 227, 234, 240, 267, 294-5,
    304-6, 331, 334, 339, 343-5
    association with control 92
    relationship to autonomy 90
    relationship to role conflict 89
    relationship with burnout 80
Job security 2, 19, 57
Job sharing 28
Job strain 35, 55-9, 90-1, 145-51
    association with alcohol abuse
        225-6, 275-6
    association with ischaemic heart
        disease 246

association with myocardial
infarction 249, 251
association with smoking 271
Karasek model of 35-7, 55-9, 145,
147-9
relationship to blood pressure 248-
52
relationship to cardiovascular disease
209-10
relationship to musculoskeletal
disorders 243
relationship to ventricular mass 248
Job tenure 19, 95
Jobs
blue-collar 48
in traditional organisations 1-2
migration of 28
part-time 5
passive jobs 35-6
quality of 5
skill requirements of 24
temporary 5
white-collar 25, 48
Jobseekers Allowance 4, 17
Joint disease, degenerative 240

K

Karoshi (death from overwork) 74, 99
Keynesian demand management 2-3, 6

L

Labour
displacement by new technology 2
flexible 14-15, 27
in traditional organisations 2
Labour Force Survey 5, 15, 18, 29,
228, 277-8

Labour governments
education policies 356-8
post-war 2
1997 onwards 4, 18, 351-63
Third Way, the 351, 371-4
welfare policies of 353-8, 374-8
see also New Labour
Labour market
degradation of 126
flexibility in 5-6, 18-9, 27-9, 158
historical perspective of 18
in Britain 20
in Ireland 20
in Netherlands 20
in New Zealand 20
polarisation in 11
social change in 24
Layoffs 152
effect on survivors 152, 155
Legal Actions, resulting from
workplace stress 231-2
Leisure 21, 99, 103
Leukocytes 213, 256
leukocytosis 256
Life expectancy 16
Lipids, plasma levels of
association with workload 247
stress effects on 250-1
Lipoprotein, low density
in arteriosclerosis 211
stress effects on 250-1
Local Education Authorities 357
Local Government Act 1988 378
Locus of Control 164-7, 176-9,
183-8, 197, 266
as correlate of mental strain 187
as stress moderator 166, 185
buffering effects of 187
effects on health 184

measurement of 165-6, 180
models of 188
relationship with burnout 185
Low Pay Commission 382
Low Pay Unit 361-2, 382
Lymph nodes 213
Lymphocytes 213-4
    B lymphocytes 213
    T lymphocytes 213-4
    levels associated with depression
      215
    cytotoxic T lymphocytes 214
    helper T lymphocytes 214
    suppressor T lymphocytes 214
Lymphocytosis 256
Lymphokines 214, 255

M

Maastricht Treaty 366, 368
Macrophages 213-4
Malignancy, *see* Cancer
Management 2
    Ashridge Management Index 157
    burnout in 120
    career progress of 154-5
    in traditional organisations 1-2
    job insecurity in 95-6, 152
    morale of 228
    psychological contract of 158
    stress in 277-8
    working hours of 100, 103
Marijuana use 226, 271, 275
Market forces
    effects on nation states 22
    modification by the state 16
Markets, financial 23
    effect on social welfare 8
    speculation by 9
Massage therapy 338

Means testing 17
Meditation 284, 292, 312, 319, 332-4,
    337, 340
Melanoma 25
    psychiatric intervention 262
Mental health 127, 219-21, 263-7
    occupational incidence 227, 263
    relationship to work demands 267
    social support 266
    stress effects 264
    workplace policies on 316, 391
    see also Anxiety, Depression
Mergers 13, 153
Michigan School *see* Person–
    Environment Fit Model
Minimum wage 361-3, 380-2
Minnesota Multiphasic Personality
    Inventory 240
Mobbing 121
    models of 121
    see also Bullying
Monetarism, effect on economy 20
Monocytes 213-4
Monotonous work 93-4, 110, 143-7,
    241
Mortality, occupational 200-2
Mortgage protection 16-17
Motor tasks, in shiftwork 103
Multinational companies 9
    effects on nation states 21
    prosperity of 23
Muscle relaxation 292, 331-2, 340
Musculoskeletal disorders 206-9,
    239-45
    aetiology 206
    association with repetitive work 93
    incidence of 228
    neuroendocrine mechanisms in
      244

risk factors 206
role of psychosocial factors 207-9
Myocardial infarction
    association with job strain 249
    association with work environment
        55
    occupational analysis of 246

N

Narcissism 276
Nation states, effects of globalisation 22
National Health Service 355, 359-60,
    376, 379
National Health Service and
    Community Care Act (1990) 17,
    360
National Insurance 17, 377
Natural Killer cells 214, 216
    stress effects on 253-4
Negative, affectivity, *see* Affectivity,
    negative
Nervous system, association with
    immune system 214, 255
Netherlands
    job demand–control study in 150
    labour market in 20
    service industry in 367
Neurological disorders, peripheral,
    association with boredom 93
Neuroticism 43-4, 81, 177-9, 182, 194
    see also Affectivity, negative
Neutrophils 213-4
New Labour 351, 353-63, 371-2,
    374-8
    approach to welfare, 353-8
    Excellence in Schools (white paper)
        374
    1997 Manifesto 371

New Ambitions for our Country
    (green paper) 376
New Deal 355, 377
    see also Blair, Tony
New Right, ideology of 16, 30
New technology 23
    effect on work 24-5
    managerial implications of 25
New Zealand, labour market in 20
Noradrenalin 54, 203, 210
Norway, bullying laws in 83
    Norwegian Employers Federation
        122
Nurses
    burnout in 115-6, 119, 138, 150
    coping strategies of 106
    musculoskeletal disorders in 244
    shiftwork tolerance of 108

O

Optimism 95
Organisational structure, relationship
    to burnout 80, 114
Organisations
    changing structures of 26-30
    response to new conditions 11-12
    traditional 1-2
    virtual organisations 25, 30
Overload, effect on cholesterol levels
    252
Overtime working 15-16, 99
Overwork 73-5, 97-103

P

Paedophiles 343
Paperworkers, coping strategies of
    106
Parasites 213, 258

Parental Leave Directive 369
Parental withdrawal 133
Part-time working 6, 14–15, 19, 29, 128
Part-time Work Directive 369
Participatory action research 305–7, 346–9
Pathophysiological processes, in disease 202
Pensions 16–17
  reduction by Conservative government 17
PERI Life Events Scale 47–8
Periodontal diseases, inflammatory
  association with stress 21
  psychosocial factors in 256
Person–Environment Fit model 37–40, 49, 59–60
  critique of 39
  versions of 60
Personal Views Survey 164
Personality
  as moderator of work stress 160–99
  association with burnout 81–2
  association with coping strategies 43–4
  association with drug/alcohol abuse 227
  disease associations of 238
  effects on anxiety and depression 136
  effects on cancer survival 204
  in predisposition to cancer 217–8, 260–1
  links with heart disease 135
  relationship to stress process 160–99
  types of 162–76, 179–99

Personality, Type A 44, 57, 64, 66, 68, 91, 163, 165, 167, 170–80, 186, 192–9, 218, 250, 291
  appraisal of work environment 17
  association with artherogenic lipid profile 250
  association with cardiovascular disease 170–2, 175, 180, 192–3, 196, 209
  association with occupation 173
  characteristics of 170
  effects on health 180
  impact on depression 192
  measurement of 172–3, 195–7
  meta-analysis 195
  personality factors underlying 172
  reactivity to work stressors 193, 195, 198–9
  smoking incidence in 270
Personality, Type B 57, 170–1, 173–6, 186, 193, 197–9
  association with breast cancer 218
  smoking incidence in 270
Personality, Type C 259–60
  association with melanoma 218
Pessimism 95
Pituitary–adrenal cortical system, role in psychopathology of stress 34, 52–54
Pneumonia, association with immune system impairment 212
Police
  job stress in 178
  post-traumatic stress disorder in 222
Positive, affectivity see Affectivity, positive
Post-traumatic stress disorder 222–3, 267–9, 299–302, 340–3

aetiology of 267
conceptual history 267
debriefing 269, 301-2
epidemiology 268
risk factors 269
treatment 268
Posture, relation to immune function 254
Poverty, effects of new technology 25
Pressure 32
five point scale (Williams) 33
tolerance of 33
Private Finance Initiative 359-60, 379
Privatisation 2, 360-1, 378-80
Prolactin 244
Promotion, in traditional organisations 2
Psoriasis, association with stress 215, 254
Psychobiology 34-5, 40, 52-3
Psychoneuroimmunology 212-16, 233, 255-7
Psychosomatic illness
association with bullying 121
association with negative affectivity 167-70, 188-92
in Type A personality 175, 196
Psychotherapy 333
Public sector bodies 1
Pulse rate 232

Q

Quality of Employment Survey 136, 274

R

Race discrimination 230
Race Relations Act 1976 230, 281

Reagan, Ronald 31
Recession 6, 13, 97
effects on work stress 352
Redundancy 25, 157, 280
effects on workforce 96-7
relation to serum cholesterol levels 248
Regional Development Agencies 377
Relaxation training 284, 291-2, 295, 298, 312, 319, 327, 330, 334, 390
relaxation with guided imagery 335
Repetitive work 35, 53, 93-4, 144-5
links with musculoskeletal disorders 206-9
Reporting of Injuries, Diseases, and Dangerous Occurrences Regulations, United Kingdom 128
Respiratory tract infections, association with stress 215
Reticular activating system 232
Revised Hardiness Scale 164
Robots 10
Role ambiguity 87-90, 135-43, 168-9, 183, 201, 273, 302, 312, 344
impact on depression 139
in Type A personality 174
Role conflict 87-90, 135-43, 168-9, 183, 201, 302, 312, 344, 347
association with bullying 122
Bedeian and Armenakis model of 138-9
effect on job performance 142
intersender role conflict 88
in Type A personality 174
meta-analysis 137-8
person-role conflict 88
role episode model 135

Role overload 86, 125, 132-3, 273
Role processes
   in work–non-work conflict 86-7
Role senders 88-9
Role stress 88, 142, 147-8, 187
   association with anxiety and
      depression 219
   effects on health 184
   moderators of 89-90
Rotter External-Internal Scale 165-6,
   180, 184

S

Sabotage 185
School, as stabilising institution 125
Self-employment 14, 29, 94
Self-blame, as coping strategy 45
Session impact methodology 296, 334
Sex discrimination 230
   Sex Discrimination Act 1973 281
   Sex Discrimination Act 1975 230
Shiftwork 75-8, 103-11, 280, 284
   association with cardiovascular
      disease 104-8
   association with myocardial
      infarction 55
   association with ulcerative disease
      204
   domestic and social disruption 77
   effect on gastrointestinal function
      76, 105-8
   health effects of 76
   injury rates of 109
   relationship to job performance 77,
      103, 105
   sleep loss in 76-7, 104
   tolerance of 77-8, 108
Single parent families 16

Sleep disturbance 99, 104, 108, 110,
   279, 284, 300
   effects on adrenal function 204
   in post-traumatic stress disorder
      222
Sleep loss 74, 100
   association with shiftwork 76, 105
   relationship to job performance
      97-8
Sleep quality 248-9
Sleep-wake rhythms 104
Small intestine, stress effects on 236
Smoking 217, 223-4, 233, 246-7,
   270-6, 308, 328, 334-5
   as stress response 212, 223
   association with coronary heart
      disease 224
   association with job stress 270
   cessation 270-1, 274-6, 283
Social Change and Economic Life
   Initiative 5, 94, 159
Social Chapter, of Treaty of Rome
   368-9
Social security
   economic impact of 31
   Social Security Act 1986 17
Social skills 234
Social support 140, 142, 148, 150,
   163, 167, 177, 181, 184-6, 199, 220-
   1, 242, 247, 256, 264-7, 270, 300,
   335-7, 344, 346
   as stress moderator 185
   effects on strain 264-5
   relation to musculoskeletal disorders
      243
   structural equations model of 188
Socialisation processes 86-7
Spillover processes 86-7
Spleen 213

State Earnings Related Pension
  Scheme (SERPS) 17
Steel industry, manufacturing methods
  in 26
Stimulants 99-100, 104
Stockholm School 34-5
Streamlined management control 12
Streptococcal infections, association
  with immune system impairment
  212
Stress
  association with cancer 216-7,
    260-1
  association with diabetes 206, 239
  association with gastrointestinal
    disorders 204-5
  association with psoriasis 254
  association with ulcers 204-5, 237
  biological responses to 202-3
  cardiovascular responses to 181,
    209-12, 245-53
  chronic 203
  cognitive appraisal of 40-1, 61-71
  controllability effects 35
  costs of 200
  definition of 32-4, 62
  effects on blood glucose level 238
  effects on blood lipids 211-2
  effects on catecholamine levels 212
  effects on cellular immunity 254
  effects on cortisol production 203
  effects on endocrine system 34-5,
    53-4, 202-4, 215, 255-7
  effects on immune system 212-5,
    253-8
  effects on incidence of autoimmune
    disease 213
  effects on interleukin levels 214-5
  effects on lymphocyte trafficking
    256
  effects on serum cholesterol and
    blood clotting 245
  effects on T- lymphocytes 253-4
  employee adjustment to 68
  exercise effects on 330
  glycaemic reactivity to 239
  health effects of 51, 200-69, 319,
    389
  in high risk occupations 50
  in repetitive work 93-4, 110,
    143-7
  in shiftworkers 75-8, 103-11
  individual differences in 160-2,
    176-9
  influence of negative affectivity
    167-70, 188-92
  influence on smoking behaviour
    223-4, 270-6
  interactional approaches to 33
  intervention strategies 284-5
  legal aspects 281-2
  male-female transmission 132
  organisational costs of 277-81
  Person–Environment Fit model
    37-40, 59-60
  psychophysiology of 54
  physiological model of 33-4, 52-4
  relationship to alcohol abuse
    224-7, 270-6
  relationship to working hours
    72-51, 97-103
  reviews of 48-52
  structural equations model of 188
  theoretical models of 33-47, 52-71
  transactional models 33, 40, 47,
    61-71, 119, 317
  vitamin model of (Warr) 37, 58
  see also Post-traumatic stress disorder
Stress audits 317-8
Stress counselling 317-8, 322-7

Stress hormones 34-5, 52-4
  role in immune system 214, 255-8
Stress inoculation training 293, 328-9,
  336, 338
Stress management 50-1, 283-350
  cost–benefit analysis 284, 323, 332-3
  crisis intervention 299-302, 340-3
  development of programmes 338
  effectiveness of interventions
    293-5, 311-2
  employee assistance programmes
    287-91, 317, 322-7
  evaluation of 289-91, 293-5, 311,
    322-7
  individual level training 291-9,
    327-40
  integrated models of 307, 318-9
  intervention frameworks 309-10
  organisational level interventions
    302-12, 343-50
Participatory Action Research 305-7,
  346-9
  personal strategies 321-2
  problem solving cycle 310, 320
  psychoeducational programmes
    337
  stress inoculation training 293,
    328-9, 336, 338
  Time-Life Stress Management
    Program 332
  total stress management 309-10,
    347
Structured Interview, measure of Type
  A personality 172-3
Suicide 98, 121
Supplies–Values fit 37-9, 60
Survivors 96-7
  guilt in 152
  survivor syndrome 159

Sweden
  bullying laws in 83
  cardiovascular disease in 247
  coronary heart disease in 36, 145
  Federation of White Collar Unions
    145
  ill health and mortality in 98
  labour federations in 233
  shiftwork in 107
  Swedish National Level of Living
    Survey 246
  Swedish Style of Living Survey
    145
  workforce surveys in 55, 91
Sympathetic nervous system 202
  in stress responses 53, 210
Sympathetic–adrenal medullary
  system, role in psychopathology of
  stress 34, 52-54, 202-3

T

Teachers
  burnout in 89, 116, 119, 140
Team cultures 235
Technological change 10-11, 24-5,
  311
Tecumseh Community Health Study
  264
Teleworking 27-8, 67
Testosterone 240, 244
  levels associated with job strain 248
Thatcher, Margaret 351, 369
  replacement of welfare state 30
  Thatcherism 30, 378
Third world, economies of 7
Threat management 125
Thymus 213
Tobacco use, see Smoking

Trade,
   globalisation of 7, 21-3
Trade unions 3, 228, 231, 354
Training and Enterprise Councils 377
Trait anxiety, *see* Affectivity, negative
Transactional stress model of appraisal
   and coping 40-7, 61-71
Transnational corporations 4, 23
Trauma 222-3, 267-9
   workplace trauma, models of
      intervention 299-302, 340-3
Triglycerides, in arteriosclerosis 211
Tuberculosis, association with immune
   system impairment 212
Two-career couples
   occupational stress in 132
   well being in 132
Tyranny
   in organisations 123

U

Ulcers, duodenal 204-5, 236-7
   association with shiftwork 105
   links with work stress 236
Unabridged Hardiness Scale 164
Unemployed
   job uptake by 20
   mass migration of 367
   welfare provisions for 355
Unemployment 3-5, 7, 16, 19, 94-5,
   100, 130, 387
   effects on families 28
   social consequences of 24
Unemployment benefits 3
   degradation of 17
United Kingdom
   bullying in 124
   economy of 20, 352-3, 364-5,
      373-4

flexible working in 28
labour market in 28
manufacturing sector in 72
social policy in 387
welfare retrenchment in 31
welfare state in 31
working hours in 102
workplace violence in 129
United States of America
   coronary heart disease in 36, 145,
      247
   Department of Health and Human
      Services 323
   Health Examination Survey 91
   job strain surveys in 15
   productivity in 26
   Quality of Employment Survey 91,
      145
   welfare retrenchment in 31
   workforce surveys in 55
   working hours in 102
   workplace violence in 85, 126-7
University for Industry 358, 375

V

Victim support 301
Violence, workplace 82-5, 125-9
   causes of 127
   consequences of 127-8
   effects of 129
   legal aspects of 126
   media glamorisation 125
   psychological effects 126
   prevention of 125, 127
   reporting of 128
   surveys of 127-9
Virtual offices 28
Viruses 213-4, 216, 234, 258

Visual display terminals,
    musculoskeletal disorders associated
    with usage 242, 244

W

Wages 7
    statutory minimum 7, 361-3, 380-2
Wages councils 3, 354, 380
Welfare reform 16-18, 30-1, 353-8,
    374-8
Welfare State 6, 16-18, 30-1, 353-8,
    374-8
    impact on living standards 31
Western Collaborative Group Study
    170
WFD/*Management Today*, working
    hours survey 73
White collar workers
    cardiovascular disease in 171,
        209-10
    effects of job insecurity 94, 153-4,
        156-7, 159
    health status of 146
    illness and behaviour correlates in
        233
    job strain in 161
    musculoskeletal disorders in 242,
        245
    working hours 73-4, 100, 102-3
Whitehall II study (psychosocial work
    characteristics) 156, 235, 266
Wife abuse 129
Winter of Discontent 1978-9 3
Women
    alcohol use 226
    bullying of 122

cardiovascular disease in 98, 209-10
carpal tunnel syndrome in 98
harassment of 122
health effects of work demands
    133
in labour market 6, 16
job strain in 151
job tenure of 95
relationship between work and
    health 131
stress responses in 253
Type A personality 173
working hours of 99, 101
working mothers 335
see also Wife abuse
Work–family conflict 85-7, 129-35,
    association with long hours culture
        74, 100-2
    in shiftwork 77
Work groups, autonomous 303-5,
    343, 345
Work–non-work conflict 85-7, 129-
    135
Work-related upper limb disorders
    206, 241-3, 245
Work schedules, effects on sleep 104
Workaholism 74
Workers, alienation of 272
    displaced 13
Working Families Tax Credit 6, 356
Working hours 73-5, 97-103, 127,
    280
    adverse health effects of 74-5,
        98-101
Working Time Regulations 1998 370
Workplace Industrial Relations Survey
    29

Author index

A

Adams, A 122
Ader, R 255
Ahlberg-Hultén, GK
  243
Aiken, O 126
Åkerstedt, T 104, 107
Albright, CL 249
Alcock, P 30
Alexander, CN 333
Alfredsson, L 55, 246
Allinson, T 323
Amick, BC 148, 151
Andersen Consulting,
  London 384
Anisman, H 261
Anonymous 381-2, 384,
  388
Apel, E 384
Armenakis, AA 137
Arnetz, BB 244
Aronowitz, S 24-5
Arroba, T 345
Arsenault, A 177, 187
Arvey, RD 127
Ashford, SJ 63, 153
Ashforth, B 123
Ashforth, BE 118
Ashridge Research 157
Atkinson, AB 31

B

Baer, PE 329
Baglioni, AJ 64, 196, 264
Baker, D 251
Baker, E 318

Bale, T 371
Barling, J 129-30, 147
Barnard, SM 183
Barnett, RC 57, 131
Baron, RA 128
Barton, J 106, 108
Bassman, ES 121
Batlis, NC 183
Baum, A 233
Baxter, V 126
Beale, D 128
Beasley, PJ 257
Beatson, M 18
Bedeian, AG 130, 137
Beehr, TA 51, 68, 137,
  265, 312
Belbin, M 27
Bemis, C 261
Benbow, N 278
Benschop, RJ 253, 256
Benson, H 327
Benson, JM 327
Bentley, T 375
Bernard, B 241
Bernier, D 121
Berridge, J 325-6
Berry, JO 134
Bertoch, MR 332
Bhagat, RS 130
Bieliauskas, LA 259
Bigos, SJ 240
Biondi, M 258
Blaney, PH 181
Blau, G 132
Blau, GJ 184
Bliese, PD 100
Blum, M 120

Blum, YC 273
Blumenthal, JA 199, 252
Bobko, P 153
Bohle, P 111
Bolger, N 64
Bongers, PM 241
Bonnet, MH 108
Booth-Kewley, S 194
Borg, V 243
Boudewyns, PA 268
Boyd, DP 193
Boyer, R 22
Brady, DS 63
Braverman, M 340
Brennan, RT 57, 266
Brennan, S 347
Breslau, N 268
Brett, JF 189
Brief, AP 188, 190, 192
Brindley, DN 251
Briner, RB 111, 317,
  349
Britton, P 138
Brivati, B 371
Brockner, J 152, 155
Brosschot, JF 253
Brown, J 178
Brown, MR 234
Brown, RK 28
Bruning, NS 330
Bryan, P 324
Bryla, CM 257
Buck, N 155
Buckle, P 245
Budd, JW 127
Bulatao, EQ 127
Bunce, D 339

Burchell, B 156, 159
Burke, MJ 190
Burke, RJ 116, 119, 140, 197, 348
Burns, JW 198
Burns, P 102
Burton, AK 244
Burton, S 138
Büssing, A 110
Buunk, BP 117
Byosiere, P 49

C

Cahill, J 346
Callan, VJ 66, 68-9
Candell, AB 29
Capelli, P 28
Caplan, RD 59, 135-6, 270
Capozzoli, TK 127
Carayon, P 148-9
Card, D 380
Carels, RA 199
Carlier, IVE 267, 269
Caroll, V 245
Carrol, C 27, 152
Cartwright, S 279, 317, 319-21, 348
Casey, B 29
Cassileth, BR 259
Cates, DS 131
Cellini, JV 184
Centre for Public Services, Sheffield 379
Champy, J 26
Chan, WF 276
Chapell, D 129
Charlesworth, EA 329
Charlesworth, K 278

Chartrand, JM 190
Chen, PY 189
Cherniss, C 112, 115
Chesney, MA 330
Christie, I 372
Clarkin, N 126
Clayton, T 27
Clegg, CW 343
Coats, M 131
Cobb, S 270
Coe, T 154
Cohen, N 255
Cohen, S 176, 234, 255-6
Colligan, MJ 105, 263
Commission of the European Communities 386-7
Confederation of British Industry, London 278, 280-1, 373
Contrada, RJ 181
Convery, P 377
Conway, N 158
Conway, TL 270
Cooper, CL 48-9, 51, 60, 64, 67, 69, 103, 145, 177-8, 196, 261, 264, 279-80, 282, 312, 317, 319-26, 348,
Cooper, ML 141, 265, 272
Cordery, JL 345
Cordes, CL 114, 120
Corrigan, PW 115
Coulson-Thomas, C 27
Cox, DJ 238
Cox, S 54, 314
Cox, T 50, 54, 62, 65-6,

128, 144, 314
Coyle, D 25
Crabbe, S 126
Crandall, R 50, 67
Crawford, N 124
Crum, RM 275
Cummings, LL 142
Cummins, R 186
Cummins, RC 185
Cunningham, G 325
Currie, D 383
Curtis, D 326
Cushway, D 151
Cutler, J 25
Czajkowski, SM 194

D

Da Silva, AM 256
Dancey, CP 237
Daniels, K 187, 266, 320
Daniels, M 258
Davidson, H 131
Davidson, JRT 268
Davies, NV 278
Davis, GC 268
Davis, H 378
Davy, J 152
de Grauwe, P 385
de Jonge, J 58
de Rijk, AE 150
Deakin, S 18
Dearing, R 374
Deary, IJ 118
DeFrank, RS 312
DeLongis, A 70
DeLucia, AG 332
Dembroski, TM 193-5
Demos Quarterly 100

Department for
    Education and
    Employment 377
Dewe, P 65-6, 317
Di Martino, V 129
Dickens, R 380, 382
DiFazio W 24
Dimsdale, JE 53
Doctor, RS 326
Dohrenwend, BS 48
Dolan, SL 177, 187
Donnelly, C 377
Dougherty, TW 114, 120
Drache, D 22
Drake, B 119
Drazen, M 328
Driscoll, RJ 126
Dunkerley, M 24
Dunning, JH 22

E

Earnshaw, J 282
Eaton, WW 277
Eden, D 232, 270
Edwards, JR 60, 64, 176,
    196-7
Einarsen, S 122
Elliott, TK 119
Elliott, TR 190
Elovainio, M 244
Elwood, M 262
Employee Assistance
    Professionals
    Association, London
    326-7
Endersen, IM 254
Erera, IP 140
Erickson, RJ 133
Etzion, D 134

Evandrou, M 31
Evans, GW 143
Everly, GS 342

F

Fabian Society 372, 377
Facione, NC 133
Fairbank, JA 268
Falkner, G 387
Faragher, EB 261
Fawzy, FI 262-3
Fawzy, NW 263
Feinleib, M 192
Feldman, LH, 346
Felstead, A 159
Felten, D 255
Fenwick, J 378
Ferguson, E 65-6
Ferrie, JE 156
Fertig, DL 257
Field, F 374
Fife, A 257
Fink, LS 150
Firth, H 138
Firth-Cozens, J 324
Fisher, CD 137
Fisher, S 54
Fitzgerald, LF 122
Flaherty, JA 276
Flannery, RB 341
Fletcher, B 55, 132, 350
Fletcher, BC 57
Folkard, S 103, 106-7,
    109, 111
Folkman, S 62-3
Ford, DL 130
Foreman, A 378
Fournier, C 155
Fox, BH 260

Fox, ML 190
Fox, RJ 237
Frankenhaeuser, M 52-3
Freedy, JR 336
French, JRP 59, 135,
    270
Frese, M 104, 146
Freudenberger, HJ 111
Frew, DR 330
Fried, Y 142
Friedman, HS, 194
Friedman, M 192, 245
Frone, MR 141, 265,
    272
Fry, FL 344
Funk, SC 182
Furnham, A 178
Fusilier, MR 144, 184,
    264

G

Gaffney, D 379
Gaillard, AWK 235
Gallagher, J 282
Ganellan, RJ 181
Ganster, DC 144, 184,
    189-90, 193, 195, 197,
    234, 264, 328
Gardell, B 233
Garron, DG 259
Geaughan, N 379
Gelpin, Y 237
George, JM 190
Gerhard, A 27
Gersons, BPR 267, 269
Giddens, A 372
Gilligan, I 236
Ginsburg, IH 254
Gio-Fitman, J 257

Gitelson, R 137
Gladstone, D 31
Glaser, R 255
Glick, WH 26
Golembiewski, RT 117
Goodspeed, RB 332
Gowing, MK 30
Granrose, CS 132
Gray, J 23
Green, F 159
Green, KL 271
Greenberg, ES 276
Greene, RL 182
Greenglass, E 116, 140
Greenglass, ER 119, 197
Greenhalgh, L 152-3
Greenhaus, JH 132
Greenlund, KJ 252
Greenwood, KM 110
Gregg, P 19-20, 156
Grobe, JE 274
Gronningsæter, H 333
Gros, D 385
Grunberg, L 276
Grunberg, NE 233
Guest, D 157-8
Guppy, A 187, 266
Gutmann, J 322

H

Haan, MN 246
Hackmann, A 333
Hagihara, A 199
Hale, R 30
Hall, EM 247, 272
Hallier, J 157
Halverson, RR 100
Hammer, M 26
Handy, C 21

Hänninen, V 242
Hanson, C 386
Hanson, SL 238
Harbin, TJ 195
Hardy, GE 324
Hargreaves, I 372
Harkins, SW 190
Harma, M 108
Harrington, C 380
Harrington, JM 98, 109
Harris, M 25
Hartley, J 154
Harvie, PL 117
Harwich, C 104
Haslam, DR 97
Havlovic, SJ 65, 67
Haynes, SG 192
Head, S 28
Heald, D 379
Heaney, CA 69
Heaney, CA 156, 276, 313, 347
Heft, LL 273
Heiskanen, M 125
Herbert, TB 256
Hertzman, C 258
Highley, JC 324-5
Highley-Marchington, C 326
Hilakivi-Clarke, L 262
Hills, H 182
Hills, J 378
Hine, D 387
HMSO, London 277
Hobfoll, SE 336
Hochschild, AR 102
Hoel, H 124
Holmes, EP 115
Holt, R 29

Hooijberg, R 139
Horning, KH 27
Houck, JW 22
House, JS 156, 236, 264
Houston, BK 131
Houtman, ILD 242, 336
Huber, GP 26
Huebner, ES 115
Hugentobler, MK 345
Hull, JG 180
Hurrell, JJ 126, 132, 145, 315-6, 319
Hutt, J 198

I

Incomes Data Services London, 281
Indvik, J 125
Inkson, K 154
Institute of Management, London 277
Irwin, J 261
Irwin, M 254
Isaacs, G 326
Iska-Golec, I 110
Israel, BA 156, 318-9, 345, 349
Ivancevich, JM 314, 330, 344
Iwata, N 142

J

Jackson, SE 118, 138, 344
Jacobson, D 154
Jamal, M 196
James, K 345
Jenkins, R 316

Jex, SM 191, 314
Jick, TD 153
Johansson, G 143, 272
Johnson, C 383
Johnson, JV 247, 271-2
Johnson, LB 68
Johnson, NW 138
Johnson, PR 125
Johnson, V 275
Jones, F 57-8, 132, 350
Jones, GE 338
Jones, J 100
Jones, KW 136
Jones, ML 141
Julkunen, J 198

K

Kagan, K 337
Kagan, NI 337
Kahn, RL 49, 135
Kalik, JA 116
Kalimo, R 198
Kandel, DB 271
Kandolin, I 106
Kannel, WB 192
Kantorowski, LA 184
Karasek, R 55, 145-6, 233, 246-7, 348
Kasdan, ML 243
Kasl, SV 233
Kassim, H 387
Kauppinen-Toropainen, K 106
Keenan, A 61, 186
Keenan, JP 67
Keita, GP 132, 316
Kelloway, EK 147
Kelly, KE 131
Kelly, S 258

Kenardy, JA 342
Kiecolt-Glaser, JK 255
Kinney, JA 125
Kinnunen, U 134
Kirk, SA 187
Kirkaldy, BD 177-8
Kivimaki, M 198
Klandermans, B 154
Klenke-Hamel, KE 138
Kline, ML 335
Kneller, R 373
Knopp, RH 247
Knutsson, A 104, 107
Kobasa, SC 179-80
Koeske, GF 113-4, 187
Koeske, RD 113-4
Kolbell, RM 337
Kompier, MAJ 71, 321, 326
Koob, GF 234
Korten, DC 21
Kozul-Wright, R 23
Kraft, JD 30
Krantz, DS 233
Krepps, MB 29
Kreuger, GP 97
Kristensen, TS 105
Kroes, WH 136
Krueger, AB 380
Kushnir, T 56-7
Kutner, M 342

L

Labour Party 371
Lacroix, AZ 247
Laker, DR 273
Lamberts, RD 269
Lamont, D 22
Landsbergis, PA 148, 251, 347-8
Lang, D 139
Latack, JC 65
Lawless, P 127
Lawrence, C 128
Lazarus, RS 61-3, 66, 69, 71
Leather, P 128-9, 314
Lee, C 153
Lee, RT 118
Lehrer, PM 334
Leino, P 240
Leino, PI 242
Leiter, M 113
Leiter, MP 64, 112-3, 117-8, 265
Levenson, JL 261
Levi, L 279
Lewin, J 237
Lewis, P 105
Lewis, S 237
Leymann, H 121
Lim, VKG 158
Lindell, J 233
Liukkonen, P 279
Loher, BT 143
Louis-Guerin, C 153, 155
Lourie, J 386, 388
Low Pay Commission 382
Luchins, D 115
Lundberg, U 145
Lunde-Jensen, P 279

M

Maddi, SR 179-80
Magni, G 240
Maiden, RP 323

Mandell, W 273
Manlove, EE 141
Manning, A 380
Marek, T 114
Margavio, A 126
Margolis, BL 136
Marmar, CR 268
Marmot, MG 328
Marsden, K 20
Marshall, NL 131
Martin, JK 271
Martin, JM 273
Martin, WH 103
Maruyama, S 100
Maslach, C 112, 114,
    118
Mason, S 103
Mathieu, JE 138
Matteson, MT 330, 344
Matthiesen, SB 122
Mattiusson, I 248
Mauno, S 134
Mayes, BT 184, 195, 264
McAllister, P 324
McCaffrey, T 343
McCann, BS 247
McFarlane, AC 267
McGee, R 262
McGrath, JE 265
McHugh, M 277, 347
McKinsey Global
    Institute 26
McLoughlin, I 25
McVey, RS 127
Meadows, P 24
Meichenbaum, D 329
Meijman, TF 71
Meir, EI 56
Melamed, S 56-7

Melmed, RN 237
Mensch, BS 271
Mermelstein, RJ 274
Metcalf, H 29
Michailow, M 27
Michie, S 326
Miller, KI 140
Miller, SM 63
Mills, JA 382
Millward, N 29
Minors, DS 107
Mitchell, JT 341-2
Molloy, GN 181
Monk, TH 103-4
Monroy, J 340
Moore, JG 105
Moore, S 276
Morgenstern, H 98
Morimoto, K 100
Moss, J 53
Moyle, P 191, 267
Mueller, WS 345
Murphy, E 28
Murphy, LR 50, 313,
    315-6, 318-9, 329,
    331, 339
Myles, G 282

N

Nadolski, JA 322
Nakano, Y 258
Netemeyer, RG 138
Neuman, JH 128
Newman, HN 256
Newman, JE 312
Newstrom, JW 343
Newton, TJ 61, 186
Niaura, R 250
Nieva, R 68

Nimmo, M 377
Norman, P 67
Norvell, N 182
Nowack, KM 182

O

O'Brien, TB 70
O'Connell, BJO 178
O'Driscoll, MP 67, 69
O'Hanlon, JF 143
O'Leary, A 253
Oakland, S 70
Oakley, DA 256
OECD (Paris) 20, 374,
    381
Ohmae, K 21
Olsson, K 106
Ong, CN 242
Ono, Y 107
Orhede, E 243
Orlans, V 49, 323
Ostell, A 70

P

Pahl, R 101
Palmer, S 338
Paoli, P 280
Parasuraman, S 132
Parker, PA 116
Parkes, KR 66, 186
Patel, C 328
Payne, P 48
Payne, R 48, 55, 176-7
Pearlin, LI 61
Pelletier, KK 331
Pennant-Rea 383
Pennebaker, JW 188
Pentti, J 245
Perkins, KA 274

Perlow, LA 101
Perraton, J 22
Perrewé, PL 50, 67
PES-ECOFIN Group 385
Peters, RK 327
Philpot, J 19
Pichert, JW 238
Pieper, C 247
Pierce, CMB 181
Pierce, JL 343
Pierson, P 31
Pollock, AM 379-80
Pond, SB 336
Poole, CJM 109
Power, KG 135
Price, KH 139
Pruitt, RH 332
Psenicka, C 188
Puccetti, MC 179

Q

Quick, JC 30, 48, 315-6, 320
Quick, JD 48
Quinn, RP 136

R

Rabinowitz, S 192
Raggatt, PTF 99
Rahim, MA 188
Raknes, BJ 122
Rao, JM 134
Rayner, C 123-4
Reed, DM 56
Repetti, RL 133
Reynolds, P 323
Reynolds, S 315, 317, 334, 350

Rhodewalt, F 198
Richards, D 341
Richardsen, AM 265
Richman, JA 274, 276
Rick, J 320
Rifkin, J 24
Riley, R 373
Ringel, N 194
Rivier, C 234
Rizkilla, A 139
Robinson, P 18
Robinson, RC 341
Robinsons Fruit and Barley 102
Rodriguez-Feuerhahn, M 256
Roman, PM 273
Rosa, RR 105, 108-9
Rosch, PJ 331
Rose, J 350
Rose, RM 233
Rosenbaum, A 129
Rosenblatt, Z 152
Rosenman, RH 192, 196, 245
Roskies, E 153, 155
Rospenda, KM 276
Roth, DL 180
Rowe, MM 120
Rowthorn, R 23
Rude, DE 192
Rush, MC 183
Russell, M 141, 265, 272
Rystedt, LW 143

S

Sachdev, S 381
Sadri, G 324
Sallis, JF 331

Sandonato, CE 322
Sargent, LD 150
Sartori, G 69
Saunders, T 338
Sauter, SJ 145
Sauter, SL 50, 316
Schabracq, MJ 51-2, 235
Schalk, R 199
Schall, PL 248, 250
Schaubroeck, J 150, 189-90, 234, 346
Schaufeli, WB 58, 114, 117
Schedlowski, M 256
Schnall, PL 251
Schoel, WA 183
Schoenborn, TF 313
Schonfeld, IS 191
Schooler, C 61
Schor, JB 99
Schreurs, PJG 58
Schuler, RS 138
Schurman, S 318
Schurman, SJ 345, 349
Schwarzer, R 119
Schweitzer, R 66
Scott, AJ 107
Selwyn, NM 282
Selye, H 52
Shadel, WG 274
Shapiro, DA 315, 334
Sharpe, R 51
Shaw, K 378
Sherwood, A 199
Shillitoe, RW 238
Shipley, P 49, 131
Shirom, A 136, 252, 270
Shulman, KR 338
Siegall, M 142

Siegel, WC 252
Siegman, AW 194–5
Sigala, K 243
Sime, WE 195
Simpson, RJ 135
Sinervo, T 244
Sklar, LS 261
Skov, T 243
Smit, I 235
Smith, D 158
Smith, JG 19
Smith, L 109
Smith, LM 345
Smith, MJ 147–8
Snow, DL 335
Social Exclusion Unit,
   London 375
Social Market
   Foundation, London
   375
Sorenson, S 331
Sparks, K 101
Spector, PE 144, 178,
   183, 185, 189, 191
Spiegel, D 260
Spurgeon, A 98
St-Yves, A 185
Stansfield, SA 235, 266
Starnaman, SM 140
Starrin, B 98
Steffy, BD 273
Stewart, TA 29
Stoner, CR 344
Storms, PL 185
Strange, S 23
Summerton, J 63
Surwit, RS 239
Sutherland, VJ 49
Suzuki, K 142

Swanson, V 135
Szabo, S 105

T

Taris, TW 58
Taylor, E 111, 334
Teasdale, P 278
Temoshok, L 259–60
Tepas, DI 104
Terry, D 68
Terry, DJ 66, 69, 150,
   328
Theorell, T 55, 146, 240,
   243, 246–9
Thomas-Peter, BA 124
Thomason, JA 336
Thompson, CA 132
Thygesen, N 385
Thyrum, ET 252
Tighavi, M 237
Toll, C 322
Tonge, L 68
Trappa, KL 243
Treasury, London 384
TSO, London 374–6,
   387
TUC, London 279
Tullett, S 281
Tylecote A, 21
Tyler, P 151

U

Uehta, T 99
Ursin, H 241

V

van Ameringen, MR
   177, 187
van Dierendonck, D 117

van Harrison, R 59–60
van Ryn, M 313
van Treuren, KR 180
van Vuuren, T 154
VandenBos, GR 127
van den Berg, PT 199
Vender, MJ 243
Vener, KJ 105
Vines, SW 335
Virnelli, S 180
Vivona-Vaughan, E 348
von Egeren, LF 250

W

Wadsworth, J 19–20
Wales, JK 239
Wall, TD 149, 343, 345
Wallace, M 110
Walsh, JJ 178
Walsh, K 239, 378
Warman, D 316
Warnick, GR 247
Warr, P 147
Warr, PB 56
Warren, E 322
Waterhouse, JM 107
Watson, D 188
Watson, MG 337
Watts, M 322
Webb, L 343
Weidner, G 198
West, MA 339
Westman, M 134, 148,
   270
WFD/Management Today
   102
Wharton, AS 133
White, HR 275
Whitehouse, O 102

Whitlam, P 30
Wickstrom, GJ 245
Wientjes, CJE 235
Wilholm, C 244
Wilkinson, F 381
Williams, BJ 329
Williams, N 382
Williams, OF 22
Williams, S 50, 262, 317, 376

Williamson, GM 234
Winnubst, J 114
Winnubst, JAM 51, 52
Wittig-Berman, U 139
Woolfolk, RL 334
World Economic Forum 20
Worrall, L 103, 280
Worthington, KA 126
Wynne, R 126

Y

Yadama, GN 119
Young, G 373

Z

Zannino, LG 258
Zegans, LS 232
Zohar, D 120
Zola, MA 180